OXFORD WORLD'S CLA

DEFENCE SPEEC

T0043433

MARCUS TULLIUS CICERO (106–43 BC) was the son of a Roman *eques* from Arpinum, some 70 miles south-east of Rome. He rose to prominence through his skill in speaking and his exceptional success in the criminal courts, where he usually spoke for the defence. Although from a family that had never produced a Roman senator, he secured election to all the major political offices at the earliest age permitted by law. His consulship fell in a year (63) in which a dangerous insurrection occurred, the Catilinarian conspiracy; by his persuasive oratory and his controversial execution of five confessed conspirators, he prevented the conspiracy from breaking out at Rome and was hailed as the father of his country. Exiled for the executions by his enemy Clodius in 58 but recalled the following year, he lost his political independence as a result of the domination of politics by the military dynasts Pompey and Caesar. His governorship of Cilicia (51–50) was exemplary in its honesty and fairness. Always a firm republican, he reluctantly supported Pompey in the Civil War, but was pardoned by Caesar. He was not let into the plot against Caesar, but was in a sense its inspiration, being seen by now as a symbol of the republic. After Caesar's assassination (44), he supported the young Octavian (the future emperor Augustus) and led the senate in its operations against Mark Antony. When Octavian and Antony formed the 'second triumvirate' with Lepidus in 43, Cicero was their most prominent victim; he met his end with great courage.

Cicero's speeches are models of eloquence and persuasion; and together with his letters they form the chief source for the history of the late republic. His philosophical treatises, written in periods when he was deprived of his political freedom, are the main vehicle by which Hellenistic philosophy was transmitted to the west. His prose style raised the Latin language to an elegance and beauty that was never surpassed.

D. H. BERRY is Senior Lecturer in Classics at the University of Edinburgh. He has published an edition of and commentary on Cicero's *Pro Sulla* (Cambridge Classical Texts and Commentaries, 1996) and a revision of M. L. Clarke's *Rhetoric at Rome* (Routledge, 1996). A companion volume to this book, *Political Speeches*, is also published in Oxford World's Classics.

OXFORD WORLD'S CLASSICS

*For almost 100 years Oxford World's Classics have brought
readers closer to the world's great literature. Now with over 700
titles—from the 4,000-year-old myths of Mesopotamia to the
twentieth century's greatest novels—the series makes available
lesser-known as well as celebrated writing.*

*The pocket-sized hardbacks of the early years contained
introductions by Virginia Woolf, T. S. Eliot, Graham Greene,
and other literary figures which enriched the experience of reading.
Today the series is recognized for its fine scholarship and
reliability in texts that span world literature, drama and poetry,
religion, philosophy and politics. Each edition includes perceptive
commentary and essential background information to meet the
changing needs of readers.*

OXFORD WORLD'S CLASSICS

═══

CICERO

Defence Speeches

═══

Translated with Introductions and Notes by
D. H. BERRY

OXFORD
UNIVERSITY PRESS

OXFORD
UNIVERSITY PRESS

Great Clarendon Street, Oxford OX2 6DP

Oxford University Press is a department of the University of Oxford.
It furthers the University's objective of excellence in research, scholarship,
and education by publishing worldwide in

Oxford New York

Athens Auckland Bangkok Bogotá Buenos Aires Calcutta
Cape Town Chennai Dar es Salaam Delhi Florence Hong Kong Istanbul
Karachi Kuala Lumpur Madrid Melbourne Mexico City Mumbai
Nairobi Paris São Paulo Shanghai Singapore Taipei Tokyo Toronto Warsaw

with associated companies in Berlin Ibadan

Oxford is a registered trade mark of Oxford University Press
in the UK and in certain other countries

Published in the United States
by Oxford University Press Inc., New York

© D. H. Berry 2000

Database right Oxford University Press (maker)

First published as an Oxford World's Classics paperback 2000

Reissued with corrections 2008

British Library Cataloguing in Publication Data

Data available

Library of Congress Cataloging in Publication Data
Cicero, Marcus Tullius.
Defence speeches/Cicero; translated with introduction and notes by D. H. Berry.
(Oxford world's classics)
Includes bibliographical references.
1. Cicero, Marcus Tullius—Translations into English. 2. Speeches, addresses, etc.,
Latin—Translations into English. 3. Defense (Criminal procedure)—Rome—Sources. I.
Berry, D. H. II. Title. III. Oxford world's classics (Oxford University Press)

PA6307.A4 B47 2001   875'.01—dc21   00–040632
ISBN 978–0–19–953790–7

17

Typeset in Ehrhardt
by RefineCatch Limited, Bungay, Suffolk
Printed in Great Britain by
Clays Ltd, Elcograf S.p.A.

To Courtenay and Sarah Latimer,
and to the memory of my mother

CONTENTS

ACKNOWLEDGEMENTS

I AM grateful to Professor Jonathan Powell and two anonymous readers for their comments on my translation of *Pro Archia*.

Special thanks to Douglas Cairns, Ian Gibson, Sunit Jilla, Paul Knox, Elizabeth Pender, and Perry Savill for their help and friendship during the writing of this book. Friends, like manuscripts, should be weighed not counted.

ABBREVIATIONS

Asc.	Asconius
Cic. *Arch.*	Cicero, *Pro Archia*
Att.	*Epistulae ad Atticum*
Brut.	*Brutus*
Cael.	*Pro Caelio*
Fam.	*Epistulae ad familiares*
Man.	*Pro lege Manilia*
Mil.	*Pro Milone*
Mur.	*Pro Murena*
Orat.	*Orator*
Phil.	*Orationes Philippicae* (*Philippics*)
Planc.	*Pro Plancio*
Sest.	*Pro Sestio*
S. Rosc.	*Pro Roscio Amerino*
Plut. *Cic.*	Plutarch, *Life of Cicero*
Quint. *Inst.*	Quintilian, *Institutio oratoria*

AC	*L'Antiquité classique*
AJAH	*American Journal of Ancient History*
AJP	*American Journal of Philology*
CJ	*Classical Journal*
CP	*Classical Philology*
CR	*Classical Review*
G&R	*Greece and Rome*
HSCP	*Harvard Studies in Classical Philology*
JRS	*Journal of Roman Studies*
LCM	*Liverpool Classical Monthly*
RhM	*Rheinisches Museum*
TAPA	*Transactions of the American Philological Association*

INTRODUCTION

IN the ancient world, for century after century, public speaking ('oratory') was central to public life, and the ability to influence people with the spoken word brought power, money, and fame to the speaker ('orator'). Assemblies could be persuaded to pass laws and decrees, declare war and peace, assign commands, provinces, and even kingdoms, or redistribute land. Debates were real, their outcomes decided by the force of argument and the power of persuasion; there were no parties, as in a modern parliament, dictating to politicians the line they should take. The courts, too, were highly politicized. Political opponents prosecuted each other for crimes real and imaginary, and in this way the persuasive speaker could influence the course of events, determining who would or would not be removed from political life, and reaping the political and financial rewards. It was not easy to become a successful orator. Years had to be spent mastering the techniques of rhetoric (the term denotes the theory, not the practice of speaking). But for those who applied themselves, and who possessed in addition an outstanding natural ability, the rewards could be great.

Of all the speakers in the ancient world, Cicero can plausibly be reckoned the best. The first-century AD rhetorician Quintilian wrote: '"Cicero" has come to be regarded as the name not of a person, but of eloquence itself', adding that 'if a student is a keen admirer of Cicero, he will know that he has made real progress' (*Inst.* 10.1.112). Cicero's dates were 106–43 BC: so he lived through the fall of the Roman republic. This was a period of national instability and unprecedented political competition, and the power of persuading others through speech became as important as it has ever been. Cicero rose to prominence not because of his birth (his non-aristocratic, Italian origin was a severe handicap to him), but because of his ability. He could persuade the ordinary citizens of Rome to vote down proposals that were in their interest, and he could (it seems) persuade just about any jury that black was white. In a gesture of triumph he published his speeches for his contemporaries and posterity to admire and imitate. Fifty-eight of these still survive today in whole or part. They are in every sense classics—works

xii																								*Introduction*

which have been read, enjoyed, quoted from, studied, and imitated by people in western societies, off and on, for two millennia. And in a world in which mass-communication becomes ever more important, they retain their interest, relevance, and vibrancy.

Cicero excelled in both of the two main types of oratory, 'forensic' (the oratory of the forum, i.e. of the law courts, also known as 'judicial') and 'deliberative' (the oratory of the political assemblies); a third type, 'epideictic' (the oratory of display), was less important at the higher political level at this period. It is just forensic that we are concerned with in this collection—and only with a subset of forensic, in fact, since all five orations are speeches for the defence (a companion volume, *Political Speeches*, will contain speeches for the prosecution, and deliberative speeches). Many of Cicero's defence speeches are masterpieces of oratory, deal with events of historical significance, and are of considerable human interest. These five have been chosen because they have historically been the best known and the most appreciated, *Pro Roscio Amerino* ('For Roscius of Ameria') and *Pro Milone* ('For Milo') for their rhetorical brilliance at, respectively, the beginning and the end of Cicero's career as an advocate; *Pro Murena* ('For Murena') and *Pro Caelio* ('For Caelius') for their humour (these are perhaps the funniest works of literature to have emerged from the ancient world); and *Pro Archia* ('For Archias') for the beautiful encomium of literature which occupies the greater part of the speech. *Pro Milone* is also of particular interest because there happens to have survived an independent account of the facts of the case—strikingly at variance with Cicero's account—written by the first-century AD scholar Quintus Asconius Pedianus. Asconius' account is also translated in this volume.

I will say something below about the courts in which Cicero's defences were given. But first an account of his public career is required.

Cicero's Public Career

Thanks to his voluminous writings, particularly his letters, we know more about Cicero than about any other person in ancient history. He was the elder son of a wealthy *eques* from Arpinum, a town about 70 miles south-east of Rome that had possessed full Roman citizenship since as early as 188 BC; his younger brother Quintus was also to pursue a public career with distinction, and share his brother's brutal end. Arpinum was notable for being the home town of Gaius Marius, the seven-times consul and in 102 and 101 the saviour of Rome from the northern invaders; Cicero's paternal grandmother was in fact a relation of Marius by marriage. In *c*.95 the Ciceros bought a house in Rome so that the two boys should have the best education possible, and Cicero studied rhetoric under the two most famous orators of the day, Lucius Licinius Crassus (consul in 95) and Marcus Antonius (consul in 99); both men were later rewarded by being given parts in one of Cicero's mature rhetorical works, *De Oratore* ('On the orator', 55 BC). During the Social War, Cicero saw military service: in 89 he served under Pompey's father, Gnaeus Pompeius Strabo, and in 88 he served under Sulla. In 87 Marius occupied Rome and murdered his opponents, including Antonius. During the Cinnan regime which followed, Cicero continued his studies at Rome, studying rhetoric and, less usually, philosophy. In 82 Sulla recaptured the city, had himself appointed dictator, and 'proscribed' his enemies by posting in the forum lists of those to be killed. It was now (81), at the age of 25, that Cicero undertook his first court case, a civil case for Publius Quinctius afterwards published as *Pro Quinctio* ('For Quinctius'). He lost; but he lost to the most distinguished advocate in Rome, Quintus Hortensius Hortalus.

The next year (80) he undertook his first criminal case, *Pro Roscio Amerino* ('For Roscius of Ameria'). This was a defence of a man, Sextus Roscius of Ameria, who had been charged with the murder of his father. The trial became sensational when Cicero boldly exposed the unscrupulous profiteering of one of Sulla's cronies, the freedman Chrysogonus, who was behind the prosecution; he won his case and became famous overnight. Among the briefs which came to him as a result of this success was the politically sensitive defence of the freedom of a woman from Arretium (a town in Etruria). This time Cicero argued successfully that Sulla had not been justified in stripping Arretium of its citizen rights. Both these cases helped Cicero to gain the support of the Italians on whom he relied throughout his political career.

From 79 to 77 Cicero studied abroad. The many cases which he had taken on immediately after the Roscius case had damaged his health (oratory was physically very demanding), and his defence of the woman from Arretium may also have made his absence from

Rome politically expedient. The two brothers travelled to Greece, Rhodes, and Asia Minor (to which Quintus, who was also to pursue a political career, would later return as governor). They studied philosophy in Athens, and Cicero studied rhetoric under Molon of Rhodes. Molon, he later maintained, helped him to make his oratory a little more restrained, less 'Asianist' (elaborate and florid) in style. This toning down of his oratorical style was in keeping with the direction in which taste at Rome was moving, and it was also sensible in view of the risk to his health.

In 76 he was elected quaestor at Rome, and he served his term of office in western Sicily the following year. Election to the quaestorship brought life membership of the senate, and Cicero was the first member of his family to attain this distinction; thus he became in Roman terms a 'new man' (*novus homo*, the first man of a family to reach the senate).

This success was followed up in 70 by his election as plebeian aedile for 69. But, more significantly, he decided in 70 to undertake a prosecution: having served as an honest quaestor in Sicily five years earlier, he was only too happy to help the Sicilians by bringing a charge of extortion against the rapacious governor, Gaius Verres, who had systematically fleeced the province from 73 to 71. Verres' defence, however, was undertaken by Hortensius, who was to be consul in 69, and he was also aided by one of the leading families in Rome, the Metelli. One Metellus had become Verres' successor in Sicily, and made it difficult for Cicero to collect evidence; another was to be Hortensius' consular colleague the following year; and a third would be praetor in charge of the court if, as the defence hoped, the case could be prolonged into 69. But in the event Cicero overcame all these obstacles. He collected his evidence quickly, delivered a brief opening speech, and then brought out his witnesses. In his speech he dwelt upon the political aspect of the case: if someone as obviously guilty as Verres were let off, the people would judge the exclusively senatorial juries (prescribed by a law of Sulla's) to be unfit to try cases, and a law would be passed handing the courts over to the *equites* instead. Once the evidence had been presented, Verres went into exile, without waiting to hear more; and Cicero then published the speeches he would have gone on to deliver—*In Verrem* ('Against Verres') or, in English, the *Verrines*, a damning and sometimes hilarious exposé of Verres' crimes. With this success Cicero took Hortensius' place as Rome's foremost advocate: Hortensius all but abandoned the courts, returning only when Cicero had reached the consulship, and then as Cicero's partner, not his opponent.

Cicero's irresistible rise continued. In 67 he was elected praetor, by all the centuries (voting units in the centuriate assembly), three times over (because the election had to be repeated), and at the earliest age permitted by law (he was by now 39). He served his year of office as praetor in charge of the extortion court, the scene of his success against Verres; and in 66 he also gave his first deliberative speech, *Pro lege Manilia* ('For the Manilian law'). Rome had recently suffered a serious reverse in the Third Mithridatic War (73–63). Public opinion wanted the command of the Roman forces, held by Lucullus since the start of the war, to be given to Pompey, who had just enjoyed a spectacular success in wiping out the pirates of the Mediterranean, and was already on the scene; the traditionalists in the senate, however, such as Hortensius, did not wish to see Pompey's career advanced any further. The tribune Gaius Manilius proposed a bill to have the command transferred to Pompey, and invited Cicero to support it. As a praetor, Cicero could not avoid expressing an opinion—and yet he did not wish to alienate either the senate or the people, given that he would shortly be standing for the consulship. His solution was to give the bill his enthusiastic support, while also taking care to compliment Lucullus. The bill was passed, Cicero published his speech, and Pompey concluded the war in 63. A non-political speech, but a celebrated one, was also delivered in 66, *Pro Cluentio* ('For Cluentius'). This was an oratorical triumph in which Cicero, as he afterwards boasted, 'threw dust in the eyes of the jury' (Quint. *Inst.* 2.17.21). The remark should make us aware of the deception which may (or may not) be taking place whenever we read one of Cicero's defences.

In 64 he was elected to the consulship for 63, again at the earliest age permitted by law (he was 43 in 63). With this success his family entered the ranks of the nobility (a 'noble' was a direct descendant of a consul through the male line). It was certainly unusual for new men to rise as high as the consulship: the last one to do so had been Gaius Norbanus twenty years previously. Cicero's consulship was an eventful one, and one that afforded further scope for the exercise of his oratorical talents. It began with Cicero in four speeches *De lege agraria* ('On the agrarian law') successfully opposing the land redistributions proposed by the tribune Publius Servilius Rullus; the speeches demonstrate Cicero's ability to persuade the people to vote down a proposal that was in their interest. He claimed to be a popular consul acting in the people's interest, but was actually taking a conservative line. Now that he had reached the highest place in the 'sequence of offices' (*cursus honorum*), he was always to follow the conservative, traditional, and republican line which by nature he preferred. Having been allowed to join the club, he would defend its rules to the death.

But the major event of Cicero's consulship, and indeed of his life, was his controversial suppression of the Catilinarian conspiracy. The conspirators were a small group of failed politicians some of whom had ruined themselves financially in their attempts to secure political advancement and live up to their social status; some, in marked contrast to Cicero, were high-ranking aristocrats. Led by the patrician Lucius Sergius Catilina ('Catiline' in English), they hoped, by assassinations, arson, and a march on Rome, to seize power; after which they would reward themselves with political office and put forward legislation for a general cancellation of debts (there is no evidence of any plans for wider reform, or of any genuine social concern). The conspiracy began in earnest with Catiline's failure to be elected consul in July, and by mid-November he had thrown in his lot with an agrarian rising in Etruria led by one Gaius Manlius, a former Sullan centurion. Cicero's vigilance and prompt action saved his own life from an assassination attempt and prevented the conspiracy from breaking out at Rome—but at the cost of executing without trial five leading conspirators (including one ex-consul, Publius Cornelius Lentulus Sura), who had been arrested and had confessed their guilt. His illegal execution of the five men on 5 December had the explicit backing of the senate and overwhelming public support (he was hailed by Cato as the father of his country), and probably saved a great many lives. Nevertheless, it was to lay him open to attack for years afterwards, and required him constantly to be justifying the action that he had taken (something which has unfairly caused him to be perceived as boastful and vain). His publication in 60 of his four magnificent speeches against Catiline (*In Catilinam* ('Against Catiline') or, in English, the *Catilinarians*) was a major exercise in self-justification. The effectiveness of his attack ensured that Catiline's name was blackened for all time. Catiline himself, together with his army, was destroyed in the field by Cicero's colleague as consul, Gaius Antonius Hybrida, at the beginning of 62.

In the midst of the Catilinarian crisis (in November) Cicero also found time to undertake the defence of one of the consuls-elect for 62, Lucius Licinius Murena, who had been prosecuted for electoral malpractice by one of the unsuccessful candidates; the law under which the case was brought was Cicero's own bribery law, the *lex Tullia de ambitu*, which he had successfully carried earlier in the year. Together with Hortensius and Crassus, Cicero secured his acquittal, arguing that, in the face of the danger from Catiline, the necessity of having as consul an experienced military man such as Murena overrode all other considerations. *Pro Murena* ('For Murena') is Cicero's funniest and most enjoyable speech (unless one prefers *Pro Caelio*). Much of it is taken up with making fun of the prosecutors, the lawyer Servius Sulpicius Rufus and the Stoic philosopher Marcus Porcius Cato, both men for whom Cicero had in reality a considerable regard.

Cicero's suppression of the Catilinarian conspiracy won him enormous prestige, and on 1 January 62 he was the first senator to be asked for his opinion in the senate: he was viewed as the leading senator present (Pompey was still in the east). We have two speeches of his from this year, *Pro Sulla* ('For Sulla') and *Pro Archia* ('For Archias'). *Pro Sulla* is a defence of a wealthy aristocrat, the nephew of the dictator Sulla (and probably the brother-in-law of Pompey), on a charge of participation in the conspiracy; Cicero secured his acquittal by arguing that he of all people would hardly have undertaken his defence if he had believed him to be guilty. In this speech we see Cicero seeking to present himself as a mild and compassionate person, to counteract his enemies' portrayal of him as cruel and vindictive in his execution of the conspirators. *Pro Archia*, by contrast, is one of the least political of Cicero's forensic speeches. A defence not of a Roman aristocrat but of a Syrian poet, Cicero's old teacher, on a charge of illegally assuming Roman citizenship, it contains not just a legal defence of Archias' claim, but a lengthy encomium of literature. This is of great interest to literary historians, and shows the degree to which Cicero had to go to present Archias' profession to a Roman jury in a favourable light. Archias was acquitted.

At the end of the year a scandal occurred at Rome which was to have disastrous consequences for Cicero. A young aristocrat, Publius Clodius Pulcher, was discovered to have dressed up in women's clothes and attended the festival of the Bona Dea, to which only women were admitted, and which was being held at the house of Caesar, the *pontifex maximus*. The suggestion was that he had taken advantage of Caesar's absence from his house to commit adultery with his wife. Caesar divorced his wife on the grounds that 'Caesar's wife must be above suspicion' (Plutarch, *Life of Caesar* 10.6). At Clodius' trial for sacrilege in May 61, Cicero gave evidence which disproved his alibi. Nevertheless, Clodius managed to bribe his way to an acquittal; and he was henceforward to be a far more troublesome enemy to Cicero than Catiline had been.

At the end of 60, Caesar, who was consul-elect for the following year, formed a political alliance with Pompey and Crassus conventionally known as the 'first triumvirate'. He tried to persuade Cicero to join the alliance: Cicero would have lost his political independence, but would have been protected from Clodius and from the increasing attacks on his execution of the Catilinarians. He preferred to keep his independence—and was to pay for it. In 59 Caesar sanctioned Clodius' adoption into a plebeian family (he was of patrician birth), thus enabling him to stand for election to the tribunate of the plebs, the office traditionally sought by popular politicians who wished to propose radical legislation or, in conservative eyes, to stir up trouble. Clodius was duly elected and, as tribune in 58, he proposed a bill outlawing anyone who had put a Roman citizen to death without trial. The senate put on mourning for Cicero and the towns of Italy passed resolutions in his favour. But Clodius, who had earlier carried a law to provide the people with free grain for the first time, had the support of the urban plebs. More importantly, he also had the tacit support of the triumvirs, who were angered at Cicero's rejection of their advances and worried that he might lead the conservatives in the senate in an attack on their position. The consuls Piso and Gabinius did as the triumvirs wanted, and instructed the senate to resume normal dress. Cicero's support melted away, and he himself left for exile in Macedonia on the day that Clodius' law was passed. His house in Rome was plundered and burned, and Clodius consecrated the site as a shrine to Libertas ('Liberty'), in order to portray Cicero as a tyrant and to prevent rebuilding.

Cicero's exile, which lasted almost eighteen months, was the biggest disaster of his life. He had saved Rome, and had been exiled for his pains. The charge was executing citizens without trial; yet he had been denied a trial himself. In his despair he thought of suicide. Publicly he represented his departure as a deliberate act of self-sacrifice, intended to save Rome from the likelihood of civil war—the second time he had saved the city. But privately he felt he should have stood his ground. He was recalled to Rome the following year, when the triumvirs concluded that Clodius had become an obstacle to their plans. His actual return was glorious and gratifying. On Pompey's motion the senate passed a decree, unanimous with the single exception of Clodius, describing Cicero as the saviour of his country; and the people passed a bill authorizing his recall. His journey through Italy resembled a triumphal procession: towns passed resolutions honouring him, and he was escorted by cheering crowds. But he never recovered from the blow to his pride; and, as the price of his recall, he had had to assure the triumvirs that in future he would serve their interests.

The speeches he gave in 57 and 56 are known as the *Post reditum* ('After his return') speeches. *Post reditum in senatu* ('in the senate', 57) and *Post reditum ad quirites* ('to the citizens', 57) offered thanks for his restoration. *De domo sua* ('On his house', 57) and *De haruspicum responsis* ('On the answers of the omen-interpreters', 56) dealt with the religious aspects of Cicero's feud with Clodius; Cicero successfully persuaded the pontiffs that Clodius' consecration of the site of his house in Rome had been invalid, and he secured compensation to allow him to rebuild. Other speeches of this period included defences of people who had campaigned for his recall and opposed Clodius. Publius Sestius and Titus Annius Milo were tribunes in 57 who had used violence against Clodius and worked tirelessly for Cicero's recall. Sestius was prosecuted in 56 by dependants of Clodius, was defended by Hortensius, Crassus, and Cicero (the same team that had defended Murena in 63), and was unanimously acquitted. Cicero's *Pro Sestio* ('For Sestius') contains a full exposition of the orator's own political standpoint: the state can be divided into patriots and traitors, with Sestius and Milo and the majority of Roman citizens of all classes belonging to the former category, and Clodius, Piso, and Gabinius to the latter.

A month later Cicero was to revenge himself on Clodius in a more personal way. A former friend of Clodius', Marcus Caelius Rufus, was prosecuted on an array of charges: violence, murder, and the attempted poisoning of Clodius' sister, Clodia Metelli, with whom Caelius had previously had an affair. Caelius had originally been a pupil of Cicero's, before switching allegiance to the Clodii, and now that he had broken with the Clodii he was to become a friend of Cicero's again. In taking on his defence, Cicero saw his chance to hurt Clodius by publicly humiliating his sister, whom he had reasons for hating: she had persecuted his family during his exile. In *Pro Caelio* ('For Caelius') the charges are largely ignored, and Cicero instead focuses on Caelius' affair with Clodia, portraying her as a common prostitute (she was a high-ranking society lady) and holding her up to ridicule. Ingeniously, he manages to do this while exempting Caelius from moral blame. The speech is wonderfully funny, and very cruel: Cicero won his case by avoiding the issue and making the jury laugh at his enemy. After the trial, Clodia (who has a one-in-three chance of being the same person as Catullus' 'Lesbia') vanishes from history.

Cicero owed his recall from exile to Pompey's influence, and in return he had reluctantly undertaken to give the triumvirs his political support. But he soon detected an apparent rift between Pompey and Caesar (who was absent in Gaul from 58 to 49), and decided to drive the two men further apart by opposing Caesar. First he published an attack on Publius Vatinius which he had made at the time of Sestius' trial (*In Vatinium*, 'Against Vatinius'): Vatinius was a legate of Caesar's who as tribune in 59 had procured for him his Gallic command. Secondly, he put a motion before the senate calling for discussion of Caesar's controversial agrarian law of 59. This challenge to Caesar's position did not split the triumvirate as Cicero had hoped: instead it drove the three men closer together. They reaffirmed their alliance, and Pompey and Crassus held a second joint consulship in 55 (they had held the consulship together in 70), with commands for each of them to follow afterwards. Caesar's command in Gaul was extended for a further five years.

Cicero now realized that resistance to the triumvirs would be futile, and in any case he needed their protection against Clodius' continuing attacks; he also felt that the conservatives in the senate, such as Hortensius, were failing to give him their full support. He therefore publicly declared his allegiance to the triumvirs: in *De provinciis consularibus* ('On the consular provinces', 56) he lavishes praise on Caesar and advocates the extension of his Gallic command.

The later 50s were unhappy years for Cicero. In 54 he had to defend Vatinius; although he won, he apparently chose not to publish his defence. Soon afterwards (in 54 or 53) he was compelled to defend Gabinius, the consul of 58 who had allowed Clodius to exile him; at least this time he had the satisfaction of losing. In his private moments he consoled himself by starting to write a series of philosophical treatises in which he explained the various philosophical systems of the Greeks (he was the first person to do this in Latin; the work involved formulating a Latin philosophical vocabulary, which then became standard). At the same time he began a series of treatises on oratory and rhetoric; some of these works also explore, in theoretical terms, his own political philosophy. In 53 (or 52) he was gratified to receive, on Hortensius' nomination, an important political honour: he was elected to a place in the college of augurs, in succession to Crassus' son, who had been killed with his father at Carrhae.

Clodius during these years had become a powerful independent force in Rome with a large popular following. He had assembled a gang of thugs and used it to attack his enemies, most of all Cicero, and to terrorize the city. His chief opponent was Titus Annius Milo, who used similar tactics against him in return. The increasing willingness of politicians to resort to violence to achieve their ends was a symptom of the collapse of the republic; in the next decade, urban violence would be superseded by civil war. Clodius and Milo had fought numerous battles against each other, Milo defending Cicero's interests; and in one such battle outside Rome on 18 January 52 Clodius was accidentally wounded, and then killed on Milo's orders. Cicero must have been overjoyed. Amid the chaotic scenes which followed, Clodius' supporters cremated his body in the senate-house, which was burned down. Pompey was appointed sole consul to restore order (the violence in Rome had prevented the elections for 52 from taking place), and Milo was put on trial and defended by Cicero. The evidence for his guilt was unimpeachable, and Pompey wanted him removed from public life, so Cicero's defence stood no chance of success: he was convicted, and went into exile at Massilia (Marseilles). But later in the year public opinion swung against Pompey and the Clodians, and in Milo's favour. Milo's accomplices were tried and acquitted, whereas Clodius' supporters, who were put on trial for the burning of the senate-house, were convicted. Cicero, who had played a leading part in these trials, now regarded himself and Milo as having been vindicated, and he wrote and published a new, more confident version of his unsuccessful defence. This is our *Pro Milone* ('For Milo'), which has always been accepted as the oratorical masterpiece that Cicero intended it to be.

During his consulship in 52 Pompey had legislation passed which ruled that consuls and praetors should have to wait at least five years before going out to govern their provinces (the purpose of the law was to discourage electoral bribery by delaying the period at which a magistrate would be able to recoup the money he had spent when standing for office). This created a short-term shortage of provincial governors, and as Cicero had not previously held a provincial governorship he was made to serve for a year (51–50) as governor of Cilicia, on the south-east coast of Asia Minor (the province also included Cyprus). He was very distressed at having to be away from the political scene at Rome: his governorship seemed like a second exile, and his greatest fear was that his term of office might be extended. But he resolved to make the best of the situation by acting as a model provincial governor—no easy matter, when fairness to the provincials ran directly counter to the financial interests of prominent men at Rome. He also led a successful campaign against the brigands of the interior; but on his return to Rome the impending civil war prevented him from obtaining the triumph he had hoped for.

At the outbreak of the Civil War in 49 Cicero agonized over what to do. He was put in charge of the Campanian coast, but, being unable to raise recruits in any number, soon gave up and retired to one of his villas. Caesar repeatedly tried to win him over to his side, even coming to visit him at home: to win the endorsement of such a senior republican would serve to legitimize his position. But Cicero could not in conscience give his support to a man who had invaded Italy and declared war on his country. On the other hand, he had little confidence in Pompey, the man into whose hands the republic had been placed: Pompey's decision to abandon Italy and cross over to Greece seemed to Cicero a catastrophic misjudgement, and he was disgusted by the motives and behaviour of Pompey's followers. Eventually he concluded, despairingly, that his duty was to join

Pompey in Greece. He crossed over to him in June 49; but once in Pompey's camp he declined to accept a command, and irritated the Pompeian leaders with his criticisms. He was not present at Pompey's defeat at Pharsalus in August 48, and after Pompey's flight and murder he was invited to assume command of the surviving republican forces, but declined. In October 48 he returned to Brundisium in Italy, but it was not until September 47 that he was pardoned by Caesar and allowed to move on to Rome.

Under Caesar's dictatorship there was no free political debate in which he could participate, and in any case his advice on political matters was not sought; he attended meetings of the senate, but without speaking. It was now that he found time to resume work on his many philosophical and rhetorical treatises, the bulk of which were written during this period; and he also taught rhetoric to aristocratic pupils. These activities helped take his mind away from the fall of the republic, Caesar's increasing autocracy, and (in 45) the death of his beloved daughter Tullia. In September 46 he broke his silence in the senate. Caesar had unexpectedly agreed to pardon an enemy, one of the most die-hard of the republican leaders, Marcus Claudius Marcellus, and Cicero made a speech of thanks. *Pro Marcello* ('For Marcellus') praises Caesar's clemency and urges him to proceed with his work of reform; it also sets out Cicero's case to be accepted as a mediator between Caesar and the former Pompeians. *Pro Ligario* ('For Ligarius', 46) and *Pro rege Deiotaro* ('For King Deiotarus', 45) are other speeches of this period in which Cicero begs Caesar to spare Pompeian enemies. In their circumstances of delivery and in their tone they are a far cry from the speeches in which Cicero addresses a jury and is free to say what he wishes. Here he is addressing a monarch in his palace.

Caesar's autocracy led of course to his assassination in the senate on the Ides (15th) of March 44, just a few weeks after he had had himself made *dictator perpetuo* ('dictator for life'). Cicero had offered discreet encouragement to the assassins, or 'liberators' as he calls them, but had not been let into the plot. He was actually present at the murder: Brutus raised his dagger and congratulated him on the recovery of their freedom. As the last of the senior republicans still surviving, Cicero had a symbolic value: he had become a token of the republic. And this time we do have evidence for his joy at the death of his enemy (if *Fam.* 6.15 does indeed refer to it).

After the assassination, political life began again. The surviving
consul, Mark Antony (in Latin, Marcus Antonius), arranged a
settlement under which Caesar's assassins would not be prosecuted,
but his laws and appointments would remain in force. In April,
however, the situation changed with the arrival in Italy of Caesar's
principal heir, his 18-year-old great-nephew Gaius Octavius (who
from his posthumous adoption as Caesar's son is known as Octavian,
and from 27 is known as the first emperor, Augustus): calling himself
Gaius Julius Caesar, he showed himself to Caesar's veterans, held
games in Caesar's honour, and began paying Caesar's legacies to the
Roman people. In September, Cicero made an enemy of Antony, for
a relatively trivial reason: Antony had denounced him for his failure
to attend a meeting of the senate at which posthumous honours for
Caesar were to be voted. Cicero replied the next day with the *First
Philippic*; Antony then delivered a bitter invective against him in the
senate in his absence; and Cicero wrote (but did not deliver) a savage
reply, the *Second Philippic*. This speech attacks and ridicules
Antony's entire career, but particularly his behaviour under Caesar
and his appropriation of state funds in the months since Caesar's
death; it closes with a warning of assassination. It was Cicero's view
that Antony ought to have been murdered at the same time as
Caesar: if Cicero had been invited to the feast (i.e. let into the plot),
there would have been no left-overs (*Fam.* 10.28.1, 12.4.1).

In November Antony left Rome for Gaul, which he had taken as
his province; and Cicero assumed unofficial leadership of the senate.
In the *Third Philippic*, he persuaded the senate to approve the refusal
of Decimus Brutus, the governor of Cisalpine Gaul and one of
Caesar's assassins, to hand over his legions to Antony; and in the
Fourth Philippic, delivered before the people on the same day, he
argued that Antony was in effect a public enemy. At the same time,
he urged both senate and people to give their support to Octavian. In
thinking that the young man could be praised, honoured, and then
disposed of (to his embarrassment, his words (*Fam.* 11.20.1) were
reported to Octavian), Cicero made a serious misjudgement. It
was also unrealistic of him to suppose that Octavian would stay for
long on the same side as Caesar's assassins. But Antony's destruction seemed to Cicero the immediate priority, and an alliance with
Octavian was the only way to bring it about.

From this point, Cicero controlled events at Rome: nineteen years after his consulship, he was once again leading the republic at a moment of supreme national crisis. In a further ten *Philippics* (January to April 43), he directed the senate in its actions against Antony, urging it not to compromise, and presented his view of events to the people. It was his 'finest hour'. In April 43 Antony was defeated near Mutina and declared a public enemy. Cicero, it seemed, had saved his country a second time. But events then took an unwelcome turn. Antony escaped and succeeded in acquiring further legions from Marcus Aemilius Lepidus, the governor of Narbonese Gaul and Nearer Spain; and Decimus Brutus was deserted by his troops and killed on Antony's orders. Octavian, though only 19, demanded the consulship (both consuls had been killed in battle); he may have considered having Cicero as his colleague, but the evidence for this is doubtful. When his demand was refused by the senate, he marched on Rome and, in August, held an irregular election and took the consulship, with his uncle as colleague. With nothing more to be got from Cicero and the senate, he then changed sides, holding a meeting with Antony and Lepidus near Bononia. The 'second triumvirate' was formed, and the three men gave themselves supreme power for five years, and divided out the empire between them. To rid themselves of their enemies and raise funds for their veterans they initiated a proscription, as Sulla had done in 82. So once again the lists of those to be killed were posted in the forum. Cicero met his end, on 7 December, with great courage. He was 63. His head and hands were cut off and displayed on the rostra in the forum—the scene of so many of his successes.

Octavian defeated Antony at Actium in 31, and in 30 he chose Cicero's son as his colleague in the consulship. Many years later, as the emperor Augustus, he happened to catch his grandson reading one of Cicero's books. He took the book, looked through it, and handed it back saying, 'He was a master of words, child, a master of words and a patriot' (Plut. *Cic.* 49.3).

The Criminal Courts

Before 149 BC trials were held before the people at assemblies. Then in 149 the first permanent court (*quaestio*, 'public inquiry') was established, to try charges of extortion. Further courts were added in time, both permanent and temporary, with different rules governing each one; from 123, the juries seem usually to have been made up exclusively of *equites*. If an individual was accused of a crime, he would be brought before the relevant court; or if no court existed to try that crime, he could be tried before the people at an assembly (for convenience, this discussion will refer to male defendants, although women could also be prosecuted). For minor offences, summary action might be taken by a magistrate.

This system of criminal justice, which had been created piecemeal, was replaced by the dictator Sulla in 81. Seven new permanent courts were established to try the major crimes, namely murder and poisoning (the first trial to take place in this court was that of Roscius); forgery; extortion; treason; electoral malpractice; embezzlement; and assault. Each court was presided over by a praetor, but the praetor had no discretion over the sentence: the penalties were fixed by law. There was no appeal to the people. The juries were composed exclusively of senators.

Sulla's courts survived virtually unchanged until the principate: they were the only reforms of his which lasted. The senatorial juries, however, proved controversial (as Cicero implies in *Pro Roscio Amerino* and explains at length in *In Verrem* I), and in 70 the *lex Aurelia* replaced them with new juries consisting of one-third senators, one-third *equites*, and one-third *tribuni aerarii* ('treasury tribunes'). It is not clear precisely what the *tribuni aerarii* were, but Cicero treats them as *equites* (there was probably a lower property qualification); essentially, then, the new 'mixed' juries were one-third senatorial and two-thirds equestrian. This happy compromise ended the bitter controversy over whether juries ought to be composed of senators or of *equites*. Roscius was tried before a senatorial jury, but Murena, Archias, Caelius, and Milo were tried before mixed juries.

Later other permanent courts were added to Sulla's original seven, for example the court for violence, the court in which Caelius was tried, established in (perhaps) 70. There were not enough praetors to preside over these courts, however, so the magistrate in charge would be a more junior *iudex quaestionis* ('court judge'), chosen from among those who had been aediles the previous year. Temporary courts continued to be set up as and when needed, for example the sacrilege court, appointed to try Clodius after the Bona Dea scandal in 61.

There was no public prosecutor at Rome: criminal prosecutions were always undertaken by private individuals. A man who had broken the law would generally be prosecuted by the person who had suffered as a result of his crime: thus Murena was prosecuted by Sulpicius, his unsuccessful rival for the consulship of 62. Sometimes, however, he might be prosecuted simply by an enemy, in pursuance of a feud (*inimicitiae*). The courts were one of the principal arenas in which the business of politics at Rome was played out: if you wanted to get rid of a political opponent, you prosecuted him and brought about his exile; if you failed, he might then prosecute you. No one could be prosecuted while holding a senior public office, so politicians would sometimes seek election to a magistracy in order to escape an impending prosecution; Clodius and Milo dodged each other in this way in the 50s.

Sometimes, again, a man who had broken the law would arrange for a friend to prosecute him: the friend would deliberately put up a weak case, and he would be acquitted of his crime. But in cases where more than one person came forward with the same charge, a *divinatio* ('inquiry') was held, and the jury would decide which one should be allowed to undertake the prosecution. It was by this means that Cicero was chosen to prosecute Verres in 70, rather than Verres' crony Caecilius.

Prosecutors were often young men, hoping to attract attention and make a name for themselves. Successful prosecutors, if senators, were awarded their victim's *insignia* ('marks of honour', such as the purple-bordered toga (*toga praetexta*) of a curule magistrate), and also acceded to his rank in the senatorial hierarchy; but this must have been an invidious honour. It was not advisable for a young man to make a habit of prosecuting: it would make him enemies, and prosecuting was in any case seen as a hateful business, to be avoided unless there were a special reason or duty requiring one to undertake it. The best policy was perhaps to prosecute once, so as to be noticed, and then keep to defence. This is what Cicero did (with the exception of one prosecution in 52 or 51); and in prosecuting Verres (in 70) he had the advantage of accusing someone whose guilt was manifest and shocking.

In fifth-century Athens, defendants spoke for themselves in court, employing a speech-writer (*logographos*) if necessary, but at Rome it was more normal to find an advocate (*patronus*) to speak on one's behalf. Patronage was a key feature of Roman society: patrons gave assistance and protection to their clients, who in return waited on their patrons at home and in the street and voted for them at elections. But of course the situation in court was different in that the defendant could be of higher social status than the advocate: Cicero was not socially of as high a rank as many of his clients. Advocates were not supposed to accept fees or gifts for their services in court (this was specifically forbidden by the *lex Cincia de donis et muneribus* of 204): they were acting as patrons, out of duty, and not for mercenary motives. Usually, therefore, an advocate would undertake a defence in order to repay a favour (Cicero defended various people who had supported him in the Catilinarian crisis or at the time of his exile); or he would do it in the hope of receiving support at an election, or even in the expectation of a legacy. If there was really no other kind of repayment that the defendant could make, a low-interest or interest-free loan might be accepted, as happened when Cicero defended Publius Sulla in 62. No one worried very much about the *lex Cincia*, which probably seemed rather quaint.

The tradition of advocacy had an important effect on the speeches that were made. It meant, first, that the speeches would be of a highly professional standard: a defendant would naturally seek out the most eloquent advocate he could find to speak for him. Secondly, advocacy introduces into the speeches an additional, complicating element. If a man is defending himself, he will merely have to present his own character in a good light and his opponent's in a bad light (Roman juries put great weight on a man's character, partly because evidence was often unreliable). But if an advocate is speaking on behalf of someone else, his speech will naturally seek to make capital out of his own character as well as that of the defendant and of his opponent. Sometimes the advocate's character and standing might compensate for his client's character failings: if the jury like the speaker and approve of him, they may perhaps give his client the benefit of the doubt. In the speeches of his consulship and afterwards, Cicero makes much of his own authority (*auctoritas*): this is something he could deploy against an opponent, particularly a young one, with devastating results.

Trials were held in the forum (hence the term 'forensic' oratory), in the open air. The presiding magistrate with his scribes and attendants sat up on a high platform (*tribunal*) at the front of the court, while the jury probably sat on benches raised only slightly off the ground (the ancient evidence on these points is unclear). Facing them and also seated on benches were the two opposing parties, the prosecutors on one side and the defendant with his advocates on the other, each party accompanied by their legal advisers (advocates were not necessarily experts in the law), family, friends, and witnesses. Behind the benches a ring (*corona*) of bystanders stood to watch the performance, allowing the speakers when they wished to turn from the jury to address the public directly.

The defendant wore the shabby dress of mourning and neglected to wash or shave. It was taken amiss if he did not comply with these requirements. Publius Rutilius Rufus, put on trial for extortion in 92, refused (being a Stoic) to put on mourning, and was convicted. The case was famous as a miscarriage of justice by an equestrian jury: Rutilius, who had protected the provincials from the exactions of the equestrian tax-farmers (*publicani*), went into exile at Smyrna, to live as an honoured citizen among the provincials he was alleged to have oppressed. Milo likewise proudly refused to put on mourning (although he had done so for Sestius in 56), and was convicted.

The prosecutors' speeches were heard first, then those of the defence, and only after the end of the speeches was the evidence taken. In his speeches we therefore find Cicero speculating about what the evidence is going to be. The only speeches in which he refers to evidence as having already been taken are extortion speeches. Trials for extortion were held in two stages (separated by an adjournment of at least one day, or *comperendinatio*), so that in the speeches of the second hearing reference could be made back to the evidence taken at the end of the first hearing. If slaves gave evidence, it had to be under torture. They were not allowed, however, to be examined against their master, except in trials for incest and in the specific case of the Catilinarian conspiracy. The value or worthlessness of evidence extracted under torture was a standard topic (*locus communis*) in oratory, and is found a number of times in Cicero's speeches. The cruelty of torture was not relevant to the orators' arguments, and receives no comment.

The number of jurors was specified individually for each court, but seventy-five seems to have been a usual number, twenty-five jurors being selected from each of the three categories. Milo, however, was tried by an entirely different method, under the *lex Pompeia de vi*: 360 jurors heard the evidence (which, contrary to usual practice, was taken first); eighty-one of them, chosen by lot, heard the speeches; each side then rejected fifteen jurors, and the remaining fifty-one (eighteen senators, seventeen *equites*, and sixteen *tribuni aerarii*) cast their votes.

The jurors were not allowed to confer amongst themselves (since some might attempt to intimidate others), and they voted in a secret ballot immediately after the evidence had been taken. The presiding magistrate gave no summing-up (he was unlikely to be an expert in the law, and was only holding his office for a single year); he had no means of determining or influencing the verdict, and did not vote. The jurors were given wax tablets with 'A' (for *absolvo*, 'I acquit') inscribed on one side and 'C' (for *condemno*, 'I convict') on the other, and they would rub out one letter or the other (or both, to abstain), and drop the tablet into an urn. The verdict was reached by a majority vote; if the votes were equal the defendant was acquitted.

If the defendant was found guilty, the penalty was officially death. But since he was at no point taken into custody, even after the pronouncement of the sentence, it was always possible for him to evade his punishment by retiring into self-imposed or 'voluntary' exile in a federate (thus technically non-Roman) state. He ceased to be a Roman citizen, and suffered *aquae et ignis interdictio* ('debarment from water and fire'), in other words outlawry. Should he ever return to Italy, he could be killed with impunity. Exile was therefore not a penalty, but a means of avoiding a penalty (and it was a recourse available only to the wealthy: humbler persons seem to have been summarily executed). Before the enfranchisement of Italy in 90–89, a convicted criminal could retire to Praeneste (only 23 miles from Rome) or Naples, but in the Ciceronian period he would have to leave Italy: Massilia (Marseilles), an oasis of Greek culture and refined living, was a favoured place, the refuge of both Verres and Milo. Criminals' property was supposed to be confiscated, but very little seems actually to have been seized. They conveyed it to their friends and relatives, and lived out their exile in luxury. To many of them perhaps, the heat of the city, the interminable debates in the senate, and the constant struggle to keep up with the Luculli were things that, in time, they could learn to live without.

NOTE ON THE TRANSLATION

CICERO's orations are not written in the language of ordinary speech: instead, they are composed in a highly artificial style which must have impressed, astonished, and mesmerized those who listened to it. Sentences are long, commonly as long as a third of a page of a modern printed text and sometimes longer. The style is 'periodic'; that is, once the sentence or 'period' has begun, the listener has to wait some time before the various subordinate clauses have been delivered and the sense is complete. While the period is evolving, the listener has certain expectations about how it is going to continue and end (grammatically, and in sense), and when it is finally completed these expectations are either fulfilled (giving the listener a sense of satisfaction) or, more rarely, cheated (startling the listener). The clauses which make up the period can sometimes be mere padding, but this is unusual; often they make the argument more impressive or powerful, and in addition they serve to delay the completion of the period, providing a greater feeling of satisfaction when the grammar and sense are finally completed. The clauses themselves and the words or groups of words within them are often arranged in carefully balanced pairs, sometimes so as to form a contrast, or sometimes in a symmetrical pattern; or they can be arranged in threes, with increasing weight placed on each item, or greater weight placed on the final or second and final item. Formal English style also uses these techniques; thus I have written 'impressed, astonished, and mesmerized' above, providing more terms than is strictly necessary for the sense ('mesmerized', the strongest term and therefore placed last, would have sufficed). In periodic style, the most important part of the period is the end (the beginning is the next most important), because it is here that the sense of completion is delivered. In accordance with the techniques of Hellenistic Greek oratory, Cicero always makes sure that the ends of his periods, and even of the more important clauses ('cola'), sound right: certain rhythmical patterns ('clausulae') are favoured and others (mainly those which resemble verse) avoided. This 'prose rhythm' is one of the most prominent features of his style. Scholars have tried to analyse it, with varying results. It must have taken a great deal of training to be able to achieve the appropriate rhythms automatically, without thinking about it, in the way that Cicero could (*Orat.* 200). Roman audiences were discriminating, and appreciated the skilful use of prose rhythm: there is an anecdote about a group of listeners bursting into applause when an orator produced some striking cadences (*Orat.* 213–14; cf. 168). Besides rhythm, there are many other techniques used by Cicero to enliven his prose, such as rhetorical questions (questions that do not expect an answer), anaphora (repetition of a word or phrase in successive clauses), asyndeton (omission of connectives), apostrophe (turning away to address an absent person or thing), exclamation, alliteration and assonance, wordplay, and metaphor.

The policy I have adopted in this translation has been to preserve as much of Cicero's style and artistry as possible; and I have tried to make the translation strike the reader in as near as possible the same way as I think the Latin text would have struck its original readership. I am emphatically not of the view that Cicero's rhetoric must be sacrificed in order to achieve readability. It may sometimes be the case that reading a translation in which the rhetoric has been preserved involves a little more effort than reading one in which it has been removed. But Cicero meant his speeches to involve some effort on the part of the reader: he was not writing in the language of ordinary speech.

I have chosen to render long Latin sentences by long English ones. If a sentence would have struck its original readers as a long one, then I think it needs to be rendered by one or more sentences that would strike a modern reader as long. So a sentence that is ten lines long (i.e. for Latin, long but not excessively long) might best be rendered by two English sentences of five lines each (i.e. two sentences that in English are long but not excessively so). To chop up the original sentence into five sentences of two lines each, or ten of one line each, may conceivably make the text more readable, but it will misrepresent the original as surely as if the wrong words are chosen in the translation.

Where possible, I have retained the periodicity of the Latin: I have tried to keep the clauses and sometimes even the actual words in the same order as they occur in the original. Each word or clause contains an idea, and in the original these ideas are conveyed to the reader in a particular order; so the translator should as far as possible avoid doing violence to that order. If a significant idea is withheld until the end of a sentence (as commonly happens in periodic style), then it is essential that the translator also withhold it until the end; shuffling the clauses around for the sake of readability will destroy the effect that the author has created.

Prose rhythm is a feature of the original that cannot normally be reproduced. But good English does avoid certain rhythms, and the translator can at least ensure that the English he is writing does not strike the ear harshly.

I have retained Cicero's rhetorical devices as far as possible. Questions have been translated as questions, exclamations as exclamations, direct speech as direct speech, and indirect speech as indirect speech. It is true that we do not use rows of rhetorical questions in normal usage, but then neither did the Romans: Roman oratory was meant to sound theatrical and high-flown, so a translation ought to sound that way too.

I have tried to reproduce the many examples of alliteration, assonance, wordplay, and metaphor that feature in Cicero's writing. It was very often impossible to provide an alliterative effect using the same letter as Cicero, and in such cases I have introduced alliteration of some other letter; the same may be said with regard to assonance. In three places it has been necessary to explain a play on words in the explanatory notes.

I have been careful not to introduce material that has no basis in the Latin: however readable such flourishes may be, they have no place in the translation. Similarly, I have been careful not to omit any of the original. The reader may be unaware of the extent to which some translators take liberties in this regard, adding or subtracting material in a misguided attempt to ease the flow, and thereby providing not translation but paraphrase. If Cicero's meaning has been correctly understood (not always an easy matter), it ought not to be necessary to ease the flow of his writing.

The translator needs to decide how he is going to render the Roman names that are mentioned in the text: prominent Romans generally had at least three names (*praenomen*, *nomen*, and *cognomen*), but normally only one or two are used when the person is referred to. My own practice has been to translate the names exactly as Cicero gives them, adding (where necessary) an explanatory note at the end of the book giving the full form of the name together with any other relevant information. This allows the translation to present an accurate reflection of the Romans' customs of naming. I have, however, made an exception in *Pro Roscio Amerino*, in the case of Roscius' relations Titus Roscius Magnus and Titus Roscius Capito. Cicero refers to the first of these men as Roscius or Titus Roscius, and to the second as Roscius, Titus Roscius, Titus Capito, or Capito. The scope for confusion here is considerable, and so I have referred to the two men as Magnus and Capito throughout.

Finally, I should mention the paragraphing—the first matter to which a translator turns his attention. The medieval manuscripts of Cicero's speeches do not preserve Cicero's original paragraphing (if there ever was any, which is unlikely), and since the text of Cicero is very difficult to divide up, modern editions tend to insert new paragraphs only every several pages. The decision as to where to start a new paragraph requires one to think very hard about the structure of the argument, and I have found this almost the most difficult aspect of my task. I have re-paragraphed all five speeches afresh, and I hope that the new paragraphing will substantially aid the understanding of these speeches.

Translating Cicero's speeches is not an easy task. It is also, I believe, a task which involves a heavy responsibility. Far more people read Latin authors in translation than in the original, and their judgement of the author will be determined by the quality of the translation. Cicero is one of the world's greatest writers; but in a poor translation his merits will not come across. In this new translation I have tried to enable the reader to see him as he really is—showy, forceful, funny, and alive.

NOTE ON THE LATIN TEXT

FOR each speech I have translated the most satisfactory existing edition of the Latin text, with occasional departures from it. These editions, and my departures from them, are listed below. The numerous differences of paragraphing and punctuation are not recorded (such features have no ancient authority, but are added by editors according to their understanding of the sense).

Pro Roscio Amerino

Text: A. C. Clark, Oxford Classical Text (Oxford, 1905).

34   *non est ferendum*: I translate *num est ferendum?*
64   *Caelium*: I translate *Cloelium.*
112   *maxime videtur grave*: I translate *minime videtur leve.*
133   *quid praeco enumeraret*: I translate *praeconem enuntiare.*
141   *fortunas arasque nostras*: I translate *fortunasque nostras.*

Pro Murena

Text: J. Adamietz, Texte zur Forschung, 55 (Darmstadt, 1989).

17   *Caeliis*: I translate *Coeliis.*
25   *ab ipsis cautis*: I translate *ab ipsis his cautis.*
31   †*si qua*: I translate *aequa.*
37   *omnis*: I translate *omni.*
42   †*catenarum*: I translate *accusatorum.*
43   *Servius*: I omit.
47   †*praerogationum*: I translate *promulgationem.*
64   †*seposuisses aut*: I translate *si dixisses.*
77   *Sin etiam <si> noris tamen . . . nomen petis quasi incertum sit*: I translate *Sin iam noris tamen<ne> . . . cum petis quasi incertus sis?*
86   *idem vos*: I translate *idem et.*
      squalore et sordibus confectus: I translate *<in> squalore et sordibus confectus morbo.*

Pro Archia

Text: A. C. Clark, Oxford Classical Text (Oxford, 1911).

5	<*et Locrenses*>: I omit.
28	*adornavi*: I translate *adoptavi*.
31	*iudiciis*: I translate *ingeniis*.

Pro Caelio

Text: T. Maslowski, Teubner (Stuttgart and Leipzig, 1995).

1	*nobilem*: I omit.
14	*facilitatis*: I translate *facultatis*.
	etiam bonis: I translate *bonis*.
18	<*eam*>: I omit.
34	*non atavum*: I translate *non abavum non atavum*.
36	*parasti*: I translate *paratos*.
38	*fili*: I translate *Caeli*.
78	*hominem . . . inquinatum*: I accept the placing of these words after *vidistis*.

Pro Milone

Text of Asconius: A. C. Clark, Oxford Classical Text (Oxford, 1907).

33.6	*Clodio*: I translate *Cloelio*.
33.23	*ac Cicero ipse*: I translate *atque ipse*.
34.13	*Leo. L. Herennius Balbus P. Clodi*: I translate *Leo, et L. Herennius Balbus. P. Clodi*.
34.14–15	*postulavit; eodem tempore Caelius familiam*: I translate *postulavit eodem tempore Caelius; et familiam*.
55.20	*Clodius*: I translate *Cloelius*.

Text of Cicero: A. C. Clark, Oxford Classical Text (Oxford, 1918²).

27	*a Lanuvinis*: I omit.
	quod erat dictator Lanuvi Milo: I omit.
	quae illo ipso die habita est: I omit.

33 *Clodi*: I translate *Cloeli*.
35 *Plotia*: I translate *Plautia*.
46 *omnes scilicet Lanuvini*: I omit.
55 *Clodius ipse Clodius*: I translate *Clodius*.
57 *terrore*: I translate *tortore*.
66 *tametsi*: I translate *quod si tamen*.
75 *Aponio*: I translate *Apinio*.
96 *arma*: I omit.

SELECT BIBLIOGRAPHY

Articles (but not books) in foreign languages are excluded.

General

Alexander, M. C., *Trials in the Late Roman Republic, 149 BC to 50 BC* (*Phoenix*, Suppl. 26; Toronto etc., 1990).

Atkinson, J. M., *Our Masters' Voices: The Language and Body Language of Politics* (London and New York, 1984).

Berry, D. H., and Heath, M., 'Oratory and declamation', in S. E. Porter (ed.), *Handbook of Classical Rhetoric in the Hellenistic Period 330 BC–AD 400* (Leiden, 1997), 393–420 (*S. Rosc., Mil.*).

Broughton, T. R. S., *The Magistrates of the Roman Republic*, i (New York, 1951), ii (New York, 1952), iii (Atlanta, 1986).

Clarke, M. L., rev. Berry, D. H., *Rhetoric at Rome: A Historical Survey*[3] (London, 1996).

Classen, C. J., *Recht-Rhetorik-Politik: Untersuchungen zu Ciceros rhetorischer Strategie* (Darmstadt, 1985) (*Mur.*).

Craig, C. P., *Form as Argument in Cicero's Speeches: A Study of Dilemma* (APA American Classical Studies, 31; Atlanta, 1993) (*S. Rosc., Cael.*).

Dorey, T. A., (ed.), *Cicero* (London, 1964), esp. ch. 3 by R. G. M. Nisbet (*S. Rosc., Cael., Mil.*).

Douglas, A. E., *Cicero*[2] (Oxford, 1979).

Greenidge, A. H. J., *The Legal Procedure of Cicero's Time* (Oxford, 1901).

Gruen, E. S., *Roman Politics and the Criminal Courts, 149–78 BC* (Cambridge, Mass., 1968).

—— *The Last Generation of the Roman Republic* (London, 1974).

Habicht, C., *Cicero the Politician* (Baltimore and London, 1990).

Jones, A. H. M., *The Criminal Courts of the Roman Republic and Principate* (Oxford, 1972).

Kennedy, G. A., 'The Rhetoric of Advocacy in Greece and Rome', *AJP* 89 (1968), 419–36 (*S. Rosc.*).

—— *The Art of Rhetoric in the Roman World, 300 BC–AD 300* (Princeton, 1972).

Laurand, L., *Études sur le style des discours de Cicéron*[4], 3 vols. (Paris, 1936–8).

Ludwig, W., and Stroh, W., (eds.), *Éloquence et rhétorique chez Cicéron* (Entretiens sur l'antiquité classique, 28; Geneva, 1982) (A. D. Leeman: *Mur.*).

MacKendrick, P., *The Speeches of Cicero: Context, Law, Rhetoric* (London, 1995) (*Mur.*, *Arch.*, *Cael.*, *Mil.*).

May, J. M., *Trials of Character: The Eloquence of Ciceronian Ethos* (Chapel Hill and London, 1988) (*S. Rosc.*, *Mur.*, *Cael.*, *Mil.*).

Mitchell, T. N., *Cicero: The Ascending Years* (New Haven and London, 1979).

—— *Cicero: The Senior Statesman* (New Haven and London, 1991).

Neumeister, C., *Grundsätze der forensischen Rhetorik gezeigt an Gerichtsreden Ciceros* (Munich, 1964).

Powell, J. G. F., and Paterson, J.J., (eds), *Cicero the Advocate* (Oxford, 2004) (D. H. Berry: *Arch.*).

Rawson, E. D., *Cicero: A Portrait* (London, 1975).

Riggsby, A. M., 'Did the Romans Believe in their Verdicts?', *Rhetorica*, 15 (1997), 235–51.

Shackleton Bailey, D. R., *Onomasticon to Cicero's Speeches*[2] (Stuttgart and Leipzig, 1992).

Solmsen, F., 'Cicero's First Speeches: A Rhetorical Analysis', *TAPA* 69 (1938), 542–56 (*S. Rosc.*).

Stockton, D. L., *Cicero: A Political Biography* (Oxford, 1971).

Stroh, W., *Taxis und Taktik: Die advokatische Dispositionskunst in Ciceros Gerichtsreden* (Stuttgart, 1975) (*S. Rosc.*, *Cael.*).

Tatum, W. J., *The Patrician Tribune: Publius Clodius Pulcher* (Chapel Hill and London, 1999).

Vasaly, A., *Representations: Images of the World in Ciceronian Oratory* (Berkeley etc., 1993) (*S. Rosc.*, *Cael.*).

Wiedemann, T. E. J., *Cicero and the End of the Roman Republic* (London, 1994).

Winterbottom, M., 'Schoolroom and Courtroom', in B. Vickers (ed.), *Rhetoric Revalued* (Medieval & Renaissance Texts & Studies, 19; New York, 1982).

Pro Roscio Amerino

The following items are additional to the bibliography given by Craig (see under 'General'), 27 n. 1.

Donkin, E. H., *Cicero: Pro Roscio Amerino*[2] (London, 1916).

Harris, W. V., *Rome in Etruria and Umbria* (Oxford, 1971), 271–4.

Kinsey, T. E., 'The Dates of the *Pro Roscio Amerino* and *Pro Quinctio*', *Mnemosyne*, 20 (1967), 61–7.

Kinsey, T. E., 'The Political Insignificance of Cicero's *Pro Roscio*', *LCM* 7 (1982), 39–40.

Kinsey, T. E., 'The Sale of the Property of Roscius of Ameria: How Illegal was it?', *AC* 57 (1988), 296–7.

Nicol, J. C., *Cicero:* Pro Roscio Amerino[2] (Cambridge, 1934).

Seager, R. J., 'The Political Significance of Cicero's *Pro Roscio*', *LCM* 7 (1982), 10–12.

Stock, St G., *Cicero:* Pro Roscio Amerino[2] (Oxford, 1901).

Pro Murena

Adamietz, J., *Cicero:* Pro Murena (Texte zur Forschung, 55; Darmstadt, 1989).

Ayers, D. M., 'Cato's Speech against Murena', *CJ* 49 (1954), 245–53.

Craig, C. P., 'Cato's Stoicism and the Understanding of Cicero's Speech for Murena', *TAPA* 116 (1986), 229–39.

Freese, J. H., *Cicero:* Pro Murena (London, 1894).

Heitland, W. E., *Cicero:* Pro Murena (Cambridge, 1874).

Macdonald, C., *Cicero:* Pro Murena (London, 1969).

Sandbach, F. H., *The Stoics*[2] (Bristol, 1989).

Pro Archia

Berry, D. H., 'The Pride and Prejudices of a Roman Jury', *Omnibus*, 38 (1999), 12–14.

Gotoff, H. C., *Cicero's Elegant Style: An Analysis of the* Pro Archia (Urbana etc., 1979).

Porter, W. M., 'Cicero's *Pro Archia* and the Responsibilities of Reading', *Rhetorica*, 8 (1990), 137–52.

Reid, J. S., *Cicero:* Pro Archia[2] (Cambridge, 1883).

Taylor, J. H., 'Political Motives in Cicero's Defense of Archias', *AJP* 73 (1952), 62–70.

Vretska, H. and K., *Cicero:* Pro Archia (Texte zur Forschung, 31; Darmstadt, 1979).

Wallach, B. P., 'Cicero's *Pro Archia* and the Topics', *RhM* 132 (1989), 313–31.

Wiseman, T. P., '*Pete nobiles amicos*: Poets and Patrons in Late Republican Rome', in B. K. Gold (ed.), *Literary and Artistic Patronage in Ancient Rome* (Austin, Tex., 1982), 28–49.

Pro Caelio

Austin, R. G., *Cicero:* Pro Caelio[3] (Oxford, 1960).

Clauss, J. J., 'The Ignoble Consistency of M. Caelius Rufus', *Athenaeum*, 78 (1990), 531–40.

Dorey, T. A., 'Cicero, Clodia, and the *Pro Caelio*', *G&R* 5 (1958), 175–80.

Geffcken, K. A., 'Comedy in the *Pro Caelio* with an Appendix on the *In Clodium et Curionem*' (*Mnemosyne*, Suppl. 30; Leiden, 1973).

Gotoff, H. C., 'Cicero's Analysis of the Prosecution Speeches in the *Pro Caelio*: An Exercise in Practical Criticism', *CP* 81 (1986), 122–32.

Ramage, E. S., 'Clodia in Cicero's *Pro Caelio*', in D. F. Bright and E. S. Ramage (eds.), *Classical Texts and their Traditions: Studies in Honor of C. R. Trahman* (Chico, Calif., 1984), 201–11.

—— 'Strategy and Methods in Cicero's *Pro Caelio*', *Atene e Roma*, 30 (1985), 1–8.

Skinner, M. B., 'Clodia Metelli', *TAPA* 113 (1983), 273–87.

Wiseman, T. P., *Catullus and his World: A Reappraisal* (Cambridge, 1985), chs. 2 and 3.

Pro Milone

Berry, D. H., 'Pompey's Legal Knowledge—or Lack of it: Cic. *Mil.* 70 and the Date of *Pro Milone*', *Historia*, 42 (1993), 502–4.

—— 'Cicero's Masterpiece?', *Omnibus*, 25 (1993), 8–10.

Clark, A. C., *Cicero:* Pro Milone (Oxford, 1895) (also contains a commentary on Asconius).

Clark, M. E., and Ruebel, J. S., 'Philosophy and Rhetoric in Cicero's *Pro Milone*', *RhM* 128 (1985), 57–72.

Colson, F. H., *Cicero:* Pro Milone (London, 1893).

Crawford, J. W., *M. Tullius Cicero: The Lost and Unpublished Orations* (*Hypomnemata*, 80; 1984), 210–18.

Dyck, A. R., 'Narrative Obfuscation, Philosophical *topoi*, and Tragic Patterning in Cicero's *Pro Milone*', *HSCP* 98 (1998), 219–41.

Lintott, A. W., 'Cicero and Milo', *JRS* 64 (1974), 62–78.

Marshall, B. A., *A Historical Commentary on Asconius* (Columbia, Mo., 1985).

Reid, J. S., *Cicero:* Pro Milone (Cambridge, 1894).

Ruebel, J. S., 'The Trial of Milo in 52 BC: A Chronological Study', *TAPA* 109 (1979), 231–49.

Settle, J. N., 'The Trial of Milo and the Other *Pro Milone*', *TAPA* 94 (1963), 268–80.

Stone, A. M., '*Pro Milone*: Cicero's Second Thoughts', *Antichthon*, 14 (1980), 88–111.

Further Reading in Oxford World's Classics

Caesar, *The Civil War*, trans. and ed. J. R. Carter.

—— *The Gallic War*, trans. and ed. Carolyn Hammond.

Catullus, *The Poems of Catullus*, trans. and ed. Guy Lee.

Cicero, *The Nature of the Gods*, trans. and ed. P. G. Walsh.

Cicero, *The Republic* and *The Laws*, trans. Niall Rudd, ed. Jonathan Powell.
Plutarch, *Roman Lives: A Selection of Eight Lives*, trans. Robin Waterfield, ed. Philip A. Stadter.

CHRONOLOGY

The dates are BC.

106   Cicero born (3 January).

91–87   Social War; Cicero serves under Gnaeus Pompeius Strabo (89) and Sulla (88); Italians win Roman citizenship (90, 89).

88   Sulla occupies Rome.

88–85   First Mithridatic War.

87   Marius and Cinna occupy Rome; domination of Cinna (87–84).

86   Marius dies.

83–81   Second Mithridatic War.

82   Sulla occupies Rome and is made dictator (82–81); proscriptions (82 to 1 June 81).

81   Sulla's reforms, including establishment of seven permanent criminal courts with senatorial juries; *Pro Quinctio*.

80   *Pro Roscio Amerino*; Cicero defends the freedom of a woman from Arretium (80 or 79).

79–77   Travels abroad; visits Molon of Rhodes.

78   Sulla dies.

75   Cicero quaestor in western Sicily; henceforward a senator.

73–71   Verres governor of Sicily.

73–63   Third Mithridatic War.

70   Pompey and Crassus consuls; *In Verrem*; *lex Aurelia* makes juries two-thirds equestrian.

69   Cicero plebeian aedile; *Pro Fonteio*.

67   Lucullus relieved of Mithridatic command; *lex Gabinia* gives Pompey command against pirates.

66   Cicero praetor in charge of extortion court; *Pro lege Manilia*; *lex Manilia* gives Pompey Mithridatic command; *Pro Cluentio*.

63   Cicero consul; *De lege agraria*; *Pro Rabirio perduellionis reo*; Catilinarian conspiracy; *Pro Murena*; execution of the conspirators (5 December).

62   Catiline defeated and killed; *Pro Sulla*; *Pro Archia*; Bona Dea scandal; Pompey returns to Italy.

DEFENCE SPEECHES

DEFENCE SPEECHES

PRO ROSCIO AMERINO
('FOR ROSCIUS OF AMERIA')

DATE: 80 BC
DEFENDANT: Sextus Roscius
LAW: *lex Cornelia de sicariis et veneficis* (Cornelian law concerning murderers and poisoners)
CHARGE: murder of Sextus Roscius (defendant's father)
PROSECUTORS: Gaius Erucius, Titus Roscius Magnus
DEFENCE ADVOCATE: Marcus Tullius Cicero
PRESIDING MAGISTRATE: Marcus Fannius
VERDICT: acquittal

Pro Roscio Amerino ('For Roscius of Ameria', so called to distinguish it from the speech for a different Roscius, *Pro Roscio comoedo*, 'For Roscius the comic actor') was Cicero's first speech in a criminal court (§ 59), given when he was just 26 years old. In it he bravely spoke out against some of the more unsavoury aspects of the Sullan regime (although taking care to absolve Sulla himself from blame), and, winning his case, made a name for himself which brought him a flood of commissions. The speech shows him in a better light than almost any other speech, with the orator placing himself in some degree of danger (just how much is disputed) in order to save an innocent man falsely accused by his enemies of murdering his father. *Pro Roscio* is also important for being closer than any of Cicero's other speeches to the artificial, florid, and often flabby 'Asianist' style which was then in fashion; soon afterwards he toned down his manner of speaking and developed the more restrained and economical style in which the great majority of his speeches are written.

The trial of Sextus Roscius took place against the background of the Sullan regime. In 82 BC Sulla recaptured Rome from the Marians, who had held it illegally since 87, and had himself appointed dictator 'to write laws and reconstitute the state'. The laws he went on to pass were designed to restore to the senate the authority and powers it had possessed in the years before the Gracchan reforms nearly half a century earlier. The criminal justice system was reorganized: seven permanent courts were set up to try the major crimes, and juries were to consist exclusively of senators. Sulla also set about the punishment of his enemies. Lists were posted in the forum of men to be killed, and bounties were offered to the killers. The property of men 'proscribed' in this way was confiscated by the state and then sold off cheaply at auction to those prepared to bid for

it. The sons and grandsons of the proscribed, besides losing their inheritance, were debarred from ever holding magisterial office. Worst of all, the
proscriptions came to be used not just to remove opponents of the new
order, but as a means of paying off old scores and satisfying private greed.
Sulla's supporters were able to amass vast fortunes at the expense of those
who were, or could be represented as being, Sulla's enemies.

The proscriptions were officially ended on 1 June 81 (§ 128). Some
months later the elder Sextus Roscius, the father of Cicero's client (father
and son shared the same name), was murdered in Rome while returning
from dinner. He was a rich man, the owner of thirteen farms at Ameria, a
hill-town in the south of Umbria, about fifty miles north of Rome. Men
like him, the leaders of Italian communities, were cultivated by the Roman
nobility: the great families relied on such men to deliver them the votes of
their communities whenever a member of the family was standing for
office. In return, the Italians could expect favours such as letters of
recommendation or support in the courts, and also presents and invitations to dinner. Roscius spent most of his time in the city courting his
patrons, and Cicero tells us that they were some of the most prominent
families in Rome: the Metelli, Servilii, and Scipiones (§ 15). His son,
meanwhile, preferred to stay in Ameria, where he looked after the family
farms. During the civil war between the Marians and Sulla (83–82 BC),
Roscius supported the winning side, that of Sulla and the nobility. This
was natural in view of the very close links that his patrons, the Metelli,
had with Sulla. Caecilia Metella, who died in 81, was Sulla's wife, and her
cousin, Quintus Caecilius Metellus Pius, was consul with Sulla in 80, the
year of the younger Roscius' trial.

Soon after his father's death, Roscius' inheritance was taken from him
by two of his relations (§§ 87, 88), Titus Roscius Magnus and Titus
Roscius Capito. This was done by enlisting the help of Chrysogonus, a
Greek freedman of Sulla's and, according to Cicero, a man of considerable
influence. After the murder, Magnus and Capito went to see Chrysogonus,
and what Cicero calls a 'partnership' was formed. Chrysogonus had the
dead man's name posthumously entered into the list of the proscribed; his
property was then confiscated and put up for sale; Chrysogonus bought it
for a token price; and Capito was given three of the farms, while Magnus
took possession of the rest on Chrysogonus' behalf. When young Roscius
attempted to recover his property and clear his father's name, his enemies
sought to remove him by the ingenious means of accusing him of his
father's murder. He therefore went for help to the Metelli. Judging from
their failure to speak for him at his trial, they refused to help him, at least
publicly. Possibly (as some scholars have suggested) the case was beneath
their notice; more likely, they did not wish to be associated with a case

which could be seen as hostile to Sulla. Roscius was, however, given material assistance by Caecilia Metella (a third cousin of the Caecilia Metella who had been Sulla's wife), and Cicero in his speech makes the most of this indication of Metellan goodwill. Even so, Roscius must have been severely disappointed at the failure of his patrons to offer him more conspicuous support.

The lack of a prominent advocate threw Roscius back on the 26-year-old Cicero, a man of no influence and, as yet, no oratorical reputation. For Cicero, the case presented a great opportunity for him to make a name for himself. Many murders had been committed in the recent past, but this was the first murder trial to be held for some considerable period of time (§§ 11, 28), and the first trial to take place in Sulla's new murder court. Public interest in the case was therefore intense—and many people were looking for a conviction. The trial also had a political dimension—Cicero would need to comment on injustices committed in Sulla's name—and this too would bring him public attention. There was certainly an element of risk involved: as we have seen, the defence could not count absolutely on the support of the Metelli (like Cicero, some scholars have exaggerated the degree of support Roscius received from the nobility). But provided he took care to dissociate Sulla from Chrysogonus' wrongdoing, Cicero might hope to escape reprisals. He doubtless also found it congenial to defend an Italian like himself; and of course he had the great advantage of having right on his side.

Roscius' enemies, then, found a prosecutor, Gaius Erucius, and brought a charge of parricide. Parricide (which originally meant the murder of any free man, but was later restricted to the murder of close relations, particularly parents) was regarded by the Romans as an especially monstrous crime. Their ancestors had therefore devised an appropriately gruesome punishment for convicted parricides: they were to be stripped, scourged, sewn up in a sack together with dog, a cock, a viper, and a monkey, and then thrown into a river or the sea to drown (see §§ 30 (with note), 70). It is extremely unlikely, however, that Roscius, if found guilty, would actually have had to undergo this punishment, since it seems only to have applied to parricides who confessed their guilt (cf. Suetonius, *Augustus* 33). Instead, he would merely have faced the normal punishment which obtained in the criminal courts, officially death, but in practice 'voluntary' exile in a federate (thus technically non-Roman) state, followed by interdiction (debarment from water and fire, in other words outlawry), to prevent him returning to Italy.

The prosecution's case against Roscius was (as far as we can judge) extremely weak. They alleged that he did not get on with his father, and had murdered him because he was afraid of being disinherited by him

(§ 52). But they do not seem to have been able to offer any evidence in support of their allegation. Moreover, they would not allow the dead man's slaves, who had been with him when he was murdered, to be interrogated, since these were now the property of Chrysogonus. The greatest weakness in their case, however, was the extraordinary contradiction between their actions prior to the trial and the charge they were now bringing. Their purchase of the elder Roscius' property assumed that he had been proscribed, and hence was lawfully killed—whereas now they were prosecuting his alleged killer for murder. If the killing of Roscius had been lawful, their accusation was false. But if his killing had been unlawful, as was implied by their prosecution, then they could be shown to have acted illegally in seizing his property. In these circumstances, it seems not a little surprising that they should have brought the charge at all; and perhaps they did, as Cicero claims, first try to murder their opponent instead (§§ 26–8). But having decided to bring the charge, their strategy had to be to avoid all mention of the alleged proscription and the sale of the property (§ 5). Evidently they felt confident that the defence would also remain silent on these matters. The defence, they reasoned, would surely not risk the argument that since Roscius was proscribed, his killing was lawful: this might seem to imply that the son did after all kill his father, and a jury would be most unlikely to look favourably on such an act, however justified in law.

The prosecution were right in predicting that Cicero would not adopt this line of defence. But they were wrong in supposing that he would be deterred by fear of Sulla from revealing their misdeeds. In the event, the strategy Cicero chose to adopt was to agree that the killing of the elder Roscius was unlawful, but nevertheless expose what the prosecution had done—that they had added his name to the proscription list for the purpose of illegally acquiring his property, and were now (inconsistently) accusing his son of murder in order to prevent him from claiming his inheritance. Nor, however, did Cicero stop there. It was a standard rhetorical tactic for defence advocates not only to maintain that their client was innocent of the crime of which he was accused, but to argue that the accusers themselves were the real perpetrators of the crime. This ploy, known as *antikategoria* (Quint. *Inst.* 3.10.4, 7.2.9), is used (in different forms) in several of Cicero's speeches. In this speech, he accuses Magnus and Capito themselves of the murder of Roscius (interestingly, however, he does not accuse Chrysogonus (§§ 108, 122): that would be going too far). He is unable, of course, to substantiate his claim, but he needs only to give it a certain plausibility to establish that it need not have been his client who committed the murder. Whether Magnus and Capito were really responsible for the murder of Roscius is unknown; it seems unlikely, however, given that the younger Roscius had not prosecuted them for it.

Cicero's sensational revelation of the background to the case had the desired effect and Roscius was acquitted. Whether he went on to recover his property is unknown. In the speech, Cicero repeatedly states that Roscius is only interested in saving his life, not in recovering his property (§§ 7, 128, 143–4), but it would be naïve to suppose (as some scholars have done) that Roscius considered himself bound by this after the trial. In any case, the argument at § 127 that technically the property has not been sold at all seems to suggest that Roscius is already thinking of claiming his inheritance.

As for Cicero, his defence was greatly admired, and he was now thought capable of taking on any case at all (*Brut.* 312). The nobles were no doubt gratified to see Chrysogonus brought low, and Sulla may have welcomed the opportunity to rid himself of a freedman who had become too powerful. After the trial, Cicero accepted a large number of commissions. These included a successful defence of the freedom of a woman from Arretium; the case was politically important, more so than the defence of Roscius, because it called into question Sulla's disenfranchisement of entire communities (*Pro Caecina* 97) The speech does not survive. Later, in 79 BC, the strain of so much work forced Cicero to go abroad for the sake of his health (Plutarch (*Cic.* 3.4) gives as Cicero's reason the need to avoid Sulla, and this may have been generally believed at the time; but Cicero himself (*Brut.* 313–14) makes it clear that ill-health was responsible). When he returned two years later, he had acquired a manner of speaking which would impose less physical strain on him and was also somewhat less Asianist in style.

At the end of his life Cicero spoke of *Pro Roscio* as a speech in which he stood up against the power of Sulla (*De officiis* 2.51):

> Defences bring the greatest glory and influence, and all the more so if the speaker happens to be helping someone who appears to be oppressed and persecuted by someone in power. This is the sort of case I have often taken on, for example when as a young man I spoke for Sextus Roscius of Ameria against the influence of Lucius Sulla when he was in power. The speech survives, as you are aware.

This is not quite an accurate representation of the case, since in his speech Cicero takes great care to distinguish between Sulla and his minion, and attribute all blame to the latter. The speech, as originally given, cannot have been in any way 'against Lucius Sulla': criticism of Sulla would have run counter to Cicero's general strategy and would have been instantly fatal to the defence. There are, however, places in the speech where the praise of Sulla seems insincere and double-edged (§§ 22, 131), and certain passages at the beginning and end of the speech (§§ 3, 152–4) go much further in criticizing the regime than merely exposing the misdeeds of Chrysogonus. But these passages, which contrast so strongly with the attitude adopted throughout the rest of the speech, are best explained as anachronistic revision. The speech was probably circulated on Cicero's return to Rome in 77, after Sulla had died, and it may have been to Cicero's advantage when writing it up to represent himself as having offered greater resistance to Sulla than had been possible for him at the time. His defence of the woman from Arretium, in which he seems genuinely to have challenged Sulla's actions, would have made his out-spokenness in certain parts of the published speech more believable.

But if Cicero did not speak out against Sulla directly in his original speech, he did nevertheless protest against the horrors which were being committed in his name. Moreover, he was the only person at the time who dared to do so. His defence of Roscius should therefore be judged an act of considerable moral courage.

PRO ROSCIO AMERINO

[1] I imagine you must be wondering, members of the jury, why it is that, when there are so many leading orators and men of the highest rank present here in court, I of all people should have stood up to address you: for neither in age, nor in ability, nor in authority do I bear comparison with these men who have remained seated. All those whom you see here supporting my client believe that in this case a wrong has been perpetrated, arising from an act of unprecedented criminality, and that it ought to be resisted; but to resist it themselves they have not the courage, considering the unfavourable times in which we live. The result is that they attend the trial because it is their duty to do so, but say nothing because they want to keep out of danger. [2] So am I the boldest man here? Far from it. Or am I more attentive to my obligations than everyone else? I am hardly so eager even for that distinction that I would wish others to be deprived of it. What is it, then, that has driven me more than anyone else to undertake the defence of Sextus Roscius? The reason is this. If any of these men whom you see here supporting my client—highly influential and distinguished figures that they are—were to speak for Roscius, and were to make any mention at all of politics, something which is unavoidable in this case, he would be assumed to be saying much more than he actually was saying. [3] With me, on the other hand, if I say openly everything that the case requires, I shall certainly not find that my speech leaks out and becomes public knowledge to the same extent. A second reason is this. With the others, their rank and distinction is such that nothing they say passes unnoticed, while because of their age and experience no allowance would be given for any indiscreet remark they might make. But if I am the one that speaks too freely, what I say will either be ignored because I have not yet embarked on a political career, or else be pardoned on account of my youth—although not only the idea of pardon but even the custom of judicial inquiry has now been abolished at Rome!* [4] There is also a third reason. It may be perhaps that the others were asked to speak in such a way that their decision seemed to them to be unaffected by any ties of obligation. In my case, however, I was applied to by men who by their friendship,

acts of kindness, and position carried the greatest weight with me, and I considered that I could never ignore their kindness to me, nor disregard their rank, nor neglect their wishes.

[5] These, then, are the reasons why I have come forward as advocate in this case. I was not singled out as the one man who could speak with the greatest skill, but was simply the only one left who could speak with relatively little danger: I was chosen not so that Sextus Roscius might have a strong enough defence, but to prevent his being abandoned altogether.

You may ask, perhaps, what that terror and what that great fear consists of which is deterring so many distinguished men from coming forward, as is their usual custom, to defend someone's life and property. It is not surprising that you should still be unaware of this, since the prosecution have deliberately omitted to mention the very circumstance which has been the reason for this trial. [6] And what is that? The property of the father of my client, Sextus Roscius, is worth six million sesterces, and it is from the valiant and illustrious* Lucius Sulla, whose name I mention with the greatest respect, that a young man, arguably the most powerful man in Rome at the present time, claims to have purchased this property for two thousand sesterces: this man is Lucius Cornelius Chrysogonus! He has a particular request to make of you, gentlemen. Seeing that he has unlawfully seized the extremely valuable and splendid property of another man, and seeing that the life of Sextus Roscius appears to him to stand in the way of and impede his access to that property, he asks that you remove all uneasiness from his mind and release him from all his fears. For as long as Sextus Roscius is still unharmed, Chrysogonus does not imagine that he can keep possession of the very large and valuable inheritance of this innocent man; with Roscius condemned and forced into exile, however, he believes that he will be free to squander and fritter away his ill-gotten gains. Chrysogonus therefore requests that you relieve him of this anxiety which worries and torments his mind night and day, and declare yourselves his accomplices in this outrageous theft which he has committed.

[7] If this request seems to you, members of the jury, to be right and proper, then I for my part should like to make a small request of my own—and one which is, I think, rather more reasonable. First of all I ask Chrysogonus to content himself with our wealth and property, and not to demand our life-blood as well. Secondly I ask you,

gentlemen, to make a stand against the wickedness of criminals, to alleviate the misfortunes of innocent men, and in the case of Sextus Roscius to repel a danger which threatens every one of us. [8] If, however, there comes to light any ground for the accusation, or any suspicion of guilt, or even the slightest reason to think that the prosecution had any justification for bringing the charge, and if, in short, you find any reason at all for the charge other than the property which I mentioned, then I have no objection to the life of Sextus Roscius being given up to satisfy the greed of these men. But if, on the other hand, the only issue is that of satisfying the desires of men who are never satisfied, and if the only object of the present struggle is to see that the seizure of such a rich and splendid property is capped, as it were, by the condemnation of Sextus Roscius, then surely not the least sordid aspect of this sordid affair is this: that you, by your verdict, given on oath, should be thought of as being the most appropriate means by which these men might lay hands on that which they have previously been accustomed to obtain by criminal violence. You have been raised from the citizen body to the senate because of your noble qualities, and have been chosen from the senate to be members of this jury because of your high character.* Is it really from men such as yourselves that these cut-throats and gladiators demand not just that they may escape punishment—for that is what they ought to fear and dread from you, considering their misdeeds—but also that they may walk out of this court enriched and loaded with spoils?

[9] I feel quite unable to do justice in my speech to these atrocious and terrible crimes, or to evoke the proper degree of sorrow at them, or to protest against them with the outspokenness that is required: I find myself hampered in attempting to do justice to them by my lack of talent; and in evoking sorrow, by my youth; and in protesting against them, by the times in which we live. I also have reasons to feel acutely afraid: there is my own shy nature, and your importance and distinction, and then the domineering force of the prosecution, and the dangers to which Sextus Roscius is exposed. I therefore beg and beseech you, gentlemen, to pay careful attention to what I have to say, and listen to me with a sympathetic ear. [10] I have put my trust in your integrity and good sense, and have taken on a greater burden than I think I can manage. If you can in any way lighten this burden for me, gentlemen, I shall shoulder it to the best

of my abilities with all the effort and commitment I can muster; but if—and I trust this will not happen—you decide to abandon me, then my courage will not fail, and the case which I have taken on I will do my best to see through to the end. But if I do not manage it, I would rather be crushed by the burden of doing my duty than treacherously throw it aside or weakly give up a task which I undertook as a matter of honour.

[11] You also, Marcus Fannius, I earnestly entreat to let both us and your country see you to be the same man now as the Roman people saw you to be when you presided over this court before.* Look at the enormous crowd of people that has come to watch this trial: you can see what everyone is hoping for, what a yearning there is for strict and severe sentences. This is the first murder trial for a long time, and in the mean time there have been a large number of truly shocking murders. Everyone is therefore hoping that under your praetorship this court will be turn out to be fully capable of dealing with the bloody crimes that are openly committed every day. [12] In other trials it is generally the prosecution who appeal for severity: today, however, it is we, the defence, who make such an appeal. We ask you, Marcus Fannius, and you, members of the jury, to punish wrongdoing with the greatest determination, to show the greatest courage in standing up to criminals, and to reflect on the fact that, unless you make your views abundantly clear by the verdict you will give in this trial, then greed, wickedness, and criminality will become so rife that murders will be committed not only in secret, but even here in the forum, before your own platform, Marcus Fannius, before your feet, gentlemen, and among the very benches of this court.

[13] Do you think that this trial has any other aim except to secure official approval for this kind of behaviour? The prosecutors are men who have seized the property of the defendant; the defendant is a man who has been left by his prosecutors with nothing except utter ruin. The prosecutors are men who stood to gain from the murder of Sextus Roscius' father; the defendant is a man whose father's death brought him not just grief but poverty as well. The prosecutors are men who were desperate to kill the defendant; the defendant is a man who has brought a bodyguard even to this court, to avoid being murdered here before your very eyes. The prosecutors, finally, are men whose punishment the people demand; and the defendant is a

man who happens to be the sole survivor of a terrible massacre which the prosecutors have perpetrated.

[14] And to help you see, members of the jury, that the actual crimes that have been committed are far more shocking than my description of them, I am going to explain to you how the whole business has come about, starting from the beginning. This will give you a better understanding of the misfortunes which have fallen on this innocent man, the criminal acts of the prosecutors, and the disastrous condition of our country.

[15] Sextus Roscius, the father of my client, was a citizen of Ameria. In birth, rank, and wealth he was easily the most prominent man not only of his town but of the entire district. Moreover, he enjoyed the favour of the most high-ranking families at Rome, and was linked to them by ties of hospitality. Indeed, he enjoyed not just ties of hospitality but had regular day-to-day contact with the Metelli, Servilii, and Scipiones*—families which I mention, as I should, out of respect for their honour and distinction. And so it was that, of all that he possessed, this connection was the only thing that he managed to bequeath to his son: for the son's inheritance was violently seized, and is currently possessed, by thieves from within his own family, and now the innocent son's life and reputation are being defended by the father's hosts and friends. [16] The elder Roscius had always been a supporter of the Roman nobility. In the recent civil disturbance,* therefore, when the position and very existence of each and every noble was under threat, he defended their cause, more than anyone else in the district, with his devoted efforts, enthusiasm, and influence. He did this because he thought it only right that he should fight to uphold the honour of those to whom he owed his position as the most honourable man among his own people. Once victory had been achieved and we were no longer at war, the proscriptions began and all over Italy men thought to have been on the opposing side were being apprehended. Throughout this period Roscius was frequently in Rome and appeared daily in the forum in full view of everyone: he looked as if he was celebrating the victory of the nobles, rather than being afraid that any disaster should happen to him as a result of it.

[17] Now the elder Roscius had a long-standing feud with two other men from Ameria, also called Roscius: one of these men I can now see sitting on the prosecutors' bench, while the other, I hear, is

in possession of three farms belonging to my client. Had the elder
Roscius been able to guard himself against their hostility as much as
he used to fear it, he would still be alive today. You see, gentlemen,
he had good reason to be afraid. Let me tell you about these two
men, Titus Roscius Capito and—the one who is here in court—
Titus Roscius Magnus. Capito is reputed to be an experienced and
celebrated gladiator, the winner of many prizes; Magnus, on the
other hand, has recently attached himself to Capito to be trained by
him. Before this particular fight Magnus was, as far as I know, a mere
beginner; but now he has easily surpassed his master in wickedness
and criminality. [18] For while my client Sextus Roscius was at Ameria, and this Magnus here was in Rome—while the son was busy on
his farms, having devoted himself, as his father wished, to a life in
the country spent managing the family estate, and Magnus was constantly at Rome—the elder Sextus Roscius was murdered one night
near the baths of Pallacina* while he was returning from dinner. I
hope that it is quite clear from the circumstances of the murder on
whom the suspicion falls; but unless the facts themselves make completely clear what is at this point still only a suspicion, then please
judge my client to be implicated in the crime.

[19] After Sextus Roscius had been killed, the first to bring the
news to Ameria was a certain Mallius Glaucia, an impoverished
freedman and a dependant and friend of Titus Magnus here. This
Glaucia brought the news not to the house of the victim's son, but to
that of his enemy, Titus Capito. Moreover, although the murder had
been committed more than an hour after nightfall, Glaucia reached
Ameria by dawn: in ten hours during the night he raced across fifty-
six miles in gigs laid on in relays. And his purpose was not simply to
be the first to bring the hoped-for news to the murdered man's
enemy, but to show him the blood of the man he hated while it was
still fresh, and present him with the dagger which had been pulled
out of the body only a few hours before.

[20] Four days later, news of these events was brought to Chrysogonus in Lucius Sulla's camp at Volaterrae.* The size of the murdered man's fortune was pointed out. The quality of his estate—
consisting of thirteen farms, nearly all of which bordered on the
Tiber*—was noticed, as was the helplessness and isolation of my
client. It was represented that, since the father, Sextus Roscius, so
worthy* and influential a figure, had been killed without any difficulty,

it would be a simple matter to do away with the son, an unsuspecting country man who was unknown at Rome—and Magnus and Capito promised their help in carrying out the task. [21] Not to detain you any longer, gentlemen, a partnership was formed. At this time the proscriptions were no longer spoken of, and even those who had been afraid of them were now returning home, judging that they were no longer in any danger. In spite of this, the name of Sextus Roscius, a fervent supporter of the nobility, was entered in the proscription lists. Chrysogonus became the purchaser. Three farms, probably the best ones, were made over to Capito, who is in possession of them today. All the rest of the property was seized by Magnus here, acting, as he himself says, for Chrysogonus.

I know for a fact, members of the jury, that all this was done without Lucius Sulla's knowledge. [22] Indeed, at a time when he is repairing the past and preparing for whatever the future might hold, when he alone possesses the means of establishing peace and the power of waging war, when everyone looks to him alone, and he alone directs everything, when he is occupied with so much important business that he scarcely even has time to breathe, it is hardly surprising if he fails to notice something—especially when there are so many men watching to see how busy he is and waiting for their opportunity so that, as soon as his attention is distracted, they can do something of this kind. Remember also that, although Sulla may be 'fortunate'*—as he truly is —there is no one so fortunate that he does not, in a large household, possess at least one dishonest slave or freedman.

[23] So, as I was saying, this excellent Magnus, Chrysogonus' agent, came to Ameria and laid hold of my client's farms. Even before the wretched man, distraught with grief, had had time to complete his father's funeral rites, Magnus threw him naked from his home and flung him headlong, gentlemen, from his ancestral hearth and household gods. And that is how Magnus became master of this great estate. He who before had lived a penny-pinching existence when living on his own restricted means became, as so often happens, arrogant and spendthrift when he acquired someone else's. He carried off much of the property to his own house in full view of everyone, but still more he took away in secret; he gave away a great deal with a lavish and unstinting hand to those who had helped him; and what was left he sold off at auction.

[24] This seemed so scandalous to the people of Ameria that there were tears and lamentation throughout the town. For a whole series of tragic events had taken place before their very eyes. There had been the brutal murder of their leading citizen, Sextus Roscius. Then there was the shocking impoverishment of his son, who had been left so large an inheritance, but whom this wicked criminal had not even granted right of access to his father's tomb. After that there had been the outrageous sale of the property, its occupation by others, theft, plunder, and rewards for accomplices! There was nobody who would not rather have seen the whole property go up in flames than witness Magnus gloating and lording it over what right-fully belonged to the excellent and well-respected Sextus Roscius. [25] The town council therefore immediately passed a decree that the ten leaders of the council should go off to see Lucius Sulla and make him aware what sort of a man Sextus Roscius had been, lodge a complaint against the criminal behaviour of these people, and ask him to restore the good name of the dead father and the property of the innocent son. Please listen to the actual decree.

(*The decree of the town council is read out.*)

The deputation, then, arrived at Sulla's camp. It is clear, gentlemen, that these crimes and outrages, as I said earlier, were all committed without Lucius Sulla's knowledge. For as soon as the delegates had arrived, Chrysogonus went to meet them himself; he also deputed certain men of high rank to dissuade them from seeing Sulla in person and promise them that he, Chrysogonus, would do every-thing that they wanted. [26] Chrysogonus, you see, would sooner have died than have Sulla made aware of what he had done. The delegates were old-fashioned men who judged other people's char-acters by their own. When, therefore, Chrysogonus promised that he would remove Sextus Roscius' name from the proscription lists and hand over the farms unoccupied to the son, and when Titus Roscius Capito (who was one of the ten delegates) also promised that this would be done, they believed it, and returned to Ameria without having put their case before Sulla.

To begin with, Chrysogonus and Capito put the matter off from one day to the next, and dragged their feet. Then they took things more casually, did nothing, and made the Amerians look like fools. Eventually, as was readily inferred, they plotted against the life of my client, Sextus Roscius, believing that they could no longer hold on to property that did not belong to them as long as its owner was still alive.

[27] As soon as Roscius was aware of the situation, he took the advice of his friends and relations and fled to Rome. There he took refuge with Caecilia,* the sister of Nepos and daughter of Baliaricus, whose name I mention with the greatest respect, and with whom his father had been on terms of close familiarity. This woman, gentlemen, is someone in whom there remain, even in this day and age, traces of that old-fashioned sense of duty, preserved as a model for others: everyone has always felt it to be so. She received Sextus Roscius into her home, destitute as he was, thrown out of his house and driven from his property, and seeking to escape the threats and weapons of thieves: when everyone else had given him up for lost, she came to the help of a friend in trouble. Thanks to her goodness, loyalty, and attentive care, his name was entered, while he still lived, in the list of the accused, rather than being added, after his murder, to the list of the proscribed.

[28] Once Sextus Roscius' enemies realized that his life was being extremely carefully protected and that they had no chance of killing him, they made a plan which was utterly criminal and reckless: they decided to accuse him of murdering his father. They would get hold of some experienced prosecutor who would be capable of finding something to say, even where there were no grounds whatever for considering the defendant to be under suspicion. Secondly, since the actual charge gave them no hope of overcoming him, they would use the times in which we live as a weapon against him. Because there had been no trial for so long, they reasoned, the first man to be accused would be certain to be condemned. Chrysogonus' influence would ensure that no one would support him. Not a word would be said about the sale of the property or about the partnership which had been formed. The mere charge of parricide, and the horrific nature of such a crime, would be sufficient to destroy him without difficulty, since no one would come forward to defend him. [29] With this plan, or rather driven on by this insanity, they have handed over to you the man they had wanted to kill, but were unable to, so that you could slaughter him yourselves.

What shall I complain of first? Where, members of the jury, should I choose to begin? What help can I summon, and from whom? Should I call on the protection of the immortal gods, or of the Roman people, or of you who at this moment exercise supreme authority?* [30] The father outrageously murdered, the family home besieged by enemies, property removed, appropriated, and plundered, the son's life endangered and repeatedly attacked by sword and treachery! From this long list of enormities, surely there is no type of crime that has been left out? Yet they cap and crown these misdeeds with further atrocities. They fabricate a charge that defies belief, they use my client's own money to bribe people to prosecute him and testify against him, and then they give the wretched man a choice whether he prefers to offer his throat to Magnus or forfeit his life in the most shameful way possible by being sewn up in a sack.* They thought he would lack defenders, and he does. But a man who is prepared to speak freely and to defend him loyally—which, in this case, is all that is needed—this he most certainly does not lack, gentlemen! [31] In taking on this case I may perhaps have acted rashly, carried away by the impetuosity of youth. But now that I have taken it on, even though—by Hercules!—all kinds of threats, terrors, and dangers surround me, I will stand up and face them. I have firmly resolved not only to say everything that I judge to be relevant to the case, but to say it willingly, boldly, and freely. There is nothing, gentlemen, that can force me to act out of fear instead of duty. [32] For who could be so unprincipled as to realize what has been going on and then keep quiet or turn a blind eye? You murdered my father,* although he was never proscribed. After you killed him, you entered his name in the proscription lists. Me you forcibly evicted from my home. And you now are in possession of my inheritance. What more do you want? Can you deny that you have come to these benches fully armed in order to achieve one of two things: to secure my conviction, or to cut my throat?

[33] By far the most reckless man that we have known in Rome in recent times was Gaius Fimbria,* and also the most deranged, as everyone agrees—except of course those who are deranged themselves. At the funeral of Gaius Marius, it was he who was responsible for the wounding of Quintus Scaevola,* the most revered and honoured man in our nation. This is not the place for an extended appreciation of Scaevola's merits, and in any case there is nothing I could add to what the Roman people are able to remember for themselves. After the attack, when Fimbria heard that Scaevola might recover from his injury, he announced his intention of prosecuting

him; and when he was asked what charge he was going to bring against a man who no one thought could ever be praised highly enough, he is said to have replied, like the madman he was, 'because he failed to take the whole of the sword into his chest'.* The Roman people never witnessed anything more disgraceful than this, except for Scaevola's actual murder, an event so disastrous that it brought ruin and destruction on one and all: for Scaevola was killed by the very people whose lives he was attempting to save by mediation.

[34] In the present case, is there not a strong resemblance to what Fimbria said and did? You are accusing Sextus Roscius. Why? Because he escaped from your hands, because he refused to be murdered. The earlier outrage, I grant you, seems the more shocking, because it was committed against Scaevola; but is this recent one to be tolerated—because it was committed by Chrysogonus? Immortal gods! What is there in this case that actually requires a defence? What point is there that calls for the expertise of an advocate, or has such need of the eloquence of an orator? All the same, members of the jury, let me unfold the entire case and, having set it out before your eyes, subject it to a full examination: this will allow you to see clearly what is the point at issue, what I ought to be discussing, and what course you ought to follow in coming to your decision.

[35] There are three obstacles, as far as I can make out, facing Sextus Roscius today: the charge his opponents have brought, their violent behaviour, and their power. The fabrication of the charge has been undertaken by the accuser Erucius; the role involving the violence has been claimed by Magnus and Capito; and Chrysogonus, whose influence is the greatest, wields his power against us. I know that I must address you on all three of these topics. [36] But how? I must not treat them all in the same way, because while the first one is my own personal responsibility, the remaining two are matters which the Roman people have appointed you to deal with. My job is to refute the charge, whereas your duty is to make a stand against violence, and to break and destroy the dangerous and unacceptable power of men of this type at the very first opportunity.

[37] Sextus Roscius stands accused of the murder of his father. Immortal gods, what an outrageously criminal act, the type of act that seems to comprise within it every crime that exists! The philosophers rightly point out that filial duty can be violated by a mere

look. What punishment, then, could be devised which would be severe enough for a man who had murdered his own parent—a person he was bound by every law, human and divine, to defend with his life if necessary? [38] In the case of such a crime as this, so immense, so terrible, and so extraordinary, and committed so rarely that, if it is ever heard of, it is thought to be a portent or a prodigy, what arguments do you, Gaius Erucius, consider you should use in your accusation? Ought you not to demonstrate the unparalleled wickedness of the man you are accusing, his savage and brutal nature, his life given up to every kind of vice and crime, a character, in short, irretrievably abandoned and depraved? Yet you have made no such accusation against Sextus Roscius, not even by way of the conventional attack on a defendant's character.

[39] Sextus Roscius murdered his father. What kind of a man is he, then? A mere youth corrupted and led on by men of bad character? Actually, he is over forty years old. I take it, then, he must be a veteran cut-throat, a man who will stop at nothing, and someone with considerable experience in committing murder. No, you have not heard this even so much as hinted at by the prosecution. Well, then, it was his extravagance, his enormous debts, and his uncontrolled greed which drove him to commit the crime. But Erucius cleared him of extravagance when he said that Roscius almost never went out to dinner; and my client has never been in debt. And as for greed, how could this exist in a man who, as the prosecutor himself critically remarked, has always lived in the country and spent his time farming his land? Such a life is far removed from greed—but is, on the contrary, very closely linked to duty. [40] So what was it, then, that prompted Sextus Roscius to commit such an act of madness as you attribute to him? 'His father', the prosecutor says, 'did not like him'. Didn't his father like him? Why ever not? There certainly must have been a valid, strong, and obvious reason: for just as it is incredible that a son should kill his father without very many, very strong motives, it is similarly unlikely that a father should hate his son unless he has many strong and compelling reasons for doing so. [41] So let me return again to my original point and ask what faults this only son can have had, serious enough to cause his father to dislike him. It is quite obvious that there were no such faults. Was the father out of his mind, then, seeing that he hated his own son without good reason? Certainly not: he was the most level-headed

man you could think of. It is perfectly clear, therefore, that if the
father was not mad and the son was not depraved, then the father
had no reason to hate his son, and the son had no motive for murdering his father.

[42] 'I do not know', the prosecutor says, 'what the reason for the
hatred was. But I do know that it existed, because previously, when
the father had two sons, he wanted the one who is now dead to be
with him all the time, whereas this one he banished to his farms in
the country.' Now, the problem that Erucius has experienced in
making a malicious and futile prosecution also applies to me in pleading the strongest of defences. He did not manage to devise any means
of backing up a charge he had fabricated, whereas I cannot possibly
find any way of disproving and refuting such a groundless allegation.
[43] But what is it that you are saying, Erucius? That Sextus Roscius
handed over so many fine and productive farms to his son to culti-
vate and oversee—in order to banish and punish him? Surely this is
what heads of families, particularly men of old Roscius' class from
the country towns, wish for most: that their sons, if they have any,
should dedicate themselves wholeheartedly to managing their property, and devote most of their time and effort to running the family
estate? [44] Or are you saying that he sent him away to confine him
in the country, giving him his food and drink at the house and
stopping all his pleasures? If, however, it turns out that he was not
only put in charge of running the family estate but was also given
some of the farms as his own while his father was still alive, then will
you still describe his life as a banishment to the country and a
removal? You see, Erucius, how far your line of reasoning differs
from the actual facts of the matter and the truth. What fathers
normally do, you stigmatize as being unprecedented; what is done
out of kindness, you accuse of having been done from hatred; what
the father granted to his son as a mark of his esteem, you make out
was done to punish him. [45] It is not as if you are unaware of all
this. The problem is rather that you are so short of arguments that
you think you had better speak not only against us, but against the
way things are, against the way people behave, and against the views
of everyone.

Nevertheless, you will say, Roscius had two sons, and kept one of
them at his side, while letting the other one live in the country. Now
please do not be offended, Erucius, at what I am about to say: I do

not mean to criticize you, but to give you a gentle reminder. [46] Even if fortune has given you no definite knowledge of who your father is,* and has thus deprived you of an understanding of how a father feels towards his children, nature has at least endowed you with your full share of human feeling, and has added a taste for culture, making you no stranger to literature. Let me therefore take an illustration from a play. Do you really think that old man in Caecilius* thinks less of Eutychus, the son of his who lives in the country, than he does of the other one—Chaerestratus, I think he is called? That he keeps the one with him in the city as a mark of his esteem, but has banished the other one to the country as a punishment? [47] 'Why are you straying into such absurdities?' you will ask. As if it would be difficult for me to give you as many names as you like of people—my fellow-tribesmen, say, or my neighbours (not to stray too far afield)—who want their favourite sons to become hard-working farmers! It would, however, be a breach of good manners to mention specific individuals by name, when it is not known whether they would be happy for their names to be used in this way. In any case, there is no one I could mention who would be more familiar to you than Eutychus, and it certainly makes no difference to my argument whether I use the name of this young man from comedy or that of someone from, say, the territory of Veii.* In fact I think that poets make up these stories so that we can see our own behaviour represented in other people, and be given a realistic depiction of our daily life. [48] Anyway, turn your attention back to the real world, if that is what you want, and consider which occupations are most highly praised by heads of families not just in Umbria* and the surrounding regions, but in the old towns closer to hand. You will see very clearly that the lack of charges that you can substantiate has led you to misrepresent as a fault and a defect what is in fact Sextus Roscius' greatest virtue.

And it is not just because their fathers want them to that sons take up farming. I happen to know a great many people—and I am sure each of you does, too—who are of their own accord fired by a passion for farming, and who are convinced that this country existence, which you think ought to be a disgrace and a crime, is the most honourable and agreeable life possible. [49] As for this Roscius here, how do you rate his enthusiasm for agricultural matters, and his skill in them? His relations you see here, good people that they are, tell me that he is just as proficient in his own profession as you are in that trade of prosecution to which you belong. I realize, however, that since Chrysogonus has thought it best to leave him without an estate, he might as well forget his profession and drop his passion for farming. This would be a great pity, and something he does not deserve. Nevertheless, he will bear it with equanimity, gentlemen, if you will allow him to keep his life and good name. What he is not able to bear, however, is that he has been plunged into this crisis because of the number and quality of his farms, and that the care with which he has cultivated them should be what is most damaging to him. It is bad enough for him to have cultivated his farms for others rather than for himself, without also being put on trial for having cultivated them in the first place.

[50] You would certainly have made a risible prosecutor, Erucius, if you had been born in the days when men were summoned from the plough to be made consul. Believing as you do that it is a crime to supervise the cultivation of land, I can imagine what you would have thought of the famous Atilius,* who was found by the men who were sent to fetch him sowing seed with his own hand: you would have judged him to be an utterly disgraceful and dishonourable man! But—by Hercules!—our ancestors took a very different view about him and others like him, and it was because they did so that, instead of an extremely small and insignificant country, they handed down to us one which is very great and prosperous. For they worked on their own lands tirelessly, rather than greedily seeking after those of others; and by acting in this way they came to acquire land, cities, and foreign peoples, and so enlarged their country, this empire, and the glory of the Roman people. [51] I am not saying this for the purpose of making a comparison with our current investigation. No, the point I want to make is this. In the days of our ancestors the most distinguished and illustrious men, although they had a duty to remain constantly seated at the helm of the state, nevertheless devoted a certain amount of time and effort to cultivating their land. I therefore believe that one ought to forgive a man who declares himself a country man, in that he has always lived in the country, especially considering that there is nothing which would have pleased his father more, or would have been more agreeable to himself, or, in actual fact, more honourable.

[52] So, Erucius, I take it that the father's intense hatred of his son

is proved by the fact that he let him live in the country! And do you
have any further proof? 'Yes', he says, 'I do: his father was planning
to disinherit him.' Ah, I see; now you are saying something which
may be relevant. For I am sure even you will agree with me that these
arguments are frivolous and silly which run as follows. 'He never
went to dinner parties with his father.' Of course he didn't, as he
never even went into town, except on very rare occasions. 'Hardly
anyone invited him to their house.' That is not surprising, given that
he did not live in Rome, and was not in a position to return the
invitation. [53] You yourself realize that arguments like that are
worthless. Let us look, then, at the argument we were starting to
consider, one which constitutes the most solid proof of hatred that
there could possibly be: 'the father was intending to disinherit his
son.' I am not going to ask you what his reason was; I will ask you
how you know it. On the subject of reasons, however, you should
really have set out and counted up all the father's motives. A conscientious prosecutor, bringing such a serious charge, would have
been duty bound to give an account of all the son's vices and misdeeds, in order to explain how the father became so angry that he
was driven to suppress his natural feelings, to banish from his heart
all the love that was buried within it, and, finally, to forget that he
was a father. I do not believe all this could happen unless my client
here had committed crimes of the greatest seriousness.

[54] However, I give you leave to pass over these misdeeds which,
since you say nothing about them, you admit are non-existent. As for
your saying that the father wanted to disinherit his son, you certainly
ought to prove it. What evidence do you have to make us think that
that was the case? You can say nothing that will be true, so at least
invent something plausible, to make it less obvious what you are
plainly doing—laughing at the misfortunes of my client and at the
dignity of this fine jury. The father wanted to disinherit his son.
Why? 'I do not know.' Did he disinherit him? 'No.' Who stopped
him? 'He was thinking about it.' Was he? Who did he mention it to?
'To no one.' To make an accusation of this kind, to bring a charge
which you are not only unable to prove but do not even attempt to
prove—how can this be described, gentlemen, except as an abuse of
the court, of the law, and of your high authority, perpetrated with a
view to greed and financial gain? [55] None of us, Erucius, is ignorant of the fact that there is no personal enmity between you and

Sextus Roscius. Everyone can see why you have appeared before this court as his enemy. They know that it is his fortune that has brought you here. So what more is there to say? I can at least say this, that however eager you may have been for financial gain, you should nevertheless have reflected that the view this jury will take of you, and the Remmian law,* were also important considerations to take into account.

[56] It is beneficial that there should be, in the state, a large number of prosecutors, so that crime may be kept in check by fear. This is, however, only beneficial so long as the prosecutors do not openly make fools of us. A man is innocent, say: he has done nothing, but nevertheless has fallen under suspicion. It is a pitiful situation. All the same, I can forgive, up to a point, the man who brings a charge against him. For because the prosecutor has something to say which gives the impression that there is a case to be answered, we do not view him as making fools of us in public and knowingly bringing a false accusation. It is for this reason that we all accept that there should be as many prosecutors as possible, because an innocent man, if he is prosecuted, can always be acquitted, whereas a guilty man cannot be convicted unless he has first been charged. It is better that an innocent man be acquitted than a guilty man escape trial. Food is contracted for at public expense for the geese on the Capitol,* and dogs are fed there too, so that they can give warning should thieves break in. They are of course unable to tell who is a thief and who is not, but they will sound the alarm if anyone at all enters the Capitol during the night, because this looks suspicious, and will err—since they are only animals—on the side of caution. But if the dogs barked during the day as well, when people come to worship the gods, I think someone would probably break their legs, for raising the alarm when there was no cause for it. [57] It is just the same with prosecutors. Some of you are geese, who only honk, and can do no actual harm, while others are dogs who can bite as well as bark. We see that you are fed. In return, you should direct your attacks against those who genuinely deserve it: that is what the people want. In cases where it is likely that someone has committed a crime, by all means give voice to your suspicion by barking: that also is permissible. If, however, you behave in such a way as to prosecute a man for the murder of his father without being able to say why or how he did it, and bark when there are no grounds whatsoever for suspicion, then

nobody is actually going to break your legs—but, if I know these jurymen at all, they will tattoo your forehead with that letter which you prosecutors find so hateful that you also detest the Kalends of every month.* And they shall do it so indelibly that you will be able to accuse nothing for ever afterwards but your own bad luck.

[58] So, what have you given me to reply to, brilliant prosecutor that you are? And what have you given this jury to make them think my client might be guilty? 'He was afraid he was going to be dis-inherited.' Ah, I see; but why he should have been afraid of this, no one will say. 'His father was contemplating it.' Prove it. There is no proof: you do not say with whom he discussed it or to whom he told it, nor do you give any reason that might have led you to suspect it. When you make this kind of accusation, Erucius, surely what you are really saying is this: 'I know what I have been paid, but I do not know what to say. I thought only of what Chrysogonus told me, that no one would come forward to defend this man, and that in times such as these no one would dare to breathe a word about the purchase of the property or about the partnership.' That misjudgement led you to make this dishonest prosecution. By Hercules, you would not have uttered one single word had you thought that anyone would answer you!

[59] I don't know, gentlemen, whether you noticed the offhand way in which Erucius launched his prosecution; it was interesting to watch. When he saw who was sitting on these benches I am sure he must have asked whether this or that person was going to undertake the defence; it certainly never occurred to him that I might do so, since I have never spoken in a criminal case before. As soon as he found out that no one with any ability or experience was going to speak he became so relaxed about it all that he behaved just as his fancy took him, sitting down, wandering about, sometimes even call-ing a boy over to him—to order dinner, I imagine. In a word, he treated this panel of jurors and this entire court as if it were one vast empty space! Eventually he finished his speech and sat down. I then stood up. [60] He seemed to breathe a sigh of relief that it was only me who was going to speak, not one of the others. I began my speech. I saw, gentlemen, that he was joking and paying no attention—until I named Chrysogonus. As soon as I mentioned the name, he instantly jumped up; he seemed astonished. I realized what had pricked him. I named Chrysogonus a second and a third time.

After that men did not stop running this way and that to inform
Chrysogonus, I assume, that there was a man in Rome who was
daring to speak out contrary to his will, that the trial was not going as
he had anticipated, that the purchase of the property had been
exposed, that the partnership was being severely criticized, that his
influence and power were being disregarded, that the jury were paying close attention, and that the people thought the whole business a
scandal. [61] You misjudged the situation, Erucius. You can see that
everything has been turned round: Sextus Roscius is being represented, if not adequately, at least with free speech; the man you
thought had been deserted is being defended; those who you
believed would hand him over to you are instead holding a proper
trial. So let us see at last that old intelligence and foresight of yours:
admit that you came here expecting that what would take place in
this court would not be a trial, but a robbery.

A trial for parricide is being held; the prosecutor, however, gives
no reason as to why the son should have killed his father. [62] In the
case of the most trivial offences and the smallest misdemeanours
such as are becoming more common and are now occurring virtually
every day, the first and most important question to be asked is what
was the motive for the crime. In a case of parricide, however, this is a
question which Erucius does not think it necessary to raise. With
this particular crime, gentlemen, even when many motives seem to
coincide and point in the same direction, the charge is not lightly
believed, nor does the matter depend on idle speculation, nor is any
attention paid to dubious witnesses, nor is the verdict determined by
the ingenuity of the prosecutor. On the contrary, it must be proved
that the defendant has committed many crimes before, and that his
life has been utterly depraved. Unparalleled wickedness must also be
demonstrated—and indeed not only wickedness, but the utmost violence and insanity. But even if all this can be proved, there must exist
in addition unmistakable indications of the crime: where, how, by
whose agency, and at what time the murder was committed. And
unless such proofs are numerous and transparently clear, a crime so
atrocious, so wicked, and so outrageous cannot possibly be believed.
[63] For men's tender feelings are strong, the ties of blood are powerful ones, and nature herself protests against suspicions of this kind.
It is without doubt unnatural and monstrous that a being of human
shape and form should so far surpass the wild animals in savagery as

to have deprived of the light of day, in the most shocking way possible, the very people to whom he owes the fact that he too can enjoy this light. Even wild animals live at peace with each other, thanks to the ties of birth and upbringing, and thanks to nature herself.

[64] It is said that not many years ago a certain Titus Cloelius from Tarracina,* quite a well-known man, went to bed after dinner in the same room as his two grown-up sons, and was discovered in the morning with his throat cut. No slave or free man was found who could possibly be suspected of the crime, while the two grown-up sons who had been sleeping next to him said that they had not even been aware of what had happened. The sons were then prosecuted for parricide. What could have been more suspicious? Was it really credible that neither of them saw anything? That someone dared to venture into that room, and at a time when the two grown-up sons were there and could have easily have seen what was happening and offered resistance? There was, moreover, no one else on whom suspicion could fall. [65] Nevertheless, once it had been proved to the jury that the sons had been found asleep when the door was opened, the young men were formally acquitted and cleared of all suspicion. For nobody believed that there could have been anyone capable of violating every human and divine law by such an outrageous crime, and then going to sleep immediately afterwards. Indeed, men who have committed so terrible a crime are unable to rest in peace or even to draw breath without fear.

[66] The poets tell of sons who killed their mothers to avenge their fathers.* Although they are said to have killed them in response to the commands and oracles of the immortal gods, you have read how the Furies hound them even so, and never let them rest, because they were unable even to fulfil their duty towards their fathers without committing a crime. And that is how it really is, gentlemen. The blood of a father or a mother has great power, it is a great bond, and it possesses great sanctity. The stain it produces, however small, can not only never be washed out, but seeps right into the mind, so that the utmost violence and insanity ensue. [67] You should not believe, of course, as you so often see in plays, that those who have committed a treacherous or criminal act are literally hounded and frightened out of their wits by the blazing torches of the Furies. No, it is above all their own wrongdoing and their own terror which torments them. Each is hounded and driven mad by the crime he has committed: his

own evil thoughts and the stings of his conscience terrify him. These
are the Furies which stay forever beside the wicked, and which day
and night exact punishment for the parents from their murderous
sons.

[68] It is the very enormity of parricide which, unless it has actually been proved, makes it impossible to believe. Unless a man's early
years have been scandalous, unless his life has been defiled with
every type of corruption, unless his expenditure has been extravagant and accompanied by shame and disgrace, and unless he has
shown violent criminal behaviour and a recklessness verging on
insanity, then a charge of parricide will simply not be believed. You
should also add to that a hatred on the part of the father, a fear of
punishment at his father's hands, friends of bad character, slaves
who were party to the crime, a favourable opportunity, and a suitable
location especially chosen. I would almost go so far as to say that the
jury should actually see the son's hands stained with the father's
blood, if they are really to believe a crime so serious, so monstrous,
and so cruel. [69] It therefore follows that the less credible it is,
unless it be proved, the more seriously it should be punished, if it is
proved.

And so, while there is plenty of evidence to show that our ancestors surpassed other nations not only in warfare but in wisdom and
good judgement too, this is especially demonstrated by the fact that
they devised a unique punishment for sons who violated their filial
duty. Consider how much more sensible our ancestors were on this
point than the men regarded by other nations as supremely wise.
[70] The leading city as far as intelligence is concerned is said to
have been Athens, during her years of greatness; and in that city the
wisest man is reputed to have been Solon,* the man who drew up the
laws which are still in force there today. He, on being asked why he
had not specified any punishment for the murder of a parent, replied
that he thought no one would ever do such a thing. People say it was
sensible of him not to lay down a penalty for an offence that at that
time had never been committed; had he done so, he might have
seemed not so much to be outlawing the crime as putting the idea
into people's heads. But how much wiser our ancestors were! Realizing that nothing is so sacred as to be exempt from the possibility of
criminal violation, they thought out a unique punishment for parricides. Their intention was that those whom nature herself had been

unable to keep on the path of filial duty should nevertheless be deterred from actually committing a crime by the horrific nature of the penalty. They therefore stipulated that parricides should be sewn up in a sack while still alive and thrown into a river.*

[71] What remarkable wisdom they showed, gentlemen! Do they not seem to have cut the parricide off and separated him from the whole realm of nature, depriving him at a stroke of sky, sun, water, and earth—and thus ensuring that he who had killed the man who gave him life should himself be denied the elements from which, it is said, all life derives? They did not want his body to be exposed to wild animals, in case the animals should turn more savage after coming into contact with such a monstrosity. Nor did they want to throw him naked into a river, for fear that his body, carried down to the sea, might pollute that very element by which all other defilements are thought to be purified. In short, there is nothing so cheap or so commonly available that they allowed parricides to share in it. [72] For what is so free as air to the living, earth to the dead, the sea to those tossed by the waves, or the land to those cast ashore? Yet these men live, while they can, without being able to draw breath from the open air; they die without earth touching their bones; they are tossed by the waves without ever being cleansed; and in the end they are cast ashore without being granted, even on the rocks, a resting-place in death.*

That is the terrible crime of which you are now accusing Sextus Roscius, a crime for which so striking a punishment has been prescribed. Do you really think, Erucius, that you can prove to men like these that such a crime has been committed, when you cannot even produce a motive? Even if you were accusing my client before the actual purchasers of his property and Chrysogonus were presiding over the court, you would still have had to come more carefully and more fully prepared. [73] Can you not see what this case is which is being tried, or before whom it is being tried? It is a trial for parricide, a crime which cannot conceivably be committed without many motives, and it is being held before highly intelligent men who are well aware that nobody commits even the most trifling offence without a reason.

So be it; you cannot produce a motive. Although I ought to be deemed at once to have won my case, I will not insist on my rights, and, since the innocence of my client gives me confidence, I will concede to you what I would not concede in any other case. I will not ask you why Sextus Roscius killed his father; instead, I will ask how he killed him. Yes, Gaius Erucius, I will ask you 'how?' and I will deal with you like this: even though it is my turn to speak,* I am going to give you leave to answer me, or to interrupt me, or even, should you wish, to ask me questions. [74] How, then, did he kill him? Did he strike the blow himself, or did he leave the actual killing to others? If you maintain that he did it himself, he was not in Rome. If you say he got others to do it, then I ask you who were they? Were they slaves or free men? If they were free men, then which men? Did they come from Ameria itself, or were they our own Roman cut-throats? If they came from Ameria, then who were they? Why are their names not given? If they came from Rome, how had Roscius got to know them, given that he had not visited Rome for many years, and never for longer than three days? Where did he meet them? How did he confer with them? What means did he use to persuade them? 'He gave them money.' Who did he give it to? Through whom did he give it? Where did he get it from, and how much was paid? Is it not by steps such as these that one normally gets to the bottom of a crime?

Do not forget, either, how you portrayed my client's way of life. You said that he was an uncouth rustic, that he never spoke to anyone, that he never went into town. [75] While we are on this point I am going to pass over what might have been a very strong argument in favour of my client's innocence: that country habits, frugal living, and a rough and uncivilized life such as Roscius leads are not the usual context in which crimes of this sort originate. Just as you do not find every crop or tree growing in every type of soil, so too not every type of crime originates in every mode of life. The city breeds extravagance; and from extravagance, greed must necessarily arise; and from greed, violent behaviour breaks out, producing all manner of crimes and misdeeds. The life of the country, on the other hand, which you call uncouth, is the teacher of thrift, honest toil, and fair dealing.

[76] But I will leave all that aside. Instead, I will put this question to you. You say yourself that my client avoided the company of others. Who, then, were the men who helped him to commit so terrible a crime, and in such secrecy—and in his absence, too? Many charges which are groundless, gentlemen, can still be made to sound plausible. But in this case, if there is anything that looks at all

suspicious, I shall be happy to concede that my client is guilty. Sextus Roscius was killed in Rome, while his son was in the country near Ameria. The son, who knew no one at Rome, sent a letter, let us say, to some assassin. 'He called someone to him.' But who, and when? 'He sent a messenger.' Which messenger, and to whom? 'He persuaded someone, using money, influence, expectations, promises.' But this is so implausible it is impossible even to fabricate such a story; and yet my client is on trial for parricide.

[77] There remains the possibility that he used slaves to kill his father. Immortal gods, what a pitiful and calamitous situation this is! With crimes of this sort, the usual means by which innocent defendants clear themselves is by offering their slaves for interrogation.* Is Sextus Roscius to be denied this opportunity? You the prosecution are in possession of all his slaves. Out of so large a household, Sextus Roscius has not been left with even so much as a single boy to bring him his meals each day. I now appeal to you, Publius Scipio, and to you, Marcus Metellus.* When you were supporting Sextus Roscius and acting for him, you will recall that he asked his opponents a number of times for two of his father's slaves, so that he could submit them for interrogation. And do you also remember Magnus' refusal? Where are those slaves, then? Gentlemen, they wait upon Chrysogonus. He holds them in high esteem, and places a high value on them. Even at this late stage, I demand that they be handed over for interrogation, and my client begs and implores that this be done.

[78] So what do you think you are playing at? Why do you refuse? Remain undecided, if you can, members of the jury, about who really killed Sextus Roscius—whether it was the man to whom Roscius' murder brought poverty and risk to his life, the man who has not even been allowed to hold an inquiry into his father's death, or whether it was those who are shunning an inquiry, who are in possession of the dead man's property, and who live as murderers and support themselves by murder. This entire case, gentlemen, is pitiful and shocking, but there is no aspect of it more cruel and unjust than this: that the son should be forbidden to interrogate his father's slaves as to how his father died. Is he not even to be master of his slaves for long enough to be able to question them about his father's death? I shall deal with this point in a moment, however: all this has to do with Magnus and Capito, and I promised I would speak about their violent behaviour as soon as I had refuted Erucius' charges.

[79] Now, Erucius, I return to you. If my client is involved in this crime, we must agree that he committed it either with his own hand (and you are not claiming this) or through other people, either free men or slaves. Were they free men? You cannot explain how he came to meet them, or how he persuaded them, or where, or through whom, or by making what promises or offering what money. I, on the other hand, am able to show not only that Sextus Roscius did none of these things, but that he was not even in a position to do them, since he had not been in Rome for many years, and had never even left his estate unless he had a particular reason to do so. Your last hope therefore seemed to be the mention of slaves, where you could take refuge as if in a safe haven, driven there by all your other false accusations. Instead of a haven, however, you have encountered a rock, and this has not only made you see the charge rebounding off my client, but has made you aware, also, that the suspicion recoils entirely upon yourselves.

[80] So where can the prosecutor take shelter from his lack of arguments? 'It was a time', he says, 'when people were constantly being killed with impunity. Because there were so many murderers about, you were able to commit the crime without any difficulty.' Sometimes, Erucius, you seem to me to be wanting two things for the price of one: to soak us in a lawsuit, but also to incriminate the very men from whom you have received your payment. What are you saying? People were constantly being killed? By whom, and on whose instructions? Surely you remember that the men who brought you here were purchasers of confiscated property? What next? Are we unaware that, during these times you mention, the breakers of necks and the brokers of property were by and large the same people? [81] They used to rush about day and night brandishing weapons, they were always in Rome, they spent all their time in plunder and bloodshed—shall men such as these hold Sextus Roscius responsible for the cruelty and wickedness of that time, and treat the prevalence of murderers, whose chiefs and leaders they were themselves, as grounds for an accusation against him? Yet Roscius not only was never at Rome, he did not even know what was going on in Rome, because, as you yourself concede, he was a man who spent all his time in the country.

[82] I am afraid I may become a nuisance to you, members of the jury, or appear to have little faith in your intelligence, if I go on

talking any longer about matters that are so transparently clear. Erucius' entire accusation has, I believe, been disproved—unless of
course you are waiting for me to refute the charge of embezzlement
and the other fabricated charges of this kind, which I have not heard
about until today, and which have only just been mentioned. Erucius
seemed to me to be rehearsing them from a different speech he was
getting up against some other defendant, since they had no connection at all either with the charge of parricide or with the man who is
now on trial. Since these accusations were made with just a word, it
will be sufficient to deny them in a word. If he is keeping anything
back until the witnesses are heard,* there too, as in this part of the
trial, he will find us better prepared than he anticipated.

[83] I turn now to a matter which I have no particular eagerness to
deal with, but which my duty to my client requires me to address. If
prosecuting was something I enjoyed, I should prefer to prosecute
other people, people whose condemnation would enable me to
advance my career.* I have decided, however, not to do this, as long as
I have a choice. In my view, it is the man who reaches a higher
position by his own merit who attains the greatest distinction, not
the man who rises as a result of the disadvantage and ruin of another.
For the time being, however, let us stop investigating charges that are
without foundation. Instead, let us try to find out where the crime
exists, and where it can be discovered. This will allow you to see,
Erucius, how many suspicious circumstances are needed to prove a
genuine accusation, even though I do not propose to mention all of
them, and will only touch upon each one. I would not of course be
doing this unless I really had to, and you will be able to tell my
unwillingness from the fact that I will not be pursuing the matter any
further than my client's safety and my duty to him require.

[84] Against Sextus Roscius you found no motive; but I find one
in Magnus. For it is you, Magnus, that I must deal with, since you
are sitting on the prosecutors' bench and openly declaring yourself
my adversary. We shall see about Capito later, if he comes forward as
a witness, as I hear he is ready to do: he will then be told about the
other such prizes that he has won, prizes he has no idea I have even
heard of.

The famous Lucius Cassius,* who was regarded by the Roman
people as an extremely fair and wise judge, always used to ask the
same question at the trials over which he presided: 'Who stood to

gain?' Human nature is such that no one attempts to commit a
crime without hope of gain. [85] Those who were threatened with
criminal prosecution used to avoid and dread Cassius when he was
the president of the court because, in spite of his love of truth, his
character seemed not so much disposed to mercy as inclined to
severity. The man who is presiding over this court today is both
courageous in his opposition to criminal behaviour and merciful
towards the innocent. Nevertheless, I would be perfectly happy to
plead Sextus Roscius' case either before the rigorous Cassius himself
or before 'Cassian' jurors—a designation which even now causes
defendants to shudder. [86] For, in this case, when the jurors saw
that the prosecution were in possession of vast wealth, but that my
client was reduced to utter destitution, they would have no need to
ask 'Who stood to gain?' It would be transparently obvious: they
would associate the suspicion of guilt with the plunder, not with the
poverty. What if, in addition, you had previously been poor? What if
you were avaricious? What if you were reckless? What if you had
been the murdered man's worst enemy? Surely we need look no
further for a motive which would have driven you to commit so
terrible a crime? And can any of these facts be denied? Your
former poverty is such that it cannot be concealed, and the more you
try to hide it, the more conspicuous it becomes. [87] Your avarice
you reveal when you team up with a complete stranger and form a
partnership to do with the property of someone who is a relation of
yours and your fellow-townsman. As for your recklessness, it can be
clearly recognized from this fact alone (I leave everything else aside),
that out of so extensive a conspiracy—by which I mean, out of so
many cut-throats—you are the only person who has been found
willing to sit on the prosecutors' bench, and not only let your face be
seen, but thrust it into view. And you cannot deny that Sextus
Roscius was your enemy, and that you had serious disputes with him
over family affairs.

[88] It remains, gentlemen, to weigh up the probabilities and
decide which of the two killed Sextus Roscius. Was it the man to
whom the murder brought wealth, or the man to whom it brought
destitution? Was it the man who was poor before the murder, or the
man who was reduced to poverty after it? Was it the man who,
burning with greed, attacked his own relations, or the man who
throughout his life knew nothing about making money but only

about the fruits of his own toil? Was it the man who was the most reckless of the purchasers of confiscated property, or the man who, being unused to the forum and the courts, shunned not only the sight of these benches, but even the city itself? Finally, gentlemen, and in my opinion this is the most relevant consideration of all: was it the murdered man's enemy, or his son?

[89] If you, Erucius, had arguments as numerous and convincing as these to use against someone you were prosecuting, how long you would speak for! How you would throw yourself about! You would run out of time—by Hercules!—long before you ran out of words. In fact, there is so much evidence that you could spend whole days on each individual point. And I too could do likewise—for without wishing to sound conceited, I do not think so little of my talents as to suppose that you could speak more fully than I.

Nevertheless, because of the number of defence advocates that there are, I may perhaps be reckoned as just one among many, while the battle of Cannae* has made you look like a tolerably good prosecutor. We have seen many men killed, not at the lake of Trasimene, but at the Servilian one.* [90] 'Who was not wounded there by Phrygian steel?'* There is no need to list everyone who was killed. There was a Curtius, a Marius, and then a Memmius,* all of whom were exempted from active service on grounds of age, and finally there was that old Priam himself, Antistius,* who was disqualified from fighting not only by his age but by the laws too. There were also the multitudes who used to prosecute in cases of murder and poisoning, whose names nobody mentions because of their insignificance. As far as I am concerned, I could wish that all these men were still alive today. For there is no harm in having as many dogs as possible when there are many people to be watched and many things to be guarded.

[91] It is quite normal, however, that amid the violence and confusion of war many things happen without the generals being aware of it. While he who had overall control* was busy with separate matters, there were other men, in the mean time, who were looking to heal the wounds inflicted on them. These men behaved as if the country were shrouded in everlasting night: they rushed around in the darkness and threw everything into confusion. In fact, I am surprised they did not also burn these benches, in order to wipe out every last trace of judicial process; they certainly struck down prosecutors and jurymen alike. Luckily, however, their way of life was such that they

could not kill every witness, even had they wished to do so. For as long as the human race exists, there will be men prepared to prosecute them; and as long as our country survives, trials will take place.

But, as I began to say, if Erucius was undertaking some different prosecution, and had available to him the arguments I mentioned, he would be in a position to go on speaking indefinitely—and I, gentlemen, could do likewise. My intention, however, as I have already indicated, is to pass over each individual point lightly, merely touching on it. By doing this, I want to make it clear to everyone that I will not be indulging a personal taste for accusing, but rather doing my duty for the defence of my client.

[92] I see, then, that there are a considerable number of motives which could have driven Magnus to commit the crime; let us now see whether he had any opportunity of committing it. Where was Sextus Roscius killed? 'At Rome.' And where were you, Magnus, at the time? 'At Rome. But what has that got to do with it? There were many others there besides me!' But the question we are asking is not who, out of the whole population of Rome, killed Sextus Roscius. No, what we are asking is this: whether a man who was killed at Rome was more likely to have been killed by someone who at that time was constantly in Rome, or by someone who had not visited Rome at all for many years.

[93] Let us now take a look at what other factors there are. There were at that time a large number of assassins, as Erucius has pointed out, and people were being killed with impunity. So who did that large number of assassins consist of? They were, I think, either those who were involved in purchasing confiscated property, or those who were paid by them to kill people. If you think that they were those who went after other people's property, then you yourself are one of them, since you have made yourself a rich man by taking what belongs to us. If, on the other hand, you think they were those whom people euphemistically describe as 'hit-men', then ask yourself to whom they are bound, and whose dependants they are: I tell you that you will find among them someone from your own circle. Say what you like to the contrary—and then compare it with my defence. This will enable you to see very clearly the contrast between Sextus Roscius' case and yours.

[94] You will say, 'Suppose I was constantly in Rome—what of it?' I shall reply, 'But I was never there at all.'* 'I admit I purchased

confiscated property, but many other people did as well.' 'But I was a farmer and country man, as you yourself criticized me for being.' 'If I have mixed with assassins, it does not necessarily follow that I am one myself.' 'But I, who don't know even a single assassin, am quite beyond suspicion on a charge of this nature.' There are a great many more points I could use which would demonstrate that you had every possible opportunity to commit the crime. I shall pass over them, however, partly because I take no pleasure in accusing you, but more importantly because, if I were to relate all the murders like that of Sextus Roscius which were committed at that time, I am afraid that my speech might appear to be directed not only against you but against others as well.

[95] Let us now look briefly—in the same way as we dealt with the other points—at what you did, Magnus, after the death of Sextus Roscius. Your actions were in fact so open and transparent that—I call heaven to witness, gentlemen!—I would rather not have to speak about them. What I am afraid of is that, whatever sort of a man you really are, Magnus, people will think I have set out to save my client by being completely ruthless towards yourself. However, just when I begin to get worried about this, and decide that I want to spare you as far as I can short of actually doing damage to my case, I suddenly change my mind. What happens is that I think of your incredible cheek. The rest of your associates were making themselves scarce and keeping out of the way, so as to give the impression that this trial would be concerned not with the plunder they had stolen, but with a crime committed by my client. And to think that while they were doing this, you, on the other hand, were demanding for yourself the role of appearing in court and sitting on the prosecutors' bench! All you are achieving by this, however, is to ensure that your wickedness and effrontery become well known to everyone.

[96] After Sextus Roscius' murder, who was the first to bring the news to Ameria? It was Mallius Glaucia, whom I mentioned earlier, a dependant and friend of yours. Why was it his business in particular to convey news which was nothing at all to do with you, unless you had already formed a plan regarding Roscius' death and his property, and had entered into a partnership with some accomplice for the purposes of crime and financial gain? 'Mallius brought the news on his own initiative.' But what, I ask you, did it have to do with him? Or, if this was not the reason why he went to Ameria, was it purely

by chance that he was the first to report what he had heard in Rome?
And what was his reason for going to Ameria? 'I really can't guess,'
says Magnus. By the time I have finished, there will be no more need
for guessing! But why was the news brought first to Titus Roscius
Capito? Sextus Roscius had a house, wife, and children* at Ameria,
and many relations and kinsmen with whom he was on the best of
terms. Why then did this dependant of yours, reporting the news of
your crime, choose to bring it to Capito before anyone else?
[97] Roscius was killed as he was returning from dinner; yet the news
of his death was known at Ameria before dawn the next morning.
What was the reason for this incredibly quick journey, this extraordinary speed and hurry? I am not asking who struck the actual
blow: you need have no worries, Glaucia, on that score. I am not
going to go through your clothes to see if you have a weapon on you.
I am not going to search you—I don't think it is any of my business.
Since I have found out who arranged the murder, I am not worried
about whose hand it was that struck the actual blow. There is just
one question which your obvious guilt and the plain facts of the case
suggest to me: where and from whom did Glaucia hear of the murder? How did he come to know of it so quickly? Suppose he heard of
it as soon as it happened. What was it that made him travel such a
long journey in a single night? And if he genuinely had reasons of his
own for going to Ameria, what great necessity was there that forced
him to set out from Rome at the time he did, and not rest at all at any
point during the night?

[98] When the facts are as clear as this, is it really necessary to seek
out arguments and draw inferences from them? Do you not seem,
members of the jury, actually to witness with your own eyes what
you have been hearing? Do you not see that poor man, unaware of his
impending doom, returning from dinner? Do you not see the
ambush in place, the sudden attack? Before your very eyes, carrying
out the murder, is that not Glaucia? And is he not there too—
Magnus? Is he not with his own hands placing that Automedon* in
his chariot, to carry the news of his terrible crime and evil victory? Is
he not begging him to stay awake all night, to show his regard for
him by trying his hardest, and to bring the news to Capito at the
earliest possible moment?

[99] And why was it that he wanted Capito to be the first to hear
the news? I do not know. But this I can see, that Capito has a share in

the property: out of the thirteen farms, he is currently in possession of the best three. [100] I hear, moreover, that this is not the first time that Capito has been suspected of such dealings. I hear that he has won many shameful prizes, but that this is the first major decoration* that has been brought to him from Rome. And I also hear that there is no means of killing a man that he has not used a number of times: he has killed many people with weapons, and many by poison. I can even tell you of one man whom—contrary to the tradition of our ancestors, since the man was less than sixty years of age—he threw from a bridge into the Tiber!* If Capito comes forward as a witness— or rather when he does, since I know that he is going to come forward—he will hear about all of this from me. [101] So let him come, and let him unroll that document of his, which I can prove was in fact written by Erucius: this is the document which Capito, it is said, waved in my client's face, threatening to submit as evidence everything it contained. What a distinguished witness, gentlemen! What stern dignity—well worth waiting to see! What an honourable character, and one whose evidence you should undoubtedly have no hesitation in allowing to determine your verdict! It is certainly true that we would not be able to see these men's crimes with such clarity if they had not themselves been blinded by avarice, cupidity, and recklessness.

[102] Immediately after the murder, one of the two* sent a fast messenger to his accomplice—or, rather, his master*—at Ameria. By this action, even if everyone had been keen to cover up the fact that they knew who was responsible for the crime, he himself would nevertheless have placed his own palpable guilt before the eyes of all. The other one,* if the immortal gods will tolerate such a thing, pro- poses to give evidence against Sextus Roscius—as though it were still a question of whether his words should be believed, and not whether his deeds should be punished! Our ancestors established the custom that, even in the most trivial cases, no one, however dis- tinguished, should give evidence where their own interests are involved. [103] Not even Africanus,* who declares by his name that he has conquered one-third of the world, would give evidence in a case which affected himself; for if such a great man as he were to give evidence, I would certainly not dare to suggest that there could be any possibility at all of its not being accepted. But consider now how everything has altered and changed for the worse. This trial is

concerned with property and with murder. Yet evidence is going to be given by someone who is both a purchaser of confiscated property and a murderer, by someone, indeed, who is the purchaser and possessor of the actual property in question, and who is also the very person who arranged the murder of the man whose death is being investigated by this court.

[104] So, my good friend,* do you have anything to say? Pay attention, then, to what I have to tell you. You must take care not to let yourself down: you too, just like my client, have a great deal at stake. You have committed many crimes, many acts of violence, and many outrages, but you have also committed one act of great stupidity, and on your own initative too, not on Erucius' advice: you should not have sat on the prosecutors' bench. Nobody, you see, has any use for a prosecutor who just sits and says nothing or, on the other hand, for a witness who gets up to speak from the prosecutors' bench. Moreover, had you not joined the prosecution, your greed would have been marginally better hidden and concealed. But as it is, what is there that anyone could possibly want to hear from you, given that your behaviour makes you appear to be deliberately acting in our interests and against your own?

[105] Now let us consider, gentlemen, what happened immediately after the murder. Four days after Sextus Roscius had been killed, news of his death was brought to Chrysogonus in Lucius Sulla's camp at Volaterrae.* Does anyone at this stage need to ask who sent the messenger? Is it not obvious that it was the same man who sent him to Ameria? Chrysogonus saw to it that Roscius' property was sold at once—although he knew neither the man nor the circumstances. But how did it enter into his head to covet the farms of a stranger that he had never set eyes on? Usually on hearing this sort of story, gentlemen, you would immediately say, 'Some fellow-townsman or neighbour must have told him. It is generally they who pass information: they are usually the ones responsible when people are betrayed.' But in this case we are not dealing with mere suspicion. [106] For I am not going to argue as follows: 'In all probability, Magnus and Capito told Chrysogonus what had happened, since they were already friends of his before this. They did have many long-standing patrons and hosts inherited from their ancestors, but they had given up treating them with any attention or respect, and had taken themselves off instead to become dependants

and clients of Chrysogonus.' [107] All this I could say with complete truth, but in this case there is no need to draw inferences in this way. In fact, I know for certain that they themselves do not deny that they were the ones who prevailed upon Chrysogonus to take the property. If you see with your own eyes the man who took his share in return for information given, then will you have any doubt, gentlemen, who supplied the information? So who, then, with respect to this particular property, are the men Chrysogonus rewarded with a share? Magnus and Capito. And who else is there besides? No one, gentlemen. Can there be any doubt, then, that the men who offered the plunder to Chrysogonus are those who have subsequently received a share in it from him?

[108] But let us now look at what Magnus and Capito did according to Chrysogonus' own judgement. If during the course of that fight they did nothing worth speaking of, why did he reward them so handsomely? If they did nothing but give him the news, surely all he needed to do was to thank them, or at most, if he wanted to be particularly generous, give them a small token of his appreciation? Why, instead, were three extremely valuable farms immediately handed over to Capito? Why is Magnus jointly in possession of everything else along with Chrysogonus? Surely it is obvious, gentlemen, that Chrysogonus granted these spoils to Magnus and Capito after looking into and finding out what they had done?

[109] Capito came to the camp as one of the ten leaders of the council.* His behaviour on this deputation will on its own reveal to you the man's character, morals, and whole way of life. Unless you come to the conclusion, gentlemen, that there is no duty and no law so sacred and inviolable that it has not been desecrated and violated by his wickedness and treachery, then please judge him to be a most honourable man. [110] He prevented Sulla from being informed about what had taken place. He told Chrysogonus about the plans and intentions of his fellow delegates, advised him to make sure that the matter was not dealt with publicly, and pointed out that, if the sale of the property were annulled, Chrysogonus would lose a great deal of money, and he himself would face trial on a capital charge. He spurred Chrysogonus on, and at the same time continued to mislead his fellow delegates. He repeatedly warned him to be on his guard, while cunningly holding out false hopes to the others. He made plans against them with Chrysogonus, and he told Chrysogonus of their

own plans. He came to an agreement with Chrysogonus as to his own
share of the proceeds, while all the time giving the delegates one
excuse after another to delay their obtaining access to Sulla. In the
end, through his recommendation, advice, and intervention Capito
managed to ensure that the delegates never did see Sulla. Deceived
by his promise—or rather his broken promise, as you will be able to
learn from the delegates themselves, if the prosecution decide to call
them as witnesses*—they went home again, taking with them a false
hope instead of a positive result.

[111] In private matters, if someone showed even minor negligence in the execution of a trust*—to say nothing of deliberate
fraud for his own profit or advantage—he was considered by our
ancestors to have acted in a highly dishonourable manner. Legal
proceedings for breach of trust were therefore established, and in the
case of a conviction the disgrace was no less extreme than it was in
cases of theft. This was no doubt because, in matters in which we are
not able to be involved personally, the good faith of our friends is
substituted for our own efforts; and if someone abuses that confidence, then he is attacking a safeguard which is common to all, and
is thus, as far as lies within his power, undermining the fabric of
society. For we cannot do everything for ourselves: each man is more
useful than the next one in some particular task. That is why friendships are formed, so that the common good may be advanced by
mutual services. [112] Why accept a trust, if you are going to neglect
it or turn it to your own advantage?* Why offer to help me, and then
under the guise of service do me a disservice and thwart my interests? Stand aside: I will find someone else to manage my business.
You are taking on a burden which you think you can support, but it is
one which seems by no means insignificant to men whose abilities are
themselves by no means insignificant.*

That is why breach of trust is a disgraceful offence, because it
violates two things that are extremely sacred: friendship and good
faith. A man does not normally choose someone to be a trustee
unless he is a friend, nor does he trust someone unless he considers
him to be true to him. It is therefore the act of a totally degraded
character both to destroy a friendship and at the same time to
deceive someone who would not have been harmed had he not
placed his trust in him. [113] Do you not agree? Even in matters of
minor importance someone who has been negligent in the execution

of a trust incurs a penalty involving the most extreme disgrace. In a case as important as the present one, therefore, when someone, entrusted with the task of safeguarding the reputation of a dead father and the fortunes of his living son, goes on instead to bring ignominy on the dead man and penury on the one who is still alive, can we really consider such a man to have a place among honourable men, or indeed among the living? In private matters of minor importance, even mere negligence is open to prosecution for breach of trust and is liable to a penalty involving official disgrace. This is because, if everything is as it should be, it is the beneficiary of the trust, and not the trustee, who can afford to be negligent. In a case as important as the present one, however, where the trust was officially commissioned and set up, we have a trustee who has not merely injured some private arrangement out of negligence but has defiled and polluted the sanctity of the entire deputation by his treachery. What penalty, I ask you, is to be inflicted on such a man, and with what sentence is he to be condemned?

[114] Suppose that Sextus Roscius had privately entrusted the matter to Capito, arranging that Capito should settle everything with Chrysogonus and come to an agreement with him, and that he had given Capito discretion to pledge Sextus' word if he judged it to be necessary. If Capito, having accepted the commission, then turned it to his own advantage in any way at all, however trivial, surely this would lead to his being convicted by an arbitrator,* and he would both be required to make restitution, and also forfeit his good name entirely? [115] As it is, however, it was not Sextus Roscius who entrusted the matter to him. It is far more serious than that: what happened was that Sextus Roscius himself, together with his reputation, his life, and all his property, was officially entrusted to Capito by the town council. And Capito, moreover, has not just turned the commission to his own advantage in some minor way: he has turned my client right out of his property, has bargained for three farms for himself, and has shown as little respect for the wishes of the town council and all his fellow-townsmen as he has for his own word.

[116] Now take a look at the rest of his actions, members of the jury, and you will see that there is no crime imaginable with which he has not defiled himself. It is considered extremely disgraceful to deceive one's partner in matters of minor importance, just as disgraceful as the case I have just been talking about. And it is right that

such deception should be so regarded, because a man who has entered into partnership with someone else assumes that he has associated himself with someone who will be a help to him. In whose good faith can he trust, if he is injured because of the bad faith of the man he has trusted? Besides, the offences which it is hardest to guard against are the ones which merit the strictest punishment. With strangers we can be reserved, but our close friends must necessarily know a great deal more about us. As for a partner, how can we possibly take precautions against one? If we even so much as feel anxious about him, then we are committing a violation against the law of duty. Because of this, our ancestors were quite right to regard the man who deceived his partner as having no place among honourable men.

[117] It was not, however, a single partner in a financial deal that Capito deceived; that, although a serious offence, might have been somehow tolerable. On the contrary, it was nine extremely honourable men, his partners in the same task, deputation, duty, and commission, that he led on, deceived, deserted, handed over to their enemies, and cheated with every kind of fraud and treachery. These men could have had no suspicion of his criminal purpose; it was not for them to feel anxious about their partner in an official duty; they were blind to his wickedness; they trusted his empty promises. And so it is that these most honourable men, as a result of his trickery, are now deemed to have shown insufficient caution and foresight. He, on the other hand, who was first a traitor and then a deserter, who first revealed the plans of his partners to their enemies and then made common cause with those enemies, continues to threaten and intimidate us, while in the mean time he has enriched himself with three farms as a reward for his crime.

In a life such as this, members of the jury, you will also find, among so many other disgraceful outrages, the crime which is the subject of this trial. [118] Your inquiry ought, I suggest, to proceed on this basis: where you discover that many acts of greed, many acts of violence, many acts of dishonesty, and many acts of treachery have been committed, you should conclude that crime, also, lies concealed among all those outrages. There is nothing concealed, though, about this particular crime. It is all so visible and open to view that it does not have to be inferred from the other crimes Capito is known to have committed. Indeed, if anyone were to question his responsibility for any of those other crimes, it could actually be proved from the fact of his having committed this one. So what do you think, gentlemen? Do you think that that trainer of gladiators has retired completely from his profession, or that this pupil of his is in any way inferior in skill to his master? No: their greed is equal, their unscrupulousness parallel, their impudence the same, their recklessness twin.

[119] Now that you have learned about the trustworthiness of the master, you must also learn about the reasonableness of the pupil. I said earlier that the prosecution have repeatedly been asked to hand over two slaves for interrogation.* But you, Magnus, have always refused. Let me put this question to you: were those who made the request unworthy of having it granted? Or did the man on whose behalf they made it fail to arouse your sympathy? Or did the request itself seem to you unjustified? Those who made it were the most high-ranking and honourable men in our nation, and I have already mentioned their names.* Their way of life and standing in the eyes of the Roman people are such that, whatever they should choose to say, there is no one who would think it unreasonable. Moreover, they made their request on behalf of an utterly wretched and unfortunate man, who would even be prepared to offer himself for interrogation under torture,* just so long as an inquiry was held into the death of his father. [120] The request, furthermore, was of a type whereby your refusal to grant it amounted to an admission of guilt. This being the case, I ask you why you refused it. When Sextus Roscius was killed the slaves were present. I am not concerned either to accuse the slaves or to exculpate them. But your opposition to their being submitted for interrogation is suspicious; and the fact that you are placing such a high value on them can only mean that they know something which would be disastrous to you were they to reveal it.

'It is unfair to interrogate slaves against their master.' But that would not be happening: it is Sextus Roscius who is on trial! And if they were interrogated about Roscius, they would not be being examined against their master, since you say that you are their master now. 'They are with Chrysogonus.' Yes, indeed: Chrysogonus is so captivated by their culture and sophistication that he wanted these men—little more than labourers, trained at Ameria by a rustic householder—to mix with his own beautifully mannered and culturally aware young boys, selected out of a large number of the most refined households. [121] No, that is not how it is, gentlemen. It is not likely that Chrysogonus admired the education and culture of these slaves, or that he appreciated their diligence and loyalty in household matters. There is something that is being concealed—and the more keen the prosecution are to suppress it and hide it from view, the more blatant and conspicuous it becomes.

[122] So is it because he wants to conceal his own crime that Chrysogonus is unwilling for the slaves to be interrogated? Far from it, members of the jury: I do not think I should be directing all my accusations at everybody. As far as I am concerned, I do not suspect Chrysogonus of anything of the kind, and this is not something which it has only just occurred to me to say. You will recall that at the outset* I divided up my case as follows. First there was the charge, which was left entirely to Erucius to undertake; and then there was the violence, that role being assigned to Magnus and Capito. Any misdeed, crime, or murder that is discovered ought therefore to be attributed to those two. As for Chrysogonus, we maintain that his excessive influence and power are obstructing our case, that it cannot possibly be tolerated, and that it should not only be checked by you, but punished, since it is in your power to do so. [123] Let me give you my own view. If a man wants witnesses to be interrogated who it is certain were present at the scene of a murder, then we can infer that he is someone who is eager for the truth to be discovered. But if a man refuses this, then by his actions he unquestionably admits his own guilt, even if he does not go so far as to admit it in words. I said at the beginning,* gentlemen, that I wished to say no more about these men's crime than the case required and necessity itself demanded. For there are many allegations which could be made, and each of them could be supported by many arguments. But I cannot spend time or pains on something that I am doing unwillingly and out of necessity. The points which simply could not be passed over in silence I have lightly touched upon, gentlemen; but those which rest on suspicion and which, if I began to discuss them, I should have to treat at length, these I leave to your intelligent conjectures.

[124] I return now to that golden name* of Chrysogonus, beneath which the whole partnership has taken shelter. On this subject, members of the jury, I do not see how I can say anything—but, equally, I do not see how I can say nothing. If I say nothing, I relinquish perhaps the most important part of my case; but if I say

anything, I am afraid that not only Chrysogonus (I am not worried about that in the least) but others too might think they are being attacked. Nevertheless, I do not think that the nature of the case requires me to say much about the purchasers of confiscated property in general: for this case is unique and unprecedented.

[125] The purchaser of Sextus Roscius' property was Chrysogonus. Let us first pose this question: on what grounds was Roscius' property sold, and how could it have been sold? In asking this question, members of the jury, I am not seeking to argue that it is shocking that the property of an innocent man should have been put up for sale. If that issue should ever be raised and freely discussed, there are more important people than Sextus Roscius on whose behalf such a complaint could be made. No, what I am asking is simply this: how, according to the law relating to proscription, whether it is the Valerian law or the Cornelian*—I am not familiar with it, and do not know—how, according to that law, could the property of Sextus Roscius have been sold? [126] The wording of the law is said to run: 'THAT THE PROPERTY, EITHER OF THOSE WHO HAVE BEEN PROSCRIBED'—and Sextus Roscius was not one of those—'OR OF THOSE WHO HAVE BEEN KILLED WITHIN THE ENEMY'S LINES, SHOULD BE SOLD.' Throughout the whole period when there were any opposing lines, Roscius was within those of Sulla; it was only afterwards, when all the fighting was over and peace had been completely restored, that he was killed, at Rome, as he was returning from dinner. If he was lawfully killed, then I admit that the sale of his property was also lawful. But if it is accepted that he was killed contrary to all the laws, the new laws as well as the old ones, then I demand to know by what right, by what means, and by what law the property was sold.

[127] Do you ask whom I am speaking against, Erucius? Not against the person you would like, and think I am actually speaking against: for Sulla has been freed from blame at every point, both by my speech from its very beginning, and by his own outstanding merit. I declare that, on the contrary, it is Chrysogonus who bears responsibility for everything—that he lied, that he pretended Sextus Roscius was a bad citizen, that he said he had been killed with the enemy, that he prevented Lucius Sulla from being made aware of the facts by the delegates from Ameria. Finally, I even have a suspicion that the property was never in fact sold at all; this I will show later on,*

gentlemen, if you will allow me to do so. [128] For I believe that the
law specifies the date up until which proscriptions and sales could
take place, namely the first of June. Some months after that, Roscius
was killed and his property is said to have been sold. Either, then, the
sale has not been entered in the public accounts, in which case we are
being cheated by this crook more cleverly than we had realized;* or
alternatively, if it has been entered in the public accounts, then these
accounts must somehow have been tampered with, since by law it
was not possible for the property to be sold.

I am aware, members of the jury, that I am examining these matters prematurely, and that I am straying from the point at issue:
when I should be trying to put Sextus Roscius' life out of danger, all
I am doing is attending to a damaged fingernail. For he is not concerned about money, nor does he take account of any advantage of
his own: he reckons that he will easily put up with his poverty, so
long as he is freed from this unwarranted suspicion and this fabricated charge. [129] But I would ask you to appreciate, gentlemen,
when listening to what little I have left to say, that I am speaking
partly for myself and partly for Sextus Roscius. The aspects which
strike me as scandalous and intolerable, and which I regard as affect-
ing all of us unless we keep a look out, all these I bring up on my own
account, because of the sense of anguish I feel in my heart. Those
matters, on the other hand, which relate to my client's life and
situation—what he wishes to be said on his behalf and the outcome
that will satisfy him—this, gentlemen, you shall hear at the very end
of my speech.

[130] Leaving Sextus Roscius aside for the moment, I have several
questions that I want to put to Chrysogonus for myself. First of all,
why has the property of a very fine citizen been sold? Next, why has
the property been sold when its owner was neither proscribed nor
killed with the enemy, given that the law specifies that these are the
only cases in which sales are to be held? Next, why was the property
sold long after the date specified in the law? Next, why was it sold for
so little? If Chrysogonus does what wicked and dishonest freedmen
usually do and tries to pin the blame for all this on his patron, he will
gain nothing by it. For everyone is well aware that many people have
committed many crimes which Lucius Sulla, being preoccupied with
his important public duties, either disapproved of or knew nothing
about. [131] Is it right, then, in situations like this, that something

should be overlooked through inadvertence? It is not right, gentlemen, but it cannot be helped. If Jupiter Best and Greatest, by whose
nod and command earth, sea, and sky are governed, has often done
harm to men by violent winds, wild storms, excessive heat, or
unbearable cold, and has destroyed their cities and ruined their
crops, we do not regard any of these disasters as arising from a divine
intention to cause destruction, but rather from the sheer size and
power of nature. But on the other hand, the blessings we share, the
light we enjoy, and the air we breathe, these we view as given and
bestowed upon us by Jupiter. During the time we are discussing,
Lucius Sulla was single-handedly ruling the country, governing the
world, and, after recovering our empire by force of arms, was
strengthening its majesty with new laws: should we therefore be
surprised, gentlemen, if, at such a time, there were certain things
that escaped his notice? One might just as soon express surprise that
human intelligence has failed to attain what divine power is unable to
achieve.

[132] But let us leave aside the past: surely it is obvious to anyone,
from what is actually happening at this very moment, that the man
who has contrived and engineered this whole business is Chrysogonus alone? It was he who arranged for a charge to be brought
against Sextus Roscius; it was out of respect for him that Erucius
said he was undertaking the prosecution . . .* [*There is a large gap in
the text here. Several fragments are preserved in the scholia as follows.*]
. . . in the district of Pallacina . . . he was very much afraid . . . he
dodges the question, however, and says that he . . . by hand, farms
with farms . . . at this point I want those men to hear . . .

[*Here the text resumes.*] . . . they think that they have a country
house which is well ordered and meets their requirements, those
men who reside in the territory of the Sallentini or the Bruttii,* where
news reaches them scarcely three times in a year.

[133] And here you have the other one,* making his way down
from his residence on the Palatine. To refresh his spirits, he also has
a delightful country seat outside Rome, and in addition a number of
farms, all very good ones, and close to the city. His house is crammed
with vessels of Corinthian and Delian bronze, including that kettle-
urn for which he recently paid so high a price that passers-by who
heard the auctioneer calling out the bids assumed that a farm was
being sold. How much embossed silver, how much embroidered

cloth, how many paintings, how many statues, and how much marble
do you suppose there is in that house of his? As much, of course, as
could be seized from many distinguished families in times of civil
disorder and pillage and piled up inside a single building!

As for his household slaves, how many he has and what their
various specialities are, what can I say? [134] I do not mention such
common-or-garden trades as cooks, bakers, litter-bearers: to refresh
his spirits and ears, he has so many slaves that the whole neighbourhood resounds every day with singing voices, strings, and pipes, and
at night with revelling. With a way of life like this, gentlemen, can
you imagine what daily expense, what extravagance is involved, and
what festivities take place? They are respectable ones, naturally, in a
house of this kind—if it can in fact be called a house, and not a
factory of vice and lodging for every type of scandal.

[135] And look at the man himself, gentlemen, how, with his hair
carefully styled and soaked in perfume, he flits about the forum,
escorted by a large band of citizens in togas!* See how he looks down
on everyone, how he thinks that no one is more important than he is,
how he considers that only he is successful, and only he is powerful.
Nevertheless, if I felt inclined to go into everything that he does, and
everything he attempts to do, then I fear, gentlemen, that someone
who has not fully grasped the facts of the case might assume that I
intended to impugn the nobility and the victory their cause has
achieved.

Of course, if there were anything in that cause that I disagreed
with, I would be fully within my rights in criticizing it. For I have no
fear that anyone could think of me as having been ill-disposed to the
interests of the nobility. [136] Those who know me are aware that,
once my greatest hope—that an agreement be reached—had
proved impossible, I then strove, in my own small way, for the victory of the side which afterwards proved victorious. For was there
anyone who failed to grasp what was happening—that the highest
honours were being disputed between inferior men and men of high
status? In such a contest, it would have been a bad citizen indeed
who failed to attach himself to those on whose survival both the
dignity of our nation at home and its authority abroad depended.
And I am delighted, gentlemen, and extremely happy that this has
been achieved, and that everyone has had their honour and rank
restored to them—and I appreciate that all this has been done by the

will of the gods, the commitment of the Roman people, and the wisdom and guidance and good fortune* of Lucius Sulla. [137] As to the fact that punishment was inflicted on those who fought against us by every means in their power, it is not my business to find fault with this; and as to the granting of rewards to the valiant men who gave outstanding service in what they did, this has my full approval. Those were the aims, in my opinion, for which we were fighting, and I am happy to declare that that was the side to which I gave my support. But if it is the case that all this happened and a war was started in order that the worst class of men should enrich themselves with other people's wealth and make an assault on the property of every single person; and if one should be forbidden not only to put a stop to it by action but even to censure it with words—if this is how the matter stands, then the Roman people have not been restored and rehabilitated by the recent war, but, on the contrary, defeated and crushed.

[138] But that is far from being the case. That is not what happened, members of the jury. If you make a stand against these men, not only will the cause of the nobility remain undamaged, it will actually be promoted. For those who want to criticize the current state of affairs complain that Chrysogonus has too much power, whereas those who wish to praise it deny that he has been given any. And there is no excuse for anyone to be either so stupid or so dishonest as to say, 'I could wish it were allowed—then I would have said this.' Well, you can say it! 'I would have done this.' You can do it: no one is stopping you. 'I would have voted this way in the senate.' Vote—only do so as justice requires, and everyone will approve. 'I would have given this verdict.' Everyone will praise you, if your verdict is right and proper.

[139] As long as it was necessary and the situation demanded it, one man controlled everything; but once he had appointed magistrates and passed laws, everyone received back the responsibility and standing they had previously held. And if those who have received it back want to hold on to it, they will be able to keep hold of it for ever. But if they commit or condone such acts of murder and looting and such excessive and prodigal extravagance—I do not want to say anything too harsh against them, if only to avoid a bad omen, but I will just say this: if those nobles of ours fail to show themselves watchful and good and valiant and merciful, then they will have to

resign their distinctions* in favour of those who do possess these qualities.

[140] They should therefore stop saying that someone who has openly spoken the truth has spoken treasonably; they should stop making common cause with Chrysogonus; they should stop thinking that, if Chrysogonus' interests are damaged, then theirs, too, are affected; they should reflect how lamentable and shameful it is that they, who could not endure the splendour of the equestrian order,* should submit to the domination of an utterly worthless slave. This domination, gentlemen, has in the past been exercised in other fields,* but now you should be able to see what road it is constructing for itself and what course it is preparing: it is aiming at your good faith, at your oath, at your verdicts, at what is virtually the only thing left in the state that is uncorrupted and intact. [141] Does Chrysogonus really imagine that he has some influence in this area too? Does his desire for power extend this far? What a lamentable and sickening state of affairs! My feeling of outrage does not—by Hercules!—arise from any fear that Chrysogonus may actually have some influence. No, my complaint is simply that he has had the audacity to suppose that he could incline men such as yourselves to bring about the destruction of an innocent man.

Did the nobility, then, fulfil our hopes and recover the country by arms and the sword simply in order to allow their freedmen and petty slaves to ransack our goods and property just as it suited them? [142] If they did, then I admit that I was wrong to prefer their cause, I admit that I was mad to have sided with them (although I did so, gentlemen, without actually taking up arms myself). But if, on the other hand, the victory of the nobles is to be seen as a glory and a blessing for our country and the Roman people, then what I am saying ought to be extremely welcome to all the finest and noblest citizens. But should anyone conclude, on hearing Chrysogonus being criticized, that his own interests and cause are being damaged, then he does not understand his cause—and he has formed a fine idea of what his interests are! For the cause, if it stands up to each and every scoundrel, will become ever more glorious; and the unprincipled supporter of Chrysogonus, who thinks that he shares a community of interest with him, is in reality damaging his own interests, because he is cutting himself off from this glory which the cause is winning.

[143] But all that I have just been saying, as I told you before, was

said in my own name: the state of our country, my own feelings of indignation, and the wrong which these men have committed all forced me to speak out. Sextus Roscius, for his part, feels no indignation at any of this, he accuses no one, he makes no complaint about the loss of his inheritance. A farmer and country man with little knowledge of the world, he believes that all these actions for which you claim that Sulla was responsible were done according to custom, law, and the universally recognized principles of justice. All he desires is to be able to walk from this court freed from blame and cleared of this outrageous charge. [144] If he can only be relieved of this unwarranted suspicion, he declares that he will bear the loss of all his property with equanimity.

Roscius begs and entreats you, Chrysogonus, if from his father's considerable fortune he has spent nothing on himself, if he has defrauded you of nothing, if he has made his entire property over to you in good faith and has counted it all out and weighed it up, if he has handed over to you the clothes in which he stood and the ring* from his finger, and if he has kept back nothing whatsoever from you with the sole exception of his own naked body—then please allow him, innocent as he is, to live out his life in poverty, dependent on the support of his friends. [145] You are in possession of my farms,* I am living on the charity of others: I accept it, both because my heart is resigned to it and because I must. My house is open to you, but closed to me: I bear it. You have the use of my large household, I have not a single slave: I put up with it and think it tolerable. What more do you want? Why do you persecute me? Why do you attack me? In what way am I thwarting your desires? What interests of yours am I blocking? How am I standing in your way? If it is for the sake of the spoils that you are wanting to kill a man, you have already despoiled him. What more are you asking for? If it is out of personal enmity, what enmity can you possibly feel towards a man whose farms you took before you even knew him? If it is out of fear, how can you fear anything from someone who, as you can see, is quite unable to defend himself on his own against such a terrible wrong? But if it is your acquisition of the property of Sextus Roscius which makes you determined to destroy his son, are you not showing yourself to be afraid of something which you have less reason to fear than anyone else*—that at some point in the future the children of the proscribed may be given their fathers' property back?

[146] You do an injustice,* Chrysogonus, if, in seeking to hold on to
what you have purchased, you place more trust in my client's death
than you do in what Lucius Sulla has achieved. But if you have no
reason for wanting this unfortunate man to be struck down by so
great a calamity, if he has already handed over to you everything he
possesses except the actual breath in his body, and has kept back out
of his father's property nothing whatsoever for himself, not even the
merest keepsake, then—by the immortal gods!—what is the purpose
of this excessive cruelty, this monstrous savagery of character? What
robber was ever so wicked, what pirate so barbaric that, when he
could have taken the spoils complete and intact without bloodshed,
he nevertheless preferred to strip them off soaked in blood?
[147] You know full well that my client has nothing, aspires to nothing, can do nothing, has never dreamt of opposing your interests; and
yet you attack him—a man whom you cannot possibly fear, nor
ought to hate, and who you see has nothing further that you can take
from him. Unless, of course, you think it shocking that the man you
threw naked from his inheritance as from a shipwreck should be
sitting here in court, as you see him, with clothes on his back! As if
you can be unaware that he is being both fed and clothed by Caecilia,*
the daughter of Baliaricus and sister of Nepos, a lady of the utmost
respectability! Despite having an illustrious father, highly exalted
uncles, and a most accomplished brother, nevertheless, woman
though she is, she has herself displayed manly distinction of her
own, and has demonstrated that, great as is the honour conferred on
her by these eminent relations, she has conferred on them, through
her noble actions, no less glory in return.

[148] Or perhaps it is the fact that my client is being properly
defended that makes you feel so outraged? Believe me, if, in return
for the generous hospitality shown by his father, his family friends
had all been willing to appear and had ventured to speak openly on
his behalf, then he really would have a proper defence. But if each of
them were to punish you in proportion to the injustice you have
done and the extent to which your prosecution is threatening the
national interest, then I can assure you—by Hercules!—you would
not be standing where you are now! As it is, however, the defence
that my client is receiving is one that the prosecution have no reason
at all to resent, and they could not possibly view themselves as being
overcome by superior force.

[149] My client's domestic needs are being seen to by Caecilia. His business in the forum and in court, on the other hand, has been undertaken, as you see, gentlemen, by Marcus Messalla.* If he were old enough, and up to the physical demands of the task, Messalla would speak for Sextus Roscius himself. But since his youth, and the natural modesty which does credit to one so young, prevent him from speaking, he has entrusted the case to me, knowing that I have his interests at heart and have a duty to be of service to him. It is, however, thanks to his perseverance, advice, influence, and hard work that the life of Sextus Roscius has been rescued from the hands of the purchasers of confiscated property and entrusted instead to the votes of a jury. Yes, gentlemen, it was for nobles such as Messalla that most of the citizens took up arms. Their aim was to restore to their rightful position in the state the sort of nobles who would act as you see Messalla doing—who would defend the rights of the innocent, who would stand up against injustice, and who would prefer to exercise whatever influence they possessed in saving rather than destroying their fellow men. If everyone who has been born into that level of society were to act like this, our country would be suffering less from them, and they themselves would be less resented.

[150] But if we cannot induce Chrysogonus, members of the jury, to be satisfied with our property and not to insist on taking our life as well; if he cannot be dissuaded, even after taking away everything that was ours, from seeking to deprive us also of the light which is common to all; and if he does not think it enough to satisfy his greed with money without blood, too, being offered to assuage his cruelty; then, gentlemen, there is only one place of refuge, only one hope left for Sextus Roscius, and it is the same as that which is left for our country—your own traditional goodness and mercy. If this holds strong, we can all, even now, be saved. But if the cruelty which is currently endemic in our country should harden and embitter your hearts as well (and that surely cannot happen), then it is all over, gentlemen. It would be better to spend one's life among wild animals than amid such savagery.

[151] Is this really the purpose for which you have been destined, is it really for this that you have been chosen—to condemn people whom purchasers of confiscated property and cut-throats have not succeeded in murdering? Good generals, when they join battle, position troops at the point where they expect the enemy to flee, so that

they can launch an unexpected attack on anyone who runs away from the battlefield. I imagine these purchasers must be thinking along the same lines, that men such as yourselves are seated here for the purpose of catching anyone who escapes from their clutches. May the gods forbid, gentlemen, that this court, to which our ancestors gave the name 'council of state',* should be thought a bastion for purchasers of confiscated property! [152] Do you not realize, gentlemen, that the sole aim of these proceedings is to get rid of the children of the proscribed by fair means or foul, and that the first step in this process is to be achieved through your sworn oath and this attack on Sextus Roscius? Is there any doubt about who the guilty party is, when on the one side you can see someone who, besides being the prosecutor, is a purchaser of confiscated property, a personal enemy of the accused, and a cut-throat, while on the other you see an impoverished son, highly esteemed by his relations, a man to whom not only no blame at all but not even the suspicion of it can possibly be attached? Can you see anything else at all that counts against Roscius, except for the fact that his father's property has been sold?

[153] But if you do indeed favour that cause and pledge your support to it, if you are sitting there precisely so that the children of those whose property has been sold may be brought before you, then—by the immortal gods!—take care, gentlemen, that you do not seem to have instigated a new and far crueller proscription.* Although the first proscription was directed against those in a position to take up arms, the senate was nevertheless unwilling to undertake it: it was afraid that the council of state might appear to have sanctioned measures more extreme than those of our ancestors. This new proscription, on the other hand, is directed against the children of the proscribed and against little babies in their cradles; and unless you reject it and repudiate it by your verdict in this trial, then—by the immortal gods!—think what may happen to our country!

[154] Men who are wise, and endowed with the authority and power which you possess, have a particular duty to cure those ills from which our country is particularly suffering. There is no one among you who is not conscious that the Roman people, who used to be thought merciful to their enemies abroad, are currently suffering from cruelty at home. Remove this cruelty from our nation, gentlemen. Do not allow it to continue any longer in this country of ours. It

is an evil thing, not only because it has done away with so many
citizens in a most dreadful manner, but because it has taken away the
feeling of compassion from even the mildest of men, by accustoming
them to troubles. For when we are witnessing or hearing of some
dreadful event every hour, even those of us who are tender-hearted
by nature find that, through constant contact with unpleasantness,
we lose all sense of humanity.

PRO MURENA
('FOR MURENA')

DATE: late November 63 BC
DEFENDANT: Lucius Licinius Murena
LAW: *lex Tullia de ambitu* (Tullian law concerning electoral malpractice)
CHARGE: electoral malpractice during campaign for consulship of 62
PROSECUTORS: Servius Sulpicius Rufus, Marcus Porcius Cato, Servius
  Sulpicius, Gaius Postumius
DEFENCE ADVOCATES: Quintus Hortensius Hortalus, Marcus Licinius
  Crassus, Marcus Tullius Cicero
PRESIDING MAGISTRATE: unknown
VERDICT: acquittal

The circumstances of *Pro Murena* are quite different from those of *Pro Roscio Amerino*. In *Pro Roscio* (80 BC) we saw the 26-year-old Cicero, not yet launched on a political career, undertaking his first criminal case. When he delivered *Pro Murena* (63 BC), on the other hand, he was one of the year's two consuls, having attained each political office in turn at the earliest age permitted by law. In *Pro Roscio* Cicero made himself known as a speaker; by the time he was consul, however, he had been established for some seven years as Rome's foremost orator. And whereas Sextus Roscius was merely a farmer from one of the Italian towns, Lucius Licinius Murena was a prominent politician and general from a senatorial family, recently elected to succeed Cicero in the consulship of 62.

There is a contrast in the guilt of the two men, too. Roscius was transparently innocent of the crime of which he was accused. Murena, on the other hand, accused of having secured his election to the consulship by bribery, was fairly evidently guilty. Fortunately for him, however, his trial coincided with a dangerous military emergency, the Catilinarian conspiracy, and Murena was a man with a proven military record. Only days before the trial began, news had arrived that Lucius Sergius Catilina ('Catiline' in English), one of Murena's unsuccessful rivals for the consulship, had taken command of a hostile army in Etruria (cf. §§ 79, 84). In these circumstances it would clearly have been an act of madness for the Romans to send one of their consuls-elect into exile (the Greeks had been accustomed to act in this way, but the Romans never). This allowed Cicero to claim, with justice, that the national security, not the technical question of Murena's guilt, was the overriding factor in the case. The jury agreed, and Murena was unanimously acquitted. Cicero, then, does appear in this speech to have used his eloquence to secure the acquittal of a guilty defendant. But *Pro Murena* is far from being a dishonourable defence.

Murena's family (like that of Titus Annius Milo) came from Lanuvium in Latium, about twenty miles south of Rome. His father, grandfather, and great-grandfather had all been praetors, but until Murena himself no member of the family had attained the consulship. This did not make Murena (like Cicero, whose family had been entirely non-senatorial) a 'new man'; but it did mean that his family was not classed as belonging to the nobility. Murena's father, also named Lucius Licinius Murena, was the general who provoked the Second Mithridatic War (83–81 BC), was defeated, and returned to Rome for a triumph (events grossly misrepresented by Cicero in this speech); it was under his command that the young Murena gained his first military experience.

In 74 Murena held the quaestorship, and spent the year serving under a provincial governor. Then from 73 he served as a legate under Lucius Licinius Lucullus, to whom he was related (*Att.* 13.6.4), in the Third Mithridatic War (73–63 BC); Lucullus placed him in charge of the sieges of Amisus in 72 and of Tigranocerta in 69. We are not told when his service came to an end, only that he served 'for many years' (§ 89); but there is no reason to suppose that he did not continue to serve under Lucullus until the latter's replacement in 67. In 66 he stood successfully for the praetorship; during his year of office (65) he held the prestigious post of *praetor urbanus* (city praetor) and gave extravagant games. He then went on to govern a province, Transalpine Gaul (64–63). Finally, in the first half of 63, he returned to Rome to stand for the consulship. Lucullus' veterans, meanwhile, had come to Rome for a triumph, and with their help, together with that of the Umbrian towns from which he had recruited soldiers on his way out to his province the year before, Murena was elected consul for 62.

The other candidates in the consular election of 63 were Servius Sulpicius Rufus, Decimus Junius Silanus, and Lucius Sergius Catilina. Sulpicius' career had been exactly contemporaneous with that of Murena. He had been quaestor in charge of the port of Ostia in 74 and praetor in charge of the embezzlement court in 65, but after his praetorship he had declined to take a province. His entire career had been spent in Rome, where he had established himself as a great jurist, a reputation he still retains among students of Roman law. Silanus' earlier career is unknown, although he had made a previous attempt at the consulship in 65 (*Att.* 1.1.2). He was fortunate, as we shall see, to have been the brother-in-law of Marcus Porcius Cato, being the husband of Cato's half-sister Servilia. As for Catiline, he had been a legate under Sulla in 82–80, praetor in 68, and governor of Africa in 67–66. In 66 he had been unable to stand for the consulship because he did not return from Africa in time; in 65 he was prevented by a trial for extortion; and in 64 he lost to Cicero. The election of 63 was to be his final attempt. Of the four candidates, two, Sulpicius and Catiline, were patricians, and so legally could not both be elected (every year at least one consul had to be a plebeian). But in the event it was the two plebeians, Murena and Silanus, who were successful.

The election campaign was notable for the bribery and other illegal practices resorted to by at least some of the candidates. The existing law on electoral malpractice was the *lex Calpurnia* (67 BC), which imposed a penalty of expulsion from the senate, permanent disqualification from public office, and payment of a fine. When, during the campaign, the extent of the candidates' malpractice became known, Cicero, as consul, was pressed into obtaining from the senate a decree which clarified the *lex Calpurnia* by enumerating the practices which would be considered violations of it. This was done at the request of all the candidates, none of whom could decently resist the decree once it had been proposed. After the decree was passed, however, the candidates continued their campaigns exactly as before. At this point Sulpicius, who was probably the only candidate to keep within the law (and who perhaps had a greater respect for law in general than his fellow candidates), began to despair of being elected. Instead, his plan became to wait until the election was over and then prosecute one of his successful rivals. If the patrician Catiline were elected, he would have to prosecute him, since Sulpicius was a patrician himself; but otherwise he would have a free choice between Murena and Silanus. Then, having unseated one of the newly elected consuls, Sulpicius would stand in the supplementary election which would be held to fill the vacancy. Such was his plan. He also demanded a new, more rigorous bribery law, and persuaded his friend Cicero, who had been supporting his campaign, to propose one. The *lex Tullia* was duly passed. It did not contain all the proposals that Sulpicius wanted, but it was an advance on the *lex Calpurnia*, and it added to the penalties of that law a further penalty, exile for ten years.

Sulpicius was not, however, the only politician who disapproved of bribery. His views were shared by the austere Cato, who had just been elected to a tribunate for 62 (his year of office would begin on 10 December 63, some weeks in advance of the consular year, which began on 1 January). Cato was a great-grandson of the elder Marcus Porcius Cato (the new man from Tusculum who became consul in 195 and censor in 184), and he resembled his distinguished ancestor in his uncompromising traditionalism and in the severity of his moral outlook. But Cato was also (unlike his ancestor) an adherent of the Stoic school of philosophy. It was not unusual for Roman aristocrats at this time to have an interest in philosophy, whether in Stoicism or in its rival, Epicureanism; what was unusual was the extent to which Cato allowed his Stoic beliefs to dictate his actions and dominate his life. It is impossible for us to tell precisely what brand of Stoicism Cato chose for his own, and therefore to what degree Cicero's portrayal of Cato's philosophy in *Pro Murena* is misrepresentation, but the strength of Cato's commitment to Stoicism is not in doubt. Cato, then, joined Sulpicius in protesting against the use of bribery, and he announced publicly that he would prosecute any candidate whom he found acting illegally—although he would make an exception, he said, in the case of Silanus, since Silanus was his brother-in-law! This qualification may seem to us laughable (since it effectively proclaimed Silanus' guilt) and hypocritical, but this is to misunderstand Roman morality: prosecuting was a hateful business, and loyalty to one's own family was a moral imperative (except, of course, in cases where it conflicted with the national interest). In ruling out the prosecution of a relation, Cato was merely conforming to the old-fashioned Roman-ness which was a mark of his character, and which no one at the time would have considered reprehensible.

Bribery, then, was one cause for concern in the run-up to the consular election of 63. Another was the alarming behaviour of Catiline. When Cato announced his intention of prosecuting Catiline, the latter replied to the effect that if he were ruined by a conviction in the courts, he would see that he brought the whole country down with him. Then, shortly before the election was due to take place, he gave an inflammatory address at his house, recommending himself as someone who was prepared to go to any lengths on behalf of the poor and desperate, among whom he included himself. This was reported to Cicero by his spies, and Cicero persuaded the senate to postpone the election in order that they could discuss the speech Catiline had made. So the senate met, and Catiline, called upon to justify himself, far from denying what he had said, made another speech in the same vein. To Cicero's dismay, the senate then declined to take any effective action, and the election therefore went ahead without further delay. Catiline attended with a gang of armed men. Cicero, who was presiding, came with a bodyguard, and ostentatiously wore a large cuirass. He did this partly to register his disagreement with the senate about the nature of the threat posed by Catiline, and partly to bring home to the people the danger that Catiline represented. The result of the election was the best that Cicero could have hoped for. His friend Sulpicius was not successful, but that had been expected. The more important objective was to keep Catiline out, and a timely swing to Murena produced this result. As in 64, when Catiline was defeated by Cicero himself, the people voted for new blood in preference to decayed and unworthy aristocracy.

It was now time for Sulpicius to prosecute one of the successful candidates, and he decided he would join forces with Cato, who was also intending to prosecute. Cato would not prosecute Silanus, and so it was Murena against whom Sulpicius brought his charge. Two others joined the prosecution: Servius Sulpicius and Gaius Postumius. Servius Sulpicius was a young man and apparently the son of one of Murena's friends (§ 56): he was not, therefore, the son of Servius Sulpicius Rufus, but was probably one of his relations. As for Gaius Postumius, he stood for the praetorship of 62, but then withdrew his candidature (§ 57). Cicero claims that he was one of his own friends (§ 54), and also that he was a long-time friend and neighbour of Murena's late father (§ 56). It has been suggested that he may have been a relation of Servius Sulpicius Rufus' wife, perhaps her brother; that would explain his presence among Murena's prosecutors.

Catiline, for his part, responded to his election defeat by forming a conspiracy against the state. He could have chosen instead to wait for Murena's conviction and then stand against Sulpicius at the supplementary election which would follow; but he had evidently run out of patience, hope, and cash. We know little of what happened in August and September; in September the senate seems to have discussed Catiline's conspiracy, but there was as yet no hard evidence against him. In October a military rising took place in Etruria under one Gaius Manlius. The senate passed the emergency decree and made military preparations; but still there was nothing to incriminate Catiline. Then on 6 November Catiline held a secret meeting at which he arranged for Cicero to be assassinated at his home early the following morning; Cicero, however, was warned beforehand by his spies, and the assassins arrived to find the consul's doors closed against them. Cicero then went to the senate, where he denounced Catiline in the *First Catilinarian*; Catiline fled from Rome the same day, and Cicero reported his departure to the people in the *Second Catilinarian* (Cicero's four *Catilinarians* have survived, but were not written up until 60 BC, and are thus in some respects anachronistic). A week or so later, the news reached Rome that Catiline had joined Manlius' army; and Catiline and Manlius were declared public enemies. It was at this crucial juncture that the trial of Murena, which had been many months in preparation, finally opened.

The Catilinarian conspiracy was a serious blow to Murena's prosecutors, since it made it difficult if not impossible for them to argue that Murena's conviction was in the national interest: the defence would be able to point out that both consuls would be needed to defend Rome against Catiline. Sulpicius, however, had set his hopes of the consulship on a successful prosecution, and was not inclined to give up yet; in any case, Catiline's conspiracy had removed a candidate from the supplementary election that would be held afterwards. One might perhaps have expected Cato to see that the defeat of Catiline was the more important priority, especially since he was shortly afterwards to prove implacable in his opposition to the conspirators. But Cato was not a man to change his mind (§§ 61–2): he had said he would prosecute, and therefore would do so.

Murena was defended by Quintus Hortensius Hortalus, Marcus Licinius Crassus, and Cicero. Hortensius had been Rome's leading orator, until he lost to Cicero in the Verres trial of 70 BC; his oratorical style was of the florid, 'Asianist' variety. He became consul in 69, and then, avoiding the courts, settled down to life as one of the senior conservatives in the senate: he supported his friend Lucullus, and in 66 opposed the appointment of Pompey to the command against Mithridates that Lucullus had held. When Cicero became consul, Hortensius returned to the courts, and the two men worked together thereafter: the defence of Murena was their second collaboration (the first being their defence of Gaius Rabirius earlier in the year). Hortensius' support for Lucullus explains his acceptance of the case: Murena was very much Lucullus' man, and Lucullus attended the trial and gave Murena his backing (§ 20).

Crassus' motives were similar to those of Hortensius: he too was a supporter of Lucullus against Pompey. He had been an enemy of Pompey's since 71, when Pompey had claimed the credit for the suppression of Spartacus, which was largely Crassus' achievement. The two men were consuls in 70 (in spite of the fact that Pompey was technically six years too young), after which Pompey went on to further commands, against the pirates in 67 and against Mithridates in 66, while Crassus remained in Rome. By the time of Murena's trial, the war against Mithridates was over, and Pompey would before long be returning to Rome. This gave Crassus cause for concern: when Sulla had returned from fighting Mithridates in 82 he had made himself dictator and proscribed his opponents. Crassus would therefore have judged it in his interest to have as consul an experienced general who had fought under Lucullus and who owed a debt of gratitude to himself. Moreover, Catiline was in the field, and the senate would have to decide who should be sent against him. With Murena as consul, there would be a suitable general available, and so Pompey, if he should return before Catiline were suppressed, would be prevented from assuming a further command.

Cicero, on the other hand, was more favourably disposed to Pompey, and had no wish to offend him (cf. § 34). Moreover, he was a friend of the prosecutor Sulpicius, and had supported him in the election campaign; and he was in addition the author of the *lex Tullia* under which Murena was charged. There were therefore good reasons for him not to take on the

case, particularly at a time when he was heavily occupied with other matters. Why, then, did he accept it? The suggestion that he wanted to have a
consul in his debt to protect him from future attacks on his handling of
the Catilinarian conspiracy seems very doubtful: the act which left Cicero
open to attack for ever afterwards, his execution of the conspirators on 5
December, had not yet taken place. So his main reason is more likely to
have been that he saw it as his responsibility as consul to ensure that two
successors would be in place on 1 January to defend Rome against Catiline
(§§ 4–5, 79–82). If Murena were convicted, the new year would open with
only Silanus as consul, and his time would be taken up with arranging the
supplementary election necessary to fill the vacancy. Moreover, Catiline
had taken up arms, and a military man, such as Murena, would be needed
to defeat him. Pompey was away in the east, and Silanus, about whom
little is known, may have been ineffectual (he vacillated in the debate of 5
December). Cicero was uniquely aware of the danger of the Catilinarian
threat. He had just survived an assassination attempt, and through his
spies he knew more of Catiline's plans than others did. It therefore seems
reasonable to accept that his determination to stand up to Catiline was the
main factor in his decision to defend Murena. But there were no doubt
secondary motives too. Cicero's partners in the defence, Hortensius and
Crassus, were prominent conservatives, and Cicero, having reached the
top of the political ladder, now wished to join their number. And yet, as a
new man, he also felt a duty towards other men of a similar background to
his own. Murena was not a new man himself, but he nevertheless came
from a family in which no one had attained the consulship. In defending
him, therefore, Cicero was in the unusual position of being able both to
help one of his own kind and to earn the goodwill of the senior
conservatives in the senate.

The speeches for the defence were given in order by Hortensius,
Crassus, and Cicero (§§ 48, 54); in speaking last, Cicero was following his
usual custom (*Brut.* 190; *Orat.* 130). Cicero's speech used both humour, to
undermine the high moral status of the prosecutors, and seriousness, to
emphasize the danger from Catiline. Cato was heard to remark, 'Gentlemen, what an amusing consul we have!' (Plutarch, *Life of Cato the Younger*
21.5; id. *Demosthenes and Cicero compared* 1.5). Cicero's delivery of the
speech, however, is said to have fallen below his usual standards, because
he had stayed up all night preparing it (Plut. *Cic.* 35.3); but this has had no
discernible effect on the speech as we have it. Murena's acquittal was
unanimous: the jury accepted that the national interest required it (*Pro
Flacco* 98; cf. Quint. *Inst.* 6.1.35).

Murena, then, was consul in 62. But by the time he took office, Cicero
had already crushed the Catilinarian conspiracy at Rome. Shortly after the

trial was over, Cicero, with Murena's help (*De domo sua* 134), acquired the documentary evidence that he needed to prove the guilt of Catiline's leading associates in the city. Five conspirators were interrogated in the senate on 3 December; they confessed their guilt and honours were voted to Cicero, who was hailed as the father of his country. That evening Cicero reported these events to the people in the *Third Catilinarian*. Then on 5 December the senate debated what was to be done with the five men. It was Cato who rallied a wavering senate and persuaded it that the men should be executed at once, forfeiting their legal right to a trial (Cicero's *Fourth Catilinarian* was delivered on this occasion). Cicero had them executed the same day. Cato then took up his tribunate on 10 December—along with his political opponent Quintus Caecilius Metellus Nepos.

Murena himself took office on 1 January. Cicero, meanwhile, was being attacked by Nepos for the executions. After a clash between the two of them on 3 January, Cato hailed Cicero as the father of his country. As for Murena, he defended Cato against Nepos and treated him with every courtesy (Plutarch, *Life of Cato the Younger* 21.6, 28.2–3). He did not, however, play any part in the final defeat of Catiline in the field: that was undertaken by Cicero's consular colleague Gaius Antonius Hybrida, whose command against Catiline (§ 84) was continued into 62.

After his consulship, nothing more is heard of Murena. Sulpicius remained a good friend of Cicero, but had to wait until 51 to become consul; and Cato never reached the consulship at all.

PRO MURENA

[1] On that day, members of the jury, on which, after taking the auspices, I informed the centuriate assembly of Lucius Murena's election to the consulship, I offered up to the immortal gods the traditional prayer established by our ancestors, that the election should augur well and happily for myself, my honour, and my office, and for the Roman people and plebs. Today I offer the same prayer to those same immortal gods, that this same man may retain his consulship together with his civil status, that your opinion and verdict may reflect the wishes and votes of the Roman people, and that the outcome for yourselves and for the Roman people may be peace, tranquillity, harmony, and concord. But if that traditional election prayer, made sacred by the consular auspices, contains as much force and religious power as the dignity of our country demands, then I have prayed that the election over which I presided should also turn out luckily, happily, and successfully for the men on whom the consulship had been bestowed. [2] Since this is the case, gentlemen, and since the full power of the immortal gods has either been made over to you or at least shared with you, I, who recently entrusted a consul to the immortal gods, now entrust him to your protection, so that he, after being both declared consul and defended by the voice of one and the same man, may preserve the gift of the Roman people and, with it, the safety of yourselves and all Roman citizens.

And since, in fulfilling this duty, my devotion to the defence, and even the fact that I have undertaken the case at all, has been criticized by the prosecution, I propose, before I begin to speak for Lucius Murena, to say a few words on my own behalf. My reason for doing this is not that I judge defending my own actions to be more important to me at this time than defending my client. Rather, I believe that, by securing your approval for the action I have taken, I will be able to repel with greater authority the attacks which my client's enemies have made on his honour, his reputation, and everything that he has.

[3] I shall reply first, on the question of where my duty lies, to Marcus Cato—a man who orders his life according to a fixed set of rules, and who weighs up the respective claims of every duty with

the greatest of care. Cato objects that it is wrong for me to have anything to do with Lucius Murena's defence, seeing that I am a consul and the author of the law on electoral malpractice,* and have displayed such severity during my consulship.* His criticism has moved me greatly, and has made me demonstrate—not only to you, gentlemen, as I am very much obliged to do, but also to Cato himself, being the stern and upright man that he is—the rational grounds for the action I have taken.

So let me ask you, Marcus Cato, who could be a more appropriate person to defend a consul than a consul? Who in our entire nation can or should be more closely connected with me than the man to whom I am now handing over this country, preserved by great efforts of mine and at great danger to myself, for him to preserve? When property that has been formally sold* by one man to another is then claimed as his own by a third party, it is the man who has sold the property, and who has undertaken to guarantee its title, who ought to take the responsibility if a court decides in the third party's favour. This being the case, it is all the more appropriate that when a consul designate is put on trial, it should be the consul, the man who announced his successor's election, who should be the person who takes responsibility for this gift of the Roman people, and also the one who guards it from danger. [4] And if, as happens in some states,* an advocate were officially appointed to undertake the defence, and the defendant were someone who had attained the highest office, then the man who would be chosen to defend him would be someone who held the same office himself, and so could bring just as much authority to his defence as he could practical skill. People who are just putting into harbour from the open sea usually make great efforts to give others who are leaving harbour information about storms, pirates, and geography. This is because nature makes us well disposed towards those who are about to undergo the same dangers through which we ourselves have passed. Now that I have come through a severe buffeting* and am nearly within sight of land, how do you expect me to feel towards this man who I see must undergo the most violent political storms himself? Accordingly, if it is the mark of a good consul not only to be aware of what is happening now but also to see what is going to happen in the future, I shall reveal at a later point how important it is for our national security that there be two consuls in place on the first of January.* [5] If this is how the situation is, it ought not to have been a case of duty summoning me to defend a personal friend so much as our country summoning the consul to defend the safety of the nation.

As for the fact that I carried the law on electoral malpractice, I did indeed carry it—but in doing so I did not repeal that other law of mine, by which I bound myself long ago, the 'law on defending citizens in danger'. If I were to accept that bribery had taken place and argue that there was nothing wrong in that, I would indeed be acting improperly, even if someone else had carried the law. But since my defence is that the law has not been broken, how does my passing of the law undermine my case?

[6] Cato objects that my present defence of Lucius Murena is inconsistent with the severity I showed* towards Catiline when he was plotting the destruction of our country from within the city walls: by my words* and virtually by my official authority, I drove him out of Rome. But I have always been happy to play the part of mercy and compassion which nature herself taught me. As for that mask of strictness and severity, I never sought it: it was thrust onto me by the state, and I wore it during the serious national crisis as the dignity of my office demanded. But if at that time, when the state required me to show force and severity, I overcame my nature and displayed, unwillingly, the sternness that was expected of me, then surely now, when every consideration urges me to show compassion and humanity, I ought to be eager to yield to my character and normal practice? But on the question of my duty to speak for the defence and your grounds for prosecuting, I shall perhaps have something to say about this in another part of my speech.

[7] But the complaint, gentlemen, of that extremely learned and distinguished man, Servius Sulpicius, has affected me no less than Cato's criticism: he says that he is deeply and bitterly hurt that I should have forgotten our close ties of friendship and defended Lucius Murena against himself. I want very much, gentlemen, to explain myself to him, and to call on you to judge between us. For it is a serious matter to be accused of violating a friendship, if the accusation is true; and even if it is not, it is not something which can simply be ignored.

In your election campaign, Servius Sulpicius, I admit that, because of our friendship, I had a duty to lend you my full support— and I believe that I did fulfil that duty. When you were campaigning for the consulship, I failed you in nothing that could have been asked of a friend, or of a man of influence, or of a consul. But that time is past. The situation is different now. This is what I think and believe: in opposing Murena's election, I owed you all the help that you ventured to ask of me; but in opposing his civil status, I owe you nothing at all. [8] Even though I supported you when you were going for the consulship, now that you are going for Murena himself it is no longer my duty to help you in the way I did. And the view that when our friends are prosecuting we may not speak for the defence is not merely a view that cannot be applauded: it is one that is completely unacceptable, even if the person we propose to defend is a total stranger. My friendship with Murena, members of the jury, is both intimate and long-standing; it will not be overridden by Servius Sulpicius, in a case involving Murena's civil status, simply because it was my friendship with Servius that I put first in an election in which the two of them were standing.

But even if Murena were not my friend, his personal standing and the distinction of the office that he has attained would nevertheless have branded me with the stigma of arrogance and cruelty had I refused to defend a man of such distinction—both his own and that conferred by the Roman people—in a case involving such risk to himself. For it would be neither permissible nor honourable for me not to devote my efforts to helping men faced with prosecution. Since I have received greater rewards for these efforts of mine than anyone before me, I feel that to abandon one's labours after obtaining the honours to which they led* would be the act of a calculating and ungrateful man. [9] If, however, I am allowed to give up my work, and if I may let you take the responsibility for my doing so, and if I can avoid criticism for being idle, or disgrace for acting arrogantly, or blame for showing a lack of humanity, then certainly I shall gladly give it up. But if shunning hard work denotes sloth, rejecting suppliants arrogance, and abandoning one's friends shamelessness, then this case is one which no one who is hard-working or compassionate or loyal to duty could possibly refuse.

There is a straightforward comparison you can make, Servius, with your own field of study. If you feel duty-bound to provide legal opinions even to your friends' opponents when they consult you, and if you feel outraged when a former opponent to whom you have given legal advice loses his case, then do not be so unfair as to maintain that my fount of knowledge should be closed even to my friends, while yours is even open to your enemies. [10] Moreover, if our friendship had prevented me from taking on this case, and if the same had happened with the illustrious Quintus Hortensius and Marcus Crassus, and also with all the others who, I know, greatly value your goodwill, then the result would be that a consul designate would have no one to defend him—and this in a country in which our ancestors intended that no one, however humble, should ever be in need of someone to stand up for his interests! For my part, gentlemen, I should consider myself wicked had I deserted a friend, cruel had I deserted a man in trouble, arrogant had I deserted a consul. Nevertheless, every concession that is owed to friendship I shall freely concede; and I shall deal with you, Servius, as though it were my own dear brother, whom I am extremely fond of, standing in your place. I do have an obligation to duty, to loyalty, and to conscience, but I shall temper this with the recollection that it is against the efforts of a friend as well as for the safety of a friend that I am speaking.

[11] I gather, members of the jury, that the prosecution is divided into three parts. The first consists of an attack on my client's private life, the second of a comparison of the merits of the rival candidates, and the third of the charges of electoral malpractice. Of these three parts, the first, which ought to have been the most damning, was in fact so flimsy and trivial that it is clear that it was the standard convention among prosecutors rather than any genuine grounds for criticism that forced the accusers to mention Lucius Murena's private life at all.

Asia* has been made an accusation against him. But he did not seek out this province for pleasure and luxurious living: he passed through it in the course of his military service. If, as a young man, he had not chosen to serve under his father, who was our commander there, people would have thought him afraid of the enemy or of his father's command, or else would have concluded that his father had disowned him. Sons who have not yet assumed the toga of manhood ride on the horses at their father's triumphs.* Do you really think, then, that Murena should have declined to honour his father's triumph with the military prizes he had won and, since his father's successes had in fact been achieved jointly by both of them, virtually to share the triumph with him? [12] Yes, gentlemen, he was indeed

in Asia, and that most valiant man, his father, found him an invalu-
able help in moments of crisis, a comfort in times of strain, and a son
to be proud of in the hour of victory. And if Asia should give rise to a
suspicion of luxurious living, it is not the fact of never having seen
Asia that deserves praise, but of having lived there modestly. It was
therefore wrong of the prosecution simply to accuse Murena with
the word 'Asia': this is a province which has brought praise to his
family, fame to his stock, and honour and glory to his name. Instead,
they should have brought up some specific outrage or dishonour that
he committed in Asia or brought home from Asia. However, by
serving in that war—the greatest and indeed the only war that the
Roman people were fighting at that time—he gave proof of his valour; by serving of his own free will under his father's command he
gave proof of his sense of duty; and by completing his service with
his father's victory and triumph he gave proof of his good fortune.
There is no place at all in any of this for slander: there is room only
for praise.

[13] Cato calls Lucius Murena a dancer. Such a reproach, if true,
denotes an energetic prosecutor—but if false, a scurrilous slanderer.
A man of your stature, Marcus Cato, ought to be above picking up
slanders from off the street or from idlers' tittle-tattle, nor should
you call a consul of the Roman people a dancer unless you can
produce strong evidence. What you need to do is to look around for
the other vices which would also have to exist in someone who could
rightly be accused of being a dancer. Hardly anyone dances when he
is sober, unless he happens to be insane, nor when alone, nor at a
respectable, decorous gathering. First there needs to be extended
partying, a charming venue, and an array of pleasures—and only
then comes dancing. Do you seize upon what must necessarily be the
culmination of all vices, but make no mention of those lesser ones
without which it could not conceivably exist? You have given evidence of no disgraceful partying, no love affairs, no carousing, no
self-indulgence, no extravagance. The fact is that you cannot find
any sign of those so-called pleasures—or rather vices. Do you really
think, then, that you can find the shadow of luxurious living where
you cannot find the substance?

[14] So there is nothing that can be said against Lucius Murena's
private life, nothing whatsoever, I tell you, gentlemen. I am defending a consul designate against whom no deceit, no greed, no treach-

ery, no cruelty, and no offensive language at any point in his life can
be alleged. So far, so good: the foundations of my defence have been
laid. I have vindicated the moral character of my client not by praising him—that can come later—but by the tacit admission of his
enemies. Having done this, it will be easier for me now to proceed to
the comparison of the merits of the rival candidates, which was the
second part of the prosecution.

[15] I am aware, Servius Sulpicius, that you possess the very
highest qualifications of birth, integrity, industry, and all the other
qualities that a man needs if he is to put himself forward for election
to the consulship. I know, too, that Lucius Murena possesses equal
qualifications—so exactly equal that his standing could not possibly
be exceeded by your own, nor yours by his. Nevertheless, you have
expressed contempt for Lucius Murena's family, while extolling
your own. If, in making this point, you put forward the argument
that nobody is well born unless he happens to be a patrician, you will
make it seem as though there ought to be another secession of the
plebs to the Aventine!* But if it is the case that distinguished and
honourable plebeian families do exist, then please note that both
Lucius Murena's great-grandfather and his grandfather were praetors,* and his father, after capping his praetorship with a magnificent
and richly deserved triumph,* smoothed Murena's way to the consulship, since, in seeking this office, the son was only claiming what had
been his father's due.

[16] As for you, Servius Sulpicius, your noble birth* is indeed
outstanding, but it is better known to literary scholars and historians; the people and the voters are not so familiar with it. Your
father was indeed only of equestrian rank, and your grandfather was
not renowned for any brilliant deed.* As a result, no one nowadays
would learn of your noble status through casual conversation: the
information has to be dug up from ancient records. This is why I
have always included you in my own circle,* because, although only
the son of a Roman equestrian, you have shown by your ability and
your own determined efforts that you are fit to be thought of as
eligible for the highest office. Moreover, I have never considered
Quintus Pompeius,* a most valiant soldier but a new man, to be of
any less merit than the extremely noble Marcus Aemilius.* For it
requires the same spirit and talent to pass on to one's descendants,
as Pompeius did, a distinction which one has not inherited as to

renew by one's own ability, like Scaurus, the almost forgotten memory of one's family.

[17] I used to think, members of the jury, that I had by my own efforts succeeded in ensuring that brave men should not have to face criticism for the inferiority of their birth; for I have often drawn attention not only to valiant men of old such as Curius, Cato, and Pompeius, but to more recent ones like Marius, Didius, and Coelius.* I myself, too, broke down the gates of the nobility, which had been shut for so many years,* so that access to the consulship should be open in the future, as it was in our ancestors' time, as much to ability as to noble birth. But when I did this I little thought that when a consul designate from an old and distinguished family was being defended by a consul who was the son of a Roman equestrian, the prosecution would be talking about newness of family.* In my case, I was standing for the consulship against two patricians, one an utterly reckless traitor, the other a forbearing and altogether excellent man; I nevertheless defeated Catiline in merit, and Galba* in popularity. If it was wrong for me as a new man to defeat them, then surely people who disliked or envied me would not have been slow in coming forward. [18] Let us, therefore, stop talking about birth, since in this respect Sulpicius and Murena are equally distinguished. Instead let us move on to other matters.

'Murena was a candidate for the quaestorship at the same time as I was, and I was elected ahead of him.'* I need not reply to every objection. You will all of course appreciate that, while there may be a number of candidates of equal merit, only one can obtain the first place. The candidates' respective merit and the order in which their election is announced are not the same thing. This is because the elections are announced serially, whereas the merit of the various candidates may very often be identical. In any case, the duties which you and Murena were allotted in your quaestorships were just about of equal importance. Murena received, under the Titian law,* a quiet, peaceful province; you were given the post which always produces an outcry when the quaestors draw lots—Ostia, a duty which does not bring one popularity and fame so much as trouble and nuisance. During your quaestorships you each became less well known to the public because the lot gave neither of you a field in which your talents could be exercised and made known.

[19] The period that followed* has been made a focus of dispute. It

was spent by each of the two men in an entirely different way. Servius soldiered with me here at Rome, giving legal opinions, drawing up documents, and providing advice—a life full of anxiety and bother. He studied civil law, stayed up all hours, spared no pains, put himself at the service of a great many people, tolerated their stupidity, stomached their arrogant behaviour, and put up with those who were awkward. He lived for others, not for himself. That one man should work so hard at a profession that will benefit so many other people is highly creditable and also widely appreciated. [20] But what of Murena meanwhile? He served as a legate under that most valiant and wise man, the great general Lucius Lucullus.* In that posting he led an army, engaged in pitched battles, joined in close combat, defeated numerous enemy forces, took some cities by storm and others by siege, and in crossing that Asia of yours, so crammed with wealth and pleasures, he left behind not a trace of avarice or luxurious living; in that greatest of wars his conduct was such that he performed many great deeds without his commander—while his commander performed none without him. This I venture to assert in Lucius Lucullus' presence, and in case you should think that he has given me leave, in view of the danger which my client is currently facing, to go further than the truth, I can assure you that everything is vouched for in official despatches. In these despatches Lucius Lucullus is far more generous in his praise of Murena than any commander who was either self-seeking or jealous would have needed to be when writing about the contributions made by the officers under him.

[21] In each of the two men there exists the greatest honour, the greatest merit; and, if Servius will allow me, I shall give them exactly equal credit. But he does not allow me. He derides the military profession, he attacks Murena's command in its entirety, and he believes that obtaining the consulship is simply a matter of unflagging devotion to these day-to-day duties of ours. 'So', he says, 'you have been off with the army, and have not set foot in the forum for years. You have been away for all that time and now, returning after such a prolonged absence, are you really going to compete for office with men who have virtually been living in the forum?'* First of all, Servius, do you not realize how sick people sometimes get of our constant presence, how fed up they become with us? In my case, it was, I admit, extremely advantageous to me that my popularity was

there for all to see, but I did have to work very hard to prevent people becoming bored with me, and you no doubt have done likewise. Nevertheless, a spell of absence—and of being missed—would have done neither of us any harm.

[22] But let us leave all that aside and return to our comparison of careers and qualifications. How could anyone possibly doubt that military distinction counts for far more, when one is aiming at the consulship, than eminence in civil law? You are up at the crack of dawn to give legal opinions to those who consult you, he to bring his army to its destination in good time. You are woken by the cry of the cock, he by that of the bugle. You set out the line you will take, he sets up his line of battle. You ensure that your clients are not taken by surprise, he that cities and camps are not taken. He has a knowledge of how to keep off the enemy's forces, you of how to keep off rainwater.* He is occupied in extending boundaries, you in defining them. And surely—I must say what I feel—military ability counts for more than ability in any other field. For it is this which has given the Roman people the brilliant name they have; it is this which has bestowed everlasting glory upon our city; it is this which has induced the world to submit to our command. All our city affairs, all these fine pursuits of ours, the applause and the hard work here in the forum, all lie beneath the guardianship and protection of military strength. The moment the slightest alarm sounds, our cultured occupations instantly fall silent.

[23] And since you appear to me to be kissing your knowledge of the law just as if it were a baby daughter of yours, I am not going to let you carry on believing—quite wrongly—that this whatever-it-is that you have worked so hard to master is in any way remarkable. It is because of your other qualities—self-control, dignity, fairness, integrity, and all the rest—that I have always considered you to be exceptionally deserving of the consulship and every other office. As for the fact that you have learned civil law, I will not say that you have wasted your time exactly, but I will say that in that field of study there lies no paved highway to the consulship.

Every skill that serves to secure for us the favour of the Roman people needs to have two things: a prestige which impresses, and a usefulness which pleases. [24] The greatest prestige resides in those with outstanding military reputations because such men are credited with protecting and upholding our entire empire and government.

They have the greatest usefulness, too, since it is by the decisions they take and the dangers they face that we are able to enjoy our national life and our own private affairs. Another skill that commands respect and carries considerable prestige, and has often proved critical in the choice of a consul, is ability in public speaking—the ability to use good judgement and eloquence to sway the minds of the senate, the people, and those who sit on juries. A consul is needed who can, when necessary, use his ability in speaking to check the frenzy of tribunes, to calm the excitement of the people, and to oppose state handouts.* It is hardly surprising that this skill has enabled many men, even those who were not nobles, to attain the consulship, especially seeing that ability in speaking produces very deep gratitude, very strong friendships, and very great popularity.

   In the profession which you practise, Sulpicius, there is nothing of any of this. [25] First of all, there can be no prestige in such a narrow field of study. For the matters with which it deals are trivial, nearly always to do with individual letters and the dots between words. Secondly, even if your profession was treated with some respect by our ancestors, it fell into contempt and was totally rejected once your secrets had been divulged. At one time, few people knew whether legal business could be transacted, since there was no calendar available.* The lawyers had enormous power, and were consulted even about the day as if they were Chaldaean astrologers. But then a scribe, one Gnaeus Flavius, came along and pecked out the crows' eyes:* by learning off the individual days he was able to supply the people with a calendar and so rob those cautious lawyers of their knowledge. The lawyers were furious. Their fear was that, with the calendar out in the public domain and known to everyone, legal business could be transacted without them. So that they could remain indispensable, they therefore thought up various legal formulas. [26] It would be perfectly possible for someone to say, 'The Sabine farm belongs to me,' and another to say, 'No, it belongs to me,' then the hearing would take place. But the lawyers wouldn't have it. 'The farm', says the lawyer, 'which is in the territory which is called Sabine.' Long-winded enough, you might think. But look what comes next. 'I declare that, according to the legal rights of the Roman citizenry, it belongs to me.' And then what? 'I therefore summon you from the court to join hands* at the property.' The defendant is at a loss to know how to reply to so verbose a litigant.

But then the very same lawyer crosses over to the other side of the court, like a Latin piper.* 'Seeing that you have summoned me from the court', he says, 'to join hands at the property, I, therefore, summon you there in turn.' Meanwhile, to stop the praetor getting too good an opinion of himself and actually saying something off his own bat, a jingle was thought up for him too. Here is a particularly ridiculous extract: 'The witnesses for both parties being present, I indicate your route. Follow the route.' Our learned friend remains on hand to point out the route to be followed. 'Return by that route.' They return, escorted by the same guide. It no doubt already seemed nonsensical, even in the days when our ancestors wore beards,* for people who had turned up at the right place to be told to go away again, and then, when they had gone away, to be told to come back at once to where they had started from. Everything was dressed up with absurdities of this kind, such as: 'Whereas I see you before the court' and 'Will you not state the grounds on which you base your claim to the property?' As long as these procedures were a secret, one had to go and consult those who knew about them; later on, however, once they had been made generally available and had been examined and turned inside out, they were found to be not only completely devoid of common sense, but also filled to the brim with trickery and foolishness. [27] A great many points had been set down in the laws with perfect clarity; but these were mostly twisted and perverted by the lawyers' ingenuity. For instance, our ancestors intended that all women, because of the weakness of their judgement, should be subject to the authority of guardians. But the lawyers thought up types of guardian which would be subject to the authority of women. Our ancestors were concerned that religious ceremonies should not die out. But the lawyers ingeniously found old men to undergo secular marriages,* in order to make the ceremonies die out. In short, in every branch of civil law, they abandoned the spirit of the law while holding fast to the letter. Thus, because they had come across the name 'Gaia' used as an example in the treatises of someone or other, they thought that all women who underwent a secular marriage were actually called 'Gaia'.* As for myself, I have long found it extraordinary that so many of the finest legal brains should not yet have managed, even after so many years, to make up their minds as to whether one ought to say 'two days from now' or 'the day after tomorrow', 'judge' or 'arbitrator', 'case' or 'lawsuit'.

[28] So, as I said, your profession—consisting as it does entirely of
fictions and fabrications—has never conferred the prestige required
for the consulship, much less the necessary popularity. Something
that is universally available, and just as accessible to my opponent as
to myself, cannot conceivably win you gratitude. You have therefore
lost not only the means to confer a favour but also the 'May I ask
your advice?' with which you were for so long approached. No one
can be thought learned if his field of knowledge is one which has no
relevance outside Rome, or even in Rome when the courts are not in
session. So no one can be considered an expert, since in a subject
with which everyone is familiar there is no scope at all for disagreement. Nor can the subject be said to be a difficult one, given that it is
entirely contained within a very small number of perfectly straightforward texts. If, therefore, you persist in provoking me, extremely
busy as I am,* I shall set myself up as a lawyer within three days. For
questions which depend on a form of words are all written down
somewhere or other—and nothing has been written so exactly that I
could not add to it 'which is the point at issue'. Oral advice, on the
other hand, can be offered with little or no risk: if you gave the right
answer, you would be seen as having made the same reply as the great
Servius,* and if you answered otherwise, people would think you had
recognized a difficult point of law and were dealing with it.

[29] Accordingly, not only does military glory—of which you
speak so slightingly—carry more prestige than those formulas and
processes of yours, but public speaking, also, far and away outstrips
the profession which you practise, so far as election to high office is
concerned. It seems to me that many men have started out with a
strong preference for my profession, but when in due course they
found they were not up to it, they sank to yours. They say of Greek
musicians that the singers who accompany the reed-pipe are the ones
who failed with the lyre.* So it is with our professions: those who do
not make it as orators resort to the study of law. Public speaking has
to do with great efforts, great questions, great prestige, and overwhelming influence. Clients consult you about their state of health,
as it were, but they consult orators about their actual life. Moreover,
your opinions and rulings are often overturned by a speech, and
cannot be upheld unless an orator speaks in their favour. On the
subject of oratory, if I had achieved very much in that department
myself I would certainly not be praising it so extravagantly. As it is,

however, I am not referring to myself at all, but to those who are now
or have in the past been great speakers.

[30] There are therefore two professions which can raise a man to
the highest peak of distinction, that of a general, and that of a good
orator. The latter maintains the beauties of peace, while the former
repels the dangers of war. There are of course other virtues which
carry considerable weight in themselves—justice, good faith, modesty, self-control—and everyone recognizes that you, Servius, possess these to an outstanding degree. But I am talking now about the
professions that lead to high office, not about the personal qualities
which each man possesses. The moment that any fresh crisis sounds
the call to arms, the other professions that we practise are all dashed
from our hands. For as that brilliant poet* and exceptional authority
declares, 'when battle is begun, from our midst is driven' not only
your long-winded pretence of knowledge but also that mistress of
the world, 'wisdom' herself. 'The question is decided by force: the
orator is thrust aside'—and not just the one who is tiresome and
wordy, but even the one who is 'good: the uncouth soldier is loved'.
Your profession lies completely abandoned: 'they do not go from
court to join hands:* it is with the sword', he says, 'that they claim
back their property.' If this is so, Sulpicius, then let the forum yield
to the camp, peace yield to war, the pen yield to the sword, the shade
yield to the sun—and may first place in our nation be given to that
profession thanks to which our nation itself occupies first place in
the world.

[31] But Cato objects that I am making too much of this in my
speech, and that I have forgotten that the whole of that war against
Mithridates* was fought against a load of women. My own view is
very different, members of the jury, but I shall be brief on this
subject, since it is not on this point that my case turns. If we are to
look down on all the wars that we have fought against the Greeks,
then we will have to scoff at the triumphs of Manius Curius over
King Pyrrhus, of Titus Flamininus over Philip, of Marcus Fulvius
over the Aetolians, of Lucius Paullus over King Perseus, of Quintus
Metellus over the false Philip, and of Lucius Mummius* over the
Corinthians. But if, on the other hand, these were wars of the greatest importance, and the victories with which they were concluded
were greatly to be welcomed, why do you deprecate the peoples of
Asia and an enemy such as Mithridates?

Historical accounts show that perhaps the greatest war fought by the Roman people was the one against Antiochus.* The victor in that war was Lucius Scipio, and the glory he thereby acquired was equal to that which had been won by his brother Publius. For Publius, after conquering Africa, boasted of his glory through the name he assumed, and Lucius, likewise, took the same glory for himself from the name of Asia. [32] Marcus Cato,* your great-grandfather, also showed outstanding bravery in that war; and since he was, I am convinced, a man who possessed the same qualities as I now see in you, he would never have gone out with Scipio had he thought that they were to fight against 'a load of women'. Moreover, the senate arranged with Publius Africanus that he should accompany his brother as a legate, and this was not long after he had himself driven Hannibal out of Italy, thrown him out of Africa, defeated Carthage and so freed our country from extreme danger. They would certainly not have done this had they not considered the war an important and difficult one.

Yet if you think carefully what Mithridates was capable of, what he actually achieved, and what kind of a man he was, you will surely rate this king more highly than any of the others that the Roman people have fought against. Lucius Sulla, an aggressive, energetic, and not inexperienced general (to say the least), the commander of an extremely large and courageous army, allowed Mithridates to go away in peace,* despite his having brought war into the whole of Asia. Lucius Murena, my client's father, pursued him* with the greatest persistence and pertinacity, and left him constrained, more or less, but not crushed. This king, after spending some years making the necessary plans and preparing his forces for war, had such high hopes for himself that he fully expected to link the Atlantic Ocean with the Black Sea and the forces of Sertorius* with his own. [33] When the war came, both consuls were sent out:* one was to go after Mithridates, the other to defend Bithynia. The operations of the latter were disastrous on both land and sea, and served greatly to enhance both the king's military strength and his reputation. Lucius Lucullus' activities, on the other hand, were so successful that it is impossible to recall any war that was fought on a larger scale or conducted with greater intelligence and bravery. The whole thrust of the war was at this stage directed against the walls of Cyzicus, since Mithridates thought that this city would become his gateway to Asia, and that when he had broken it down and forced it open the entire province would lie at his feet. Lucullus, however, succeeded in ensuring that the city of our most loyal allies held out against the king, and that his forces were all used up on the protracted siege. And what about that naval battle off Tenedos? The enemy fleet, led by the most determined commanders, was making for Italy* at full speed, puffed up by hope and courage: do you really think that this was a small-scale encounter, a trivial skirmish? I leave out the battles, I pass over the assaults on towns; even after he was at long last driven from his kingdom, Mithridates still had sufficient intelligence and influence to be able to win over the king of the Armenians and thus make good his position again with fresh troops and resources.

If it were now my task to talk about our army and its commander, there are a great many important battles of which I could remind you; but that is not our present concern. [34] I do say this, however: if this war, if this enemy, if that king had really been so contemptible, then the senate and Roman people would not have thought it necessary to take such trouble over it when it broke out; nor would Lucius Lucullus have pursued it, and with such distinction, over so many years; nor would the Roman people have been so enthusiastic in bestowing on Gnaeus Pompeius the task of bringing it to an end. Out of all the countless battles which Pompeius has fought, the fiercest and most strongly contested was, I think, the one that he fought against the king.* And after escaping from this battle and taking refuge in the Bosporus* where our army could not reach him, nevertheless, in desperate straits and on the run, Mithridates kept his royal title. That is why Pompeius, despite having driven the enemy from his borders and all his known bases and having taken over his kingdom,* nevertheless set so much store by the life of this one man. Although everything that Mithridates had ever controlled, come near to controlling, or aspired to control had fallen into his victorious hands, even so Pompeius did not consider the war to be won until he had driven him from life itself.

Is this, Cato, the enemy you scorn? One whom so many generals have fought against in so many battles over so many years? One whose very existence, even after he had been ejected and thrown out of his kingdom, was thought to pose so serious a threat that it was not until his death had been reported that the war was judged truly over? Such, then, was the war in which my client Lucius Murena was acknowledged to be an officer of the most outstanding courage, the highest intelligence, and the greatest industry; and I maintain that the service he gave was at least as strong a qualification for the consulship as my own efforts here in the forum.

[35] But, you say, in the election for the praetorship Servius was declared elected ahead of Murena.* Are you really trying to tell the people that once it has placed a man in a certain position in the poll in one election, it is then obliged, as if under contract, to place him in the same position in all subsequent elections? What strait, what Euripus* can you think of that has so many eddies, such great and multifarious movements of current as would compare with the great turbulences and tides that elections have? A day's interruption or night's intervention often throws everything into confusion, and it is not unknown for the merest whisper of a rumour to make everyone change their mind. Often, and for no apparent reason, things do not go the way you expect, and sometimes even the people are surprised at the way something turns out—as if they had not themselves been responsible. [36] There is nothing more fickle than the masses, nothing more unfathomable than people's intentions, nothing more misleading than the entire process of an election. Who would have thought that Lucius Philippus, a man of the highest ability, industry, popularity, and nobility, could be defeated by Marcus Herennius?* That Quintus Catulus, so outstandingly cultured, wise, and honourable, could be defeated by Gnaeus Mallius?* That Marcus Scaurus, a man of the greatest dignity, an outstanding citizen, and a truly courageous senator, could be defeated by Quintus Maximus?* Not only were these outcomes totally unexpected, but even once they had occurred no one could understand why they had come about. Storms often occur when there is some recognized indication in the sky, but they also quite often happen without warning, for no obvious reason and without any apparent cause. In the same way, in this tempest of popular elections, there is often some indication which enables you to see what has caused it, but often, too, the reason is unclear, and the storm seems to have blown up purely by chance.

[37] But if I must provide an explanation, there were two things which Murena, in his campaign for the praetorship, suffered seriously from the lack of, but which were both of considerable benefit to him when he came to stand for the consulship. One was games, the

expectation of which had been brought about by certain rumours and by the deliberate suggestion of his rivals for office. The other thing he lacked was the presence in Rome of those who had been with him in his province and throughout his period of service* and who had seen his generosity and courage at first hand: for they had not yet returned home. Both of these advantages fortune held back for him until he stood for the consulship. When the time came for that, Lucius Lucullus' army, which had come to Rome for his triumph,* was on hand to support Lucius Murena at the elections; and as for his not having put on games, a factor which had hampered Murena in his campaign for the praetorship, this deficiency had been made up for by the extremely lavish games he put on in the course of his year as praetor.

[38] You surely do not regard the backing of the soldiers and the military vote as being of negligible use and help when one is standing for the consulship? In terms of sheer numbers the soldiers are important, then one must take into account the influence they have over those they know, and then there is also the fact that all Roman citizens are strongly inclined to follow the lead of the soldiers when electing a consul. At the consular elections it is generals that are elected, not interpreters of words. So talk of this kind carries great weight: 'He looked after me when I was wounded. He gave me a share of the spoils. He was our general when we took that camp, when we fought that battle. He never made a soldier put up with more hardship than he was prepared to endure himself. He was brave, and he had luck on his side.' How important do you think this sort of talk is for securing a reputation and backing? If at these elections people are so superstitious that up to now the vote of the first century has always proved a sure omen of the final result,* is it any wonder that in this case a much talked-about reputation for luck has proved decisive?

It may be that you consider such matters trivial (although they are in fact of the first importance) and attach more weight to the urban vote than to that of the soldiers. But, if so, you can hardly show the same contempt for the high quality of Murena's games and the magnificence of the spectacle, since this was unquestionably of enormous help to him. Do I need to point out that the people and the ignorant masses adore games? It is hardly surprising that they do. And yet this point on its own proves my case: for elections, like games, have to do with the people and the masses. So if the people derive pleasure from magnificent games, it is hardly surprising that Lucius Murena's, which were indeed magnificent, improved his standing with the people. [39] As for us, pressure of work keeps us away from the pleasures enjoyed by the people, and in any case our work itself provides us with many alternative sources of pleasure; but, despite this, we do in fact enjoy the games, and find ourselves drawn to them. And if we enjoy the games, why should you be surprised that the uneducated masses enjoy them? [40] It was not just its status that my friend the valiant Lucius Otho* gave back to the equestrian order, but its source of enjoyment too. That is why his law about the games is the most popular law of all—because it restored to that most honourable order, along with its prestige, the full enjoyment of its pleasure. Games, then, do give people pleasure, believe me, and not only those who admit it, but even those who pretend otherwise. I was aware of this when I was standing myself, because I too had a rival who had put on games. But if I, who had myself put on three sets of games when I was aedile, was nevertheless alarmed by Antonius' games,* do you really think that that silver spectacle of Murena's, which you scoff at, did you no damage, especially when you, as it happened, had put on no games at all?

[41] Let us assume, however, that all these factors are equal, that service in the forum counts for the same as service in the army, that the urban vote counts for the same as the military, and that having given extremely magnificent games is equivalent to never having given any games at all. But would you then go on to maintain that in your respective praetorships there was no difference between what you and Murena were assigned?* Murena was allotted the post which all your friends wanted for you, that of civil jurisdiction. This is a post in which the importance of the task wins one glory, and the dispensing of justice wins one gratitude; in this office a wise praetor, such as Murena was, avoids causing offence by judging impartially, and attracts goodwill by listening to the litigants sympathetically. It is an excellent job to get, and one which fits the holder for the consulship: it enables him to win a reputation for fairness, honesty, and helpfulness, and all this is ultimately crowned by enjoyable public games. [42] And what were you allotted? Dismal and grim, the embezzlement court. On the one side you find nothing but tears and filth,* on the other accusers and informers. Unwilling jurors must be

compulsorily summoned and kept on against their will. A scribe is found guilty, and you alienate the entire profession. A favour from Sulla* is criticized, and many brave veterans, practically an entire section of society, turn against you. Heavy damages are awarded: the winner forgets, the loser remembers.

Lastly, you refused to take a province. Having done the same myself when I was a praetor and again in my consulship, I am in no position to criticize. All the same, Lucius Murena's province* won him many useful favours and a glorious reputation. On his way out, he raised troops in Umbria; the political situation gave him the opportunity to show generosity, and this allowed him to acquire the support of the many tribes which are made up of Umbrian towns.* Then, while in Gaul, by his sense of fairness and his dedication to the task he enabled our men to recover debts which they had previously written off. You, meanwhile, were at Rome and, naturally, were helping your friends. I do not deny it. But just think for a moment: the support of friends does sometimes tend to become less enthusiastic when they see those they have been supporting turning down provinces.*

[43] What I have shown, members of the jury, is that Murena and Sulpicius were equally well qualified to stand for the consulship, but were not equally lucky as regards the official duties they were allotted. I shall now state explicitly the respects in which my friend was the weaker of the candidates, and now that he has lost the election I shall say in your hearing what I often said to him in private when he still had a chance.

I repeatedly told you, Servius, that you had no idea how to campaign for the consulship, and I used to say to you that in everything that I saw you say and do—and with such spirit and resolution, too—you gave me the impression of being a courageous prosecutor rather than a serious candidate. First, the terrifying threats of prosecution which you used to utter daily may be the mark of a man of spirit, but they make the people think you have no chance of winning and they weaken the enthusiasm of your friends. I do not know how, but it always turns out—and this has been noticed not once or twice, but a great many times—that as soon as a candidate for office is understood to be contemplating a prosecution, he is believed to have given up all hope of being elected. [44] So, then, do I not approve of seeking redress when one has been wronged? Of course I approve, very strongly; but there is a time for campaigning and a time for bringing prosecutions. I like a candidate, particularly a candidate for the consulship, to be escorted to the forum and to the Campus Martius with great hopes, great enthusiasm, and great crowds. I do not like him to be looking for evidence: that's a sure sign of impending defeat. Nor do I want him to be gathering witnesses instead of voters, or making threats instead of compliments, or protests instead of greetings, especially given this new practice according to which almost everyone now chases round the houses of all the candidates trying to tell from their faces how much confidence and potential each one seems to have. [45] 'Do you see how downcast and despondent he is? He's down, he has given up hope, he has thrown his spears away.' The rumour spreads. 'Have you heard? He's planning a prosecution, looking for evidence against the other candidates, trying to find witnesses. I'm voting for someone else: this one's obviously given up.' Close friends of this type of candidate are dismayed and their enthusiasm cools; they give the whole thing up for lost, or else keep back their help and influence for the trial and the prosecution.

A further consequence is that the candidate cannot put his whole heart into his campaign, or devote all his time, trouble, and effort to it. He has to be thinking about his prosecution; and this is no trivial concern for him, but unquestionably the most important one he has. It is no small matter to collect together everything you need to drive a man from his country,* particularly if he is neither weak nor defenceless, and can rely on the help that he can provide himself, and that of his friends, and even that of people he does not know. For all of us rush to defend those in danger, and as long as we are not openly declared enemies we will fulfil, even to perfect strangers if they are in danger of forfeiting their civil status, the duties and responsibilities that we otherwise owe only to our closest friends. [46] I myself have first-hand experience of the trouble involved in campaigning for office, in mounting a defence, and in preparing a prosecution, and I can tell you what is the chief feature of each of these tasks: in campaigning it is commitment, in defending it is duty, and in prosecuting it is sheer hard work. That is why I am certain that it is quite impossible for the same man to organize and marshal a prosecution and a campaign for the consulship at the same time, and do justice to both of them. Few men can manage either one of these tasks, no one both. In your case, when you had turned aside from the race for office and had switched your attention to prosecuting, you imagined that you could carry out both tasks at once. How wrong you were! In fact, once you had set about giving notice of your prosecution, was there ever a single day which was not completely taken up with that project?

You demanded a law against electoral malpractice—quite unnecessarily, since there was already in existence the very strictly worded Calpurnian law.* Nevertheless, your wishes and standing were deferred to. That law,* taken as a whole, would perhaps have fortified your case, had you been prosecuting a guilty defendant. As it happened, all it did was wreck your campaign. [47] You were heard to demand a stricter penalty for the masses:* this merely stirred up the poorer classes against you. You wanted exile for our order: the senate acceded to your demand, although it was not happy about imposing, at your insistence, a harsher penalty for senators in general. The plea of ill-health* was also penalized. This alienated a good many people: some would be required to exert themselves to the detriment of their health, while others, in addition to suffering from ill-health, would also have to forfeit* whatever enjoyment their lives still held for them.

So who was it, then, who brought in these measures? It was someone who deferred to the senate's authority and to your own personal wish—and who also had least to gain from them himself.* As for the further proposals which a packed senate rejected (as I very much hoped it would), do you seriously believe that they did you only trivial damage in your campaign? You demanded that the votes be mixed up, that the Manilian law be proposed, and that influence, rank, and votes be equalized.* Respectable men, men of influence in their neighbourhoods and towns, took it badly that a man such as yourself should be fighting to abolish all distinctions of rank and prestige. You also wanted the jury to be nominated by the prosecution,* so that people's private hostilities, which are currently contained within silent feuds, should burst out into the open and attack all our finest men. [48] All these proposals of yours paved your way to a prosecution, but blocked your path to the consulship.

That was the greatest of all the blows inflicted on your campaign, as I warned you at the time; and my most able and fluent friend, Quintus Hortensius, has discussed it fully and authoritatively.

Indeed, my task has been made harder by the place I have been given in the order of speaking: for both Hortensius and Marcus Crassus, a man of the greatest rank and diligence and oratorical skill, have spoken before me. In giving the last of the speeches, I am not dealing with any particular part of the defence, but am saying whatever I think appropriate about the case as a whole. Inevitably, therefore, I am covering the same points, more or less, as my partners covered, but I am doing my best, members of the jury, not to bore you.

But what sort of an axe-blow, Servius, do you think you inflicted on your campaign when you terrified the Roman people into being afraid that Catiline* would be elected consul? You were busy preparing your prosecution, and had abandoned and jettisoned your campaign. [49] People saw you making enquiries; you looked glum yourself, and your friends looked downcast. People noticed the spying, the taking of evidence, the quiet words with witnesses, the meetings with assistant prosecutors—activities which undeniably raise doubts about a candidate's intentions. At the same time they could see Catiline, lively and enthusiastic, escorted by a crowd of young men, guarded by informers and cut-throats, buoyed up by the hopes of his soldiers and the promises he claimed my colleague* had made to him, and borne along by an army of colonists from Arretium and Faesulae*—a uniform rabble, but distinguished by the inclusion of men of a very different sort, those ruined in the time of Sulla.* The rage in his face, the criminality in his eyes, and the insolence in his speech gave the impression that the consulship was already confirmed as his and laid down for him at his house. Murena he looked on with contempt. As for Sulpicius, he counted him more as his prosecutor than as a rival, threatening him with violence and menacing the state.

[50] You do not need me to remind you of the fear which this inspired in all loyal citizens, or the despair that the whole country felt at the prospect of Catiline's election: you can remember it yourselves. You will recall what that unspeakable gladiator was widely reported to have said at a meeting held at his house—that there could be no true defender of the poor who was not also poor himself; that people who were poor and in trouble should not trust the promises of the rich and trouble-free; that those who wished to recoup what they had spent and recover what they had forfeited* should look at the size of his debts, the limits of his possessions, and the lengths

to which he was prepared to go; and that the man who was to be the leader and standard-bearer of the desperate should be the one who was the least afraid and most desperate himself.

[51] When this speech had become public knowledge, you will recall that the senate, on my proposal, passed a decree calling off the following day's election in order to give us the opportunity to debate these matters in the senate. On the next day, therefore, at a well-attended meeting of the senate I called on Catiline to rise and asked him to comment, should he wish to do so, on the matters that had been reported to me. But he, forthright as ever, instead of attempting to clear his name, incriminated and trapped himself. After that he said that the state had two bodies, one feeble with a weak head, and the other one strong but with no head at all, and that this latter body, provided that it showed itself deserving of him, would never be without a head so long as he lived. The packed senate gave a groan, but nevertheless failed to pass a decree severe enough to reflect the shocking nature of what had taken place. Some of the senators failed to take a strong line because they saw nothing to fear, others because they were afraid of everything. Catiline, jubilant, rushed out of the senate-house in triumph—a man who should never have been allowed to leave it alive, especially in view of the fact that, at a meeting of the senate only a few days before, he had told the valiant Cato, who was threatening him and announcing his intention of prosecuting him, that if his own fortunes should be set on fire, he would put out the flames not with water but by destruction.*

[52] I was extremely worried by this, and I knew, moreover, that Catiline had already formed a conspiracy and was bringing men armed with swords down to the Campus Martius. I therefore went down to the Campus Martius myself with a very strong bodyguard of the bravest men, and wearing that large and conspicuous cuirass. I wore this not in order to protect myself, since I knew that Catiline's practice was not to strike at the flank or the stomach, but at the head and neck. My aim was, rather, to make all loyal citizens aware of the situation. When they saw their consul afraid and in danger, they would surely rush to his aid and protection—and this is exactly what happened.

People thought that you, Servius, were not really bothering with your campaign, and they could see that Catiline was ablaze with lust for power and the expectation of it. Everyone who wanted to rid the country of that pestilential villain therefore went over at once to Murena. [53] In consular elections, sudden swings of opinion are important, particularly when the swing is towards a good man who has many other points in his favour. Murena had the advantage of an extremely honourable father and ancestors, a youth entirely beyond reproach, a most distinguished period as a legate, and a praetorship in which his dispensing of justice had won him approval, his games popularity, and his province distinction. He had worked hard at his campaign, nor had he given way to anyone's threats, or made threats against anyone himself. Is it any wonder, then, that Catiline's sudden hope of being elected proved an enormous boost for Murena?

[54] It now remains for me to deal with the third subject of my speech, the charges of electoral malpractice. These have already been disposed of by those who spoke before me, but I am going to go over them again, because this is what Murena wants. In dealing with this subject I shall reply to Gaius Postumius—a friend of mine and a man of great distinction—on the evidence of the distributing agents and on the money that has been seized. I shall also reply to that talented and loyal young man, Servius Sulpicius, on the equestrian centuries.* And I shall reply to Marcus Cato, a man who excels in every virtue, on the charge that he has personally brought, on the decree of the senate,* and on the national interest.

[55] But before I do this I must briefly voice the distress that has suddenly come over me at Lucius Murena's plight. I have often before been led, members of the jury, by the troubles of others as well as my own day-to-day worries and labours to regard as fortunate those who, free from the pursuit of ambition, follow a life of ease and tranquillity. And in this particular case, when I see the terrible and totally unexpected dangers that Lucius Murena is now facing, I am so affected that I cannot deplore strongly enough either the common lot of all of us or the unhappy situation in which Murena finds himself. All that he was trying to do was to rise one step higher than the office* repeatedly attained by his family and his ancestors; yet this has caused him to risk losing everything that he has inherited as well as all that he has won for himself. In this way his eagerness to win new honours has brought him to the point where he is in danger of losing even those he already possesses. [56] And if that were not bad enough, gentlemen, this is particularly painful to him, that his accusers are not men who have turned to prosecuting out of personal

feelings of enmity, but men who have turned to enmity out of a personal desire for prosecuting. I leave out Servius Sulpicius,* who, I know, is motivated not by any wrong that Lucius Murena has done to him but by their rivalry for office. Apart from him, the prosecutors include a friend of Murena's father, Gaius Postumius, a long-time neighbour and friend, as he himself admits: he mentioned a number of reasons for their friendship, but could offer none at all why they should be enemies. The prosecutors include Servius Sulpicius,* the son of Murena's close companion, who ought to be devoting his abilities instead to protecting his father's friends. And the prosecutors include Marcus Cato, who has never been at odds with Murena over anything at all, and who has been born into such an elevated position in our nation that he ought to be devoting his talents and his resources to the defence of many people, of strangers even, and scarcely ever to the destruction even of an enemy.

[57] I shall reply, then, to Postumius first, who as a candidate for the praetorship throwing himself at a candidate for the consulship seems to me somehow like a circus rider throwing himself at a four-horse chariot.* If his fellow candidates did not violate the law, then he acknowledged their superior claims when he withdrew his candidature. But if, on the other hand, one of them did commit an act of bribery, then he is indeed a friend worth having, who would seek to avenge an injury done to someone else, but not one done to himself!

(*On the charges of Postumius, and those of the young Servius.*)*

[58] I come now to Marcus Cato, who is the mainstay and bulwark of the entire prosecution. This man is in fact such a stern and force-ful prosecutor that I am far more afraid of his influence than I am of his allegations. With such a prosecutor as this, members of the jury, my first prayer shall be that his rank, that his impending tribunate,* and that the impressiveness and dignity of his whole life may do no harm whatsoever to Lucius Murena; and next I shall pray that those sterling qualities of Marcus Cato's, acquired by him expressly for the purpose of helping many people, may not be used to hurt Murena alone. When Publius Africanus prosecuted Lucius Cotta,* he had been consul twice and had destroyed the two terrors which threat-ened our empire, Carthage and Numantia. He was, in addition, a man of the greatest eloquence, the greatest devotion to duty, and the greatest integrity; and the authority he possessed equalled that of the entire Roman empire—an empire upheld, indeed, by his own

exertions. And yet I have often heard people older than myself say that this overwhelming power and status that Africanus possessed proved in the event to be a factor very much in Lucius Cotta's favour. For what happened was that the wise men who were serving as jurors at the time were not prepared to see a man apparently convicted as a result of the excessive power of his opponent. [59] And what about Servius Galba?* Was it not the case, as history relates, that the Roman people rescued him from the clutches of your great-grandfather, the valiant and successful Marcus Cato, who was doing his best to destroy him? In our country, both the entire people and its wise and far-sighted jurors have always been opposed to prosecutors with too much power. For my part, I do not think a prosecutor should impose his dominance on a court, or any strong pressure that he may have, or his overwhelming authority, or his excessive influence. Such advantages should all be used for saving the innocent, for protecting the powerless, and for helping people in trouble: for imperilling and for ruining Roman citizens they should be cast aside. [60] If someone, then, were perhaps to say that Cato would not have elected to prosecute unless he had already come to a judgement about the case, my answer is this: it will be creating an unfair precedent, gentlemen, and an appalling situation for men on trial if a prosecutor's opinion is to count as some sort of presumption of guilt against the defendant.

Holding, as I do, Cato, a very high opinion of your moral standards, I could not possibly fault your judgement; but there are perhaps a few respects in which I could shape and improve it slightly. 'You do not make many mistakes,' the old teacher said to the great warrior, 'but some mistakes you do make. I can put you right.'* But I cannot put you right. In fact, I could say with complete truth that you make no mistakes whatsoever, nor is there anything at all in which you appear to need correction—only a little gentle modification. Nature herself has made you a great and elevated human being, fashioned for integrity, seriousness, self-control, greatness of character, fairness, and for every virtue. And yet she has added to all that a philosophy which is neither moderate nor mild but, it seems to me, rather more harsh and inflexible than either reality or human nature can tolerate.

[61] Now, since I am not making this speech before an ignorant rabble* or before some gathering of rustics, I shall be a little more

bold in discussing those cultural studies with which you and I are so familiar, and which we find so agreeable. You should be aware, members of the jury, that these superlative, godlike qualities which we see in Marcus Cato are his very own; but as for the qualities which we sometimes find lacking in him, their absence is due not to nature, but to his teacher. For there was once an extremely intelligent man, Zeno,* whose disciples are known as Stoics. Let me quote you some typical sayings and precepts of his. 'The wise man is never influenced by favour, and never forgives someone who has done wrong.' 'No one ever feels pity unless he is a fool or an idiot.' 'A true man is never prevailed upon or appeased.' 'Only wise men are handsome, however deformed they may be; rich, however destitute; kings, however much a slave.' As for those of us who are not wise men, they call us runaways, exiles, enemies, lunatics even. 'All misdeeds are equal: every transgression is an unspeakable crime. The man who strangles a farmyard cock without good reason commits no less a crime than the man who strangles his father.' 'The wise man never supposes anything, never regrets anything, is never mistaken, never changes his mind.'

[62] Marcus Cato, a man of the greatest intelligence, was induced by the most learned authorities to seize on this philosophy not, like most people, simply as a topic for discussion, but as a guide to life. The tax-farmers make some request.* 'Make sure you are not influenced by favour!' Some wretched and desperate people come to beg for help. 'You will be an unspeakable criminal if you are led by pity to do anything for them.' Someone admits he has done wrong and asks forgiveness for what he has done. 'It is an unspeakable crime to forgive.' But it was only a small transgression. 'All misdeeds are equal.' You made some remark. 'It is fixed and unalterable.' But your remark was not based on fact, but on supposition. 'The wise man never supposes anything.' All right, you went wrong somewhere: he thinks you spoke maliciously. It is from philosophy like that that we arrive at this sort of thing: 'I declared in the senate that I would prosecute a candidate for the consulship.' But you spoke in anger. 'The wise man', he says, 'is never angry.' All right, you said it because you had to at the time. 'It is dishonest', he says, 'to deceive by lying; to change one's mind is shameful; to be prevailed upon is criminal; to feel pity is disgraceful.'

[63] My own teachers, on the other hand—for I will admit, Cato,

that I too as a young man lacked confidence in my own abilities and sought the reassurance of philosophy—my own teachers, I tell you, were moderate and reasonable men, followers of Plato and Aristotle. Their view is that the wise man can sometimes be influenced by favour; that a good man does feel pity; that there are distinct classes of misdeed which merit different punishments; that a man of consistent principles does have room for forgiveness; that the wise man himself often supposes something which he does not know for certain, that he is angry once in a while, but yet can be prevailed upon and appeased, that he does occasionally alter what he has said if that is the better course, and that he does sometimes change his mind. All virtues, they believe, are tempered by what they call the 'mean'.*

[64] If some happy chance had brought you, Cato, with all your great qualities, to these teachers, you would not have turned out better or more courageous or more self-controlled or more just*—such a thing is impossible!—but you would have been a little more disposed to kindness. You would not have prosecuted a thoroughly decent man of the highest rank and integrity who is not a personal enemy of yours and has never harmed you in any way. You would instead have judged that, because fortune had appointed Lucius Murena and yourself as guardians of the same year,* you and he were consequently tied together by a kind of political bond. And as for those heated words which you spoke in the senate, either you would not have said them at all, or, if you had said them, you would afterwards have interpreted them in a more conciliatory way.

[65] You yourself have of late been stirred up by some mental impulse, carried away by the force of your character and ability, and set ablaze by your recent philosophical studies; but I venture to predict that in due course experience will influence you, time will soften you, age will mellow you. In fact those masters of yours and teachers of virtue seem to me to have deliberately extended the bounds of moral duty a little further than nature intended, their purpose being that in our minds we should strive for perfection, and so at least make it to the point we ought to reach. 'Never forgive!' No, forgive some things, but not everything. 'Never be influenced by favour!' No, stand fast against favour, when duty and good faith require. 'Do not be moved by pity!' Certainly not, if this means relaxing your rigour; but there is nevertheless some merit in

compassion. 'Hold fast to your opinion!' Of course, unless your opinion is trumped by a better one.

[66] The great Scipio* is a case in point. He was not ashamed to do what you are doing and keep a man of great learning, Panaetius,* in his household. However, Panaetius' conversation and teachings, although precisely the same as those in which you take such pleasure, did not make Scipio stricter but, as old men have told me, much milder. And out of those who shared that same philosophy, who was more affable than Gaius Laelius, who more charming? Who was more dignified than he was, who wiser? I could say exactly the same about Lucius Philus and about Gaius Galus;* but let me take you back now to your own house. Can you think of anyone more obliging, more sociable, and more temperate, in every sphere of human society, than your great-grandfather Cato?* When you were speaking impressively and truly about his outstanding virtue you said that you had a model at home for you to imitate. You do indeed have that model set before you at home, although it has been easier for his character to pass to you, who are descended from him, than it has been for it to come to any of us. All the same, it is there as a model for me to imitate just as much as for you. If, however, you were to sprinkle some of Cato's ease and affability onto your own sternness and severity, those qualities of yours would not become better— since they are perfect already—but they would at least be more agreeably seasoned.

[67] So, to return to the point at which I began: strike Cato's name out of the case, set his power to one side, ignore his influence— influence which in a trial should either be used for an acquittal or not at all—and come to grips with me on the actual charges. What is your accusation, Cato, what charge are you bringing to the court, what do you allege? Electoral malpractice? That is not something I defend. You criticize me for defending the crime which I penalized by law.* But it was malpractice that I penalized, not innocence: malpractice I will gladly join you in prosecuting, if that is what you want. You pointed out that the senate, on my proposal, passed a decree* that it should be deemed a violation of the Calpurnian law if men were paid to meet the candidates, if they were hired to escort them, if seats at gladiatorial games were given out wholesale by tribes, or if lunches were likewise given out wholesale. So the senate ruled that these practices, if engaged in, should be deemed violations

of the law. This decree, while it humoured the candidates, was quite unnecessary. For the crucial question is whether these practices did in fact take place: if they did, then no one doubts that they were illegal. [68] It is absurd to leave as uncertain something that is doubtful but make a ruling on something that no one is in any doubt about. Moreover, this decree of the senate was passed at the request of all the candidates, so one cannot tell from it whom it benefited and whom it hurt. Prove, therefore, that these practices were engaged in by Lucius Murena: if you can, I shall gladly concede that they were illegal.

'Large numbers of people went out to meet him on his return from his province.'* This is quite normal when the man is someone who is standing for the consulship—and in any case people surely go out to meet anyone who is coming back home? 'What did that huge crowd consist of?' First of all, even if I were unable to give you a complete account of it, what is so surprising about large numbers of people having gone out to meet such a great man on his arrival, and particularly a candidate for the consulship? It would have been far more surprising if they had not gone out to meet him. [69] And if I were to tell you that many of them had been asked to go—something which is in no way out of the ordinary—surely that would hardly be a crime, or even surprising? In our country, where it is common practice for us, when asked, to escort the sons of the humblest citizens almost at the crack of dawn from the furthest parts of the city to the forum,* would people really be unwilling to go to the Campus Martius at eight o'clock, especially when asked in the name of such a great man? And if all the trading companies went too—those to which many of the jurors* sitting here belong? And if there were many members of our own most honourable order? And if that entire race of office-seekers, so eager to please and so determined that nobody should enter the city without due honour, if finally our own prosecutor Postumius himself went to meet him with a hefty following of his own, then what is so surprising about the huge crowd that resulted? I need not mention Murena's clients, his neighbours, his fellow-tribesmen, and Lucullus' entire army, which had come to Rome at that time for a triumph.* I will say just this: crowds have never been unwilling to provide this service without payment, and not just for men of high standing, but for anyone at all who might want it.

[70] 'But he was escorted by large numbers of people.' Prove that they were paid, and I will admit the charge. That apart, what do you find to criticize? 'What does he need an escort for?' he says. Are you asking me why he needs something that all of us have always made use of? Poor people have only one means available to them of earning favours from our order or of paying us back, and that is by helping us and escorting us around when we are standing for office. It is neither realistic nor fair to expect members of the equestrian order or our own to spend whole days attending those of their friends who are candidates. If our house happens to be crowded with such people, or if we are sometimes accompanied down to the forum by them, or if they deign to walk the length of a public hall with us, we think that they are paying us great attention and respect. It is by contrast our humbler friends with time on their hands who provide the sort of constant attendance that is generally given to men of substance who are in a position to confer a favour. [71] So do not take away from the lower class of men this fruit of their devotion, Cato. Allow those who look to us for everything to have something which they can give us in return. If poor people have nothing except their votes, then their support counts for nothing, regardless of whether or not they do vote.* As they are always saying themselves, they cannot give speeches for us, act as our guarantors, or invite us to their homes. All these are things they ask for from us, and they think that what we give them cannot be repaid in any other way except by their service. This is why they opposed the Fabian law, which concerns the number of people in an escort, as well as the decree of the senate passed in the consulship of Lucius Caesar.* There is in fact no penalty which could prevent the poorer people from respecting this time-honoured way of fulfilling their obligations.

[72] 'But seating was given out by tribes and invitations to lunch distributed wholesale.' Murena abstained entirely from such practices, members of the jury, and his friends engaged in them only in moderation, and as far as custom allows. Nevertheless, this reminds me how many votes, Servius, these complaints in the senate lost us.* For when was there ever a time, in living memory or in the memory of our fathers, when people did not want, whether from self-interested motives or out of simple generosity, to give their friends and fellow-tribesmen seats in the circus or the forum?* These are the rewards and benefits that poorer people receive from their fellow-

tribesmen by time-honoured custom. [73] [*A few words are missing.*]
... gave seats to his fellow-tribesmen on one occasion when he was
an aide-de-camp, what will they make of our leading men who have
provided whole blocks of seats in the circus for theirs?

All these charges to do with escorts, seating, and lunches were
attributed by the public to an excessive keenness on your part,
Servius, and Murena is defended against them by a senatorial
decree.* 'How so?' The senate surely does not regard it as a crime if
people go out to meet a candidate, does it? 'No, but it does if they are
paid to do so.' So, prove that they were. And if a crowd escorts a
candidate? 'No, but it does if it has been hired.' So, show that it was.
And if seats are provided at shows or invitations to lunch given out?
'Not at all, but it does if they have been given out wholesale, all
over the place.' And what do you mean by 'wholesale'? 'To all and
sundry.' So if Lucius Natta,* a young man of the highest social
standing—and we can see where his loyalties lie already, and what a
great man he is destined to become—wanted to show generosity to
the equestrian centuries* both because of his tie of kinship with
Murena and with an eye to his future prospects, that cannot reflect
adversely on his stepfather, or form the basis of any charge against
him. Likewise, if a Vestal virgin, a relation of Murena's and his close
friend, gave him her seat at the gladiatorial games,* then she acted out
of a sense of duty, and he is free from blame. All such favours are the
duties required of friends, the benefits that are owed to the poor, and
the obligations expected of candidates.

[74] But Cato disputes with me coldly, like a Stoic. He says that it
is wrong to purchase goodwill with food; he says that in choosing
magistrates men's judgement should not be perverted by pleasure.
So if a man invites someone to dinner because he is standing for
election, is he to be condemned? 'Of course,' he says. 'Are you telling
me that you would seek the supreme power, the supreme authority,
and the government of the country by pandering to men's senses,
making their characters go soft, and tempting them with pleasures?
Was it', he continues, 'a job as a pimp that you were seeking from a
bevy of pampered young boys, or power over the whole world from
the Roman people?' That is a revolting way of talking: it is alien to
our custom, way of life, habits, and our very nation. For neither the
Spartans, the originators of your way of life and speech,* who recline
on bare wood for their daily meals, nor the Cretans, who do not even

recline at all when they eat, have done any better in preserving their states than the Romans, who set aside time for pleasure as well as for work. Indeed, the latter were destroyed by our army in a single attack, while the former* hold onto their discipline and laws only thanks to the protection afforded by our empire. [75] So do not speak with such excessive harshness, Cato, against the customs of our ancestors. These customs are vindicated both by the facts of the matter and by the great length of time that our empire has endured.

There was in our fathers' time a learned man from the same philosophical school as yourself, an honourable and noble man, Quintus Tubero.* When Publius Africanus died, his nephew Quintus Maximus provided a banquet for the Roman people in his honour; and since Tubero was the son of Africanus' sister, Maximus asked him if he would provide covers for the couches. But Tubero, being an extremely learned man and a Stoic, covered the Carthaginian couches* with goatskins and put out Samian crockery,* as if it was the death of Diogenes the Cynic* that was being commemorated, not that of the godlike Africanus—a man, indeed, whom Maximus praised at his funeral by thanking the immortal gods that he had been born into this country rather than any other, since it was inevitable that wherever Africanus was, there the seat of empire would be. Such a man was Africanus; and in the commemoration of his death the Roman people objected to Tubero's ill-judged philosophy. [76] And so it was that a very fine and honourable citizen, despite being the grandson of Lucius Paullus and, as I said, the son of Publius Africanus' sister, was defeated in the election for the praetorship thanks to those goatskins. For although the Roman people cannot abide private extravagance, they love public display. They do not care for lavish banquets, but they like shabbiness and penny-pinching even less. And they distinguish as to the appropriateness of duties and occasions, observing an alternation of work and pleasure.

You say that in choosing magistrates people should not be influenced by anything except a candidate's merit. You, however, although a man of the highest merit yourself, do not observe this rule in your own case. Why otherwise do you ask people to help you and give you their support? You ask me to entrust myself to you, so that you will be put in charge of me.* But do you really think the request ought to be coming from you? Should it not be the other way round—me asking you to undergo toil and danger for my protection? [77] And what about your use of a prompter?* This involves cheating and deceiving people. For if we accept that it is honourable to address your fellow citizens by name, then it follows that it must be shameful if your slave knows them better than you do. But if you do already know them, do you really have to address them with the help of a prompter, while you are standing for election, as though you did not know them?* And what about your greeting them as if you knew them personally when you have in fact been prompted? And again, your greeting them in a much more offhand way once you have been safely elected? These practices, if judged by the normal rules of political life, are all right and proper; it is only if carefully weighed against the precepts of philosophy that they would be found to be corrupt.

The Roman plebs, therefore, should not be deprived of the benefits of games, gladiatorial shows, and banquets, all of which were instituted by our ancestors; nor should the liberality of candidates—the sort that represents bounty, not bribery—be disallowed.

[78] But it was the national interest that led you to undertake the prosecution. I accept, Cato, that that was your feeling and supposition when you came here, but you have slipped up through a lack of wisdom.* What I am doing, members of the jury, I am doing partly because of Lucius Murena's position and my friendship with him, but I also declare and proclaim that I am doing it for the sake of peace, tranquillity, concord, freedom, security, and the lives of all of us. Listen, listen to a consul, gentlemen—I shall not be presumptuous, I shall only say a consul who spends all his days and nights thinking about the national interest!

Lucius Catilina did not so scorn and despise our country as to think he could destroy the state merely with the forces he took out with him. The infection of his criminality is spreading more widely than anyone realizes, and affects more people. The Trojan horse is within our walls, within our walls I tell you—but it will never overwhelm us as we sleep so long as I am consul. [79] You ask me whether I have any fear of Catiline. I have none, and I have taken steps to ensure that no one else need fear him either. But his forces I see here, these, I tell you, are very much to be feared; and it is not so much the army of Lucius Catilina of which we should now be afraid as those men who are said to have deserted that army. For they have not in fact deserted it at all. Posted by him on the look-out and in ambush, they remain behind, poised above our heads and necks. These people want to use your votes to dislodge an honest consul, a fine general, and someone by nature and personal circumstances bound up with the security of this country, and to topple him from his guardianship of the city and his protection of the state. Their weapons and treachery I have rebuffed in the Campus Martius,* undermined in the forum,* and frequently thwarted even in my own home,* gentlemen; and if you hand over one of the consuls to these men, they will have achieved far more through your votes than by their own swords.

It is very important, members of the jury, that there be two consuls in place on the first of January, and I have worked hard in the face of considerable opposition to bring this about. [80] You should not imagine that it is by ordinary plans or routine methods or [*a few words are missing*]. It is not a mischievous law that these men are aiming at, or a pernicious distribution,* or some damage to the state that has at some point been rumoured. No; in this very country, gentlemen, plans are under way for the destruction of the city, the massacre of the citizens, and the obliteration of the name of Rome. And it is citizens, citizens I tell you—if it is right to call them by that name—that have plotted and are still plotting these actions against their country. Every day I counter their plans, undermine their treachery, and resist their crimes. But I warn you, gentlemen: my consulship is now coming to an end. Do not take away from me the man whose diligence should succeed mine! Do not remove the man to whom I am eager to hand over the country unharmed, for him to defend against these terrible dangers!

[81] And do you not see, members of the jury, what further evil is being added to this? It is you, Cato, you to whom I am speaking: surely you can see the stormy year of office that you have ahead of you? Already at yesterday's public meeting there was thundering the pernicious voice of a tribune designate,* your colleague in office—the man against whom your own prescient mind took many precautions, as did all those loyal citizens who urged you to stand for the tribunate yourself. All the stirrings of the past three years—since the time when, as you know, Lucius Catilina and Gnaeus Piso* formed a plot to murder the senate—are bursting out during these days, during these months, and at this very moment. [82] What place is there, gentlemen, what time, what day, what night, when I am not snatched

away and flee away from the traps and swords of those men,* saved
not just by my own personal precautions, but far more by those of
the gods? It is not on my own account that they want me killed: what
they want is for a vigilant consul to be removed from the defence of
the country. They would want just as much to get rid of you too,
Cato, if they could find some means of doing so; and, believe me,
that is what they are aiming at and striving to achieve. They see how
much courage you have, how much brilliance, how much authority,
and how much power to defend our country. But when they see a
tribune's power deprived of a consul's influence and support, they
conclude that, once you are disarmed and weakened, they will have
less difficulty in destroying you. They are not afraid of the vacant
consulship* being filled: they see that your colleagues in office will be
able to prevent this happening. What they hope is that the illustrious
Decimus Silanus can be thrown to them without a colleague, yourself without a consul, and the country without any means of defence.

[83] In such a critical and dangerous situation as this, it is your
duty, Marcus Cato—as someone, it seems to me, born to serve your
country rather than yourself—to recognize what is going on and to
preserve in public life a man who will be your helper, protector, and
ally. He will not be a self-seeking consul, but a consul such as the
country is crying out for at the present time—fitted by his personal
circumstances to uphold peace, by his expertise to wage war, and by
his character and experience to undertake whatever duties you could
ask of him.

And yet complete power over this situation rests with you, members of the jury. In this trial you hold the whole country in your
hands: it is yours to direct. If Lucius Catilina with the council of
criminals that he has taken with him from Rome were able to judge
the case, he would condemn Lucius Murena; if he were able to kill
him, he would do so. For his plans require that the country be
robbed of its defences, that the number of generals available to counter his madness be reduced, and that greater power to stir up sedi-
tion and discord be granted to the tribunes of the plebs, by the
removal of their opponent. So shall the most honourable and learned
gentlemen, chosen from the most distinguished orders,* reach the
same verdict that that relentless gladiator and public enemy would
reach?

[84] Believe me, gentlemen, in this trial you will be voting not just

about Lucius Murena's survival, but about your own as well. We have reached the moment of reckoning. There is no longer any place from which we can restore our strength or in which, having fallen, we can make a final stand. It is not enough to ensure that our present forces are not reduced: we must also acquire fresh ones,* if we can. For the enemy is not on the Anio,* which in the Punic War seemed terrible enough, but in the city, in the forum—immortal gods! I can scarcely say it without shuddering—there are even some enemies in our country's very sanctuary, some enemies, I tell you, in the senate-house itself. May the gods grant that my most valiant colleague,* as general, may destroy Catiline's unspeakable band of brigands! Meanwhile, I, as a civilian, with your help and that of all loyal citizens, will by my careful planning scatter and crush this danger which the country has conceived and to which it is now on the point of giving birth.

[85] But, I must ask you, what will happen if this crisis slips out of our control and is carried over into next year? There will be only one consul, and he will be preoccupied not with managing the war but with arranging for the vacant consulship to be filled. Already those who will hinder him . . . [*There are gaps in the text here and below.*] . . . that relentless, pestilential monster that is Catiline will burst forth, where . . . threatens, will suddenly swoop down on the country areas outside the city. Frenzy will be found on the rostra, terror in the senate-house, conspiracy in the forum, an army in the Campus Martius, and devastation in the countryside. In every home and every place we shall fear fire and the sword. All these threats, however, so long in preparation, will easily be crushed by the responsible action of the magistrates and the watchfulness of private citizens, provided that the country is furnished with its proper defences.

[86] That, gentlemen, is how the matter stands. First of all, then, for the sake of the country—which ought to be the most important consideration for each one of us—by virtue of my diligent and widely recognized watchfulness over the state I warn you, by virtue of my position as consul I urge you, and by virtue of the extreme danger that we face I implore you, defend the tranquillity, peace, security, and lives of yourselves and the rest of the citizens! Secondly, led by the duty not just of an advocate, but of a friend too, I beg and beseech you, gentlemen, to spare a thought for Lucius Murena, that unhappy man, exhausted as he is by physical illness* and mental

torment. Do not overwhelm with fresh grief the congratulations* he
has recently received! Only a short time ago, honoured by the greatest gift that the Roman people can bestow, he seemed blessed by
fortune, being the first man to bring the consulship to an old family,
and the first to bring it to an extremely ancient town.* Now, however,
dressed in filth and rags,* exhausted by illness, and devastated by
tears and grief, he is your suppliant, gentlemen, he calls on your
good faith, he appeals to your compassion, and he looks to your
power and your protection. [87] By the immortal gods, gentlemen,
do not deprive him of the very thing which he judged would enhance
his personal honour, and do not take away all the other distinctions
that he has won in the past, together with all his rank and fortune!
Lucius Murena begs and beseeches you, gentlemen, if he has never
wronged anyone unjustly, if he has never offended anyone's ears or
acted against their wishes, if he has never been an object of hatred (to
say the least) either at home or on campaign, then, gentlemen, may
there be a place in your hearts for modesty, may there be a refuge for
the downcast, and may there be a protection for blameless conduct.
Having the consulship wrested from one's grasp ought to excite
considerable pity, gentlemen, for when the consulship is lost, everything else is lost too. At the present time, however, the office of
consul can attract no envy, for it is exposed to the harangues of
trouble-makers, the traps set by conspirators, and the weapons of
Catiline: in short, it alone stands against every danger and against
every assault.

[88] I therefore fail to see, gentlemen, what there is in this glorious
office of consul to cause anyone to envy Murena or indeed any of us;
but as for this piteous spectacle, it is actually taking place before my
eyes, and you yourselves are also able to see it and gaze upon it. If
you strike him down with your votes—may Jupiter avert the
omen!—where will the poor man turn? To his home? To see the
mask* of his illustrious father, which a few days ago he beheld
wreathed with laurel in his honour, now grieving and disfigured with
shame? Or to his mother, who only a short time ago, poor woman,
was kissing a consul when she kissed her son, but is now tormented
by the worry that she is shortly to behold her son stripped of all his
honour? [89] But why do I mention his mother and his home when
the penalty of the new law* deprives him of his home, his parent, and
the company and sight of all his friends? Shall the poor man go into

exile, then? Where? To the east, where for many years he served as a legate, led armies, and performed heroic deeds? But it is deeply painful to return in disgrace to a place from which you departed in high honour. Or shall he hide himself away at the other end of the world, and let Transalpine Gaul, which a short time ago was delighted to have him as its governor, see him once again, grieving, mourning, an exile? And if he goes to that province, how will he feel when he meets his brother, Gaius Murena?* Imagine the pain of the one, the sorrow of the other, and the grief of both of them, imagine the change in their fortunes and in their conversation! Only a few days earlier, messengers and letters had spread the news there that Murena had been elected consul, and his friends and hosts were rushing off to Rome to offer their congratulations—then suddenly he appears on the scene in person, announcing his own downfall!

[90] If such an outcome would be cruel, if it would be pitiable, if it would be heartbreaking, if it would be totally out of keeping with your clemency and compassion, gentlemen, then preserve the gift which the Roman people have bestowed, give the country back its consul, and grant this for the sake of Murena's decency, grant it for his late father, grant it for his family and stock, and grant it also for the highly respectable town of Lanuvium, whose sorrowful representatives you have seen in large numbers here throughout this trial. Do not tear from the ancestral rites of Juno Sospita,* to whom all consuls are required to sacrifice, a consul who is her own fellow-townsman and hers above all others! If my commendation carries any weight at all or my backing any influence, gentlemen, I, a consul, commend Murena, a consul, to you; and I can promise and guarantee that he will be eager for public harmony, active in his support of loyal citizens, relentless against civil discord, courageous in war, and an implacable enemy of this conspiracy which is now rocking the country.

PRO ARCHIA
('FOR ARCHIAS')

DATE: 62 BC
DEFENDANT: Aulus Licinius Archias
LAW: *lex Papia de peregrinis* (Papian law concerning aliens)
CHARGE: illegal exercise of citizen rights
PROSECUTOR: Grattius
DEFENCE ADVOCATE: Marcus Tullius Cicero
PRESIDING MAGISTRATE: Quintus Tullius Cicero
VERDICT: acquittal

Pro Archia is probably the least typical of Cicero's speeches, and is one of his most admired. It is a defence, not of a Roman aristocrat, but of a Syrian poet whose claim to Roman citizenship was disputed. The prosecution seem not to have had much of a case, and Cicero is therefore able to establish the technical grounds of Archias' claim within a few paragraphs (§§ 4–11). The rest of the speech is then devoted to an encomium of literature and this, coupled with the fact that *Pro Archia* is itself a literary product of the highest order, has ensured the speech's continuing popularity.

Archias was born at Antioch in Syria, probably in the mid-120s BC. At an early age he became famous throughout the east as a professional poet (writing in Greek), travelling from city to city; some of his poems were selected at around this time by Meleager for inclusion in his anthology, the *Garland* (although, since there were several poets named Archias, we cannot now be certain which poems are his). In the course of his travels Archias came to southern Italy (he was probably doing a round of festivals), and was granted honorary citizenship by some of the cities he visited. He finally arrived at Rome in 102, and was accepted into the household of the Luculli. The head of the family, Lucius Licinius Lucullus, went into exile, probably in 102, after being convicted of misconduct during his command in Sicily the previous year, but he had two teenage sons at home, Lucius and Marcus, and Archias no doubt assisted with their education. His connections were not, however, limited to the Luculli. He was sought out by many of the leading men in Rome, among them the Metelli, Marcus Aemilius Scaurus, the Catuli, and Lucius Crassus, and Cicero tells us that even the great Marius, who otherwise had little time for literature, was pleased with Archias' poem on the war against the Cimbri. During this period the young Cicero was also lucky enough to receive instruction from Archias; gratitude towards his old Greek teacher is the reason he gives for defending him in this speech.

Some time later, Archias accompanied Marcus Lucullus on a visit to Sicily, and on their return journey Lucullus arranged for him to be granted honorary citizenship at Heraclea, a Greek city in Lucania. He continued, however, to live in Rome. In 91 the Social War broke out: Rome's allies (*socii*) were demanding Roman citizenship, which was quickly conceded. The first law by which this was done was the *lex Iulia* in 90. This was followed in 89 by a further measure, the *lex Plautia Papiria*, which among other provisions extended the citizenship to honorary citizens of federate states not resident in those states but nevertheless resident in Italy, provided that they reported to one of the praetors at Rome within sixty days. As an honorary citizen of Heraclea, which had been allied to Rome since 278, and being long resident in Rome, Archias duly reported to the praetor Metellus Pius within the specified period. Thus he became a Roman citizen, calling himself, in the Roman fashion, Aulus Licinius Archias (the family name Licinius was adopted out of respect for his patrons the Luculli).

He continued to live with the Luculli, accompanying Lucius Lucullus to the east in the 80s and again during the Third Mithridatic War (73–63 BC), in the period when Lucullus was in command of the Roman forces (73–67). Lucullus' command proved to be highly successful in the early stages of the war, but after pursuing Mithridates into Armenia in 69 he began to lose the support of his troops; when his subordinate Gaius Valerius Triarius was heavily defeated in 67, he was relieved of his command, and Pompey was appointed the following year to bring the war to a successful conclusion. These events gave rise to great hostility between Lucullus and Pompey, and the poem which Archias composed in praise of Lucullus' conduct of the war would have served to remind public opinion at Rome of the crucial part played by Lucullus in the defeat of Mithridates.

In 62 Archias became the object of a criminal prosecution. In 65 the tribune Gaius Papius had carried a law expelling from Rome all non-citizens who did not have a fixed residence in Italy: residents of Rome, therefore, who could not prove themselves Roman citizens, were liable to be prosecuted under the law and expelled from the city. The reason why Archias should have been prosecuted under this law is uncertain. The prosecutor, Grattius, is not otherwise known, but in view of the hostility between Lucullus and Pompey he is usually assumed to have been one of Pompey's supporters, and the prosecution is therefore interpreted as an attack by a supporter of Pompey on the protégé of Pompey's enemy Lucullus. This seems plausible: it is difficult to see why anyone should

otherwise have wished to call into question Archias' citizenship, which
had gone unchallenged for twenty-seven years. But Archias was only a
poet, and it would be too much to suppose that the trial had any great
political significance. It is perhaps most likely that Grattius was acting on
his own initiative to avenge an imagined slight to his patron (who was still
away in Asia)—the slight being simply that Archias had given Lucullus
extravagant praise in his poem on the Mithridatic War.

It used to be assumed that Cicero's defence was an act of hostility
towards Pompey, but Cicero's policy during this period was, on the
contrary, to keep in both with the conservatives in the senate, such as
Lucullus, and with Pompey. In this same year he also defended Publius
Sulla, probably Pompey's brother-in-law, and in April he was seeking to
form closer ties with Pompey (*Fam.* 5.7); the one reference to him in *Pro
Archia* (§ 24) is complimentary. Cicero knew well how to serve one side
without offending the other: he had done it before in *Pro lege Manilia* (66),
in which praise for Pompey is combined with a generous appreciation of
Lucullus' achievements. In *Pro Archia*, he successfully avoids political
controversy by concentrating on the status of literature, and insisting on
that as the deciding factor in the case. Thus he is able to oblige the
Luculli, and do a good turn to his old teacher—from whom he expected
a laudatory poem in return (§§ 28, 31)—without risk of damaging his
relations with Pompey.

Archias was acquitted, as he surely deserved to be: of Cicero's clients,
Archias is one of those of whom we can say with most certainty that he
was innocent of the crime of which he was charged. We hear of him again
in 61, presumably still living in Rome, and contemplating writing a poem
for the Metelli (*Att.* 1.16.15). He appears, however, never to have finished
the poem on Cicero's consulship to which his former pupil looked forward
so eagerly. In the end, therefore, Cicero had to make do with only a Latin
poem—written by himself (*De consulatu suo*, 60 BC).

PRO ARCHIA

[1] If I have any natural talent, members of the jury—and I am aware how limited it is; or if I have any experience in public speaking—in which I do not deny that I am moderately well practised; or if there is any technical skill in my oratory which has been derived from application and training in the liberal arts—and I admit that I have never at any period of my life been averse to such training: if I do have any of these capabilities, then Aulus Licinius* here is entitled almost as of right to be among the very first to claim from me the benefits which they may bring. For when I look back in my mind over the time I have lived and recollect the remotest memories of my childhood, I am aware that from the earliest point that I can recall it was he who was my guide as I undertook and entered upon the course of my studies. So if this voice of mine, trained by his encouragement and teaching, has sometimes brought safety to other people, I must indeed do all I can to bring help and safety to the very man from whom I received the gift which has enabled me to help others and to save some.

[2] But in case anyone is surprised to hear me say this, given that my client's talents lie not in the theory and practice of oratory but in another direction, I should point out that I have never devoted myself exclusively to this one art. For all branches of culture are linked by a sort of common bond and have a certain kinship with one another. [3] Some of you may also be surprised that, in a statutory court and at a public trial, when a case is being heard before a praetor of the Roman people, a most excellent man,* and before the most principled jurors, and with such a large crowd of listeners, I should be using a manner of speaking which is out of keeping not only with the tradition of the courts but also with the customary style of forensic pleading. If this is so, then I beg of you that you will grant me an indulgence in this trial which is appropriate to this defendant here, and, I trust, not disagreeable to you—that you will allow me, speaking as I am on behalf of an eminent poet and a most learned man and before this crowd of highly educated people, this civilized jury, and such a praetor as is now presiding, to speak rather more freely on cultural and literary matters, and, as befits the character of a man

who because of his life of seclusion and study has had very little to do with the hazards of the courts, to employ a somewhat novel and unconventional manner of speaking. [4] If I feel that you have allowed and granted me this indulgence, I shall certainly convince you that Aulus Licinius here should not only not be removed from the list of Roman citizens, since he is indeed a citizen, but, were he not one, ought to have been added to it.

As soon as Archias had grown out of childhood and those studies which mould the years of boyhood with an outline of culture, he devoted himself to literary composition. At Antioch,* first of all, then a bustling and wealthy city and overflowing with liberal culture and men of the greatest learning (and where he was born, to high-ranking parents), he quickly began to outshine everybody else by his exceptional talents. Later in the other parts of Asia and all over Greece his arrival used to cause such a stir that the fame of his talents was exceeded by the eagerness with which he was awaited, and that in turn was exceeded by the admiration which he excited when he finally arrived. [5] Italy* was at that time full of Greek teaching and culture, and in Latium these studies were pursued more enthusiastically than they are in the same towns today; while here at Rome they were not neglected either, thanks to the untroubled political situation. The people of Tarentum, Rhegium, and Neapolis accordingly bestowed upon Archias citizenship and other honours, and all those who were able to recognize outstanding talent thought him worthy of their hospitality and acquaintance.

It was now, when his enormous fame had spread to places where he had never been seen in person, that he arrived in Rome; this was when Marius was consul with Catulus.* In these two consuls he found men of whom one could supply him with the greatest achievements to write about, while the other could give him not only achievements but also an appreciative ear. The Luculli* straight away received Archias into their house, although even at this time he was still of the age when the toga of boyhood is worn.* Indeed, it is a tribute not just to his literary talent but to his excellence of character that the house which first received him as a very young man is also the house which is most familiar to him in his old age. [6] Back in those days Archias was regarded with affection by the famous Quintus Metellus Numidicus and his son Pius;* his recitations were attended by Marcus Aemilius;* he was constantly in the company of

Quintus Catulus and his son;* his friendship was cultivated by Lucius
Crassus;* and as for the Luculli, Drusus, the Octavii, Cato, and the
entire family of the Hortensii,* he was on the closest terms with all of
them and was treated by them with the greatest respect. In fact, he
was courted not only by those who were eager to learn and listen, but
also by such as pretended to be.

Some time later, after he had set out for Sicily with Marcus
Lucullus* and was on his way back from that province with the same
Lucullus, Archias arrived at Heraclea.* Since this was a town which
enjoyed the fullest treaty rights with Rome, he wished to be enrolled
among its citizens; and, being in any case considered worthy of the
honour on his own merits, he obtained it from the Heracleans
thanks also to the authority and influence of Lucullus. [7] Roman
citizenship was then bestowed upon him by the law of Silvanus and
Carbo, which reads: 'IF ANY PERSONS HAVE BEEN ENROLLED AS
CITIZENS OF THE FEDERATE STATES, IF THEY HAVE HAD A
FIXED RESIDENCE IN ITALY AT THE TIME WHEN THE LAW WAS
PASSED, AND IF THEY HAVE DECLARED THEMSELVES BEFORE A
PRAETOR WITHIN SIXTY DAYS . . . '* Since by this time Archias
had had a fixed residence in Rome for many years, he declared
himself before the praetor Quintus Metellus,* who was a close
friend of his.

[8] If I am to speak about nothing except Archias' citizenship and
the law, I have nothing more to say, and I rest my defence. So which
of these facts, Grattius, do you think you can disprove? Do you deny
that Archias was enrolled at Heraclea at the time stated? We have
present here in court a man of the highest standing and the greatest
possible conscientiousness and honour, Marcus Lucullus, who
declares not that he thinks it, but that he knows it; not that he heard
it, but that he saw it; not that he was present when it was done, but
that he actually did it himself. We also have here representatives
from Heraclea, men of the highest rank, who have made the journey
to Rome specially to attend this trial and have come with written
instructions and official evidence: they confirm that Archias was
enrolled at Heraclea. Do you ask me at this point for the public
records of the Heracleans, which everybody knows were destroyed
when the public record office was burnt down in the Italian War?* It is
absurd to say nothing of the proof which we have, but demand the
proof which is not to be had; to keep quiet about what men can

remember, but insist on documentary evidence; and, when you have
the conscientious evidence of a highly distinguished man and the
oath and good faith of a most honourable town, to reject what cannot
possibly be tampered with, but ask for records which you yourself
say are often falsified. [9] Or did he not have a fixed residence at
Rome—he who for so many years before obtaining the citizenship
had made Rome the seat of all his possessions and his fortune? Or
perhaps he failed to declare himself? On the contrary, he did do so,
and his declaration was registered in records which, of all the records
resulting from the declarations made before the board of praetors,*
were the only ones to possess the full authority of public documents.
For it is said that the citizen-lists of Appius* were carelessly maintained, and that no trust could be placed in any such records because
of the unreliability of Gabinius* before he was prosecuted, and
because of his downfall once he had been condemned. Yet Metellus,
on the other hand, the most conscientious and orderly of men, was
so painstaking that he actually went to the praetor Lucius Lentulus*
and the panel of judges to say that he was worried at the erasure of a
single name. These, then, are the lists of Metellus, and in them you
will find no erasure over the name of Aulus Licinius.

[10] That is how the matter stands. What reason do you have,
then, for doubting his citizenship—especially given that he had been
enrolled in the citizen-lists of other towns too? When Greek communities were giving out their citizenship for nothing to numerous
undistinguished individuals, people with low-grade skills or with
none at all, I suppose that the people of Rhegium or Locri* or Neapolis or Tarentum, who were used to giving their citizenship to stage
performers, were unwilling to bestow it upon a man whose talent had
earned him the greatest glory! And a second point: when the other
people had somehow smuggled their names into their towns' citizen-
lists not only after the general granting of Roman citizenship* but
even after the enactment of the Papian law,* and when he by contrast
did not even make use of those other lists in which he is enrolled,
because he always wanted to be counted as a Heraclean—under
circumstances such as these, is Archias really to be driven out?

[11] You miss his name on the Roman census lists.* It is, I take it, a
closely guarded secret that at the time of the last census Archias was
on campaign with the illustrious general Lucius Lucullus; that during the previous one he was away in Asia with the same man who was

then quaestor; and that at the first census after his enfranchisement, the one held by Julius and Crassus, no section of the population was in fact registered at all. In any case, since the census does not constitute proof of citizenship, but only shows that someone who is registered was claiming to be a citizen at the time, I should add this: in the period in which you allege that Archias even in his own eyes did not have the rights of a Roman citizen, he nevertheless frequently made a will according to our laws, entered upon inheritances bequeathed to him by Roman citizens, and was nominated for a reward from the treasury by Lucius Lucullus as proconsul. Go and find some stronger arguments, then, if you can—because you are never going to be able to refute Archias' claim by citing his own opinions or those of his friends.

[12] You will no doubt ask me, Grattius, why I am so delighted with this man. The answer is that it is he who enables my mind to recover from the din of the courts and gives my tired ears a rest from the shouting and abuse. How do you imagine I could find material for my daily speeches on so many different subjects if I did not train my mind with literary study, and how could my mind cope with so much strain if I did not use such study to help it unwind? Yes, I for one am not ashamed to admit that I am devoted to the study of literature. Let others be ashamed if they have buried their heads in books and have not been able to find anything in them which could either be applied to the common good or brought out into the open and the light of day. But why should I be ashamed, gentlemen, given that in all the years I have lived my private pastimes have never distracted me, my own pleasures have never prevented me, and not even the need for sleep has ever called me away from helping anyone in his hour of danger or of need? [13] Who, then, can justly censure or reproach me if I allow myself the same amount of time for pursuing these studies as others set aside for dealing with their own personal affairs, celebrating festivals and games, indulging in other pleasures, and resting their minds and bodies, or as much as they devote to extended partying and to playing dice and ball? And I have all the more right to engage in such studies because it is from them that I am able to improve such oratorical ability as I have, an ability which has always been at the disposal of my friends when faced with prosecution. But even if my oratorical powers seem not to amount to much, I do at least recognize the source from which all that is highest

in them has been drawn. [14] For had I not in my youth been led by the teachings of many, and by all that I read, to the belief that there is nothing in life to be sought after more earnestly than excellence and honour, and that in the pursuit of these every physical torture and every risk of death or banishment should be held of little account, I would certainly never have exposed myself to so many great struggles and to the daily attacks from desperate men* which I have been facing, for the sake of your security. But all books, all the words of the wise and all history are full of examples which teach this lesson—examples which would all be lying in obscurity, had not the light of the written word been brought to them. How many finely executed portraits of the most valiant men have the Greek and Latin writers left us, and not only for our contemplation but for our emulation! Indeed, I myself, when serving as a magistrate, have always kept these men before my eyes, and have modelled myself on them, heart and mind, by meditating on their excellences.

[15] Someone will no doubt ask: 'Were those great men, then, whose virtues have been recorded in books—were they themselves experts in that learning which you praise so highly?' It would be difficult to state categorically that all of them were. Nevertheless, I am sure what my answer should be. I do admit that there have been many men of outstanding temperament and ability who were not well-read, but who achieved a natural self-possession and dignity of character because of their innate, almost godlike endowments. Moreover, I would even go so far as to say that character without learning has made for excellence and ability more often than learning without character. And yet I also firmly maintain this, that when a natural disposition which is noble and elevated is given in addition a systematic training in cultural knowledge, then something remarkable and unique comes about. [16] There were examples of this in our fathers' time, the younger Africanus,* a godlike man, and Gaius Laelius and Lucius Furius, men of the greatest moderation and self-control, also the elder Marcus Cato,* a most valiant man and the most learned of his day. These great men would surely never have taken up the study of literature had it not been of help to them in attaining and practising excellence. But suppose one could not point to this great benefit, suppose that the study of literature conferred only enjoyment: even then, I believe, you would agree that this form of mental relaxation broadens and enlightens the mind like no other.

For other forms of mental relaxation are in no way suited to every time, age, and place. But the study of literature sharpens youth and delights old age; it enhances prosperity and provides a refuge and comfort in adversity; it gives enjoyment at home without being a hindrance in the wider world; at night, and when travelling, and on country visits, it is an unfailing companion.

[17] It might be that we ourselves have no expertise in literary matters, and no taste for them. Even so, we should surely have to admire literary attainments when we recognize them in others. Is there anyone here who was so oafish and insensitive that he was not seriously affected when Roscius* died? Although he was an old man at the time of his death, his outstanding skill and pleasing manner made us think that he was wholly exempt from our common lot. Yet Roscius won such love from all of us merely because of the motions of his body: are we, then, to fail to respond to extraordinary motions of the mind and quickness of the intellect?

[18] How many times, members of the jury, have I seen this Archias—I am going to presume upon your kindness, since you are paying such close attention to me as I speak in this unconventional manner—how many times have I seen him, without his having written down so much as a single letter, improvise a large number of the finest verses about the topics of the day, and then, when asked to do it again, repeat his performance but with different words and expressions!* As for his written compositions, which were carefully and thoughtfully produced, I have seen them so highly acclaimed as to equal the praise given to the ancient writers. Should I not love such a man, should I not admire him, and should I not think it my duty to defend him by every means possible? Indeed, we have it on the highest and most learned authority that, whereas the other arts are made up of knowledge, rules, and technique, a poet is created by nature itself, activated by the force of his own mind, and inspired, as it were, by a kind of divine spirit. Rightly, therefore, does our own great Ennius* call poets 'sacred', because they seem to us to be marked out by a special gift and endowment of the gods. [19] So let the name of poet, gentlemen, which no barbarian race has ever treated with disrespect, be a sacred name among you, the most enlightened of men. Rocks and deserts respond to the poet's voice; ferocious wild animals are often turned aside by singing and stopped in their tracks:* shall we, then,

who have been brought up to all that is best, remain unmoved by the voice of a poet?

The people of Colophon say that Homer was a citizen of their city, the Chians claim him as theirs, the Salaminians put in a counter-claim, while the people of Smyrna are so confident that he belongs to them that they have even set up a shrine to him within their town; and there are a great many other places, too, which dispute the honour among themselves and fight over it. These cities, then, even go so far as to search out a foreigner who is dead, because he was a poet: are we, on the other hand, to turn away this man who is alive, and who belongs to us both in law and by his own choice? Are we to turn away a man who has for long now devoted all his efforts and all his talents to celebrating the glory and renown of the Roman people? For in his youth Archias touched on the war against the Cimbri,* and even won the approval of the famous Gaius Marius himself, who was thought to have little respect for literature. [20] But there is in fact nobody who is so hostile to the Muses that he would not readily allow his own deeds to be immortalized in verse. The famous Themistocles, the greatest of the Athenians, when asked which singer or performer he most enjoyed listening to, is said to have replied that he preferred 'the one who best proclaimed Themistocles' greatness'. It was for the same reason that Marius was so fond of Lucius Plotius:* he thought that his achievements could be made famous by Plotius' talent.

[21] The Mithridatic War,* a great and difficult undertaking pursued with many changes of fortune on land and sea, has been treated by Archias in its entirety. The books he wrote on it cast glory not only on the valiant and illustrious Lucius Lucullus, but also on the reputation of the Roman people. For it was the Roman people who, under Lucullus' leadership, opened up Pontus, fortified though it was by the resources of its king and by its geographical position. It was an army of the Roman people, led by the same general, which, although small in number, routed the countless forces of the Armenians. And it is to the Roman people, again under Lucullus' direction, that the glory belongs of having rescued and preserved the loyal city of Cyzicus from all the assaults of the king and from the very mouth and jaws of war. That astonishing naval battle off Tenedos, when Lucius Lucullus killed the enemy commanders and sank their fleet, will always be spoken of and proclaimed as ours: ours are the

trophies, ours the monuments, ours the triumphs. Those who use their talents to write about such events serve therefore to increase the fame of the Roman people.

[22] Our own Ennius was held in affection by the elder Africanus,* and it is even thought that a marble statue of him was placed on the tomb of the Scipios. Yet the praises of a poet shed glory not only on the person who is praised, but on the reputation of the Roman people also. Cato, the great-grandfather of our Cato,* was praised to the skies, and great honour was paid to Rome because of it. In short, all those great men like Maximus, Marcellus, and Fulvius* were praised, but not without each of us having a share in their glory. It was because of this that our ancestors bestowed Roman citizenship on the poet who had written these laudations, a man from Rudiae: are we, on the other hand, to disenfranchise this man of Heraclea who has been sought after by many communities, and legally enrolled in ours?

[23] But if anyone thinks that there is a smaller harvest of glory to be reaped from Greek verse than from Latin, he is seriously mistaken. Greek is read by almost every nation on earth, whereas Latin is confined to its own geographical limits, which are, you must admit, narrow. If, therefore, our achievements are limited only by the boundaries of the world, then we ought to desire that our glory and fame may penetrate as far as our weapons have reached. For literary commemoration not only brings honour to the nations whose achievements are described, it also acts as the strongest incentive to those who risk their lives for the sake of glory, driving them on to face danger and endure toil. [24] How many writers Alexander the Great is said to have kept with him to record his deeds! And yet, when standing before the tomb of Achilles at Sigeum, he said: 'Lucky young man, to have had Homer to proclaim your valour!' And rightly—because, had it not been for the *Iliad*, the tomb which covered Achilles' body would also have buried his memory. Again, the man whom we today call Great,* whose good fortune has been equal to his valour, did he not confer Roman citizenship upon Theophanes of Mytilene, who wrote about his deeds, before a full assembly of soldiers? And were not those brave men of ours, country men and soldiers though they were, so swayed by their love of glory that they shouted their approval with a great roar, feeling that they too had a share in the praise which had been heaped on their leader?

[25] If Archias, therefore, had not already been a Roman citizen by law, he could not, I take it, have succeeded in being awarded the citizenship by some general! Sulla, when giving the citizenship to Spaniards and Gauls, would no doubt have turned down his request! And yet we ourselves saw what Sulla did when a third-rate poet of the people passed up to him a booklet containing an epigram about him, merely something set out as elegiacs: he immediately ordered a reward to be given to him from the proceeds of the property he was engaged in selling,* but on condition that the poet never wrote anything again. Sulla thought that the efforts of a bad poet nevertheless deserved some reward: would he not therefore have actively sought out the talent, literary skill, and fluency of Archias? [26] Again, would Archias have failed to obtain what he wanted, either at his own request or through the Luculli, from Quintus Metellus Pius, a close friend of his who had given Roman citizenship to many other people? Especially when Metellus was so anxious for his own deeds to be written about that he even gave a hearing to some poets from Corduba,* whose style was somewhat coarse and foreign?

This is in fact something which cannot be denied, and so must not be concealed, but should be openly admitted: we are all motivated by the desire for praise, and the best people are the ones who are most attracted by glory. The philosophers who write treatises 'on despising glory' actually inscribe their own names on those very books! In the actual writings in which they scorn publicity and fame they want to be publicized and named! [27] Decimus Brutus,* a leading citizen and a great general, decorated the entrances to his temples and monuments with poems by Accius, who was a close friend of his. Then again, the great Fulvius,* who took Ennius with him on his staff when he fought against the Aetolians, showed no hesitation in devoting the spoils of Mars to the Muses. In a city, therefore, in which generals, scarcely before putting aside their arms, have given honour to the name of poet and the shrines of the Muses, it would indeed be wrong for jurors, wearing the toga of peacetime, to fail to respect the honour of the Muses and the well-being of poets.

[28] So that you will do this all the more readily, members of the jury, I shall now reveal my feelings to you and own up to what I may call my passion for glory—a passion too intense, perhaps, but nevertheless an honourable one. The measures which I took during my consulship, with your collaboration, for the security of this city and

empire, for the lives of our citizens, and for the country as a whole, these have become the subject of a poem on which Archias has now started work.* When I heard what he had written I thought it was an important project and an agreeable one, and so I engaged him to complete the task. For merit looks for no reward for the toil and danger which it has to face, save only praise and glory. If you take that away, gentlemen, what incentive do we have, in life's brief and transitory career, to involve ourselves in great undertakings? [29] Certainly, if the mind had no prior conception of posterity, and if it were to confine all its thoughts within those same bounds in which the span of our life is contained, then it would not crush itself under such enormous labours, nor would it be troubled by so many sleepless responsibilities, nor have to fight so often for life itself. But as things are, there exists in every good man a kind of noble instinct which excites the mind night and day with the spur of fame and reminds it that the memory of our name must not be allowed to disappear when our life is ended, but must be made to last for ever. [30] Or are we all to appear so small-minded as to think that all our achievements will cease to exist at the same moment as we do ourselves—we who undergo toil and mortal danger in the service of the state, and who throughout our whole lives never once stop to draw breath in peace and tranquillity? Many distinguished men have been careful to leave statues and portraits behind them, likenesses not of their minds, but of their bodies: ought we not greatly to prefer to leave behind us a representation of our designs and characters, moulded and finished by artists of the highest ability? For my part, even when I was actually carrying out the actions I took, I considered that I was spreading and disseminating a knowledge of them for the world to remember for ever. And whether I shall have no awareness, after I have died, of the world's memory of me, or whether, as the wisest men have maintained, that recollection will indeed touch some part of my being, I do at least derive pleasure at this moment from the thought and hope that my achievements will be remembered.

[31] Therefore, members of the jury, protect a man whose honourable character you see confirmed by the high rank of his friends and their long-standing friendship with him; whose talent is such as you may judge it to be when you observe that it has been sought out by men whose own talents are outstanding; and whose case is one

which is supported by the sanction of the law, the authority of a town, the testimony of Lucullus, and the citizen-lists of Metellus. Under these circumstances, gentlemen, if you consider that talents such as his deserve the blessing not only of men, but of the gods as well, then I entreat you to take him under your protection. He is a man who has always done honour to you, to your generals, and to the achievements of the Roman people, who has undertaken to give an everlasting testimonial of praise to these civil dangers which you and I recently faced together, and who follows that calling which has always been declared and believed by all men to be sacred: let him therefore be seen to have been rescued by your humanity rather than injured by your severity.

[32] As regards the technicalities of the case, I have spoken briefly and in a straightforward manner, as is my custom, and I trust that you are all satisfied, gentlemen, with what I have said. As for the part of my speech which was out of keeping with the forum and the tradition of the courts—when I discussed my client's talents and literary studies in general—I hope that this has been received in good part by you, gentlemen, as I know it has been by the man who is presiding over this court.

PRO CAELIO
('FOR CAELIUS')

DATE: 4 April 56 BC (trial held on 3–4 April)
DEFENDANT: Marcus Caelius Rufus
LAW: *lex Plautia de vi* (Plautian law concerning violence)
CHARGE: civil disturbances at Naples; assault on Alexandrians at Puteoli;
  damage to property of Palla; taking gold for attempted murder of Dio,
  then attempted poisoning of Clodia; murder of Dio
PROSECUTORS: Lucius Sempronius Atratinus, Publius Clodius (not the
  famous Clodius), Lucius Herennius Balbus
DEFENCE ADVOCATES: Marcus Caelius Rufus, Marcus Licinius Crassus,
  Marcus Tullius Cicero
PRESIDING MAGISTRATE: Gnaeus Domitius
VERDICT: acquittal

Pro Caelio was delivered exactly seven months after Cicero's return from
exile. His exile, for having executed five captured Catilinarian conspirators without trial in 63 BC (in Cicero's eyes his greatest achievement), was
a public humiliation which could not be wholly effaced by his recall,
however glorious. In the years that followed, Cicero therefore lost no
opportunity of reinforcing his own stature by publicly attacking the man
who had exiled him, Publius Clodius Pulcher; and Clodius lost no
opportunity of harming Cicero.

Marcus Caelius Rufus was an ambitious young socialite who had initially been Cicero's pupil and protégé, but had later become a friend of
Clodius and the lover of Clodius' sister Clodia Metelli—a powerful society lady who may or may not have been the 'Lesbia' loved by the poet
Catullus. In 56 BC, however, Caelius had broken with the Clodii and was
prosecuted by them for violence; Cicero successfully defended him. The
case allowed Cicero to recapture the allegiance of a promising young politician and, even more satisfyingly, to damage the reputation of Clodius'
sister. The speech is highly dishonest in its refusal to address the matters
at issue (the charges of violence and murder), but is unquestionably a
masterpiece.

Caelius was born in (probably) 88 or 87 BC, at Interamnia in Picenum.
His father was an *eques* who had possessions in Africa (§ 73); there are
indications that he did not indulge his spendthrift son as generously as the
latter may have wished. From *c.*73 to 63 Caelius served a kind of political
apprenticeship under Crassus and Cicero: he accompanied them as they

went about their business in Rome, and became familiar with the life of the forum. In 63, however, he broke away from Cicero to support Catiline, who was making a last bid for the consulship (Crassus was also supporting his candidature). But it does not seem likely that he continued to favour Catiline once Catiline had lost the election and taken up arms. At all events, Caelius was not among those prosecuted for involvement in the conspiracy.

Caelius spent the years 62 to 60 in Africa, in the service of the governor Quintus Pompeius Rufus. For well-connected young men who wished to see the world and perhaps make some money at the same time, such service was a prized opportunity: Catullus was shortly afterwards to follow the same path when he served under the governor of Bithynia, Gaius Memmius, in 57–56. But Caelius still needed to make a name for himself before the public at Rome. In April 59 he therefore brought a prosecution, probably for extortion, against Gaius Antonius Hybrida, Cicero's colleague in the consulship of 63. Although he had reason to dislike Antonius, Cicero disapproved of the prosecution (Antonius had after all been the general nominally responsible for the defeat of Catiline in the field, and so an attack on Antonius would be seen as an attack on Cicero's consulship). He therefore undertook Antonius' defence; but Caelius won.

Flushed with this success, Caelius decided it was now time to leave his father's house and take up residence in the most fashionable part of the city, on the Palatine. He rented an apartment there from Clodius, close by the residence of Clodia. Clodia was at this time about 36, and recently widowed (her husband Quintus Caecilius Metellus Celer died in 59); and she accepted Caelius as her lover. In 58 Clodius was tribune, and succeeded in exiling Cicero; and in 57 Cicero was recalled. In one of these years it is likely that Caelius became quaestor and entered the senate, although Cicero says nothing about this in the course of the speech. Then at the end of 57, or the beginning of 56, Caelius broke with the Clodii. We do not know for certain what happened; but Clodius and his sister determined to punish him.

On 11 February 56 Caelius and Cicero again found themselves opposing each other in court, Caelius prosecuting and Cicero speaking for the defence. The defendant was Lucius Calpurnius Bestia, whom Caelius accused of electoral malpractice in the praetorian elections of 57, in which Bestia had stood unsuccessfully. Cicero had secured his acquittal on four previous occasions (we do not know when or on what charges), and this time he did so again. But Caelius would not accept defeat. Bestia was making a further attempt at the praetorship, and so Caelius brought a second charge against him, presumably for malpractice in the forthcoming election (that of 56); Cicero prepared to defend him a sixth time. At this point Bestia's 17-year-old son Lucius Sempronius Atratinus sought to prevent his father's trial from taking place by bringing a charge against Caelius: if Caelius were convicted, he would be unable to proceed with his action against Bestia. But time was of the essence, and so Atratinus prosecuted Caelius in the violence court (*quaestio de vi*): in contrast to other cases, trials for violence (*vis*) could take place even on public holidays. Atratinus was joined by two assistant prosecutors, Publius Clodius (not the famous Clodius, but a relation or perhaps a freedman) and Lucius Herennius Balbus, a friend of Atratinus' father (§ 56).

Being an experienced orator, Caelius decided to speak on his own behalf. But he also arranged for his old mentor Crassus to defend him, and for the third member of the team he succeeded in winning over Cicero. Cicero may have been difficult to persuade, given Caelius' past links with Catiline and Clodius, and his prosecutions of Antonius and Bestia. But Caelius was now an enemy of Clodius, and Cicero perhaps felt no deep affection for Bestia (cf. *Phil.* 11.11). Cicero would have been attracted by the prospect of placing so talented a politician as Caelius in his debt; and the case offered him a heaven-sent opportunity to revenge himself on Clodia, who had persecuted his family during his exile (§ 50). So he agreed.

There was an array of charges, most or all of them connected with the attempt of the deposed King Ptolemy Auletes of Egypt to recover his throne, so we must now turn to consider this, one of the more unsavoury episodes in the history of the period.

In 80 BC Alexander II of Egypt died, bequeathing his kingdom to Rome. The throne was usurped, however, by Ptolemy XII Auletes ('the Piper'), who ruled in the knowledge that Rome might lay claim to his kingdom, which was very wealthy, at any time. For the next twenty years he cultivated the Romans' favour in order to retain his throne—which made him unpopular with his subjects, who hated the Romans. Then in 59 he seized the opportunity presented by the 'first triumvirate' to secure for himself formal recognition as king, and 6,000 talents, a year's revenue, was paid to Pompey and Caesar. When Ptolemy tried to exact this sum from his people, however, he was deposed and fled to Rome. Once there, he borrowed heavily and tried to persuade the senate to provide an army to restore him to his throne. But the Alexandrians did not want him back, and in 57 they sent to Rome a deputation of one hundred citizens, led by the Academic philosopher Dio, to put their case before the senate. Ptolemy's reaction was to bribe, intimidate, or kill the members of the deputation: some were assaulted at Puteoli, and at Naples some sort of uprising may have been organized against them. These events caused great indignation at Rome. As for Dio, he succeeded in reaching Rome, where he stayed at the house of the senator Lucius Lucceius. But during his stay there an attempt was made to bribe Lucceius' slaves to murder him, and he therefore moved on to the house of Titus Coponius.

At the end of 57, the senate finally decreed that Ptolemy should be restored by the consul Publius Cornelius Lentulus Spinther (a friend of Cicero's). But it was then discovered that an oracle in the Sibylline Books forbade Ptolemy's restoration, and the senate rescinded its decree; Ptolemy at this point retired to Ephesus. Pompey, meanwhile, was agitating for the command to be given to himself, and early in 56 Dio, still staying with Coponius, was murdered. Public anger flared up again, and was directed particularly against Pompey, who was thought to have been responsible for the murder.

Various prosecutions then took place. Publius Asicius, said to have been Ptolemy's agent, was prosecuted for the murder of Dio, and was successfully defended by Cicero (§ 23). Then Caelius was accused, by Atratinus and Balbus, and by Publius Clodius. Atratinus, as we have seen, was anxious to bring about the exile of the man who was prosecuting his father. For the Clodii, on the other hand, the trial was an indirect attack on Pompey: it seems likely that Caelius had switched his allegiance from the Clodii to Ptolemy and Pompey, and that this was the cause of his rupture with the Clodii.

The actual charges brought against Caelius were as follows:

(i) civil disturbances at Naples, and (ii) assault on the Alexandrians at Puteoli. These were probably incidents of violence directed against members of the deputation from Alexandria on their arrival in Italy;

(iii) damage to the property of Palla. Nothing is known of this charge, or of Palla; it is possible that his property was damaged in the course of the attacks on the deputation;

(iv) taking gold for the attempted murder of Dio, then the attempted poisoning of Clodia. We know much more about these charges, since these are the ones that Cicero chooses to answer in his speech. Caelius was accused of having borrowed gold from Clodia under false pretences, with the intention of bribing Lucceius' slaves to murder Dio at Lucceius' house (§§ 51–5). It was further alleged that Clodia discovered what Caelius was plotting, and that he, wishing to conceal the crime, attempted to poison her with the help of her own slaves (§§ 56–69);

(v) the murder of Dio. Caelius was accused of having been in league with Asicius in the actual murder of Dio at Coponius' house (although Asicius had been acquitted).

The trial took place on 3–4 April 56. For the prosecution, Atratinus spoke first, then Clodius, then Balbus. Atratinus' speech was devoted to an attack on Caelius' character and morals: he represented him as effeminate (a 'pretty-boy Jason'), loose-living, immoral, profligate, a lover of luxury, and well used to committing crimes of bribery and violence. Clodius' speech probably went over the charges in detail: he would have deplored the treatment of the Alexandrian deputation, criticized Pompey for his support of Ptolemy, and referred to the evidence that Clodia would give against Caelius at the end of the trial. In particular, she would reveal how Caelius' friend Publius Licinius had been caught handing over poison to her slaves at the Senian baths. It seems most likely that the prosecution indicated that Caelius was on familiar terms with Clodia, but not that he had been her lover. Evidently they calculated that the defence would also say nothing about this, since it would reflect badly on Caelius' character (the situation resembles that at the trial of Sextus Roscius, at which the prosecution said nothing about Chrysogonus or the proscription lists, confident that the defence would not mention them either). Balbus, in closing the case for the prosecution, returned to the subject of Caelius' moral delinquency, and also voiced his indignation at Caelius' continuing persecution of his friend Bestia.

The speeches for the defence were given in order by Caelius, Crassus, and Cicero; in speaking last, Cicero was again following his usual custom (*Brut.* 190; *Orat.* 130). Caelius' speech was vigorous and full of witty gibes: it contained a reference to Clodia as 'the one-penny Clytemnestra', i.e. a husband-murderer who sells her sexual favours cheaply (she was suspected of having poisoned her husband Metellus Celer). Although Caelius attacked Clodia's morals in this way, it seems unlikely that he admitted to having been her lover—just as the prosecution calculated he would not. Caelius and Crassus, it is reasonable to assume, must have made some defence against the actual charges, particularly perhaps those ones which Cicero does not discuss.

Cicero's speech, the final speech of the trial, took place on the second day, 4 April. This happened to be the first day of the Megalesian games, when the rest of Rome was on holiday. He therefore decided to compensate the jurors for missing the games by providing them with a speech that would be at least as entertaining: this is the speech that we have. In it he says little about the charges but concentrates on attacking Clodia (so as to discredit the evidence that she will give), sensationally revealing that Caelius had formerly been her lover (indeed, Cicero may even exaggerate their intimacy). If Caelius was Jason, as Atratinus had rashly claimed, then Clodia was Medea (§ 18): it was Caelius, like Jason, who had terminated the affair, and now Clodia, like Medea, was hell-bent on revenge. Hence the present trial. The prosecution had been confident that Cicero would reject this line, since it would surely damn Caelius; but Cicero manages to assign all the moral delinquency to Clodia, while admitting Caelius' involvement with her only obliquely, and not in any memorable or easily quotable form. This strategy was completely successful. Cicero made it seem as if the charges were a mere pretext: the only reason his client was facing them was because he had had the good sense to dissociate himself from a woman who was no better than a prostitute. The light-hearted tone, well suited to the holiday atmosphere in Rome, was used to ridicule Clodia and her hangers-on (who might also testify), so that the prosecution's most high-ranking witness, and hence their entire case, would simply be laughed out of court. The strategy adopted was also useful to Cicero in that it minimized the trial's political dimension. Public opinion was outraged at the murder of Dio and the treatment of the Alexandrian deputation, and yet Pompey was openly supporting Ptolemy's cause. Cicero's decision to restrict his attention to the character of Clodia enabled him to avoid taking a stance which would set him at odds with public opinion or damage his relations with Pompey.

Caelius was acquitted. This allowed him to proceed with his second prosecution of Bestia. Cicero defended Bestia a sixth time and lost; Bestia was sent into exile. In the next year, 55, Ptolemy secured his restoration to the Egyptian throne by bribing the governor of Syria, Aulus Gabinius, with 10,000 talents (Gabinius was in due course convicted and exiled for this, in spite of being defended by a reluctant Cicero). Ptolemy then ruled until his death in 51, upon which he was succeeded by his daughter Cleopatra, the last of the Ptolemies.

Caelius became tribune in 52; this was the year in which Publius Clodius was murdered, and Caelius was active in helping Cicero defend his killers and prosecute his supporters. Then in 50 he was aedile. Cicero was away serving as governor of Cilicia at the time, and Caelius sent him all the news from Rome in a lively correspondence which has survived (*Fam.* 8). (Everyone who has read this correspondence remembers Caelius' repeated but ultimately unsuccessful pleas to Cicero to send him panthers from his province for his games.) When the Civil War broke out in 49 Caelius supported Caesar, and was rewarded with the office of *praetor peregrinus* (foreign praetor) in 48. But then things went wrong. He put forward radical measures for debt relief against the opposition of his colleagues, caused a riot, and was suspended from office. Fleeing Rome, he tried, with Titus Annius Milo, to raise southern Italy in revolt against Caesar, but was killed by Caesar's troops at Thurii (48 BC).

Atratinus, on the other hand, enjoyed a long and distinguished career, becoming consul in 34, and later governor of Africa, being granted a triumph on his return from there in 21. He died in AD 7, having very nearly outlived Augustus.

And Clodia? In 45 Cicero unsuccessfully tried to induce her to sell him her pleasure-gardens on the Tiber. But apart from that we hear nothing about her at all. She simply vanishes from history.

PRO CAELIO

[1] If, members of the jury, there should happen to be present among us here today anyone who is unfamiliar with our laws, courts, and way of doing things, I am sure he would wonder what terrible enormity this case involves, since on a day of festivities and public games,* when all other legal business is suspended, this court alone remains in session—and he would have no doubt at all that the defendant must be guilty of a crime so terrible that, unless action were taken, the state could not possibly survive! And if he were then to be informed that there is a law* for rebellious and criminal Roman citizens who have besieged the senate-house with arms, used violence against the magistrates, and attacked their country, and that under this law trials may be held on any day of the year without exception, he would not object to the law, but would enquire what charge it is that is before this court. If he were then to be told that no crime, no enormity, and no act of violence has been brought before the court, but that a brilliantly able, hard-working, and popular young man is being accused by the son of someone he has prosecuted once and is now prosecuting again,* and that this attack on him is being financed by a prostitute,* he would find no fault with the prosecutor's sense of filial duty, he would consider that a woman's passions should be kept under control, and he would conclude that you yourselves are over-worked, since even on a public holiday you are not allowed the day off! [2] In fact, if you are prepared to pay close attention and form an accurate view of the case as a whole, you will realize, gentlemen, that none of the accusers would have taken on this prosecution if they had had any choice, nor, having taken it on, would they have had any hope of winning, were it not for their reliance on the insupportable passion and bitter hatred of some other person.* I shall forgive Atratinus, however, a civilized and altogether excellent young man and a friend of mine. He can plead as his excuse either filial duty, or compulsion, or his tender years. If he brought the charge voluntarily, I put it down to his sense of filial duty, if he was acting under orders, I put it down to compulsion, and if he expected to gain something from it, I put it down to his youthful naïvety. As for the other accusers, they deserve no such indulgence, and must be vigorously opposed.

[3] I think, gentlemen, that the best way of beginning my defence, in view of the youth of Marcus Caelius, is to reply to those slanders which the prosecutors have come up with in order to discredit him and deprive and despoil him of his good name. His father has been cited against him in various ways, either as not himself living in a manner befitting an equestrian, or as having been treated with insufficient respect by his son. As regards the first of these points, those who know Marcus Caelius* and the older ones among us will appreciate that he needs no words of mine to rebut the charge, in silence, himself. Those of us, on the other hand, who are not so well acquainted with him (since his advanced years have long prevented him from mixing with us much or coming into the forum) may rest assured that whatever distinction a Roman equestrian may possess—and it can undoubtedly be very great—has always been judged as belonging to Marcus Caelius in the fullest measure, and is still so judged today, and not just by his own circle but by all those who may for whatever reason have come into contact with him. [4] In any case, being the son of a Roman equestrian is something that the prosecution should never have used as a slur before these jurors, or before myself as advocate.*

As regards your point about my client's respect for his father, we have our own opinion about that, but the verdict surely lies with the parent. Our own opinion you shall hear from witnesses on oath. As for what his parents feel, that is made clear by his mother's tears and her indescribable grief, and by his father's filth* and all the sorrow and distress that you see in front of you.

[5] Regarding the further objection that the young man is held in low esteem by his fellow-townsmen, the Praetuttians* have never conferred greater honours on anyone in their presence, gentlemen, than they have on Marcus Caelius in his absence. Indeed, they elected him, while he was away, to their senate and granted him, without his asking, certain honours which they refused to the many who did ask for them. They have also sent to this trial a deputation of the most high-ranking men, fellow senators of mine and Roman equestrians too, and these delegates have brought with them an extremely impressive and eloquent testimonial.

I believe I have now laid the foundations of my defence—which will be very secure if based on the verdict of my client's own people. For this young man would hardly come before you with an adequate recommendation if he had incurred the disapproval of a man such as his father is, or of a town so distinguished and so important. [6] Indeed, if I may turn to my own situation, it is from just such a source that I issued forth to make my own reputation, and this forensic labour of mine and my career in general have found a rather wider course to public recognition as a result of the recommendation and approval of my friends.

Now as for the slur on his sexual morals and the slanderous insults—for they were not proper charges—levelled at him by each of the prosecutors, these will never upset Marcus Caelius enough to make him wish he had been born ugly! For slanders of this kind are commonly directed against any young man of becoming figure and appearance. But slander is one thing, prosecution another. Prosecution requires a basis for a charge, and then to determine the facts, to identify the person responsible, to prove the case by argument, and back it up with evidence. Slander, on the other hand, has no object except to insult. If its character is coarse, it is termed abuse, but if sophisticated, it is termed wit.

[7] Indeed, I was surprised and disappointed that this part of the prosecution was given to Atratinus. For it did not suit him, nor was it appropriate for one so young, nor, as you will have noticed yourselves, did this fine young man's sense of decency allow him to feel at home with language of this sort. I should have preferred it if one of the more hardened prosecutors among you had taken on the task of slandering my client; then I could have contradicted this unfettered slander in rather more free, forcible, and natural terms. But with you, Atratinus, I shall deal more leniently. Your sense of decency leads me to moderate my words, and I ought also to take into account the kindness I have shown towards you and your father.*

[8] I should like, however, to give you a word of advice. First, to prevent anyone forming a wrong impression of the sort of person that you are, you must be as strict in avoiding intemperate words as you are in avoiding shameful deeds. Secondly, you should not say against someone else things that you would blush to hear falsely said against yourself. For who is there who cannot go down that road if they choose? Who is there who cannot direct against your youth and grace the coarsest slanders that he pleases? There may be no grounds whatever for the suspicion—but there will be grounds for an accusation! The blame for the part you have played lies, however, with

those who wanted you to take it on. Credit, on the other hand, is due
to your sense of decency, because we saw how reluctantly you spoke,
and also to your talent, because your speech was elegant and
polished.

[9] That speech, however, requires only a brief reply. In so far as
Marcus Caelius' youth could have given any grounds for suspicion,
let me assure you that it was well protected, first by his own sense of
decency, and then by the strict upbringing that he received from his
father. After that, as soon as his father had given him the toga of
manhood*—and here I will say nothing about myself, leaving you to
be the judge of that: I shall only say that his father immediately put
him in my charge. During this early period of his youth, no one ever
saw Marcus Caelius in the company of anyone other than his father
or myself, or at the highly respectable home of Marcus Crassus; and
all the while he was receiving a principled education.

[10] As for the charge that Caelius was a friend of Catiline,* he
should by rights be wholly above any suspicion of that kind. You
know that he was still very young when Catiline, together with
myself, was standing for the consulship.* If he ever attached himself
to Catiline or detached himself from me—even though there were
many patriotic young men who did become supporters of that vile
traitor—then let Caelius be reckoned to have been too friendly with
Catiline. 'But we know that later on* he even became a political
adherent of his: we could see it with our own eyes.' Who is denying
it? But at the moment I am only defending that period of youth that
is by itself unstable, yet threatened by the passions of others. In that
period, when I was praetor,* Caelius was constantly by my side, and
did not know Catiline, who was serving as praetor in Africa.* In the
year that followed Catiline was tried for extortion;* Caelius stayed
with me, and did not even appear in support of Catiline at his trial.
The next year was the year in which I stood for the consulship;
Catiline also stood alongside me. Caelius never attached himself to
him, and never separated himself from me.

[11] So it was only after he had spent many years in the forum
without any suspicion or any ill repute that he became a supporter of
Catiline, when Catiline was standing for the second time.* How long
do you think his youth should have gone on being protected? Back in
my day a single year sufficed for keeping our arms inside our togas,*
and for our physical training on the Campus Martius, when we wore

our tunics;* and if we went straight into the army we served a similar
probationary period, in the camp and on campaign. At that age,
unless a young man could defend himself by his own strictness of
conduct and purity of morals, coupled with a stern upbringing and a
certain inborn virtue, he could not escape a bad reputation (and
justified, too), however closely his own people kept guard over him.
But a man who preserved those first beginnings of youth pure and
undefiled never had aspersions cast on his reputation and morals,
once he had finally grown up and become a man among men.

[12] Yes, he did support Catiline, after he had spent a number of
years in the forum, Caelius that is—just as many others did, from
every class and of every age. For Catiline had, as I am sure you
remember, a great many indications of the highest qualities*—not
fully developed, mind you, but sketched in outline. He mixed with
numerous individuals of bad character; yet he pretended to be
devoted to the best of men. He had the effect of degrading those
around him; yet he could also stimulate them to effort and hard
work. The fires of passion burned within him; yet he was a keen
student of military affairs. For my part I do not think the world has
ever seen a creature made up of such contrary, divergent, and mutu-
ally incompatible interests and appetites.

[13] Who was more agreeable, at one particular time, to men of
high rank,* and who more intimate with scoundrels? Who at one time
a more patriotic citizen, and who a more loathsome enemy of this
country? Who more corrupt in his pleasures, and who more able to
endure hard work? Who more avaricious in rapacity, and who more
lavish in generosity? That man, gentlemen, had many features that
were paradoxical. He had a wide circle of friends, and he looked after
them well. What he had, he shared with everyone. He helped all his
friends in times of need with money, influence, physical exertion,
even, if necessary, with recklessness and crime. He could adapt and
control the way he was to suit the occasion, and twist and turn his
nature this way and that. He could be stern with the serious, relaxed
with the free-and-easy, grave with the old, affable with the young,
daring with criminals, and dissolute with the depraved. [14] And so
this complex, ever-changing character, even when he had collected
all the wicked traitors from far and wide, still held many loyal, brave
men in his grasp by a sort of pretended semblance of virtue. Indeed,
that dastardly attempt to destroy this empire could never have come

into being had not that monstrous concentration of so many vices
been rooted in certain qualities of skill and endurance.

Therefore, members of the jury, you should reject the prosecution's argument, and refuse to allow my client's association with
Catiline to count against him: this is something he has in common
with many other people, including some fine patriots. I, I myself, I
tell you, was almost taken in by him on one occasion,* when I took
him to be a loyal citizen, eager to be on good terms with all the best
people, and a dependable and faithful friend. I did not believe his
crimes until I came upon them with my eyes, or suspect them until I
had laid my hands on them. If Caelius was also among his wide circle
of friends, it is better that he should be angry with himself at his own
mistake (just as I sometimes am about my own misjudgement of
Catiline) than that he should have to fear a charge of having been a
friend of his.

[15] So your speech has gone from slanders about my client's
sexual morality to using the conspiracy to stir up prejudice against
him. For you implied, although in a hesitant and sketchy manner,
that because of his friendship with Catiline, he must have been a
member of the conspiracy. At this point not only did the charge fail
to hang together, but this fluent young man's speech scarcely did so
either. So let me ask you, what terrible madness was there that came
over Caelius? What terrible wound had he suffered, either psycho-
logically or in his personal circumstances? And when was Caelius'
name ever mentioned in connection with the conspiracy? I do not
wish to go on for too long discussing matters about which there is
not the slightest doubt, but this I will say: if Caelius had been a
member of the conspiracy, or even if he had been anything other
than implacably opposed to it, he would surely never have used a
charge of conspiracy* as his preferred means of promoting his youthful abilities.

[16] Apropos of this, I rather think that the question of electoral
malpractice and the charges relating to political clubs and the distribution of bribes* (since this is the point I have reached) can be
disposed of in the same way. For if Caelius had really sullied his
reputation with the unstinted bribery that you speak of, he would
hardly have been so insane as to prosecute another person* for the
same crime. Nor would he deliberately cause someone else to be
suspected of this crime if he wanted to have the freedom to do it

himself in the future. Nor indeed, if he thought that he would run the risk of being prosecuted for bribery once, would he have prosecuted someone else for it a second time. In doing this I admit that he has acted unwisely and without my approval. Yet it is the mark of this type of ambition that it pursues the innocence of another person instead of betraying any apprehension on its own account.

[17] As for the charge of debt, the complaints of extravagance, the demands for account-books—see how brief is my reply. A man who is under his father's legal authority does not keep accounts. Caelius has never once borrowed money from one creditor to pay off another. It is one particular form of extravagance that he is charged with, his accommodation. This, you say, costs him 30,000 sesterces a year. Ah, now I understand! The block in which my client rents an apartment for, I think, 10,000 a year has been put up for sale by Publius Clodius. You, wishing to do him a favour, have adjusted your lie to suit his purpose.*

[18] You have criticized Caelius for moving away from his father's house. But at his age that is scarcely something to be criticized. He had just won a success in a political case* which, although unwelcome to me, was a great victory for him, and he was also at an age when he could stand for public office. Moreover, it was not only with his father's permission but with his active encouragement that he moved away from home. For his father lives a long way from the forum, and in order to be able both to visit our houses* more easily and to be visited himself by his own people* he took an apartment on the Palatine at a moderate rent.

While on this subject I can repeat what the illustrious Marcus Crassus said a little while ago, when he was deploring the arrival of King Ptolemy: 'Would that never in Pelion's forest . . .'* And I could go on with the quotation: 'for never would a wandering woman' have caused us all this trouble, 'Medea, sick at heart, wounded by a wild passion'. For you will find out, gentlemen, what I shall show you when I come to that point—that this Medea of the Palatine* and the change of residence was the cause of all this young man's difficulties, or rather of all the talk.

[19] So, since I have every confidence in your judgement, gentlemen, I am not in the least afraid of those charges which the prosecution, as I inferred from their speeches, are fabricating to bolster their case. For they gave out that they had a senator* who would testify that

he had been assaulted by Caelius at the pontifical elections. If this person comes forward, I will ask him first of all why he did not take legal action there and then; and secondly, if he says he preferred to make a complaint rather than go to law, I will ask him why he has been produced by yourselves rather than coming forward on his own initiative, and why he wished to make his complaint so long after the event rather than at the time. If he can supply me with acute and astute answers to these questions, I will then ask, finally, from what source that senator springs. If it emerges that he himself is his own source and origin, I may well be impressed by this, as I generally am. But if it turns out that he is merely a rivulet drawn off and derived from that very fountain-head* of your prosecution, I shall be delighted that, although you have such great influence and resources at your disposal, you could nevertheless find only a single senator who was prepared to do your bidding.

(*On the witness Fufius.*)*

[20] Nor, on the other hand, am I in any way frightened of that other type of witness—those who operate by night. For the prosecution said there would be witnesses who would testify that their wives were assaulted by Caelius when returning from dinner. What impressive witnesses they will be, who will dare to swear this on oath, when they will also have to admit that they never started legal proceedings regarding these terrible wrongs, even to the extent of requesting a meeting and out-of-court settlement!

You are now in a position, gentlemen, to foresee the whole nature of this attack, and when it is launched it will be your duty to beat it back. For the accusers of Marcus Caelius are not the same people as those who are attacking him: the weapons that are hurled at him in public are supplied by an unseen hand. [21] I am not saying this to discredit the prosecutors, who are entitled even to feel proud of what they are doing. They are doing their duty, defending those near to them, acting as men of spirit do. When injured, they feel aggrieved; when angered, they let fly; they fight back when provoked. Men of spirit may indeed have just cause for attacking Marcus Caelius. But you in your wisdom, gentlemen, will appreciate that you should not on this account be guided by other people's grievances rather than by your own sense of honour.

You can see what a mass of people there is in the forum, of how many different classes and occupations, what a variety of humankind. From such a crowd, how many people do you think there are who are used to offering their services, exerting themselves, and promising their evidence, on their own initiative, to powerful, influential, and persuasive individuals, when they believe that there is something those individuals want? [22] If there happen to be some such people who have forced their way into the present trial, then use your wisdom, gentlemen, to put a stop to their greed! In this way you will show that you have taken consideration at one and the same time for the safety of my client, for your own consciences, and for the general public welfare against dangerous and powerful individuals.

For my part, I intend to draw you away from witnesses. I will not allow the facts of the case, which are unalterable, to be made to rely on witnesses' personal inclinations, which can so easily be manipulated, and which can be twisted and distorted with no difficulty at all. Instead, I shall proceed by means of proofs, and shall refute the charges with indications that are clearer than the light of day. Fact will be pitted against fact, reason against reason, argument against argument!

[23] I am very pleased, therefore, that Marcus Crassus has dealt so impressively and eloquently with the part of the case that has to do with the civil disturbances at Naples, the assault on the Alexandrians at Puteoli, and the property of Palla. I could wish that he had also spoken about Dio.* But on this last point what can you possibly be expecting to hear, given that the perpetrator of the crime has no fear of punishment, or even admits his responsibility?* After all, he is a king! The man, on the other hand, who is said to have been his agent and accomplice, Publius Asicius,* has been acquitted of the deed in a criminal trial. So here we have a charge which the guilty party does not deny, whereas the man who did deny it has been acquitted of it. In these circumstances, do you really think my client has any reason to be afraid of the charge when he not only had no involvement in the crime but was not even suspected of being involved in it? And if the help Asicius received from the strength of his case outweighed the harm done to him by the odium of the charge, what harm can your slander possibly do to Caelius, who not only has not been suspected of this particular crime, but has not even been tainted with a bad reputation?

[24] 'But Asicius was acquitted as a result of collusion.' This point is an extremely easy one to answer, especially for me since I was the

defence advocate. But Caelius' view is that however strong Asicius'
case is (and he thinks it is very strong indeed), it nevertheless has no
bearing on his. Nor is this the view of Caelius alone: it is shared by
two highly civilized and cultured young men, possessed of the most
virtuous principles and the best literary training, Titus and Gaius
Coponius, who were more upset than anyone at Dio's death, and
who were attached to him both by their common devotion to culture
and civilized values and by the ties of hospitality. Dio, as you have
heard, was living at Titus' house, and had known him in Alexandria.
What he or his most worthy brother thinks of Marcus Caelius you
will discover from themselves, if they are brought forward to testify.
[25] So let us put all this to one side, and turn at last to the points on
which the case depends.

I noticed, members of the jury, that you were listening to my
friend Lucius Herennius with close attention. Although it was pri-
marily his ability and his particular manner of speaking that held
your attention, I was nevertheless afraid at times that that speech of
his, carefully contrived to suggest guilt, might imperceptibly and
gently insinuate itself into your minds. For he had a great deal to say
about luxurious living, a great deal about self-indulgence, a great
deal about the vices of the young, and a great deal about morals. In
his life away from the court Herennius is a gentle soul, and elegantly
exemplifies the familiar charm and good manners which just about
everyone admires nowadays; but in this trial he has shown himself
the grimmest type of uncle, moralist, and schoolmaster. He casti-
gated Marcus Caelius as no father ever did his own son; he gave a
long lecture on licentiousness and profligacy. In short, gentlemen, I
began to excuse your listening so attentively because I myself was
shuddering at so grim and so severe a way of talking.

[26] The first part of his speech, however, troubled me less. He
claimed that Caelius was on familiar terms with my friend Bestia,
that he dined at his house, that he visited him frequently, and that he
supported his campaign for the praetorship.* These allegations do not
trouble me because they are patently false. For the people that
Herennius claimed were present at these dinner parties are all people
who are either unavailable or else under an obligation to back him up.
I am not troubled, either, by his assertion that Caelius is a colleague
of his in the Luperci.* Clearly the fraternity of the Luperci must be a
savage brotherhood, rustic and wild, an association of backwoods-

men formed before the invention of laws and civilization, if its members today not only prosecute one another but even allude to their common membership in the course of their prosecution, apparently afraid in case anyone should be unaware of the connection! [27] But I am going to leave out all of this, and pass on to the points that trouble me more.

Herennius' castigation of pleasures was lengthy; it was also calmly delivered, more like a disputation than a harangue, which is why it was listened to so attentively. As for my friend Publius Clodius,* although he threw his weight about very impressively and energetically and gave a fiery speech in the strongest language and at the top of his voice, I found that I thought highly of his oratory without, however, being alarmed by it—for I had seen him in a number of cases on the losing side. No, it is you, Balbus,* that I must reply to first, in all humility, if you will allow me, if it is lawful, that is, for me to defend a man who has never refused an invitation to a dinner party, who has visited a pleasure-garden, who has used perfume, and who has set eyes on Baiae!*

[28] I have in fact seen and heard of many men in our nation who have not merely taken a sip of this kind of life and touched it with their fingertips, so to speak, but have devoted the whole period of their youth to the pleasures of the flesh, and who even so have eventually risen above it all and turned over a new leaf, going on to become respected and famous citizens. Everyone agrees that the young should be allowed to play around a little, and nature herself has been generous in supplying them with youthful passions; and if these passions should burst out into the open, then so long as they do not upset anyone's life or break up anyone's home they are generally regarded as unproblematic and easy to put up with. [29] But it seemed to me that what you were trying to do was to use the bad reputation of young men in general to stir up prejudice specifically against Caelius. So all that silent attention which was paid to your speech can be put down to the fact that, while there was a single defendant on trial, we were reflecting on the vices of many.

It is easy to attack luxurious living. Daylight would soon fail me if I tried to set forth everything that could be said on the topic: corruption, adultery, wantonness, extravagance—it's a vast subject! Even if you have no defendant to accuse but just the vices in general, the subject in itself offers scope for a full and damning attack. But wise men like yourselves, gentlemen, should not be diverted from the person of the defendant himself. Your own strictness and stern responsibility give you barbs that you can deploy. The prosecutor has aimed these barbs at an abstraction—at vices, at morals, at the age in which we live. You, on the other hand, ought not to deploy them against an individual defendant, when he has been subjected to an unwarranted prejudice not through any fault of his own, but because of the failings of many others.

[30] I shall not venture, therefore, to reply to your criticisms as I ought. For I could ask you to make an exception for the young, and beg your pardon. But, as I say, I shall not do this: I shall not take refuge in my client's youth, and I give up the rights to which anyone would be entitled. All I ask is that, whatever general disapproval there may currently be concerning young men's debts, dissipation, and licentious behaviour—and I know that on this subject there is considerable disapproval—my client should not be made to suffer for other people's misdemeanours, or for the vices of youth and of the age in which we live. And yet, although I am making this request, I have no objection to providing the most conscientious answers to those charges which actually relate to my client specifically.

There are two charges, one about gold and one about poison;* and behind both of them one and the same person is to be found. Gold was taken from Clodia, and poison was sought to be given to Clodia—or so the prosecution claim. All the other accusations are not charges but slanders, more appropriate to an abusive slanging-match than to a public trial. 'Adulterer, pervert, dealer in bribes!'—this is the language of slander, not of prosecution. There is no basis for such charges, no foundation; they are insulting remarks thoughtlessly spouted by an angry prosecutor who has no authority for what he says. [31] But as for the two charges, I can see their originator, I can see their source, I can see the specific individual who is their fountain-head. Caelius needed gold: he took it from Clodia, he took it without any witness being present, and he kept it as long as he wanted it. Here I detect the strongest evidence of an extremely close friendship! He wanted to kill Clodia: he sought poison, pestered those he could for it, somehow obtained it, fixed on a place, and conveyed the poison there. Here I detect a bitter hatred, following upon a cruel rupture!

In this trial, members of the jury, everything has to do with

Clodia, a woman who is not only of noble birth, but notorious. In talking about this woman, I shall say only what I need to say to rebut the charge. [32] You with your remarkable understanding, Gnaeus Domitius,* will appreciate that we are concerned with this woman alone. If she denies that she lent gold to Caelius, if she does not allege that he obtained poison to use against her, then I am behaving outrageously in referring to a respectable mother in terms other than those due to a saintly Roman matron. But if this woman is eliminated from the case, the prosecution are left with neither charges nor resources with which to attack Marcus Caelius—so surely I as his advocate have no choice but to repel those who are assailing him? Indeed, I would do this more vigorously, were it not for the fact that I am restrained by my personal enmity with this woman's husband, I mean her brother*—I'm always making that mistake! I shall treat her gently, then, and go no further than my duty to my client and the demands of the case require. Indeed, I never thought I would be getting involved in quarrels with women, especially with one who is always thought of as every man's friend rather than any man's enemy!

[33] But I should like to ask her first whether she would prefer me to deal with her in a stern, solemn, old-fashioned way or in a relaxed, easy-going, modern way. If she chooses the severe mode of address, then I must call up from the underworld one of those bearded ancients—not with the modern type of goatee beard that she takes such pleasure in, but the rough type such as we see on antique statues and masks*—to castigate the woman and speak in my place (for otherwise she might become angry with me!). Let me therefore summon up a member of her own family—and who better than the famous Caecus?* He, at any rate, will be the least shocked at her, since he will not be able to see her!

[34] If he appears, this is, I am sure, how he will treat her, this is what he will say: 'Woman! What do you think you are doing with Caelius, with a man much younger than yourself, with someone from outside your own family? Why have you been either such a friend to him that you lent him gold or such an enemy that you were afraid of poison? Did you not notice that your father, or hear that your uncle, your grandfather, your great-grandfather, your great-great-grandfather and your great-great-great-grandfather were all consuls? And were you not aware that you were recently the wife of

Quintus Metellus,* that illustrious and valiant lover of his country,
who only had to step out of his front door to surpass virtually every
one of his fellow citizens in excellence, fame, and standing? Coming
from such a distinguished family yourself, and marrying into one so
illustrious, what reason did you have for linking yourself so closely to
Caelius? Was he a blood-relation, a relation by marriage, a friend of
your husband? He was none of these. What, then, was the reason—
unless it was some reckless infatuation? And if you were not
influenced by the masks of the men in our family, did my own
descendant, the famous Quinta Claudia,* not inspire you to rival our
family's glory in the splendid achievements of its women? Or were
you not inspired by the famous Vestal virgin Claudia* who, at her
father's triumph, held him in her arms and so prevented him from
being pulled down from his chariot by a hostile tribune of the plebs?
Why was it your brother's vices that influenced you, rather than the
virtues of your father and ancestors, virtues that have been repeated
down the generations from my own time not only in the men but
particularly in the women of our family? Did I destroy the peace
treaty with Pyrrhus so that you could strike the most disgraceful
sexual bargains on a daily basis? Did I bring water to the city for you
to foul with your incestuous practices? Did I build a road so that you
could parade up and down it in the company of other women's
husbands?'

[35] But why, members of the jury, have I brought on this solemn
character when there is a danger that Appius might suddenly turn
round and start accusing Caelius with that censorial severity of his?
But I shall take care of that later on; and I am confident, gentlemen,
that I shall be able to defend Marcus Caelius' private life before even
the strictest judges. But as for you, woman (I am no longer using a
character, but am speaking to you directly), if you intend to justify
your actions, your assertions, your charges, your intrigues, your allegations, then you must give a full account and explanation of this
familiarity, this intimacy, this entire relationship. The prosecutors go
on about orgies, love-affairs, adultery, Baiae, beach parties, dinner
parties, carousing, singing, musical entertainments, pleasure-boats—
and they imply that they have your approval for everything they say.
And since in what appears to be a moment of sheer, unbridled madness you have wanted all this brought up in the forum and in court,
you must therefore either explain it away and show it to be untrue or

else admit that neither your charge nor your evidence is to be believed.

[36] You may, on the other hand, prefer me to deal with you in a smart, modern way; if so, this is what I shall do. I shall get rid of that harsh and almost rustic old man, and choose instead a different member of your family: your youngest brother.* He is the very model of smart, modern manners, and he is exceedingly fond of you. Indeed, when he was a little boy, being, I assume, of a somewhat timid nature and inclined to feel frightened at night for no reason, he always used to sleep with you, his elder sister!* So imagine what he would say to you: 'What's all this fuss about, sister? Why have you gone mad? Why do you protest so much, and make so much of nothing?* You happened to notice a boy who lives nearby. You were attracted by his fair complexion, his tall figure, his face, his eyes. You wanted to see him more often. You sometimes spent some time with him in the same pleasure-gardens. You are a noble lady and he has a stingy, parsimonious father. You want to keep him tied to you with your money, but you can't: he kicks against the goad, spurns and rejects you, and thinks nothing of your presents. Try somewhere else, then! You own pleasure-gardens on the Tiber carefully sited where all the young men like to come for a swim. You can pick up whatever you fancy there any day you like. So why go on bothering this man who is not interested in you?'

[37] I come to you now, Caelius: it is your turn; and I am going to assume a father's authority and strictness. But I am unsure which particular father I ought to choose—the harsh, overbearing one in Caecilius:* 'Now at last my mind is ablaze, now my heart is heaped with anger,' or perhaps this one: 'You wretch, you villain!' Those fathers must be made of iron: 'What am I to say? What am I to wish for? By doing such disgraceful deeds, you make all my wishes vain'—intolerable! A father like that would say, 'Why did you go to live so near to that prostitute? Why did you not flee the moment you became aware of her allurements?* Why have you got to know a woman who is a stranger to us? Scatter and squander for all I care! If you run out of money, it'll be you that suffers; I have enough to see me through the years I have left.'

[38] To this blunt and morose old man Caelius would reply that no passion had led him astray, nor had he deviated from the straight and narrow. And what evidence did he have? There had been no

extravagance, no waste, no borrowing from one creditor to pay off another. But there were rumours. How many of us can escape such rumours, particularly in a city so full of slanderers? And are you surprised that this woman's neighbour acquired a bad reputation when her own brother was unable to escape unkind gossip?*

But to a mild and lenient father—the sort who would say, 'He has broken open a door: it can be repaired; he has torn someone's clothes: they can be mended'*—Caelius' case is an extremely easy one to make. For what charge could there possibly be that he would not find it easy to defend himself against? I am not at this point saying anything against that woman.* But if there were some woman quite unlike her who made herself available to everyone, who always had some man that she had openly designated as her lover, whose pleasure-gardens, house, and place at Baiae were open as of right to every lecher, who even kept young men and made up for their fathers' stinginess by paying them herself; if there were a widowed woman living shamelessly, a wayward woman living wantonly, a wealthy woman living extravagantly, and a lustful woman living like a prostitute, then am I really to think of it as criminal if some man should happen to have greeted her a little too freely?

[39] But someone will object: 'Is this, then, your way of bringing up the young? Is this how you educate them? Was it this that the boy's father had in mind when he entrusted his son to your care and handed him over to you—for him to devote his youth to lustful pleasures, and for you to defend that kind of life and pursuits?' For my part, members of the jury, if there ever existed a man with so firm a mind and a character of such virtue and self-control as to reject every pleasure and to dedicate the whole course of his life to physical toil and mental exertion, a man who took no pleasure in rest, in relaxation, in the pursuits of his contemporaries, in making love, or in partying, and who considered that nothing in life was worth striving for unless it led to glory and renown—such a man, it seems to me, must have been endowed and distinguished with qualities that are more than human. There have indeed been men like that, or so I believe—men like Camillus, Fabricius, and Curius,* and all the others who built Rome's greatness out of nothing.

[40] But virtues of that kind are not much in evidence nowadays: you can scarcely now find them in books. The pages which recorded the ancient austerity have themselves wasted away. And this is true

not just of us Romans, who have adopted this approach to life in practice more than we have in theory, but of the Greeks also, men of considerable learning who, although not up to achieving great deeds, were nevertheless capable of speaking and writing with integrity and brilliance; and now that times have changed for Greece,* different moral rules have come to prevail. [41] For there are some* who have asserted that the wise man does everything for the sake of pleasure, and learned men have not refrained from talking in this disgraceful way. Then there are others who have supposed that virtue can be combined with pleasure, thus joining by verbal cleverness two things that are entirely incompatible. As for those who have demonstrated that the only direct road to glory consists in hard work, they have now been virtually abandoned in their lecture-rooms.

It is certainly true that nature herself has provided us with many temptations which sometimes cause virtue to slumber and lie still. She has presented the young with many slippery paths on which they can scarcely set foot or walk upon without some accident or fall. She has set out a large assortment of delightful charms to which not only the young but even those of maturer years can sometimes succumb. [42] So if you should happen to come across anyone who shuns the sight of beauty, who is never attracted by any fragrance or touch or taste, who blocks all sweet sounds from his ears, I, perhaps, and some of you might consider him the recipient of the gods' favour, but most people will reckon him the object of their wrath.

So let us abandon this unused and neglected path, now blocked with branches and undergrowth. Let some allowance be made for youth, some freedom given to the young. Let pleasure be not always denied, and true and unbending reason not always prevail. Let desire and pleasure sometimes triumph over reason, provided that in such cases the following rule and limitation be observed. A young man should guard his own reputation, and not attack anyone else's. He should not squander his inheritance nor cripple himself with high-interest loans. He should not assault anyone's home and family. He should not bring shame upon the virtuous, dishonour upon the respectable, or disgrace upon the good. He should threaten no one with violence, have nothing to do with plots, and steer clear of crime. And finally, when he has heeded the call of pleasure and devoted a moderate amount of time to playing around and to the empty desires of youth, he should turn at last to his duties at home, to his work in the courts, and to public life. In this way he will show that satiety has caused him to reject, and experience to despise, those things which reason, at an earlier time, had not enabled him to disdain.

[43] Indeed, gentlemen, there have been many leading men and illustrious citizens, both in our own times and within the memory of our fathers and ancestors, who, once their youthful desires had simmered down, went on in their maturity to exemplify the very highest virtues. I prefer not to mention any of them by name: you will recall them for yourselves. It is not my intention to associate the great renown of any valiant and distinguished personage* with even the slightest misdemeanour. But if I did wish to do this, I could point to many eminent and leading men who were notorious during their youth for their licentious behaviour or for their reckless extravagance, the size of their debts, their lavish expenditure, and their wanton passions, but whose vices were later so completely eclipsed by their many virtues that anyone who wished could explain them away on the score of youth.

[44] But in Marcus Caelius—for I shall now speak more boldly about his honourable pursuits, since I also have sufficient trust in your wisdom to make certain other admissions to you—in Marcus Caelius you will discover no extravagance, no lavish expenditure, no debts, and no passion for parties and dens of vice. As for the vice of excessive eating and drinking, that is something which not only does not diminish but actually increases as a man's life goes on. And as for love-affairs and what are called 'amours'—which do not generally trouble men of strong character for long (for such passions wither away rapidly and soon)—these have never held him prisoner within their grasp.

[45] You have heard him speaking in his own defence, and you have heard him speaking before as a prosecutor* (I say this for his defence, not as a boast): with your customary discernment you have taken note of his oratorical style, his technical ability, and the richness of his thought and expression. And it was not merely his natural talent that you saw shining out in his oratory—something which, even if not backed up by hard work, can nevertheless make its mark on its own by its sheer power; no, his oratory contained (unless my partiality has clouded my judgement) a theoretical foundation based on a sound liberal education and perfected by careful and unremitting toil.

And yet you should realize, gentlemen, that the passions with which Caelius is charged and these pursuits about which I have been speaking cannot easily exist in one and the same person. For it is impossible that a mind given over to passion and hampered by love, desire, greed, often by too much money, but sometimes by too little, can possibly undertake whatever it is that we manage to achieve in speaking, and in the way that we achieve it, and not only as regards the physical exertion, but also in terms of the mental effort needed. [46] Can you think of any other reason why, when public speaking brings such rewards, such personal satisfaction, such renown, such influence, and such honour, there are and always have been so few people willing to undertake this burdensome profession? All pleasures have to be trampled underfoot, enjoyable recreations, amusements, fun, and parties have to be renounced, and even conversation with one's friends virtually given up. It is therefore the work required that puts people off public speaking and discourages them from taking it up, not any lack of talent or childhood training.

[47] So if Caelius had really given himself up to the kind of life that is alleged, would he, when still a young man, have brought a prosecution against an ex-consul?* If he shied away from hard work, if he were enslaved to pleasure, would he do battle here every day, go in search of personal enmities, bring prosecutions, and run the risk of being prosecuted himself, and would he also maintain for so many months now and in full view of the entire Roman people a struggle* for one of two things—his own political survival, or glory?

'So are you honestly saying, then, that that neighbourhood* gives off no tell-tale scent, that public gossip amounts to nothing, that Baiae itself has no tale to tell?' Certainly, Baiae talks all right, and not only that, it resounds with this report—that the lusts of a single woman have sunk to such depths that she does not merely decline to seek seclusion and darkness with which to veil her immoralities, but openly revels in the most disgusting practices amid crowds of onlookers and in the broadest light of day!

[48] But if there is anyone who believes that young men should not be allowed to have relations even with prostitutes, his view is undoubtedly a strict one (I will not deny that), but also one that deviates both from the permissiveness of the present age and from the custom and allowances of our ancestors. For when was such a thing not common practice, when was it ever criticized, when was

it ever forbidden, and when was what is allowed now ever not allowed?

At this point I want to explain what I will be talking about. I shall mention no woman by name: that much I shall leave unclear. [49] But if a woman without a husband throws open her home to every lecher and publicly leads the life of a prostitute, if she is used to attending dinner parties given by men to whom she is completely unconnected, if she carries on like this at Rome, in her pleasure-gardens, and among the crowds at Baiae, and if she conducts herself in such a way that not only her bearing but also her dress and entourage, not only her blazing eyes* and her loose language but also her embraces, her kisses, her beach parties, her boating parties, and her dinner parties all declare her to be not simply a prostitute but a lewd and lascivious prostitute at that—and if some young man should chance to take up with her, then would you, Lucius Herennius, regard that man as an adulterer or as merely a lover, as someone who intended to violate her chastity or merely to satiate his own appetite?

[50] I am forgetting the wrongs you have done me, Clodia. I am putting aside the memory of the pain you have caused me. The cruelties you inflicted on my family when I was away* I choose to ignore. So do not think what I said was directed against you. But I do want you to answer me this yourself, since the prosecution declare that you are responsible for the charge, and that you are also their witness to it. If a woman did exist like the one I have just been describing, a woman quite unlike yourself I hasten to add, one with the life and habits of a prostitute, would you consider it so very shocking and disgraceful if a young man should have had some dealings with her? If, then, you are not this woman, as I prefer to believe, what criticism can the prosecution possibly make of Caelius? But if they would have it that you are, then what reason do we have to be afraid of this charge, when you think nothing of it? Show us, therefore, the line we must take in our defence. For either your own fundamental decency will make it clear that Caelius has not acted immorally, or else your utter lack of decency will provide both him and all the rest with an ample means of justifying their behaviour.

[51] Since my speech seems now to have got clear of the shallows and avoided the rocks, the rest of what I have to say should all be plain sailing. Two very serious charges are brought against Caelius,

both involving the same woman. First there is the gold, which he is alleged to have taken from Clodia. And then there is the poison, which he is charged with having procured to bring about this same Clodia's death.*

He took the gold, you say, to give to the slaves of Lucius Lucceius,* so that they could murder Dio of Alexandria, who was at that time staying at Lucceius' house. It is certainly a serious charge, to allege that someone plotted to kill envoys or incited slaves to murder their master's guest—a plot full of wickedness, full of criminality! [52] And in reply to such a charge I should first like to ask whether Caelius told Clodia his reason for taking the gold or whether he did not. If he did not, then why did she hand it over? If he did, then she too is implicated in the crime. Did you dare, then, to fetch the gold from out of your chest, to strip of its adornments that Venus of yours,* loaded with the spoils from your other lovers, when you knew what a terrible crime this gold was wanted for—to bring about the murder of an envoy, and to cast on Lucius Lucceius, a man with the most scrupulous sense of honour, the everlasting taint of criminality? That welcoming heart of yours should never have consented to so horrific a crime, that open house of yours should never have aided it, that hospitable Venus of yours should never have abetted it. [53] Balbus was aware of this point. That is why he said that Clodia was kept in the dark, and that Caelius gave her the excuse that he needed the gold to pay for some games. But if he was as close a friend of Clodia's as you made out when you were lecturing us on his morals, then he did without question tell her why he wanted the gold; if, on the other hand, he was not so close a friend, then she did not give it to him. So if Caelius told you the truth, you shameless woman, you knowingly gave him gold to commit a crime; and if he did not bring himself to tell you, you never gave it!

Why, then, do I need to counter this charge with endless arguments? I could point out that the character of Marcus Caelius is entirely incompatible with such an atrocious and terrible crime, and that it is scarcely credible that such an intelligent and sensible man did not realize how stupid it would be to entrust a criminal act of this magnitude to unknown slaves belonging to another master. I could also put to the prosecution the usual questions regularly asked by myself and other advocates: where did the meeting between Caelius and Lucceius' slaves take place, and how did Caelius make contact

with them? If it was in person, how rash of him! If it was through
someone else, then through whom? I could talk you through every
possible hiding-place where suspicion could lurk, but no motive, no
location, no opportunity, no accomplice, no prospect of bringing off
the crime or covering it up, no rational scheme, and no trace whatever of such a serious undertaking would come to light.

[54] These are the sort of proofs that orators use, and they could
have brought me some benefit (not because of any talent I might
have, but simply because of my experience and practice in public
speaking): they would give the impression of having been worked up
by me on my own and presented in evidence. But to keep matters
brief I will forgo all such arguments. For I have instead, members of
the jury, a man whom you will readily accept as a partner in the
sacred bond of your oath, Lucius Lucceius, a man of complete integrity and a most impressive witness.* If so terrible a crime really had
been directed against his position and his good name by Marcus
Caelius, he could not have failed to hear of it, could not have ignored
it, and could not have tolerated it. Or is it conceivable that so civilized a man, with those scholarly interests of his, with all that culture
and learning, could have ignored a danger which threatened that
very person to whom he was devoted precisely because of those
interests that they shared? And would he have failed to protect his
own guest against a crime which, even if intended against someone
he did not know, he would have viewed with the utmost seriousness?
Would he have ignored his own slaves' attempt to commit an act
which, even if he discovered that strangers were responsible for it,
would have caused him great distress? Would he have taken a relaxed
view of a deed undertaken at Rome and in his own house which, even
if it had been committed in the country or in a public place, he would
have denounced in the strongest terms? Would he, as an educated
man himself, have thought it proper to conceal a plot against a man
of learning which, even if it were some rustic who was in danger, he
would not have let pass?

[55] But why do I detain you any longer, gentlemen? He himself
has sworn a statement on oath. Please take note of its solemnity, and
mark carefully every word of his evidence. Read out the evidence of
Lucius Lucceius.

(*The evidence of Lucius Lucceius is read to the court.*)

What more do you want? Or perhaps you are waiting for the case

itself, and for truth, to speak out with a voice of their own? No, it is
this that is the defence of the innocent, this is the speech of the case
itself, this is the sole voice of truth!

The charge itself offers no grounds for suspicion, the facts no
proof of guilt. The business that is alleged to have been transacted
has left no trace of what was said or where or when. No witness, no
accomplice has been named. The entire charge arises out of a
malevolent, disreputable, vindictive, crime-ridden, lust-ridden
house. The house which is alleged to have attempted this unspeakable crime, on the other hand, is a house of principle, honour, duty,
and conscience. From this house you have just heard a statement
made under solemn oath. This will leave you in not the slightest
doubt about the matter in dispute—whether an impetuous, capri-
cious, and angry woman has fabricated a charge, or whether a
serious, scholarly, and temperate gentleman has given his evidence
conscientiously.*

[56] There remains the charge about poison.* But with this I am
unable either to discover a beginning or to unravel an end. For what
reason could Caelius possibly have had for wanting to poison that
woman? So that he would not have to return the gold? But did she
ever ask for it back? To avoid being accused?* But did anyone ever
consider him to be guilty? And would anyone ever have mentioned
his name at all if he had not brought a prosecution against somebody
himself?* Moreover, you heard Lucius Herennius say that he would
not have had a single word to say against Caelius were it not for the
fact that Caelius has now brought a second prosecution against his
friend on the same charge as that on which he has already been
acquitted.* Is it really credible, then, that so horrific a crime* was
committed for no reason at all? And can you not see that an
extremely serious charge* has been fabricated simply in order to
provide a motive for the second of the two alleged crimes?

[57] Finally, in whom did he confide, whom did he use as his
helper, who was his assistant, who was his accomplice, to whom did
he entrust so great an undertaking, entrust himself, entrust his own
life? The woman's slaves? For that is what has been claimed. But do
you think that my client—whom you certainly credit with some
intelligence, even though your hostile language denies him other
qualities—do you think he was really so stupid as to entrust his
entire fate to someone else's slaves? But what type of slaves were they

(and this is a very important point): were they slaves whom he knew were treated not as other slaves are, but were permitted to enjoy a free, easy, and intimate relationship with their mistress? For who is not aware, gentlemen, that in a household like this in which the lady of the house behaves like a prostitute, in which nothing that goes on is fit to be made public, in which perverted lusts, extravagant living, and all kinds of outlandish vices and outrages are rife—who does not realize that in such a household the slaves are slaves no longer? In that household every trust is placed in them, everything is left to them, they indulge themselves in the same pleasures as their mistress, they are let into her secrets, and they do quite well for themselves out of the spending and extravagance that goes on on a daily basis. [58] So was Caelius unaware of all this? If he was as intimate with the woman as you make out, then he would of course have been aware that her slaves were intimate with her too. But if his relationship with her was not as close as you would have us believe, then how could he possibly have been on such close terms with the slaves?

Now regarding the actual poison, what theory is made up about that? Where was it sought from, how was it obtained, how, to whom, and where was it handed over? The prosecution claim that Caelius already had it at home, that he tried it out beforehand on some slave that he had bought for the purpose, and that the speedy death of the slave demonstrated the poison's effectiveness. [59] Immortal gods! Why, when people commit the most terrible crimes, do you sometimes overlook what they have done, or else postpone retribution to some future time? For I saw, I saw with my own eyes and drank down that bitter grief—the most bitter, perhaps, that I ever experienced— on the day when Quintus Metellus* was snatched from the bosom and embrace of his country, when that great man, who considered himself born for the service of our empire, only two days after he had been at the height of his powers in the senate-house, on the rostra, and in our public affairs, when in the prime of his life, in the best of health, and in full bodily vigour, was most shamefully torn from the company of every loyal citizen and the entire nation. At that moment, as he lay dying and his mind in all other respects was already overpowered, he kept back his final thought for his country, and fixing his eyes on me as I wept he signified to me in halting and dying words how terrible a storm was hanging over my head, and how violent a tempest threatened the state.* Then, striking again and

again the wall which divided his house from the one where Quintus
Catulus* had lived, he repeatedly called out Catulus' name, and often
my own, but most often that of Rome, bewailing not so much the fact
that he was dying as that Rome, and I too, would henceforward be
robbed of his protection. [60] And had not so great a man been
struck down by a sudden, violent crime, just think how he, as a
senator of consular rank, would have stood up to his deranged
cousin*—especially given that, when he was consul and his cousin
was only just starting his revolutionary madness and beginning to
stir up trouble, he had declared in the senate's very hearing that he
would kill him with his own hand! So does that woman, coming from
this of all houses, really have the gall to start debating about the
celerity* of poison? Will she not rather be terrified of that house, in
case it should cry out her guilt? Will she not shudder at the walls
which know her secret and tremble at the memory of that deadly,
mournful night? But I return to the charge. Indeed, the reference I
have made to that illustrious and valiant gentleman has caused grief
to weaken my voice and sorrow to cloud my mind.

[61] It is not stated, however, where the poison came from, or how
it was obtained. The prosecution allege that it was given to Publius
Licinius who is here in court, a decent and patriotic young man and a
friend of Caelius; that an arrangement was made with the slaves for
them to come to the Senian baths; and that Licinius would join them
there and hand over the box of poison to them. At this point I want
to ask first, why was it necessary to arrange to meet at the baths?
Why did the slaves not simply go to Caelius at his home? If Caelius
and Clodia were still seeing so much of each other, and were still on
such friendly terms, then surely there could be nothing suspicious
about a slave of Clodia's being seen at Caelius' apartment? But if by
this time a quarrel had arisen between them, their relationship was
over, and they had split up, then 'that explains the tears'* and there we
have the reason for all these crimes and charges.

[62] 'On the contrary,' he says, 'when the slaves reported the plot
to their mistress and told her of Caelius' treachery, that intelligent
lady instructed them to promise him whatever he asked. But so that
Licinius could be caught in the act of handing over the poison, she
also ordered that the Senian baths be specified as a meeting-place:
she would send some of her friends there to lie in wait and then
suddenly, when Licinius had arrived and was handing over the

poison, they would jump out from their hiding-places and arrest him.'

All this, members of the jury, is extremely easy to refute. For why had she fixed upon the public baths of all places? I cannot see that there would have been any hiding-places there for men in togas! For if they were in the forecourt of the baths, they would not have been hidden from view; but if they were prepared to stow themselves away inside, it would have been rather awkward for them in their shoes and outdoor dress, and they might even have been refused entry—unless of course that influential lady had made friends with the attendant beforehand by means of her usual one-penny transaction!*

[63] It was, let me tell you, with an eager sense of anticipation that I kept waiting to discover the identities of those fine fellows who are alleged to have witnessed the interception of the poison; and we have still not been informed of their names. But I have no doubt that they are very responsible characters. For one thing they are intimate friends of this great lady. Then again, they willingly took on the job of being packed away inside the baths, something she could never have prevailed on them to do, however influential she might be, had they not been men of the very highest honour and respectability. But why do I need to discuss the respectability of these witnesses? You can judge their character and their diligence for yourselves. 'They hid in the baths.' What admirable witnesses! 'Then they jumped out by mistake.' What self-control! For the story you have made up is that when Licinius had arrived on the scene with the box in his hand and was endeavouring to hand it over but had not yet actually done so, then all of a sudden out flew these highly distinguished but anonymous witnesses; at which point Licinius, having already stretched out his arm to hand over the box, drew it back again at this sudden attack and took to his heels.

How great is the power of truth! How easily it can defend itself, unaided, against the ingenuity, craftiness, and cunning of human beings, and against their lies and plots! [64] Take, for instance, this little drama, the work of an experienced poetess with a great many plays to her credit:* how devoid it is of plot, how lacking in any proper dénouement! What about all those men (and there must have been more than a few of them if they were to arrest Licinius without difficulty and also provide sufficient eye-witness evidence): why did they let Licinius slip through their hands? Why should it have been more difficult to arrest Licinius after he had drawn back from handing over the box than it would have been if he had actually handed it over? The men were, after all, posted where they were precisely in order to arrest Licinius, to catch Licinius* in the act either when he had the poison on his person or after he had handed it over. That was the woman's whole idea, and that was the job of the men she asked to help her. And why you say that they mistakenly jumped out too soon, I simply cannot fathom. They had been asked to do this and had been stationed there specifically for this purpose, to expose the poison, the plot, and the crime that was being committed. [65] Could they in fact have chosen a better moment to jump out than when Licinius had arrived on the scene and was holding the box of poison in his hand? Indeed, if Licinius had already handed it over to the slaves, and the woman's friends had immediately gone out of the baths and arrested him, he would surely then have been imploring their protection and strenuously denying that it was he who had handed over the box. And how would they have proved him wrong? By saying that they had seen him? In the first place, that would only have served to bring down on themselves the suspicion of having committed so terrible a crime. And secondly, they would be claiming to have seen what they could not possibly have seen from the point where they had been stationed. That is why they revealed themselves, instead, at the moment when Licinius had arrived on the scene and was getting out the box, stretching out his arm, and handing over the poison. So here we have the conclusion, not of a proper play, but of a mime—of the sort in which, when no one has managed to devise a satisfactory ending, someone escapes from somebody else's clutches, the clappers sound, and up goes the curtain.*

[66] I ask, then, why it was that, when Licinius was hesitating, dithering, retreating, and trying to flee, those woman-led warriors allowed him to slip through their hands? Why did they not arrest him, why did they not use his own confession, the testimony of the many eye-witnesses who were present, and the cry of the deed itself to press home the charge of so terrible a crime? Could they really have been afraid that they would not be able to overcome him, they being numerous and he all on his own, they strong and he weak, they confident and he terrified?

No arguments counting against my client can be found in the facts of the case, nor any grounds for suspicion, nor does the charge itself give rise to any conclusion. In the absence, therefore, of arguments, of inferences, and of those indications which normally shed light on the truth, this case is thrown back entirely upon the witnesses. These witnesses, gentlemen, I now await not just without any trepidation, but even with some expectation of amusement. [67] I am bursting to set eyes on those elegant young men, the friends of a wealthy and noble lady, and on those valiant warriors stationed by their commandress in a fortified ambush at the baths. I intend to ask them how and where they hid themselves, whether it was the famous bath-tub or a Trojan horse that carried and concealed so many invincible heroes waging a woman's war. I shall also make them answer this, why so many big, strong men failed either to arrest this single, defenceless person (whom you see here) when he was standing still or else catch up with him when he was running away. If they do come forward to testify, I do not see how they will ever succeed in extricating themselves. They may be witty and clever at dinner parties, and sometimes even eloquent over a glass of wine. But a dining-room is one thing and the forum another; the couches there and the benches here are altogether different; the sight of revellers and the sight of jurors is not the same; and the light of lamps is quite unlike the light of day. We will therefore shake all their frippery and tomfoolery out of them—if, that is, they come forward. But let them take my advice: let them turn their energies in another direction, let them ingratiate themselves by a different means, let them show off in some other way, let them impress that woman by their elegance, let them outdo all others in their extravagance, let them cleave to her side, lie at her feet, be her slaves—but let them also spare the life and fortunes of an innocent man!

[68] 'But these slaves have been given their freedom on the advice of the woman's relations, illustrious men of the very highest rank.' At last we have found something that she is supposed to have done on the advice and authority of her valiant relations! But I am curious to know what is behind this act of liberation. It must mean either that a charge had been fabricated against Caelius, or that the prosecution wished to prevent the slaves being interrogated, or that the slaves who were party to so many of her secrets were receiving their well-earned pay-off.* 'Nevertheless', the prosecution say, 'her relations did approve.' And why should they not, since, as you told us

yourself, the information that you presented them with was not brought to you by others but was personally discovered by you?

[69] At this point are we even surprised if that fictitious box has given rise to a highly indecent story?* With a woman like that, anything is possible. Everyone has heard the story and talked about it. For some time now, gentlemen, you have been aware of what I would like—or rather would prefer not—to say. But even if what I am referring to did take place, then it is quite certain that Caelius, at least, was not responsible for it (for what did it have to do with him?): it was no doubt the work of some young man whose sense of humour was more highly developed than his sense of propriety. But if the tale is an invention, it is of course quite improper—but also quite funny! And certainly people would never have spoken of it and believed it as true were it not for the fact that every story involving a pennyworth of scandal* seems to square perfectly with that woman's reputation.

[70] My defence is over, members of the jury, and I have come to the end. You will now be able to appreciate the importance of the decision you have to make and the seriousness of the case before you. You are investigating a charge of violence. The law concerned is one that has to do with the dominion, the sovereignty, the condition of our country, and the safety of us all, the law which Quintus Catulus carried at a time of armed civil strife and almost desperate national crisis, and the law which, after those fires which blazed during my consulship had been brought under control, extinguished the smoking embers of the conspiracy.* And now it is under this same law that demands are made for the young life of Caelius, not because the national interest requires his punishment, but to gratify the whim of a licentious woman!

[71] In this context the prosecution also cite the conviction of Marcus Camurtius and Gaius Caesernius.* How stupid of them! Or should I call it not stupidity but bare-faced cheek? Do you really have the nerve to come from that woman and mention the names of those men? Do you have the nerve to revive the memory of so shocking an outrage—a memory that had not been not wholly effaced, I admit, but one that had at least faded with time? For what was the charge and what the offence for which those men were condemned? Surely it was because they avenged that woman's spite and resentment by committing an unspeakable sexual attack on Vettius? So was

the trial of Camurtius and Caesernius brought up again just so that Vettius' name could be mentioned and that veteran tale about the coppers be re-told? Although these two men were certainly not liable under the violence law, the crime in which they were implicated was so shocking that, whatever law they were charged under, they could hardly have extricated themselves from its meshes.

[72] But returning to Marcus Caelius, why has he been summoned before this court? No charge appropriate to this court has been brought against him, nor indeed any charge that is outside the scope of the law but nevertheless within the range of your own just censure.* His early years were devoted to training, and to those studies which prepare us for work such as this in the courts, for public service, and for honour, glory, and position. He also made friends with older men* whose qualities of hard work and self-restraint he was very anxious to imitate, and this, together with the pursuits he shared with his contemporaries, showed him to be following the same course of renown as the best and most high-ranking of our citizens. [73] When he had grown a little older and more mature, he went out to Africa on the staff of the governor Quintus Pompeius,* a highly moral man, and a man who performs all his duties with the greatest conscientiousness. Africa was a province in which Caelius' father had business interests and property, and Caelius himself acquired some experience of provincial government there at an age which our ancestors rightly considered suitable. When he left the province he was very highly regarded by Pompeius, as you will hear from Pompeius' own testimony.

It was now Caelius' wish to undertake some spectacular prosecution, so that his hard work should receive its due recognition from the Roman people; and in doing this he was following the long-established custom and precedent set by those young men who afterwards went on to become the most distinguished and illustrious citizens in the state. [74] I should have preferred it, in fact, if his thirst for glory had taken him in some other direction; but it is no use complaining about that now. He prosecuted my colleague Gaius Antonius, whose misfortune it was that the memory of a signal service to our country proved of no avail to him, while speculation about an intended crime did him harm.* From that point on, Caelius never yielded to any of his contemporaries in his attendance in the forum, in his dedication to court cases and the defence of his friends, and in the strength of his influence over those with whom he was connected. All the benefits that men are unable to obtain unless they are alert, sober, and hard-working were obtained by Caelius as a result of his industry and application.

[75] At this turning-point in his life (I am going to trust to your sympathy and wisdom, gentlemen, and keep nothing from you), his youthful reputation did briefly come a cropper. This was the result of his recent acquaintance with that woman, the unfortunate proximity of their houses, and his unfamiliarity with those forms of pleasure which, when they have long been bottled up and have been repressed and restrained during one's early years, are sometimes apt to burst out and pour forth all of a sudden. But from this way of life—or rather, I should say, from this chatter (since the reality was nothing like as bad as people said)—anyway, from this, whatever it was, he emerged unscathed and completely broke free and escaped. And today he is so far removed from the disgrace of being associated with that woman that he is actually having to defend himself against her enmity and hatred!

[76] To put a stop to the gossip about idleness and pleasure that had arisen in the mean time—and he did this against my wishes, by Hercules, and against my strong opposition, but still he did it—he prosecuted a friend of mine* for electoral malpractice. My friend was acquitted, but Caelius is now returning to the attack and prosecuting him again; he is not listening to any of us, and is showing himself more violent than I could have wished. But I am not considering his wisdom, a quality not to be expected in a man of his age: it is his impetuous spirit, his thirst for success, and his burning desire for glory that I am speaking of. In men of our age, such passions are best kept in their place, but in young men, as in plants, they give an indication of what that virtue will become when it is ripe, and how great the fruits of industry will one day be. It has always been the case that highly talented young men have had to be reined back from glory rather than spurred on towards it; at that age, if their brilliant ability bursts into flower, it is not so much grafting as cutting back that is required. [77] So if anyone feels that Caelius' energy, spirit, and persistence in taking up and pursuing hostilities has gone too far, or if even such trivial details as the shade of purple he wears, the following he attracts, and the brilliance and sparkle he displays have offended anyone, then let me assure you that in due course all these

traits will have subsided, and age, experience, and time will have mellowed them all.

I ask you, then, members of the jury, to preserve for our country a citizen of sound education, sound principles, and sound loyalties. I promise you this and I make this pledge to our country that if I myself have served the country adequately, Caelius will never deviate from my own political standpoint. This I feel able to promise partly because of the friendship that exists between the two of us, but also because Caelius has already bound himself personally by the strongest guarantees. [78] For it is impossible that a man who has prosecuted a senator of consular rank,* alleging that he had done damage to our country, should himself turn out to be an unruly citizen of our country; and it is equally impossible that a man who will not accept the acquittal even of someone already acquitted of bribery* should himself go unpunished were he ever to commit that crime. So, gentlemen, our country has received from Marcus Caelius two prosecutions, to serve either as hostages against dangerous behaviour or as pledges of his good intentions.

This, gentlemen, is a city in which only a few days ago Sextus Cloelius* was acquitted—a man whom for two years now you have observed as either a participant in civil discord or else its originator, a man without money, without credit, without hope, without home, and without resources, whose lips, tongue, hands, and entire way of life are defiled, a man who personally set fire to a sacred temple,* to the census of the Roman people, and to the public records, who knocked down the monument of Catulus, demolished my own house, and set fire to that of my brother,* and who on the Palatine, in full view of the whole of Rome, incited slaves to commit a massacre and to burn down the city. In this same city I therefore beg and beseech you not to allow Cloelius to be acquitted through a woman's influence while at the same time allowing Marcus Caelius to be sacrificed to her lust, nor to let it be said that this same woman, together with her brother and husband,* has succeeded both in rescuing a depraved brigand and in crushing a young man of the very highest sense of honour.

[79] But when you have set the picture of this young man in front of you, place before your eyes also the picture of his old and unhappy father here; he totally depends on this his only son, he places all his hopes on him, and he is afraid for him alone. This old man is a

suppliant before your compassion, a slave before your power, and a
beggar not so much before your feet as before your instincts and your
sensibilities. Recall the memories you have of your parents or the
delight you take in your children and raise this man up, so that in
assuaging another person's grief you may indulge your own filial
duty or else your own fatherly love. Do not desire, gentlemen, that
this old man, who is already in his declining years, should meet his
end prematurely from a wound dealt not by his own fate but by
yourselves! Do not strike down, as by some sudden storm or tornado,
this young man who is now in the first flower of his prime and whose
excellent qualities have already taken root! [80] Save the son for the
father, the father for the son! Never let it be thought that you have
scorned an old man whose hopes are now almost at an end, or that
you have not only failed to help but have actually cast down and
ruined a young man with the brightest prospects! If you restore
Caelius to me, to his family, and to the country, you will have a man
who is dedicated, devoted, and bound to you and your children; and
from all his exertions and labours, it is you in particular, gentlemen,
who shall reap the abundant and lasting fruits.

PRO MILONE
('FOR MILO')

DATE: 7 April 52 BC (trial held on 4–7 April)
DEFENDANT: Titus Annius Milo
LAW: *lex Pompeia de vi* (Pompeian law concerning violence)
CHARGE: murder of Publius Clodius Pulcher
PROSECUTORS: Appius Claudius Pulcher, Marcus Antonius, Publius Valerius Nepos
DEFENCE ADVOCATE: Marcus Tullius Cicero
PRESIDING MAGISTRATE: Lucius Domitius Ahenobarbus
VERDICT: conviction (by a vote of 38 to 13)

In *Pro Caelio* (56 BC) we witnessed one incident in the long-running feud between Cicero and Publius Clodius Pulcher, the man who had exiled him. That feud continued until 52 BC, when Clodius was unexpectedly murdered by another of his enemies, Cicero's friend Titus Annius Milo, at a chance encounter on the Appian Way outside Rome. In the trial which followed, Cicero defended Milo and, unusually, lost; Milo went into exile. Despite this failure, subsequent events persuaded Cicero that he had won a moral victory. He therefore wrote and published an improved (and anachronistic) version of the speech he had given: this is our *Pro Milone*, Cicero's last surviving forensic speech. It is a magnificent rhetorical set piece, and has usually been considered his masterpiece.

What makes the speech of particular interest, however, is the survival of what we should dearly like to have for all of Cicero's forensic speeches, an independent account of the facts of the case. This is contained in the commentary by the first-century AD scholar Quintus Asconius Pedianus (the narrative parts of which are translated below). Asconius lived probably from AD 3 to 88, and wrote under Nero (AD 54–68). He produced various works. We know of a book on Virgil, a biography of Sallust, an essay on old people—and commentaries on a number of speeches of Cicero (how many is not known). These commentaries were written for the education of his two sons, to prepare them for a senatorial career; presumably he was then persuaded to publish them. Five of the commentaries survive: on *In Pisonem*, *Pro Scauro*, and *Pro Milone* (extant speeches), and on *Pro Cornelio* and *In toga candida* (lost speeches—although Asconius' quotations restore them to us in part). His commentary on *Pro Milone* explains the political background, the precise facts of the case, what happened at the trial, and what the result was, while also providing information as to how the speech as later published by Cicero relates to what Cicero said on the day. From Asconius' account we can appreciate just how untruthful and misleading Cicero's speech is. If we had similarly revealing commentaries on his other speeches, we might well view Cicero in an entirely different light. But we cannot know.

Like Lucius Licinius Murena, Milo came from Lanuvium in Latium. He seems to have been an opponent of Clodius from at least 57, the year in which he held the tribunate. On 23 January that year, Clodius used a force of gladiators to block a move to recall Cicero from exile (Clodius as tribune the previous year had brought about his exile on the grounds of Cicero's illegal execution of the Catilinarian conspirators when consul in 63). Milo arrested Clodius' gladiators, was attacked by Clodius' gangs, attempted to prosecute Clodius for violence and then, after failing in this, recruited gangs of his own, probably with the encouragement of Cicero's friends. From this point on, Clodius' and Milo's gangs regularly clashed with each other on the streets of Rome, and these battles continued after Cicero's triumphant return on 4 September. Milo brought a further prosecution for violence against Clodius at the end of the year; but Clodius managed to escape by being elected aedile for 56 (magistrates were immune from prosecution while holding a senior public office).

In 56 Clodius in his turn attempted to prosecute Milo (who was no longer tribune and therefore open to prosecution). Milo received support from Pompey and Cicero; eventually the trial was broken up with violence and was not resumed. From this point on we find that Milo and Cicero are close political allies. Cicero defended another of the tribunes of 57, Publius Sestius, on a charge of violence, and used the occasion to issue a rallying-call to all patriots, men such as Sestius and Milo, to defend the state, by whatever means necessary, from traitors such as Clodius. Pompey also helped with the defence, and Sestius was unanimously acquitted. Shortly after this Milo provided Cicero with a guard for his house: Clodius had demolished it during Cicero's exile, and had been using his gangs to attack the workmen who were now rebuilding it.

In April 56 the 'conference at Luca' took place, a renewal of the alliance between the three dominant political figures of the age, Pompey, Caesar, and Crassus. This resulted in a political re-alignment at Rome. Clodius became reconciled with Pompey—but not, however, with Milo or Cicero. The vendetta between Milo and Clodius therefore continued. Milo was praetor in 55, but we know nothing about his tenure of the office. In 54 there is evidence that Milo and Pompey were drifting apart; and in 53 Milo and Clodius were both standing for high office, Milo for the consulship and Clodius for the praetorship. Cicero was strongly supporting Milo's campaign: if Milo became consul, he would be in a position to control Clodius as praetor. Every attempt to hold the elections, however, was frustrated by violence, and 52 therefore opened with no curule magistrates in place. Matters came to a head at around 1.30 p.m. on 18 January 52, when Clodius was murdered by Milo's gang near Bovillae, 12 miles south of Rome on the Appian Way.

Asconius relates what happened (Cicero's version is greatly distorted). On the day of the murder, Milo left Rome and set off in a coach down the Appian Way towards Lanuvium, where he was due to install a priest the next day. His wife was travelling with him, and he also had a bodyguard of more than 300 armed slaves, including a number of gladiators. When he had passed Bovillae, he met Clodius coming the other way, returning to Rome from Aricia, where he had been addressing the town council. Clodius was on horseback and had a much smaller bodyguard, a mere twenty-six armed slaves (Asc. 34 C). Once the parties had passed each other, Clodius looked back and happened to catch the attention of one of Milo's gladiators, who threw a spear at him and wounded him in the shoulder. A full-scale fight then broke out in which Clodius' slaves were all either killed or seriously wounded. Clodius himself was carried into a nearby inn. Asconius explicitly states (41 C) that the incident had arisen by chance. However, when Milo heard that Clodius was wounded, he decided that it would be safer to kill him than to leave him alive; so he had him taken out of the inn, killed, and left lying in the road. All this was done under the direction of Milo's gang-leader, Marcus Saufeius.

The events which followed are also related by Asconius. Clodius' body was discovered by a senator, Sextus Teidius, who had it conveyed to Rome. It arrived there at dusk (4.30 p.m.), was taken to Clodius' house, and was displayed to the crowd by his widow Fulvia. Next day it was carried into the forum at the suggestion of two Clodian tribunes, Titus Munatius Plancus Bursa and Quintus Pompeius Rufus, who held a public meeting at which they stirred up popular feeling against Milo. Then Clodius' gang-leader Sextus Cloelius persuaded the people to carry the body into the senate-house and cremate it there. This they did, using the senate-house furniture and records to make a pyre, and burning down the senate-house in the process. Asconius says that the burning of the senate-house caused far greater indignation among the general public than the murder of Clodius. Encouraged by this, Milo returned to Rome and resumed his campaign for the consulship.

A few days later, a public meeting was held by another tribune, but a supporter of Milo, Marcus Caelius Rufus (the Caelius defended by Cicero in 56). Caelius and Milo both claimed that the encounter on the Appian Way had not arisen by chance: Clodius had set a trap for Milo, who had then killed him in self-defence. This false account was to form the basis of

Cicero's defence of Milo when Milo was eventually brought to trial. The grounds for this version are given by Asconius (54 C): three days before the incident, a senator named Marcus Favonius had reported to Marcus Porcius Cato that Clodius had said that Milo would be dead within three days. The story is referred to twice in the course of our speech (§§ 26, 44).

During January, because of the lack of consuls, a series of *interreges* held office for five days each. Probably in early February the emergency decree (*senatus consultum ultimum*) was passed, together with a further decree directing Pompey as proconsul to levy troops. Soon afterwards the Clodians began legal proceedings against Milo. Two sons of Clodius' brother Gaius Claudius Pulcher, both named Appius Claudius Pulcher, made a preliminary summons of Milo's slaves. The defence was undertaken by Quintus Hortensius Hortalus, Cicero, Cato, and other prominent conservatives. The line they took was that Milo's slaves could not be summoned since they were no longer slaves: Milo had freed them in gratitude for saving his life! This reflects the version of events put about by Caelius and Milo, that Clodius had set a trap for Milo, but that Milo's spirited resistance had allowed him to escape with his life. In addition, Caelius summoned the slaves of Clodius and of two other opponents; proceedings continued into the intercalary month of twenty-seven days which was added this year between February and March (the Julian calendar had not yet been adopted).

About thirty days after the murder, one of Milo's rivals for the consulship, Quintus Metellus Scipio, addressed the senate with a version unfavourable to Milo (34–5 C). This is similar to Asconius' (presumably truthful) narrative, but with one important difference: Scipio claimed that Milo had set a trap for Clodius on his return from Aricia. Both sides therefore agreed, contrary to fact, that a trap had been set, but they disagreed as to which of the parties was the plotter and which the victim.

Meanwhile, there was pressure in Rome to appoint Pompey dictator to restore order. But the office of dictator had unpleasant associations, evoking memories of Sulla and the proscriptions, and so the senate instead made Pompey sole consul. This happened on the twenty-fourth day of the intercalary month. Three days later Pompey proposed two new laws under which those responsible for the recent acts of lawlessness could be tried, a violence law relating specifically to the incident on the Appian Way and subsequent events, and a law on electoral malpractice. These laws laid down special procedures designed to reduce the possibility of corruption, and imposed heavier penalties. Witnesses were to be produced first (in contrast to the normal practice), and all speeches were then to take place within a single day, two hours being allowed for the prosecution and three for the defence. Character references were to be disallowed. Eighty-one jurors would sit on the case, but just before the vote prosecution and defence would each reject fifteen, leaving a total of fifty-one to decide the verdict. These new laws were vigorously resisted by Caelius on the grounds that they represented a personal attack on Milo (there already existed suitable laws under which Milo could be tried); but ultimately they were passed, on 26 March.

Legal proceedings against Milo began immediately, instituted by Clodius' nephews, Appius Claudius Pulcher and his brother of the same name. Three actions were lodged at this point, a fourth being added later (Asc. 38 C, 54 C). First, Milo was accused under Pompey's violence law (*lex Pompeia de vi*) of the murder of Clodius. Secondly, he was accused under Pompey's law on electoral malpractice (*lex Pompeia de ambitu*) of bribery in his campaign for the consulship. Thirdly, he was accused under the law on illegal association (*lex Licinia de sodaliciis*) of malpractice in his campaign. If Milo was found guilty on any one charge, he would retire into exile and lose the subsequent cases by default.

So Milo's trial finally went ahead, under the *lex Pompeia de vi*, on 4–7 April. The evidence was taken on the first three days, and the speeches given on the fourth day. On the first day, a prosecution witness, Gaius Causinius Schola, gave evidence designed to whip up feeling against Milo (Asc. 40 C). Marcus Claudius Marcellus (working with Cicero for the defence) tried to cross-examine him, but was shouted down by the Clodians. Marcellus and Milo therefore asked that an armed guard attend the remainder of the trial (cf. §§ 1–3). On the second and third days evidence was taken from various parties such as the inhabitants of Bovillae, some virgins (probably priestesses) from Alba, and members of Clodius' family (the view that Cato gave evidence is in my opinion mistaken; Marcus Favonius may have done).

The speeches were given on the fourth day, and all the shops in the city were closed. Troops were posted in the forum, and Pompey waited in front of the treasury (in the north-west corner of the forum) with a military guard. The prosecution—the elder Appius Claudius Pulcher, the young Mark Antony (the future triumvir), and Publius Valerius Nepos— spoke first, within the two hours allotted to them. They claimed that the incident on the Appian Way had not arisen by chance: Milo had deliberately set out to kill Clodius (as claimed earlier by Scipio). For the defence, Cicero alone spoke, within his three hours. According to Asconius (41 C), some people thought that the best line of defence would be that Clodius' murder was justified by the public interest, and Marcus Junius Brutus afterwards wrote up and circulated a hypothetical speech for Milo on these lines (cf. Quint. *Inst.* 3.6.93, 10.1.23, 10.5.20). Cicero, however, disagreed: if Clodius' removal had been in the public interest, then prosecution in the courts, not murder, would have been the proper response. Instead, therefore, he based his entire speech (Asc. 41 C) on the argument that Clodius had set a trap for Milo, and had then been killed by him in self-defence; this was the line which Caelius and Milo had been promoting since within a few days of the murder. This original trial speech is not the same as the speech which has come down to us. A pirate version of the trial speech was still surviving in Asconius' day (Asc. 42 C), and indeed for some centuries afterwards, but it has long since been lost.

The ancient sources disagree over how well Cicero performed on the day. Asconius (41–2 C) says that his speech was received with shouting from the Clodians, and that this made him speak 'without his customary resolution'. Plutarch and Dio (Greek writers of the first/second and third centuries AD respectively) go further. According to Plutarch (*Cic.* 35), Milo arranged for Cicero to be taken early to the court in a litter, so that he would not be intimidated by the sight of the soldiers. However, when he emerged from the litter and saw the soldiers, 'he was utterly confused and hardly began his speech—his body shook and his voice choked', while Milo by contrast showed no trace of fear. Dio (40.54.2) tells a similar tale. When Cicero saw the soldiers he 'was stunned and filled with alarm, and so said nothing of what he had prepared, but after uttering with difficulty a few words that died on his lips, was glad to retire'. Both these accounts exaggerate Cicero's discomfiture. Plutarch is making a contrast with Milo's courage, and Dio is concerned throughout to portray Cicero in the worst possible light. The statement of both writers that Cicero uttered just a few words cannot be accepted in view of Asconius' evidence that a version of the trial speech was still surviving in his day. But it is no doubt true that Cicero's performance fell short of his usual standards, as Asconius says.

After the speeches were concluded, each side rejected fifteen jurors, and Milo was convicted by a vote of thirty-eight to thirteen. The jury realized that neither Milo nor Clodius had plotted to kill the other; but they found that after Clodius had been wounded he was then killed on Milo's orders. Milo went into exile at Massilia (Marseilles) soon afterwards, and his property was confiscated and sold.

The remaining actions against Milo now went ahead, and in each one he was convicted in his absence. On 8 April he was convicted under Pompey's law on electoral malpractice (*lex Pompeia de ambitu*) of bribery in his campaign for the consulship. Then on 11 April he was convicted of malpractice under the law on illegal association (*lex Licinia de sodaliciis*); and on the same day he was convicted of the murder of Clodius under the ordinary violence law, the *lex Plautia de vi* (to which Pompey's law had provided an alternative, but which it had not replaced).

This was not, however, the end of the story: in the courts the battle
between Milo's and Clodius' supporters continued unabated. Milo's
gang-leader Marcus Saufeius, who had supervised the attack on the inn
and Clodius' actual murder, was prosecuted under the *lex Pompeia de vi*.
Cicero and Caelius defended him, and he was acquitted by one vote
(twenty-six votes to twenty-five). He was then charged again, this time
under the *lex Plautia*; Cicero defended him, and he was acquitted by a
larger majority (thirty-two votes to nineteen). On the other hand, Clodius'
gang-leader Sextus Cloelius was prosecuted under the *lex Pompeia* for
taking Clodius' body into the senate-house, and was convicted by a near-
unanimous verdict (forty-six votes to five). A number of others were also
convicted, the majority of them Clodians (Asc. 56 C). Clearly public opinion, previously hostile to Milo, had turned around. Milo had been punished enough: now the Clodians had to pay for their part in the breakdown
of law and order.

On 10 December the new tribunes took office: their predecessors
became private citizens once again, and so were open to prosecution.
First, Quintus Pompeius Rufus was prosecuted by Caelius under the *lex
Pompeia de vi* for the burning of the senate-house; he was convicted and
went into exile. This gave Cicero considerable personal satisfaction
because Pompeius had been claiming that Cicero was the moving force
behind Clodius' murder (§ 47). Next, Titus Munatius Plancus Bursa was
prosecuted by Cicero under the *lex Pompeia*, also for the burning of the
senate-house (both these trials probably took place in January 51). Pompey, whose sympathies had been with the Clodians throughout, tried to
use the force of his authority to save him, by submitting a character
reference in his favour. But under the *lex Pompeia*, of course, such
character references were forbidden, and Cato, who was a juror, ostentatiously blocked his ears so that he would not hear the offending
testimonial (naturally, Cato was among the jurors rejected by the defence
before the vote was taken). Pompey's interference seems to have counted
against Plancus: he was convicted unanimously (*Phil.* 6.10), and went
into exile.

Plancus' conviction delighted Cicero. In a letter to his friend Marcus
Marius (*Fam.* 7.2.2–3), he wrote:

> I ask you to believe that this trial gave me more satisfaction than the
> death of my enemy [Clodius]. To begin with, I prefer to get my revenge
> in a court of law than at swordpoint. Secondly, I prefer my friend [Milo]
> to come out of it with credit than with ruin. I was especially pleased at
> the display of good-will towards me on the part of the honest men in
> the face of an astonishing amount of pressure from a very grand and

powerful personage [Pompey]. Lastly, and this may seem hard to credit, I detested this fellow far more than Clodius himself. . . . I tell you to rejoice and be glad. It is a great victory. No braver Romans ever lived than those jurymen who dared to find him guilty in spite of all the power of the very personage who had empanelled them [Pompey]. They would never have done that if they had not felt my grievance as their own. (tr. D. R. Shackleton Bailey)

How, then, does the speech which we have fit into this sequence of events? We have seen that there were two speeches *Pro Milone*, the original trial speech and the speech which has come down to us. Asconius (42 C) distinguishes between the two, and says that a version of the trial speech was still surviving in his day, having been 'taken down' (*excepta*). Plutarch and Dio, as we have seen, were unaware of the existence of the trial speech. It was known to Quintilian (second half of the first century AD), however. At one place (*Inst.* 4.3.17) he states that he knows the original speech, and at another (*Inst.* 9.2.54) he quotes a passage from a defence of Milo by Cicero that does not occur in our *Pro Milone*; this could be from the trial speech, or from a different speech, *De aere alieno Milonis* ('On Milo's debts'). The trial speech is also referred to by the Bobbio scholiast on *Pro Milone* (fourth/fifth century AD). At one place (112 Stangl) he says of it: 'in it you can see that everything is broken, unpolished, and rough, and filled with the utmost terror', and at another (173 Stangl) he quotes a passage which connects with the passage quoted by Quintilian. It is clear, then, that the trial speech survived to Quintilian's time and beyond, and we may even have two passages from it. It was no doubt a pirate version, 'taken down' and circulated without Cicero's approval. It may have been broken, unpolished, and rough because that is how Cicero's delivery was, or, more probably perhaps, because it was hurriedly taken down in court and not, like Cicero's other speeches, carefully written up afterwards by Cicero himself.

The speech which has come down to us, on the other hand, was written by Cicero at a later date, and at his leisure (Dio 40.54.2). Dio has a charming anecdote to tell about it (40.54.3). When Cicero had finished the speech which has come down to us, he sent a copy of it to Milo in exile; and Milo wrote back saying that it was lucky for him that the speech had not been made in that form in court, because if any defence of that kind had been made he would not now be enjoying the excellent mullets of Massilia. (Dio goes on to spoil the story by taking Milo's remark, perversely, as a joke at Cicero's expense. It is of course a gracious compliment, implying both that Milo has a high opinion of Cicero's oratorical ability and that he does not mind at all that Cicero has failed to secure his acquittal (after all, Cicero had done the best he could for him under the circumstances; cf. § 100).)

So what were the differences between the trial speech and our *Pro Milone*? Some scholars have thought that the difference was simply a matter of style, a case of a little touching-up, a bit of polishing here and there. This clearly cannot be correct, however, because we know from Dio that Milo noticed a big difference—one, he thought, which could have made the verdict go the other way. Moreover, Asconius states that Cicero's 'entire speech' (Asc. 41 C) was based on the self-defence argument, that Clodius had set a trap for Milo, and yet the last third of our speech (§§ 72–105) is based on the argument that Clodius' murder was justified by the public interest. The last third must therefore have been added later, as in all probability were §§ 67–71 (see my note on § 67). The first two-thirds of the speech (§§ 1–66), on the other hand, do correspond in content to what Asconius claims was actually said, and so may well reflect the trial speech. Perhaps in these sections the revision did simply consist of a little touching-up, although one also needs to bear in mind the passages from Quintilian and the Bobbio scholiast which Cicero may have excised when writing up the speech for publication.

Finally, when was our *Pro Milone* written? A. M. Stone has noticed that there is a difference in Cicero's attitude to Pompey (and also to Milo's rivals for the consulship Quintus Metellus Scipio and Publius Plautius Hypsaeus) in the two parts of the speech (*Antichthon*, 14 (1980), 88–111; further points added by myself, *Historia*, 42 (1993), 502–4). In §§ 1–66 Cicero gives Pompey unqualified praise, insisting that Pompey is Milo's friend and wishes the jury to acquit him. But from § 67 to the end of the speech he treats him with barely concealed hostility. He complains that Pompey's suspicions regarding Milo are unjustified (§§ 67–8); he warns him that he will come to regret his desertion of Milo (§ 69); he makes an ironic hint that Pompey lacks expertise in constitutional and political matters (§ 70); he implies that Pompey failed to stand up to Clodius (§ 73); he declares that Milo has done more for his country than any other man in history, including the most distinguished contemporary generals (§ 77); he suggests that Pompey is being hypocritical in setting up a court to try Milo when he must surely have welcomed Clodius' death (§ 79); and he implies that Pompey owed allegiance to Clodius and was therefore unprepared to act in the public interest (§ 88). These passages confirm what we already knew from Asconius, that the last third of the speech is an anachronistic addition. The flattering view of Pompey found in the first two-thirds of the speech reflects the stance taken by Cicero at Milo's actual trial, when there was still a chance that Milo might be acquitted. The hostile view of Pompey in the last third, on the other hand, reflects Cicero's bitterness towards Pompey after Milo had been convicted.

It looks very much as if the speech was revised and published at a time when public opinion had turned against Pompey. The revision must have taken place at some point after Milo's trial, and after he had become settled in Massilia, but before May 51, when Cicero left Italy on good terms with Pompey and went out to govern Cilicia. Within this period it will have happened at a time when Milo's reputation had recovered sufficiently for the public interest defence to have force, and when Pompey had become discredited through his continuing association with the Clodians. According to Stone, the most suitable context is the trial of Plancus in (probably) January 51: this was the occasion when Pompey, in a vain attempt to save a Clodian ex-tribune whom Cicero himself was prosecuting, broke his own law by submitting a character reference. At § 70, as we have seen, Cicero makes a hint that Pompey lacks expertise in constitutional and political matters. If this is a reference to Pompey's action at the trial of Plancus, as I believe it is (see my first note on § 70), then we have confirmation of Stone's hypothesis. The hypothesis is further supported by the letter of Cicero to Marius quoted earlier (*Fam.* 7.2.2–3). In the letter, Cicero regards himself as having defeated Pompey and vindicated Milo by having secured a unanimous verdict against Plancus. The triumphalism of the letter, and its bitterness towards Pompey, matches exactly the tone of defiance in the last third of *Pro Milone*. Cicero believed that by securing Plancus' conviction he had won a moral victory, and it is reasonable to infer that it was this which prompted him to write up and publish a new, bolder defence of Milo. This new *Pro Milone* would expunge the memory of Cicero's earlier oratorical failure (he may have hoped to drive the pirate version out of circulation), and proclaim the ultimate success of his and Milo's cause.

So much, then, for the status and historical context of the published speech. Milo remained in Massilia until the Civil War. Although now an enemy of Pompey's, he was also opposed to Caesar, and when Caesar arrived in Rome in 49 all the exiles were recalled except him. Then in 48 Milo went to Campania to join his friend Caelius, taking with him such gladiators as he still possessed; together they hoped to raise southern Italy in revolt against Caesar. But the attempt failed, and at Compsa Milo met his end, killed by a stone thrown from the city walls. Caelius was killed by Caesar's troops shortly afterwards.

Asconius' account of Clodius' murder, Milo's trial, and the background to these events is given below (the reader should read this before proceeding to Cicero's speech). This account is contained in the narrative sections

which introduce and conclude Asconius' detailed commentary on various
passages in the speech. For the commentary itself, not given here, the
reader is referred to the translation by S. Squires, *Asconius: Commentaries
on Five Speeches of Cicero* (Bristol and Wauconda, Ill., 1990). Asconius'
commentary notes are cited where necessary in my explanatory notes on
the speech. (Readers who consult the Latin should note that the mistrans-
lation of several dates by Squires and other translators arises out of the
fact that in 52 BC some of the months had an abnormal number of days.)

Passages in Asconius are usually referred to by the page number in A.
C. Clark's Oxford Classical Text (Oxford, 1907). Thus 'Asc. 30 C' denotes
page 30 in Clark's Latin text ('C' standing for 'Clark').

Asconius' account is as follows.

[30 C]   ON *PRO MILONE*

He gave this speech on 7 April in the third consulship of Gnaeus
Pompeius. While the trial was in progress, Gnaeus Pompeius had
posted troops in the forum and all the temples surrounding it, a fact
which emerges not only from the speech and from histories of the
period, but also from the book *On the Best Type of Orator*, which
goes under Cicero's name.

THE ARGUMENT

Titus Annius Milo, Publius Plautius Hypsaeus, and Quintus Metellus Scipio were standing for the consulship, and not only did they
use large-scale bribery without the slightest concealment but they
also surrounded themselves with gangs of armed men. Milo and
Clodius were deadly enemies, since Milo was a close friend of Cicero
and as tribune of the plebs had worked hard for his recall, while
Publius Clodius remained implacably opposed to Cicero after his
restoration and for this reason was strongly supporting Hypsaeus
and Scipio against Milo. Milo and Clodius with their gangs fought
continual battles with each other at Rome: each was as ruthless as the
other, though Milo stood for the better sort of people. Besides, in the
same year as Milo was standing for the consulship, Clodius was
standing for the praetorship, and he was well aware that his praetorship would be powerless if Milo were consul at the same time.

The consular elections had been long drawn out and could not be
completed because of this desperate feuding among the candidates.
[31 C] Hence in the month of January there were no consuls or

praetors, and the day of the election was continually put off by the same means as before. Milo wanted the elections completed as soon as possible, believing that he enjoyed the support both of the respectable classes, because of his opposition to Clodius, and of the people, because of his lavish bribery and his enormous expenditure on theatrical performances and gladiatorial games (on which, Cicero tells us, he used up three inheritances). His fellow candidates, on the other hand, wanted the elections put off, and so Pompeius (who was Scipio's son-in-law) and the tribune of the plebs Titus Munatius had refused to allow a motion to be put before the senate for a calling-together of patricians to nominate an *interrex* (the custom was that an *interrex* should be nominated).

On 18 January (I think that the *Proceedings of the Senate* and *Pro Milone* itself, which agrees with it, should be followed, rather than Fenestella, who says 17 January) Milo set out for Lanuvium (his home town, of which he was at that time dictator) in order to install a priest on the following day. At around 1.30 p.m., a little beyond Bovillae (near the place where there is a shrine of the Good Goddess), he came across Clodius, who was returning from Aricia, where he had been addressing the town council. Clodius was on horseback and was accompanied, as was normal for travellers in those days, by about thirty slaves, unencumbered and armed with swords. He also had three companions with him, a Roman equestrian, Gaius Causinius Schola, and two well-known plebeians, Publius Pomponius and Gaius Clodius. Milo was travelling in a coach with his wife Fausta, the daughter of Lucius Sulla the dictator, and his friend Marcus Fufius. Following them [32 C] was a large column of slaves and also some gladiators, including two well-known ones, Eudamus and Birria. These were moving slowly at the rear of the column, and started an altercation with Publius Clodius' slaves. As Clodius looked back menacingly at the disturbance, Birria pierced his shoulder with a spear. Then a fight began, and more of Milo's men ran up. The wounded Clodius, meanwhile, was carried into a nearby inn in the territory of Bovillae.

When Milo found out that Clodius had been wounded, he realized that it would be dangerous for him if Clodius were to remain alive, whereas his death would be a huge relief to him, even if he would then have to face punishment as a result. He therefore gave orders for him to be turfed out of the inn. (The leader of Milo's slaves was

Marcus Saufeius.) So Clodius was brought out from hiding and finished off with many wounds. His body was left lying in the road, because Clodius' slaves were all either dead or seriously wounded and in hiding. It was then picked up by a senator, Sextus Teidius, who happened to be returning to Rome from the country: he had it taken on to Rome in his litter, while he himself went back to the place from which he had come. Clodius' body reached Rome at 4.30 p.m. It was placed in the atrium of his house, and was surrounded by a very large crowd of the lowest classes and slaves, weeping profusely. Clodius' wife Fulvia heightened the sense of anger at the deed by displaying his wounds and giving her grief full rein.

At dawn the next day an even larger crowd gathered, but of the same sort of people, although several men of distinction were observed. Clodius' house, which he had bought from Marcus Scaurus some months earlier, was on the Palatine. Here the tribunes of the plebs Titus Munatius Plancus (brother of the orator Lucius Plancus) and Quintus Pompeius Rufus (grandson of Sulla the dictator through his daughter) [33 C] came rushing. At their instigation the ignorant mob carried the naked and trampled body down to the forum—positioned as it had been on the couch, so that the wounds would be clearly visible—and placed it on the rostra. There Plancus and Pompeius, who were supporting Milo's rivals, held a public meeting and stirred up anger against Milo. Then the people, led by the scribe Sextus Cloelius, carried Publius Clodius' body into the senate-house and cremated it using the benches, platforms, tables, and scribes' notebooks. This set fire to the senate-house itself, and the Basilica Porcia which adjoined it was also burnt. The same crowd of Clodians also made an attack on the houses of the *interrex* Marcus Lepidus (who had been appointed to a curule magistracy) and Milo (who was away), but it was driven off with arrows. Then they got hold of the rods of office from the grove of Libitina and took them to the houses of Scipio and Hypsaeus, then to Gnaeus Pompeius' property in the suburbs, calling on him as consul one moment and as dictator the next.

The burning of the senate-house caused far greater indignation among the general public than the killing of Clodius. Milo was assumed to have gone into voluntary exile but, encouraged by the unpopularity of his opponents, he had returned to Rome on the night on which the senate-house was burnt. Undeterred, he carried on with his campaign for the consulship, after openly giving 1,000 *asses* to each voter by tribe. A few days later the tribune of the plebs Marcus Caelius accorded him a public meeting, and himself pleaded his cause before the people. Both men claimed that Clodius had set a trap for Milo.

Meanwhile one *interrex* after another was appointed, since the consular elections [34 C] could not be held because of the candidates' continuing disruption and their continuing use of armed gangs. So first of all a decree of the senate was passed that the *interrex*, tribunes of the plebs, and Gnaeus Pompeius (who as proconsul remained outside the city) should 'take heed that the state should come to no harm', and that Pompeius should levy troops throughout Italy. He raised a force very rapidly, and then two young men, both named Appius Claudius, lodged with him summonses for the slaves of Milo, and those of his wife Fausta, to be produced. (These men were the sons of Gaius Claudius, who had been Clodius' brother, and this is why they were investigating their uncle's death as if on their father's authority.) Two Valerii, Nepos and Leo, and Lucius Herennius Balbus also lodged summonses for the same slaves of Fausta and Milo. At the same time Caelius lodged a summons for the slaves for Publius Clodius and those who were with him; he also lodged summonses for the slaves of Hypsaeus and Quintus Pompeius. The following spoke for Milo: Quintus Hortensius, Marcus Cicero, Marcus Marcellus, Marcus Calidius, Marcus Cato, and Faustus Sulla. Quintus Hortensius said just a few words to the effect that those who had been summoned as slaves were in fact free men, since after the recent act of violence Milo had freed them for the reason that they had saved his life. All this took place during the intercalary month.

About thirty days after Clodius had been killed, Quintus Metellus Scipio took issue with Quintus Caepio in the senate over Publius Clodius' murder. He said that what Milo was saying in his own defence was not true; that Clodius had set out with twenty-six slaves to address the town council of Aricia; that [35 C] after the senate had risen Milo had suddenly hurried off at 10.30 a.m. to meet him with more than three hundred armed slaves, and when he was above Bovillae had attacked him unexpectedly on the road; that Publius Clodius had received three wounds and been carried to Bovillae; that Milo had stormed the inn in which he had taken refuge; and that Clodius had been dragged out half-dead, killed on the Appian Way, and had his ring removed as he was dying. Milo had then gone to Clodius' house at Alba, knowing that his young son was there, and, finding him already taken away, had interrogated the slave Halicor by cutting off his limbs one by one, also murdering the bailiff and two other slaves. Of the slaves of Clodius who defended their master eleven had been killed, while only two of Milo's had been hurt. On the next day Milo had therefore freed twelve slaves who had shown the best service and had given 1,000 *asses* to each citizen by tribe in an attempt to silence the rumours about himself. It was claimed that Milo had sent to Gnaeus Pompeius (who was strongly supporting Hypsaeus because he had been his quaestor) and had offered to give up his campaign for the consulship should he so desire; but Pompeius had replied that it was not up to him whether anyone chose to stand or not to stand, and he would not obstruct the power of the Roman people by offering advice or opinion. Then he had apparently told Milo through Gaius Lucilius, who because of his friendship with Marcus Cicero was a friend also of Milo's, that he was not to make him unpopular by asking his advice in this matter.

Meanwhile people were increasingly saying that Gnaeus Pompeius should be made dictator, and that there was no other way of solving the the country's problems. [36 C] But the leading senators thought it would be safer if he were made consul without a colleague. The question was then debated in the senate, a decree of the senate was passed on the motion of Marcus Bibulus, and Pompeius was made consul by the *interrex* Servius Sulpicius on the twenty-fourth day of the intercalary month; he entered upon his consulship immediately.

Three days later, he put new legislation before the senate. He published two bills by decree of the senate, one concerning violence, specifically citing the incident on the Appian Way, the burning of the senate-house, and the attack on the house of the *interrex* Marcus Lepidus, and a second concerning electoral malpractice: a heavier penalty and a shorter form of procedure were prescribed. Each law laid down that witnesses were to be produced first, and that the prosecution and defence should each complete their speeches within a single day, two hours being allowed to the prosecution and three to the defence. The tribune of the plebs Marcus Caelius, an ardent supporter of Milo, tried to block these laws on the grounds that they represented a personal attack on Milo and would be the ruin of the courts. Caelius doggedly kept up his attack on the laws, and Pompeius grew so angry that he declared that, if driven to it, he would defend the state by force of arms.

Pompeius was actually afraid of Milo, or else pretended to be afraid. For the most part he stayed not at his house but at his property in the suburbs, and he kept to the upper parts of it, with a large body of troops keeping guard all the way around. Pompeius also on one occasion suddenly dismissed the senate, saying he was afraid of Milo's arrival. Then at the next meeting of the senate Publius Cornificius said that Milo had a dagger strapped to his thigh under his tunic. He asked him to bare his thigh, and Milo without hesitation lifted his tunic. Marcus Cicero then exclaimed that all the other charges alleged against Milo were of a similar character.

[37 C] After this the tribune of the plebs Titus Munatius Plancus brought Marcus Aemilius Philemon, a freedman of Marcus Lepidus and a well-known man, before a public meeting. Philemon said that he had been travelling with four free men and that they had arrived on the scene when Clodius was killed: when they raised an outcry, they were kidnapped and taken away, and were confined for two months in a country house of Milo's. This story, whether true or false, gave rise to considerable ill-feeling against Milo. In addition, the same Munatius and Pompeius, tribunes of the plebs, brought a *triumvir capitalis* onto the rostra and asked him whether he had arrested Galata, a slave of Milo's, in the act of committing murder. He replied that the slave had been discovered asleep at the inn, and had been arrested as a runaway and brought before him. They ordered the *triumvir* not to return the slave, but next day the tribune of the plebs Caelius and his colleague Manilius Cumanus stole him from the *triumvir*'s house and gave him back to Milo. Cicero makes no mention of these crimes in his speech, but even so I thought I should set them down, seeing that I had found out about them.

The tribunes of the plebs Quintus Pompeius, Gaius Sallustius, and Titus Munatius Plancus were the main people who held hostile public meetings relating to Milo, and these meetings were also unfavourable to Cicero, because he was defending Milo so vigorously. Indeed, most of the people were opposed not just to Milo but to Cicero too, as a result of his unpopular advocacy of Milo. Later, Pompeius and Sallustius fell under suspicion of having settled their differences with Milo and Cicero; but Plancus kept up his hostility, and [38 C] also stirred up the masses against Cicero. In addition he made Pompeius suspicious of Milo, shouting that Milo was preparing a force to destroy him; as a result, Pompeius constantly complained that plots were being made against him, and openly too, and he protected himself with a larger body of troops. Plancus also threatened to prosecute Cicero, something previously contemplated by Quintus Pompeius. So strong, however, was Cicero's loyalty and resolve that neither loss of popularity, nor the suspicions of Gnaeus Pompeius, nor the danger of prosecution, nor the weapons which had openly been taken up against Milo could induce him not to defend him—even though, if he had only defended him slightly less enthusiastically, he could have escaped all danger to himself and the outrage of the hostile masses, while also winning back the favour of Gnaeus Pompeius.

Pompeius' law was then carried. It contained a clause which said that a presiding magistrate should be appointed by a vote of the people from among those who had held the consulship; the election was held at once, and Lucius Domitius Ahenobarbus was appointed presiding magistrate. As for the panel of jurors for the court, Pompeius proposed men who everyone agreed were more distinguished and upright than any who had previously been proposed.

Immediately afterwards, Milo was charged under the new law by the two young Appii Claudii, the same men who had previously summoned his slaves. They also brought a charge of electoral malpractice, as did Gaius Ateius and Lucius Cornificius; and Publius Fulvius Neratus brought a charge of illegal association. [39 C] The last two charges were brought in the expectation that the violence trial would take place first and then, it was hoped, Milo would be convicted and hence be unable to appear at the later trials.

There was then an inquiry, presided over by Aulus Torquatus, to decide which of the prosecutors should bring the electoral malpractice charge. Both presiding magistrates, Torquatus and Domitius, ordered the defendant to appear on 4 April. On that day Milo presented himself at Domitius' court, and sent friends to Torquatus' court on his behalf; at the latter, Marcus Marcellus pleaded for him and secured permission for him not to answer the charge of electoral malpractice until the violence trial was concluded. At Domitius' court, on the other hand, the elder Appius lodged a summons for Milo to produce fifty-four slaves, and when he replied that the slaves

named were not in his possession, Domitius, on the advice of the
jurors, ruled that the prosecutor could select as many of Milo's slaves
as he wished. The witnesses were then summoned in accordance
with the law which, as I said earlier, prescribed that witnesses should
be heard during the three days before the trial took place, that a
record of their statements should be sealed by the jury, that the
jurors should all be given notice to appear on the fourth day, and that
balls with their names written on them should be checked in the
presence of the prosecution and the defence. Then on the next day
eighty-one jurors should be selected by lot: those chosen should take
their seats at once. The prosecution should have two hours for speaking and the defence three hours, and the verdict be declared on the
same day; but before the votes were cast the prosecution and the
defence should each reject five jurors from each of the orders, leaving a total of fifty-one to cast their votes.

[40 C] On the first day Gaius Causinius Schola appeared as a
witness against Milo. He said that he had been with Publius Clodius
when he was killed, and he magnified the horror of the deed as much
as he could. Marcus Marcellus, when he began to question him,
became so terrified by the shouting from the Clodian crowd surrounding him that, fearing for his life, he was allowed by Domitius to
take refuge on his platform. Because of this, Marcellus and Milo
himself begged Domitius for an armed guard. Gnaeus Pompeius was
waiting at this time in front of the treasury, and he too was concerned at the uproar. He therefore promised Domitius that on the
following day he would come down to the forum with a military
guard, which he did. This frightened the Clodians into allowing the
witnesses to be heard in silence for the next two days. The witnesses
were questioned by Marcus Cicero, Marcus Marcellus, and Milo
himself. Many of the inhabitants of Bovillae gave evidence about
what had taken place there—the killing of the innkeeper, the storming of the inn, and the dragging of Clodius' body out into the open.
In addition, the virgins of Alba stated that a woman they did not
know had come to them on Milo's instructions to pay a vow, because
Clodius had been killed. The last to give evidence were Sempronia,
daughter of Tuditanus and Publius Clodius' mother-in-law, and his
wife Fulvia; their tears greatly affected those who were standing
nearby. The court was adjourned at around 3.15 p.m., and then
Titus Munatius held a public meeting and urged the people to turn

up in force the next day and not allow Milo to escape, and to show their feelings and their grief to the jurors as they went to cast their votes.

On the next day, 7 April, the last day of the trial, [41 C] all the shops in the city were closed. Pompeius posted guards in the forum and at all its entrances, while he himself took up position, as he had done the day before, in front of the treasury, surrounded by a hand-picked body of troops. Then, at dawn, the jurors were selected by lot, and afterwards the whole forum was as near to silent as any forum can be. Next, before 8 a.m., the prosecutors—the elder Appius, Marcus Antonius, and Publius Valerius Nepos—began their speeches, taking up the two hours allowed by the law.

For the defence, only Marcus Cicero spoke. Certain people had thought that the charge should be defended on the grounds that Clodius' killing was in the country's interest—a line followed by Marcus Brutus in the speech which he composed for Milo and pub-lished as if he had actually delivered it. But Cicero did not agree with the view that someone whose conviction would be in the public interest could simply be killed without being convicted. So when the prosecution claimed (falsely, since the fight had come about by chance) that Milo had set a trap for Clodius, Cicero took this up and maintained that, on the contrary, Clodius had set a trap for Milo; and he based his entire speech on that assertion. In actual fact the inci-dent occurred as I have described: neither of them had planned the fighting on that day, but it had arisen by chance, starting with a brawl among the slaves and ending up with the murder. However, it was well known that each of them had often threatened the other with death, and while Milo was suspected because his entourage had been larger than that of Clodius, Clodius' entourage had been less en-cumbered and better prepared for battle than Milo's. As for Cicero, on beginning his speech he was received with shouting from the Clodians, who could not be restrained even by fear of the soldiers standing round. [42 C] This made him speak without his customary resolution. That speech of his which was taken down is still in exist-ence, but this one which we are reading at the moment is so perfectly written that it can rightly be considered his best.

[*Asconius' commentary: not translated here.*]

[53 C] When both sides had finished their speeches, the prosecu-tion and defence each rejected five senators and the same number of equestrians and *tribuni aerarii*, so that fifty-one jurors voted. Of the senators, twelve voted for conviction and six for acquittal; of the equestrians, thirteen voted for conviction and four for acquittal; and of the *tribuni aerarii*, thirteen voted for conviction and three for acquittal. It appears that the jury were well aware that Clodius had originally been wounded without Milo's knowledge, but they found that once he had been wounded, he was then killed on Milo's orders. Some people believed that Marcus Cato voted for acquittal, [54 C] since he had not concealed his opinion that the state had gained by Publius Clodius' death, and he was also supporting Milo in his campaign for the consulship and had helped with his defence. Moreover, Cicero had referred to him by name in his presence, and had appealed to him as a witness to the fact that he had heard from Marcus Favonius three days before the murder that Clodius had said that Milo would be dead within three days. But on the other hand it seemed expedient that a man so notoriously violent as Milo be removed from public life. However, no one was ever able to discover which way Cato had voted. A verdict of guilty was pronounced, largely thanks to the efforts of Appius Claudius.

On the next day Milo was prosecuted for electoral malpractice before Manlius Torquatus and convicted in his absence. In this trial, too, the prosecutor was Appius Claudius, who was given the reward prescribed by the law, but declined to accept it. His assistant prosecutors in this electoral malpractice trial were Publius Valerius Leo and Gnaeus Domitius, son of Gnaeus. A few days later Milo was also convicted of illegal association before the presiding magistrate Marcus Favonius; the prosecutor was Publius Fulvius Neratus, who was given the reward prescribed by the law. Then before the presiding magistrate Lucius Fabius he was again convicted of violence in his absence; the prosecutors were Lucius Cornificius and Quintus Patulcius. Within a very few days Milo set out for exile at Massilia. His property realized a twenty-fourth of its value because of the size of his debts.

After Milo, the first to be prosecuted under the same law of Pompeius' was [55 C] Marcus Saufeius, son of Marcus, who had supervised the storming of the inn at Bovillae and Clodius' murder. He was prosecuted by Lucius Cassius, Lucius Fulcinius, son of Gaius, and Gaius Valerius; he was defended by Marcus Cicero and Marcus Caelius, who secured his acquittal by one vote. Ten senators voted for conviction and eight for acquittal; nine Roman equestrians for conviction and eight for acquittal; but ten of the *tribuni aerarii* voted for acquittal and only six for conviction. It was clearly hatred of Clodius which saved Saufeius, since his case was even weaker than Milo's had been, given that he had openly led the storming of the inn. A few days later he was then prosecuted again before the presiding magistrate Gaius Considius under the Plautian law concerning violence, with the charge that he had occupied a commanding position and had been armed (he had of course been Milo's gangleader). He was prosecuted by Gaius Fidius, Gnaeus Aponius, son of Gnaeus, Marcus Seius . . . son of Sextus; he was defended by Marcus Cicero and Marcus Terentius Varro Gibba. He was acquitted by more votes this time than before, nineteen for conviction but thirty-two for acquittal; but the situation was the reverse of what it had been in the first trial, because this time the equestrians and senators voted for acquittal, whereas the *tribuni aerarii* voted for conviction.

Sextus Cloelius, at whose suggestion Clodius' body had been carried into the senate-house, was prosecuted by Gaius Caesennius Philo and Marcus Alfidius and defended by Titus Flacconius. He was convicted by a large majority, [56 C] forty-six votes; in all there were only five votes for acquittal, two from senators and three from equestrians.

Many others were convicted as well, some attending their trials and others failing to answer their summonses. Most of them were Clodians.

PRO MILONE

[1] I realize, members of the jury, that it is disgraceful, when beginning a speech in defence of a man of great courage, to show fear oneself, and that it is highly unbecoming, when Titus Annius is less concerned for his own survival than for that of his country, not to be able to show equal strength of character in pleading his case. But even so, the unfamiliar look of this unfamiliar court alarms my very eyes, and wherever they happen to light, they search in vain for the traditional activity of the forum and the long-established procedure of the courts. You the jury are not hemmed in by a ring of spectators, as you used to be, nor are we surrounded by the usual packed crowd. [2] Those guards which you can see in front of all the temples, although stationed there to prevent violence, cannot fail to cause a speaker a twinge of alarm. The result is that despite being here in the forum and in court, and despite our being surrounded by troops who are meant for our protection and are indeed very much needed, we are nevertheless unable even to be free from fear without also being somewhat afraid.

If I thought that these precautions were directed against Milo, I should bow to the inevitable, gentlemen, and conclude that amid so great a force of arms speech has no place. But I am relieved and reassured by the good sense of the wise and fair-minded Gnaeus Pompeius. He would undoubtedly consider it incompatible with his own fair-mindedness to abandon to the weapons of the soldiers someone whom he had already entrusted to the votes of a jury, and he would likewise see it as incompatible with his own wisdom to arm with official authority the hysteria of an excited mob. [3] That is why those arms, centurions, and cohorts speak to me not of danger but of defence; they encourage me to be not only calm in my mind but courageous too; and they promise me not merely protection as I make this defence but also a silent hearing.

As for the rest of the crowd gathered here, it is, inasmuch as it consists of Roman citizens,* entirely on our side. You can see the people looking on from every direction, from wherever any part of the forum happens to be visible. They are eagerly awaiting the outcome of this trial; and there is not a man among them who does not support Milo's courage and believe that himself, his children, his country, and his fortunes are this very day at stake.

Our opponents and ill-wishers, on the other hand, fall into a single class: they are those whom the frenzy of Publius Clodius has fed with plunder, arson, and every type of national calamity, and who at yesterday's public meeting were urged to dictate to you your verdict in this trial. If any shouting should be heard from that quarter, it will serve to remind you of the necessity of preserving a citizen who has always regarded that class of men and their loud yelling as nothing in comparison with your own personal welfare.

[4] So give me your attention, gentlemen, and lay aside any fear that you may have. For if you have ever had the power of judging loyal and valiant men, if you have ever had the power of judging meritorious citizens, and if specially selected men from the most distinguished orders have ever been given the opportunity of demonstrating, by their actions and their votes, that approval of valiant and loyal citizens which they have so often expressed in the past by looks and words; if that is how it is, then you have at this moment complete power to decide whether we who have always upheld your authority should linger on in adversity for all time, or whether, after being persecuted for years by the most degraded citizens, we are at long last to be revived by your good selves, and by your honour, your courage, and your wisdom.

[5] Can you point to or imagine anything, gentlemen, more difficult, worrying, and trying than the situation in which the two of us have been placed? Called to public service by hopes of the most honourable rewards, we find ourselves instead living in fear of the cruellest punishments. For my part I always believed that Milo would have to undergo many other storms and tempests—or at least the billows of the public meetings—because he had always taken the side of patriots against the disruptive elements. But at a public trial and in a court in which the most distinguished men from all the orders would be deciding the verdict, I never supposed for a moment that Milo's enemies would have the slightest hope of damaging his high reputation, still less of bringing about his total ruin, by the decision of such jurors as yourselves.

[6] In this trial, gentlemen, I shall not seek to defend Titus Annius against the charge by making use of his tribunate and all the things he has done to protect the state. Unless you actually see with your

own eyes that Clodius set a trap for Milo, I shall not beg you to waive the charge for us in consideration of Milo's many outstanding public services, nor shall I insist that, since the death of Publius Clodius has proved to be your salvation, you should put it down to the merits of Milo rather than to the good fortune of the Roman people. But if I succeed in making it as clear as day that it was Clodius who set the trap, then I shall go on to beseech and implore you, gentlemen, that, even if we lose everything else, we may at least retain the right of defending our lives, without fear of punishment, against the weapons and criminality of our enemies.

[7] But before I begin talking about the events which you are charged with investigating, I feel I need to rebut the views that have been repeatedly aired by our enemies in the senate, by trouble-makers in public meetings, and just now by the prosecutors; when I have stripped away the various misapprehensions you will have a clear view of the issue that is before the court. What these people are maintaining is that a man who admits to having killed another person should automatically forfeit the right to look upon the light of day. I ask you, what city is it in which people put forward such an idiotic point of view? It is of course the city which witnessed as its very first capital case the trial of the valiant Marcus Horatius!* He admitted to having killed his sister with his own hands, but even so was freed by an assembly of the Roman people—and this at a time when our country had not yet gained its freedom.

[8] Surely everyone knows that, when someone is being tried for murder, the deed is either categorically denied, or justified as right and lawful? Unless of course you think that Publius Africanus was out of his mind when, on being maliciously asked at a public meeting by Gaius Carbo, who was tribune of the plebs, what he thought about the death of Tiberius Gracchus, he replied that in his view he had been lawfully killed!* And if it is automatically wrong to kill Roman citizens who are criminals, then the famous Servilius Ahala, Publius Nasica, Lucius Opimius, Gaius Marius, and indeed the whole senate in the time of my consulship would all have to be considered beyond the pale!* And so, gentlemen, it is not without good reason that, even in the realm of fiction, the most learned writers have handed down the story of one who killed his mother* to avenge his father and who, when the votes of the human jury were split, was acquitted not merely by the vote of a god, but by that of

the wisest of all the gods. [9] The Twelve Tables,* moreover, laid down that a thief caught at night might be killed with impunity whatever the circumstances, and likewise one caught by day if he put up an armed resistance. So who can possibly maintain that any act of killing, whatever the circumstances, deserves punishment, when sometimes the laws themselves hold out a sword to us for the killing of a fellow man?

If, then, there are circumstances (and there are many) in which it is lawful to kill a fellow man, then in situations in which a violent attack is violently resisted, killing is obviously not only right, but unavoidable. A military tribune* in the army of Gaius Marius, a relation of his in fact, once sexually assaulted a fellow soldier. The soldier killed him: decent young man that he was, he preferred to risk punishment rather than submit to humiliation. And the great Marius freed him from his danger by acquitting him of the crime. [10] But when it is a bandit and a brigand that we are concerned with, how could the killing of such a person not be justified? After all, what is the point of our bodyguards, our swords? If their use was forbidden in all circumstances, we would surely not be allowed to have them in the first place.

There is therefore a law, gentlemen, not one written down anywhere but a natural law, not one that we have learned, inherited, and read, but one that we have seized, imbibed, and extracted from nature herself, a law for which we were not taught, but made, which we know not from instruction but from intuition, the law which states that, if any attempt is made upon our lives, if we encounter violence and weapons, whether of brigands or enemies, then every method of saving ourselves is morally justifiable. [11] When swords are drawn the laws fall silent; they do not require you to wait for them, because the man who chooses to wait will have to pay an undeserved penalty before he can exact a deserved one. And yet the law, with great wisdom, tacitly concedes the right of self-defence in that it is not the killing of a man that it forbids, but the carrying of a weapon for the purpose of killing. Thus, when a court looks not simply at the weapon but at the motive, a man who has used a weapon to defend himself is not considered to have had it for the purpose of killing. So let the point apply in this particular trial, gentlemen; for I am confident that I will convince you of my case, if you will only keep in mind the fact (which you could hardly forget) that a bandit may indeed be law-fully killed.

[12] The next point is one repeatedly brought up by Milo's enemies, that the act of violence in which Publius Clodius was killed was ruled by the senate to have been against the interests of the state. But the senate approved that act, not only by the opinions it expressed but by its active endorsement. How often I have pleaded this very cause in the senate! And how vociferous and unreserved was the approbation of that entire order! For when have there ever been, at the best-attended meetings of the senate, as many as four or at most five people who did not take Milo's side? Those defunct harangues delivered by this scorched tribune of the plebs* prove as much: every day he stirred up resentment against my 'power', saying that the senate decreed not what it felt but what I dictated. As for this 'power' of mine, I do wonder whether it ought not to be called 'modest influence for the good acquired as a result of great services to the country' or 'some degree of popularity among loyal citizens resulting from this hard work that I do in the courts'; but I do not mind what you call it, so long as I can use it to save loyal citizens from the madness of traitors.

[13] But as for this court, I am not complaining that it is unfair; but the senate never thought it should have been specially set up. There were already laws in existence, there were already courts for murder and violence, and Publius Clodius' death hardly caused the senate so much grief and sorrow that a new court needed to be established! When it was a case of his sacrilege and immorality,* the senate was denied the power of deciding on the court; now that it is his death that we are concerned with, can anyone seriously believe that the senate thought that a new court should be set up?

So why did the senate decree that the burning of the senate-house, the assault on Marcus Lepidus' house,* and the killing itself were against the interests of the state? Simply because in a free country acts of violence between citizens are always against the interests of the state. [14] Self-defence against violence, although sometimes unavoidable, is never something one would wish for. The day on which Tiberius Gracchus was killed, the one on which Gaius Gracchus died, and the arms of Saturninus* all did harm to the state, despite the fact that the suppression of these men was in the public interest. So that is why, once it was established that a killing had

taken place on the Appian Way, I did not myself vote that the man
who had acted in self-defence had acted against the interests of the
state. Instead, since violence and the setting of a trap were involved,
I voiced my disapproval of what had occurred, while leaving the
question of guilt to be decided by a court.

But if that demented tribune of the plebs* had allowed the senate
to do as it wished, we should not now have a new court. The senate
wanted to decree that a trial be held under the existing laws, but with
special priority given to it. The motion was split in two at the request
of someone or other (I see no reason to expose everyone's misdeeds),
and the second part, expressing the senate's wish, failed when it was
blocked by a purchased veto.*

[15] 'But Gnaeus Pompeius, as is shown by his proposing his bill,
has already pronounced his verdict both on the facts and on the
whole issue: for the bill which he carried specifically concerned the
act of violence on the Appian Way in which Publius Clodius was
killed.' So what was it that he proposed? Obviously, that an inquiry
should be held. And what is to be the subject of this inquiry?
Whether the deed was committed? But everyone agrees that it was.
Or by whom it was committed? But that is perfectly obvious. He
appreciated, therefore, that even where the deed was admitted it was
still possible to argue a plea of justification. Had he not appreciated
this (that the man who admitted the deed could be acquitted), he
would not, on seeing that we did admit it, have ordered an inquiry,
nor would he have given you the letter of acquittal with which to
record your vote as well as the letter of condemnation.* As I see it,
Gnaeus Pompeius has not only refrained from making any unfavourable judgement about Milo, but has actually laid down what it is that
you ought to be considering as you ponder your verdict. For what he
has given to the man who admits the deed is not punishment, but the
chance to clear himself; and this shows that it is not the mere fact of
the killing which he thinks should be investigated, but the motive.
[16] And no doubt he will tell us himself whether his action, which
he took on his own initiative, was meant as a tribute to Publius
Clodius or simply as a response to the exigencies of the situation.

A man was once murdered in his own home. He was a man of the
highest rank, the senate's champion and in those dark days almost its
patron, the uncle of this juryman of ours the valiant Cato: I am
referring, of course, to the tribune of the plebs Marcus Drusus.* No

bill relating to his death was put before the people, and no special
inquiry was decreed by the senate. Our fathers have told us what an
outpouring of grief there was in this city when Publius Africanus*
was struck down one night while resting at his home. Who at that
time was not grieved, who did not blaze with indignation that the
man whom everyone wanted to live for ever, if such a thing were
possible, should not even have been allowed to live out the natural
term of his life? So was any inquiry set up into the death of Africanus? No. [17] And why not? Because the crime is the same whether a
murdered man is famous or unknown. Let there be, in life, a distinction between the highest and the lowest; but deaths resulting from
crime should be subject to laws and punishments that are the same
for all. Unless of course you think that a man who murders his father
is more guilty of parricide if his father has held the consulship than
if he is of humble rank! Or that the death of Publius Clodius is a
more serious crime because he happened to have been killed (as the
prosecution keep reminding us) among the monuments of his
ancestors—as if the famous Appius Caecus* built his road not for the
use of the public, but as a place where his own descendants might
attack passers-by with impunity! [18] That, I suppose, must be why,
when Publius Clodius killed a most distinguished equestrian, Marcus Papirius,* on this same Appian Way, the crime was never thought
to call for punishment. The man, you see, was a noble, among his
family's monuments, and the man he killed a mere equestrian! But
now what histrionics are set in motion by this name 'the Appian
Way'! When that road was bloodied by the murder of an honourable
and blameless man, the road was never mentioned, but now that it
has been stained by the blood of a brigand and a murderer, it is
harped upon incessantly!

But why do I need to cite such examples as these? A slave of
Publius Clodius was arrested in the temple of Castor: Clodius had
posted him there to murder Gnaeus Pompeius.* A dagger was
wrenched from his hand and he confessed all. From then on Pompeius kept away from the forum, away from the senate, and away
from the public eye; he sought protection behind his own door and
walls, and not in his rights under the laws and courts. [19] But was
any new bill passed, was any special inquiry decreed? And yet if ever
the situation, the person, or the times called for such measures, they
did so with the greatest urgency in this instance. The conspirator

had been posted in the forum and at the very entrance to the senate; death was being plotted for the one man on whose life the safety of the state depended; and this was taking place at such a time of national crisis that, if Pompeius alone had succumbed, not only Rome herself but all the nations of the world would have fallen in ruin. Unless of course you think that this crime did not deserve punishment because it was not actually brought to completion, as if it were the outcome of events, and not men's intentions, that the laws take into account! The fact that the plot did not succeed meant there was less cause for grief; it certainly did not mean there was less cause for punishment. [20] How many times, gentlemen, have I myself escaped from the weapons of Publius Clodius and from his bloody hands! But suppose my own good fortune, or that of the country, had not preserved me from them: do you really imagine that anyone would have set up an inquiry into my death?

But how idiotic of me to think of comparing Drusus, Africanus, Pompeius, and myself with Publius Clodius! What happened in their cases could easily be put up with; but no one could calmly accept Publius Clodius' death! The senate is grief-stricken, the equestrian order is inconsolable, the whole country is worn out with sorrow, the towns of Italy are in mourning, the colonies are prostrate, and the very fields bewail the loss of a citizen so kind, so good, and so gentle!

[21] No, members of the jury, that was certainly not the reason why Pompeius thought that a special inquiry should be set up. As a man of great wisdom with a lofty and almost divine mind, he took account of many considerations. He saw that Clodius had been his enemy and Milo his friend, and that if he were to participate in the general rejoicing himself, there would be a danger that the sincerity of his past reconciliation with Clodius* might be called into question. There were many other factors of which he took note, but this one he was particularly aware of, that however strict the terms of his bill were, you yourselves would nevertheless deliver a courageous verdict. It was for this reason that he chose the brightest luminaries from the most distinguished orders; and it is quite inaccurate to say, as some people persist in doing, that in selecting the jurors he excluded my own friends. Being a man of the highest principles, he never contemplated such a thing, and even if he had wished it he could never, in choosing good men as jurors, have succeeded. This is because my influence is not confined to close friendships. Such

friendships can never be very numerous because it is simply impossible for social intimacies to be kept up with a large number of
people. But if I do have a measure of influence, this is due to the fact
that the interests of the state have linked me with all loyal citizens.
So when Pompeius was selecting the best men from among these
loyal citizens, realizing as he did that his own reputation would be
directly affected by the choice he would make, he could not help but
choose men who were my supporters.

[22] As for his special wish that you, Lucius Domitius,* should
preside over this court, he was looking for nothing but fairness,
decorum, humanity, and good faith. He proposed that the presiding
magistrate should be a man of consular rank because, I take it, he
considered that our leading men have a duty to stand up equally to
the fickleness of the mob and to the boldness of traitors. And from
those of consular rank you were the man he chose to appoint because
ever since your youth you had given the clearest evidence of your
contempt for the madness of rabble-rousers.

[23] So, members of the jury, we finally come to the charge and
the actual issue. If it is not altogether unprecedented for a defendant
to admit the deed, and the senate has passed no judgement on the
case which is not to our liking, and the man who actually proposed
the law, even though the facts of the case were not in doubt, nevertheless wanted the legal question discussed, and jurors were chosen
and a president appointed who would judge the case fairly and
wisely—then, gentlemen, it only remains for you to decide which of
the two set a trap for the other. And to ensure that you will have a
clear picture of this from the arguments I will be putting forward,
please listen carefully while I give you a brief account of what took
place.

[24] Publius Clodius had decided to devote his praetorship to
terrorizing the country with every type of criminal behaviour. But he
saw that the previous year's elections had been so long delayed* that
when he finally attained the office he would not hold it for more than
a few months. He cared nothing, as other people do, for the
advancement in rank that the praetorship would confer: his only
concern was to avoid having that excellent citizen Lucius Paullus* as
his colleague, and to have a complete year for tearing the country
apart. He therefore suddenly gave up his candidature for his proper
year and transferred it to the following year instead—not, as is usual

in such cases, because of any religious scruple, but, as he openly admitted, so that he should have for his praetorship (that is, for ruining the country) a full and complete year.

[25] It occurred to him, however, that his praetorship would be weak and powerless if Milo were consul at the same time; and he saw that Milo was on his way to becoming consul, by the unanimous vote of the Roman people. He therefore attached himself to the candidates who were standing against Milo, but he did so in such a way that he was single-handedly in control of their entire campaigns, whether they liked it or not—or, as he frequently put it himself, he bore the weight of the entire election on his own shoulders. He called the tribes together, acted as agent,* and by recruiting the most disreputable of the citizens enlisted a new Colline tribe.* But the more he carried on like this, the stronger Milo's position became. So when Clodius, who would stop at nothing, realized that a courageous man who was his bitterest enemy would undoubtedly be elected consul, when he understood that this had often been signified not just by common gossip but by the actual votes of the Roman people,* he began to come out into the open and declare publicly that Milo had to be killed. [26] He had already brought down from the Apennines some savage and barbaric slaves—you saw them yourselves—and used them to devastate the public forests and ravage Etruria. His intentions were perfectly clear, for he used to assert repeatedly and publicly that if Milo's consulship could not be taken from him, at least his life could. On many occasions he implied as much in the senate, and he said so explicitly in public meetings. And this was not all. When the valiant Marcus Favonius* asked him what purpose he hoped his violence would serve when Milo was alive to resist it, he replied that within three days, or four at the most, Milo would be dead. This remark Favonius immediately reported to Marcus Cato here.

[27] Meanwhile Clodius knew (it was not hard to find out) that Milo was required by both ritual and law to travel to Lanuvium on 18 January to nominate a priest.* So he suddenly set out from Rome the day before in order (as the sequel showed) to set a trap for Milo in a spot opposite his own estate. His departure from Rome meant that he had to abandon a rowdy public meeting* at which his usual violence was sadly missed—a meeting he would never have abandoned had he not particularly wished to be present at the scene of the crime at the crucial moment.

[28] Milo, on the other hand, attended the senate that day* and stayed until the meeting was concluded. He then went home, changed his clothes and shoes, waited for a bit while his wife (as they do!) got herself ready, then finally set off at an hour when Clodius could easily have returned to Rome, had he really intended to do so that day. He was met by Clodius travelling light and on horseback, with no coach, no baggage, none of the usual Greek companions, and without his wife, who almost invariably went with him. By contrast, this bandit here,* who had undertaken that journey specifically for the purpose of committing a murder, was riding in a coach with his wife, wrapped up in a heavy cloak, and accompanied by a large, cumbersome, ladylike, and unmilitary array of serving-girls and young boys. [29] He came across Clodius opposite Clodius' estate at around 3 p.m. or thereabouts.* Immediately a number of armed men launched an attack on him from the higher ground, and those of them that were in front of him killed the coachman. But Milo threw off his cloak, jumped down from the coach, and defended himself bravely. The men who were with Clodius had all drawn their swords. Some of them ran over to the coach to attack Milo from behind, while others, thinking that he had already been murdered, began cutting down the slaves of his who were following in the rear. Of the ones who kept their heads and showed themselves loyal to their master, some were killed, while others, seeing that a fight was taking place at the coach, but prevented from going to their master's aid, and hearing from Clodius' own lips that Milo had been killed and accepting it as true—these slaves of Milo's (and I shall state this openly, not in order to deny the charge, but because this is how it happened), without their master's command, knowledge, or even his presence, did what every man would have wanted his own slaves to do in such a situation.

[30] These events took place exactly as I have described, members of the jury. The man who set the trap was overcome, force was defeated by force or rather wickedness crushed by virtue. I say nothing of the benefit to our country, the benefit to you, and the benefit to all loyal citizens. Nor am I arguing that this should count in Milo's favour—a man whose fate made him incapable of saving even himself without simultaneously saving both the country and yourselves! If there was no defence in law for what he did, then I have no defence to offer. But if it is true that civilized men are taught by reason,

barbarians by necessity, peoples by custom, and wild beasts by nature herself that they should always defend themselves by every possible means against all violence to their bodies, persons, and lives, then you cannot judge this act to have been wrong without at the same time judging that all who fall among brigands deserve to die— whether it be by those brigands' weapons or by your very own votes! [31] If Milo had taken that view himself, it would surely have been preferable to him to offer his throat to Publius Clodius (who had attacked him not just once, or then for the first time) rather than have it cut by yourselves on the grounds that he had not offered it to Clodius for him to cut.

But I assume that none of you would take that view. The question before this court therefore becomes not whether Clodius was killed—for we admit that he was—but whether he was killed lawfully or unlawfully; and this is a question which has been the subject of many trials in the past. It is agreed that a trap was set, and it is this which the senate has ruled to have been against the interests of the state. But it is not clear which of the two men set the trap. This, then, is the matter which you have been appointed to investigate. In exactly the same way, the senate censured the deed and not the individual, and Pompeius set up an inquiry into the justification, not into the facts of the case. So surely the only question before this court is which of the two set the trap against the other? That is all. If Milo set the trap, let him be punished. But if Clodius set it, my client should be acquitted.

[32] How, therefore, can it be proved that it was Clodius who set a trap for Milo? In the case of such a wicked and unspeakable monster as Clodius, it is sufficient merely to show that he had a powerful motive, and that Milo's death would have presented him with great aspirations and great advantages. Accordingly, let Cassius' famous test* 'Who stood to gain?' be applied to both these men—although we should also bear in mind that no inducement, however great, will make a good man commit a crime, whereas a bad man will often be made to do so by even a trivial inducement. Now, Clodius did indeed stand to benefit in the event of Milo's being killed. For not only would he avoid having to serve his praetorship under a consul who would suppress his criminal designs, but he would actually serve it under consuls* who, he hoped, if they did not actively help him, would at least allow him a free hand in carrying out those mad

schemes of his that he was contemplating. He reasoned that they
would have no desire to put a stop to his plans, even if it was within
their power to do so, since they would be well aware how deeply they
were obliged to him. And even if they were of a mind to stop him,
they would perhaps be scarcely capable of suppressing the hardened
criminality of a man of such long-standing wickedness.

[33] Or can it really be, gentlemen, that you alone are unaware,
that you are strangers in this city, that your ears have gone for a walk
and have failed to pick up the most widespread talk of the town—
that you are ignorant of the laws that that villain was going to have
foisted and branded on us all? If, that is, you can call them laws,
rather than firebrands for the burning of our city or plagues to infect
our country! Show us, show us, please, Sextus Cloelius, that dossier
of laws that you have, which you are said to have snatched from
Clodius' house and to have carried off, like the Palladium,* from amid
the clashing of arms and the chaos of the night! You clearly intended
to present this wonderful gift, the tribunate's stock-in-trade, to anyone you could find who would be prepared to hold that office under
your direction. See! He looked at me with that menacing glance of
his that he always used to give when making all manner of threats
against everyone. That shining light of the senate-house* disturbs
me! Do you think, then, that I am angry with you, Sextus, when you
in fact took a far more cruel revenge on my bitterest enemy than my
own sense of decency would have allowed me to demand? You flung
Publius Clodius' bloody corpse out of doors, you threw it out into
the street, you deprived it of masks,* funeral rites, procession, and
eulogy and left it half-burnt on some ill-omened timber to be torn to
pieces by dogs in the night. This was a shocking thing to do, and I
therefore cannot condone it. But since it was against my enemy that
your cruelty was directed, it would certainly be unreasonable of me
to be angry with you.

[34] You have heard, members of the jury, how much it was in
Clodius' interest for Milo to be killed. So I ask you now to turn to
consider Milo's situation. How was Clodius' death in his interest?
What reason was there for him to have wished for Clodius' death, let
alone to have brought it about? 'Clodius stood in the way of his
hopes of becoming consul.' But he was well on his way to being
elected in spite of Clodius' opposition—or rather because of it! In
fact, Clodius was just as much of a help to him as the support I gave

him myself. You were moved, gentlemen, by the recollection of Milo's past services to me and to our country, you were moved by my tearful appeals, which, as I saw at the time, affected you deeply, and you were moved above all by the fear of pressing danger. For was there any Roman citizen who could contemplate the prospect of Publius Clodius' unfettered praetorship and not be terrified of a revolution taking place? And you saw that his praetorship would indeed be unfettered, unless there were a consul who possessed both the courage and the ability to keep it in check. The entire Roman people realized that Milo was the one man who could do this: so how could anyone think twice about using his vote to free himself from fear and his country from danger?

But now that Clodius is no longer with us, Milo is thrown back on more normal means of safeguarding his position. That unique glory, enjoyed by him alone, which was increased every day by his opposition to Clodius' insane violence, has now, as a result of Clodius' death, been taken from him. You have been placed in the happy position of no longer having to fear any citizen; but he has lost the opportunity of showing his bravery, the means of securing his election, and the eternal source of his glory. For this reason Milo's campaign for the consulship, which could not fail while Clodius was alive, has begun to suffer now that he is dead. Clodius' death, then, is not merely something that brings Milo no benefit: it is actually doing him harm.

[35] 'But it was his hatred of Clodius that was his motive; he acted in anger, and out of spite; he took revenge for the wrong done to him, and exacted punishment for his injuries.' If I say not that these motives were stronger for Clodius than they were for Milo, but that they were overpowering in Clodius' case and non-existent in Milo's, then what more could you ask for? If we leave aside the patriotic hatred with which we loathe all traitors, what reason could Milo possibly have had for hating Clodius, the raw material of his glory? As for Clodius, on the other hand, he had every reason to hate the man who had fought for my safety, opposed his mad violence, defeated his armed attacks, and also brought an accusation against him (Clodius right up until his death was facing a prosecution by Milo under the Plautian law*). How do you think that that tyrant would have reacted to Milo doing all that to him? How intense must his hatred of Milo have been, and, in the case of such an unjust man as Clodius, how well justified!

[36] There remains the argument that Clodius' character and way of life speak in his favour, whereas Milo's count against him. 'Clodius never did anything by violence: Milo did everything by violence.' So, gentlemen, when I departed from Rome,* to your great distress, was it a trial that I went in fear of, and not slaves, weapons, and violence? And how could there have been a just reason for my restoration if the reason for my expulsion had not been an unjust one? He had, I suppose, served a summons on me, proposed a fine, or brought a charge of treason against me! And I, I take it, had had to fear a verdict in a case that was shameful or of relevance only to me, instead of one that was both glorious and of great concern to yourselves! No: I was not prepared to allow my fellow citizens, who had been saved, at great danger to myself, by my quick thinking,* then to have to face, for my sake, the weapons of slaves and poverty-stricken criminals. [37] Indeed I saw, I saw with my own eyes that distinguished luminary of the state, Quintus Hortensius here, almost murdered by some slaves while he was acting in my support;* and in the same disturbance that excellent senator Gaius Vibienus,* who was with him, was so badly beaten up that he afterwards died. And from that point on, when did that dagger of his, which he had inherited from Catiline, ever rest? This is a dagger which has been aimed at me, and to which I did not allow you to be exposed on my behalf; a dagger which plotted against Pompeius;* a dagger which caused the Appian Way, the monument of his own family, to be stained with the blood of the murdered Papirius;* and a dagger which much later was turned back again on me. For not long ago, as you are aware, it very nearly made an end of me outside the Regia.*

[38] What did Milo ever do like that? The violence that came from him was aimed solely at preventing Publius Clodius from holding the country in the grip of violence, and was resorted to only because it was impossible to bring Clodius to trial. And if he had wanted to kill him, just think how many excellent opportunities he had, and how glorious they would have been! Could he not lawfully have avenged himself when he was defending his home and household gods from Clodius' attacks? Could he not have done so when his own colleague, the valiant and outstanding Publius Sestius,* had been wounded? Could he not have done so when the excellent Quintus Fabricius was driven away while proposing a law for my recall, and a terrible massacre was perpetrated in the forum? Could he not have

done so when the home of the valiant and fair-minded praetor
Lucius Caecilius was placed under attack? Could he not have done so
on that day* on which the law concerning myself was carried, when
the entire people of Italy, united by their concern for my welfare,
would have freely acknowledged the heroism of the deed—and when
even if Milo alone had struck the blow the entire nation would have
claimed the glory for themselves?

[39] What a moment that was! There was as consul the illustrious
and valiant Publius Lentulus,* the enemy of Clodius and avenger of
his crimes, the defender of the senate, the champion of your wishes,
the guardian of national harmony, and the restorer of my own welfare. There were seven praetors and eight tribunes of the plebs who
opposed Clodius and supported me.* And there was Gnaeus Pompeius, the originator and leader of my restoration, and enemy of
Clodius. He made an impressive and eloquent pronouncement
concerning my welfare which commanded the assent of the entire
senate; he spurred on the Roman people; and he issued a decree
about me at Capua and thus personally gave the signal to all Italy to
converge on Rome and bring about my restoration (something for
which the Italians were most eager, and had been imploring him to
do). At that time, all Roman citizens, because they were missing me,
were ablaze with hatred for Clodius, and if anyone had taken it into
their heads to kill him, the ensuing debate would not have been
about immunity from prosecution, but about rewards. [40] Yet even
so Milo restrained himself. Twice he summoned Publius Clodius to
court;* but not once did he summon him to a trial of force.

Again, when Milo had returned to being a private citizen and was
charged before the people by Publius Clodius,* and Gnaeus Pompeius
was attacked as he was speaking in Milo's support, surely then there
was not just an opportunity for suppressing Clodius but a reason to
do so? And recently, when Marcus Antonius* had given all loyal
citizens the strongest grounds for confidence in our future salvation,
when that young man of the highest rank had bravely taken on an
important public duty and had netted the monster Clodius as he
recoiled from the meshes of a trial, what a chance there was,
immortal gods, what an opportunity! When Clodius had fled and
taken refuge in a dark hidey-hole beneath the stairs, would it have
been a difficult job for Milo just to finish off that pestilential villain,
incurring no blame whatsoever for himself but bestowing the

greatest glory on Marcus Antonius? [41] Again, at the elections in the Campus Martius think how many chances Milo had! Clodius had broken into the voting enclosures and ordered his men to draw their swords and start throwing stones. But when he caught sight of the expression on Milo's face he was suddenly seized with panic and fled in the direction of the Tiber—while you and all loyal citizens prayed that Milo might choose to give a practical demonstration of his innate courage.

So if he was unwilling to kill Clodius at a time when everyone would have approved, would he really have wanted to do so at a time when some would have objected? And if he did not venture to kill him when he could have done so lawfully, at the perfect time, in an ideal place, and without fear of punishment, would he not have hesitated to do so unlawfully, at the wrong time, in an unfavourable place, and at risk to his life? [42] Moreover, gentlemen, this was at a time when the struggle for the highest office* was under way and the day of the elections was at hand, a time when we are afraid not just of all the adverse comments that might be made about us but of every hidden thought (yes, I know well how fearful ambitious men are, and also how unbounded and how anxious their longing for the consulship is!), when we are terrified of any rumour, any untrue, made-up, or silly story, and when we look searchingly into everyone's eyes and expression. There is nothing so weak, so delicate, so fragile or changeable as the feeling and attitude of Roman citizens towards us politicians. Indeed, it is not only dishonesty on the part of the candidates that makes them angry: they are prone to take exception even to exemplary behaviour.

[43] So here was Milo, with the prospect of the election day before him, on which he had placed all his hopes. Did he really intend to present himself at the solemn taking of the auspices before the centuriate assembly with bloody hands that proclaimed and confessed the wicked crime he had committed? For a man like Milo, that is simply incredible. But in the case of Clodius it is not to be doubted, since he believed that, with Milo dead, he himself would rule over all! Again (and this, gentlemen, is the key to criminal behaviour), is there anyone who does not know that the greatest temptation to crime is the hope that one will escape punishment? So which of the two nursed such a hope? Milo, who at this very moment is on trial for doing a deed that was glorious, or at least unavoidable?

Or Clodius, who held courts and punishments in such complete contempt that nothing that nature sanctioned or the laws allowed could ever satisfy him?

[44] But why do I go on producing arguments, why discuss the matter further? I call on you, Quintus Petillius,* fine and valiant citizen that you are, and I appeal to you as a witness, Marcus Cato— both of you allotted to me as jurors by some heaven-sent piece of good luck. You both heard from Marcus Favonius that Clodius told him that Milo would be dead within three days;* and you heard this from Favonius before Clodius was killed. Three days after the remark was made, the incident occurred. Since Clodius did not hesitate to reveal what he was thinking, can you hesitate to judge what he was doing?

[45] So how was it that Clodius was right about the day? I have already told you. It was a straightforward matter for him to find out the dates of the regular sacrifices that the dictator of Lanuvium* had to perform. He saw that Milo would have to set out for Lanuvium on the day he did, and so he left before him. But on which day?* As I have already explained, it was the day of the hysterical public meeting whipped up by a tribune of the plebs in Clodius' pay. And Clodius would never have abandoned such an occasion, such a meeting, and such a riot unless he were hurrying to commit a premeditated crime. So not only did he have no reason for travelling, he actually had a reason for staying in Rome. Milo, on the other hand, had no means of staying, as he had not only a reason for leaving Rome but an obligation to do so.

Now what if, just as Clodius knew that Milo would be on the road that day, Milo could have had no idea that Clodius would be? [46] I should like to ask first, how could he have known it? You cannot ask that question about Clodius. For even if he had asked no one except his close friend Titus Patina,* he could still have known that Milo was obliged, in his capacity as dictator, to nominate a priest at Lanuvium on that very day.* Indeed, there were a great many others from whom he could easily have found this out. But returning to Milo, who could he have asked about the date of Clodius' return? Let us suppose that he actually did ask (see how much I am willing to concede!), even that he bribed a slave, as my friend Quintus Arrius* has alleged. But you only need to read the testimony of your own witnesses. There you will find that Gaius Causinius Schola of

Interamna,* a close friend of Clodius who accompanied him on the journey, has stated that Publius Clodius was intending to stay at his estate at Alba that day, and only when he was unexpectedly informed of the death of Cyrus the architect* did he suddenly decide to set out for Rome. And this has been confirmed by another of Publius Clodius' fellow-travellers, Gaius Clodius.*

[47] Members of the jury, please note the important points which emerge from this testimony. In the first place, Milo is clearly freed from the suspicion of having set out from Rome with the intention of setting a trap for Clodius on the road—obviously so, if there was no way he was actually going to run into Clodius. The second point concerns me (I do not see why I should not deal with my own business as well as Milo's). You are aware, gentlemen, that there was someone who, in advocating the bill which set up this court, claimed that although the killing was done by Milo's hand, the mind which plotted it belonged to someone greater. And I, let me tell you, was the brigand and cut-throat to whom those abandoned and degraded individuals* were referring. But they are refuted by their own witnesses who maintain that Clodius would not have returned to Rome that day had he not heard the news about Cyrus. I can breathe again. I am cleared. I need not be afraid of appearing to have based my plans on something that I could not possibly have foreseen.

[48] I will now move on to the other points. An objection could be raised: 'But it follows from your argument that Clodius was not planning to set a trap either, since he was intending to stay at his estate at Alba.' That would hold true—had he not intended to leave the house to commit the murder. It is perfectly clear that the person who is said to have brought the news of Cyrus' death did not report that at all: instead he reported that Milo was approaching. For what was there to report about Cyrus, when Clodius, on departing from Rome, had left him already on his death-bed? I also witnessed his will: I was there with Clodius. Cyrus had made a will, and did not hide its terms from us: he had named Clodius and myself as his heirs.* Is it really credible that Clodius should have left Cyrus breathing his last at 9 a.m. on one day, and then be informed of his death as late as 2.15 p.m. on the following day?

[49] All right, let us suppose that it is. What was Clodius' reason, then, for rushing off to Rome? Why did he need to take off into the night?* Did the fact that he was an heir give him a reason for

hurrying? In the first place, there was no reason for him to have to
hurry. And even if there had been, what could he have gained by
reaching Rome that night, or lost by not arriving until the following
morning? Moreover, while Clodius ought to have avoided rather
than desired entering the city at night, Milo, if he was the bandit you
say he was, and if he knew that Clodius would reach the city after
dark, ought to have concealed himself and lain in wait for him.
[50] He could have killed him by night, and in a dangerous spot
infested with brigands. If he then denied killing him, no one would
have disbelieved him—just as now, when he admits it, everyone
hopes that he will be acquitted. The locality itself, the haunt and
hiding-place of brigands, would have taken responsibility for the
crime, the mute emptiness would have made no accusation, nor
would the blind night have given Milo away. The finger of suspicion
would have pointed at the many people whom Clodius had outraged,
ravaged, and ejected from their property, and at the many more who
feared the same fate. Indeed, the whole of Etruria would have been
summoned to answer the charge! [51] Moreover, it is a fact that on
the day in question Clodius did look in on his estate at Alba on his
way back from Aricia. Now let us suppose that Milo knew that he
had been visiting Aricia. In that case he ought to have suspected that
Clodius, even if he planned to return to Rome that same day, would
stop off at his country house, which was next to the road. Why,
then, did he not intercept him before he reached the safety of his
house or else lie in wait for him at the spot which he would reach at
nightfall?*

[52] Members of the jury, everything points in the same direction.
To Milo it was even advantageous that Clodius should stay alive, but
to Clodius the death of Milo was highly desirable, since it would help
him achieve his ambitions. Clodius had a burning hatred of Milo,
but Milo had no hatred of Clodius. Clodius was well used to initiat-
ing violence, but Milo was used only to repelling it. Clodius had
publicly announced and proclaimed Milo's imminent death, but
nothing of the kind was ever heard from Milo.* Clodius knew the day
on which Milo would be setting off, but Milo did not know the day
on which Clodius would be returning. Milo's journey was unavoidable, but Clodius' on the other hand was even inconvenient. Milo
had openly declared that he would be leaving Rome on the day in
question, but Clodius concealed the fact that he would be returning

on that day. Milo did not make a single change to his plans, but Clodius invented an excuse for changing his. Milo, if he were setting a trap, would have waited for nightfall close to the city, but Clodius, even if he had no fear of Milo, ought still to have been afraid of approaching the city after dark.

[53] Let us now examine the central point—whether the place at which they actually met was better suited to Milo or to Clodius as a place of ambush. On this point, gentlemen, can there be any further doubt or need for reflection? The incident took place in front of Clodius' house, where at least a thousand strong men were occupied in excavating a basement, a megalomaniac scheme.* In this location, and with his enemy occupying a commanding position on the higher ground, did Milo really imagine that his own situation was superior, and therefore make this spot his particular choice for the battle that ensued? Is it not more likely that someone who knew that the situation was favourable to himself was lying in wait for him here and planning an attack? The facts speak for themselves, gentlemen: they always carry the greatest weight.

[54] Now suppose you were not listening to this narrative of events but were looking at a painted representation of them: it would still be apparent which of the two was the plotter and which had no evil intentions. One of the men was riding in a coach, wrapped up in a heavy cloak, and had his wife sitting beside him. Which of these— the clothing, the vehicle, or the travelling-companion—was not a serious inconvenience? Could anyone be less prepared for battle than a man trussed up in his cloak, encumbered with his coach, and virtually tied down by the presence of his wife? Now look at the other man, sallying forth from his house, without warning—why? And in the evening—what's the need for that? And at a leisurely pace—where's the sense in that, especially at that hour? 'He was calling in at Pompeius' house.'* To see Pompeius? But he knew he was away at his place at Alsium. To look at the house, then? But he had been there a thousand times before. Well why then? Simply to delay and use up time: he was determined not to leave the area until my client should appear on the scene.

[55] Now please compare the unencumbered brigand's way of travelling with Milo's unwieldy entourage. Normally Clodius always travelled with his wife, but this time he was without her. Normally he travelled in a coach, but this time he was on horseback. He used to

take some wee Greeks with him wherever he went, even when hurrying off to his outposts in Etruria, but this time there were no such time-wasters with him. Milo, who normally never travelled with such people, happened on this occasion to have some of his wife's music boys, and bevies of slave girls. Clodius, on the other hand, who normally took prostitutes, rent boys, and tarts with him, on this occasion had no one, except such people as you might say had each been selected by his fellow.*

Why, then, was he defeated? Because the traveller is not always killed by the highwayman, and sometimes the highwayman is even killed by the traveller; and because, although Clodius was well prepared and had taken his victims unawares, he could nevertheless be described as a woman that had fallen among men.* [56] Moreover, Milo was never so poorly prepared against him that he did not maintain at least a minimum level of preparedness. At the back of his mind there was always the thought of how useful his death would be to Publius Clodius, how much Clodius hated him, and how Clodius would stop at nothing. He knew that a price had been set on his life, a price so enormous that he could scarcely call his life his own any longer. He therefore made sure never to expose himself to danger without taking precautions to protect himself. Remember, too, the part that chance plays, remember the unpredictable outcomes that battles have and the fact that Mars fights on both sides: often Mars has taken the side of the fallen soldier, overcoming and striking down the victor even as he strips off the spoils and shouts the cry of triumph. Remember also the stupidity of a leader who had just emerged from lunch, drunk, his mouth hanging open. He had left his enemy cut off in the rear, but it never occurred to him to take account of the followers at the end of Milo's line. They had given up their master's life as lost and were ablaze with anger; and when Clodius launched into them he met with the punishment which those loyal slaves exacted from him in return for their master's death.

[57] Why, then, did he give them their freedom? I suppose he was afraid that they might incriminate him, that they might not be able to hold out against the pain, that they might be forced by torture to admit that Milo's slaves killed Publius Clodius on the Appian Way!* But why should you need a torturer? What is it that you want to find out? Whether he killed him? But he did. Whether it was lawful or

not? That is not the torturer's job. It is facts that are elicited on the
rack: points of law are established in a court. So the point that has to
be established in court we are dealing with here, and the fact that you
want elicited by torture we have already admitted.

In choosing to ask why Milo freed his slaves instead of why he
rewarded them so inadequately, you show that you have no idea how
to fault your opponent. [58] Marcus Cato here, whose utterances are
invariably resolute and forthright, declared to a rowdy public
meeting—a meeting brought under control, I should add, by his
distinguished presence—that slaves who had saved their master's life
deserved to be given not just their freedom but every kind of reward.
For when a man owes his life to slaves so devoted, so good, and so
loyal, what reward can possibly be generous enough? More important, though, than the saving of his life is the fact that his slaves have
successfully prevented his cruellest enemies from glutting their eyes
and hearts on his blood and wounds. Had he not given them their
freedom, they would have had to be handed over for torture—the
men who had saved their master, avenged a terrible crime, and prevented a murder. In all his present troubles, there is nothing that
brings Milo such consolation as the thought that, if anything should
happen to himself, at least his slaves will have been given the reward
they deserve.

[59] But the interrogations that have now taken place in the Hall
of Liberty* are prejudicial to Milo. Whose slaves are they, then, that
have been interrogated? 'Do you need to ask? Publius Clodius', of
course.' Who called for them to give evidence? 'Appius.'* Who produced them? 'Appius.' From where? 'From Appius.' Great gods!
Could any procedure be more rigorous? Clodius really has come
close to joining the gods (more so than on the occasion when he
forced himself on their presence) when the inquiry that is held into
his death is the same as for acts of sacrilege!* Now the reason our
ancestors were not prepared to have slaves examined against their
master was not because finding out the truth would be impossible,
but because the practice seemed unworthy, and more repellent even
than the master's death. But when the prosecutor's own slave is
examined against the man he is prosecuting, how can the truth
possibly be obtained?

[60] Well then, what was the interrogation like and how did it
proceed? 'Hey Rufio,'—I pick a name at random—'be sure and tell

the truth: did Clodius set a trap for Milo?'* 'Yes.' Off he goes to be crucified! 'No.' He gets the freedom he longs for! What, I ask you, could be more reliable than this kind of examination? Even when slaves are taken away for interrogation the moment a crime has been committed, they are still kept apart and put into cells to prevent anyone talking to them. These slaves, on the other hand, have been kept in the custody of the prosecutor for a hundred days, and were then produced by the prosecutor himself. What could be less prejudiced than this kind of examination, what could be less corrupt?

[61] But it may be that, in spite of the clarity and number of the proofs and indications which shed light on the situation, you do not yet fully accept that Milo, when he returned to Rome, did so with a completely clear conscience, and was not affected by any taint of crime, alarmed by any fear, or prostrated by any sense of guilt. If this is so, then please recollect—by the immortal gods!—the promptness of his return to the city, his entry into the forum when the senate-house was on fire,* the character he displayed, the expression on his face, the words he spoke. He entrusted himself not just to the people but to the senate, and not just to the senate but to the protection of the public arms, and not just to these but to the power of him* to whom the senate had committed the whole country, the entire man-power of Italy, and all the arms of the Roman people. He would certainly never have placed himself in the hands of that person unless he had total confidence in his own cause—in the hands, especially, of someone who heard everything, entertained many fears and suspicions, and did believe some of the things that were reported to him. Great is the power of conscience, gentlemen, great whether one's conscience is clear or guilty! Those who have done nothing wrong it renders fearless; but it causes those who have done wrong to imagine punishment ever before their eyes.

[62] Nor was it without good reason that Milo's cause was consistently approved by the senate: being the intelligent men they were, they appreciated the grounds for what he did, his presence of mind, and the firmness he showed in defending himself. Or have you forgotten, members of the jury, the rumours and speculations that were put about not just by Milo's enemies but even by certain ignorant individuals at the time when we had only just received the news of Clodius' death? These people asserted that Milo would not venture to come back to Rome. [63] For they reckoned that if he had acted in

a fit of anger and excitement and murdered his enemy in a sudden
blaze of hatred, then he would no doubt have considered the loss of
his country to be a price worth paying for the death of Publius
Clodius, since he had had the satisfaction of glutting his hatred with
the blood of his enemy. Or if he had killed Clodius with the aim of
setting his country free, then so brave a man would not hesitate, after
risking his own life to save the Roman people, quietly to submit to
the laws,* taking with him an undying glory, and leaving to you the
enjoyment of those blessings which he himself had preserved. There
were quite a number of people who went so far as to make compari-
sons with Catiline and those monstrosities who followed him. 'He's
going to burst out,' people said, 'he's going to take up position
somewhere and declare war on his country.' How unlucky sometimes
are those citizens who have deserved well of their country, when
people do not merely fail to remember their distinguished services,
but even suspect them of treachery! [64] All these rumours that were
put about were quite groundless; but had Milo committed any act at
all which he could not honourably and truthfully defend, then I
agree they would indeed have been true.

   Then as for those slanders that were afterwards heaped upon him,
slanders which would have overwhelmed anyone conscious of having
committed even trivial misdemeanours—immortal gods, how stead-
fastly he endured them! Endured them? He did more than that, he
despised them and thought nothing of them, in a way that no guilty
man could ever have done, however strong his character, or any
innocent man, unless he were a person of supreme courage. It was
suggested that a large quantity of shields, swords, javelins, and even
bridles might be seized; it was alleged that there was no district in
the city, no alleyway in which a house had not been rented for Milo;
that weapons had been transported down the Tiber to his house at
Ocriculum,* that a house on the slope of the Capitol was crammed
with shields, and that every place was filled with fire-arrows for
burning the city. These slanders were not only reported, they were
almost believed, and not rejected as false until investigation had
shown them to be so.

   [65] For my part I was full of admiration for the exceptional care-
fulness of Gnaeus Pompeius, but I am going to speak my mind,
gentlemen. Those to whom the entire government of our country
has been entrusted are made to hear too much: they cannot avoid it.

In fact, Pompeius even had to listen to an attendant who slaughters the victims at sacrifices, one Licinius from the Circus Maximus. This Licinius claimed that Milo's slaves had got drunk at his place and told him that they were involved in a plot to assassinate Gnaeus Pompeius; later, he said, one of them had stabbed him with a sword to stop him revealing what he had been told. Word was sent to Pompeius at his property in the suburbs. I was among the first to be summoned, and on the advice of his friends Pompeius referred the matter to the senate. Naturally, when our country's and my protector was nursing so terrible a suspicion, I could not but be frightened out of my wits myself. All the same, I was very surprised that the slaughterman was believed, that the slaves' admission was taken seriously, and that the wound to Licinius' side, a mere pinprick, should be treated as a gladiator's blow. [66] I gather, though, that Pompeius was not so much taking fright as simply taking care; and he took care not just about those matters for which there were grounds for fear, but about everything, so that you yourselves should have to fear nothing. For example, it was reported that the house of the illustrious and valiant Gaius Caesar had been under siege for a large part of the night. No one had heard anything, busy though the place was, and no one had been aware of anything; and yet the report was taken seriously. I could never have suspected so very brave a man as Gnaeus Pompeius of being afraid; indeed, my view was that in the case of the entire government of our country, a burden that he himself had taken on, no amount of vigilance could ever be regarded as excessive. Again, at a well-attended meeting of the senate recently held on the Capitol, one senator* was produced who declared that Milo was carrying a weapon. Then and there, in that most sacred temple,* Milo stripped naked. Since the past life of so fine an individual and citizen was not enough to demonstrate his innocence, Milo, without a word, allowed the facts to speak. All such stories, then, have been found to be groundless and malicious fabrications.

[67] But if Milo is still even now to be feared, what we for our part are afraid of is not any longer the charge of murdering Clodius, but your own suspicions, Gnaeus Pompeius (yes, I am addressing you, and loud enough for you to hear me):* your suspicions, I repeat, are what terrify us. If you are afraid of Milo, if you think he is now contemplating or has ever engineered any criminal attempt upon your life, if the call-ups in Italy (as some of your recruiting officers

persist in claiming), if these weapons, if the cohorts posted on the
Capitol, if the watches, if the patrols, if the picked troops who guard
your house and person have all been mobilized to counter an attack
from Milo, and if all these precautions have been planned, organized, and directed against this single individual, then surely you
must reckon that he possesses enormous energy, unbelievable courage, and power and resources beyond the capacity of a single individual if, that is, it is against him alone that the most eminent general
has been appointed and the entire state placed under arms. [68] But
is there anyone who does not appreciate that all the sick and ailing
parts of the state have been placed in your hands so that you may use
these weapons to bring them back to health and strength?

As for Milo, if he had been given the opportunity, he would
unquestionably have made it clear to you personally that there has
never been any greater affection between men than that which he
feels for you; that he has never shirked any danger in defending your
standing; that time and again he fought it out with that pestilential
scourge* in defence of your glory; that his tribunate* had, under your
guidance, been directed towards my restoration, a cause which was
close to your own heart; that he had later been defended by you in a
criminal trial and received your support in his campaign for the
praetorship;* and that he had always hoped that two men would
remain his closest friends—you, because of all that you had done for
him, and I, because of all that he had done for me.

But if he should have failed to make this clear to you, if that
suspicion of yours had implanted itself in your mind so deeply that it
could never be uprooted, if there was genuinely no way that Italy
could be free of call-ups and Rome of weapons without Milo suffering disaster, then without a doubt Milo would surely have departed
from his country, such is his disposition and character. He would,
however, have appealed to you, Magnus,* just as he does now:
[69] 'You see how changeable and contrary human life is, how fickle
and fast-flowing fortune is, what faithlessness there is in friendships,
what pretences to suit the moment, what desertions by one's nearest
and dearest in times of trial, and what faint hearts! Yet a time will
surely come and a day at last will dawn (not, I hope, because of any
personal misfortune to yourself, but rather in one of those national
crises with which we ought by now to be well familiar) when you will
look in vain for the support of a true friend, the loyalty of a person of

complete integrity, and the heroism of the single most courageous man in history.'

[70] Gnaeus Pompeius is an expert in constitutional law, historical precedent, and the workings of politics,* and he was commissioned by the senate 'to see that the state comes to no harm'*—that brief formula which has always given the consuls all the weapons they need, even when they have been granted no actual arms. Could anyone seriously believe that such a man, when an army and the power to raise troops had actually been granted to him, would have considered it necessary to await the decision of a court before taking action to suppress someone who was using violence to overthrow those very courts? Clearly Pompeius is fully and completely satisfied that such allegations against Milo are false, since he proposed a law which, as I believe, requires you to acquit Milo, and as everyone concedes, at least allows you to do so. [71] But the fact that he is sitting over there surrounded by an official bodyguard is enough to show that he has no wish to intimidate you. For what would be more demeaning than for him to force you to convict a man whom he was entitled by law and precedent to punish himself? No, he and his bodyguard are there for your protection, to make it clear to you that, in spite of yesterday's public meeting,* you are free to cast your votes as you see fit.

[72] The charge of murdering Clodius, members of the jury, gives me no cause for concern.* I am not so deranged or so ignorant and unaware of your feelings as not to know your thoughts on Clodius' death. Suppose that I were not prepared* to refute the charge as I have done. It would then be open to Milo, without harming his defence, publicly to proclaim a glorious untruth: 'I admit I killed him! But the man I killed was not a Spurius Maelius* who, by lowering the price of corn and squandering his own property, appeared to have sided too strongly with the plebs and was therefore suspected of aiming at tyranny. Nor was he a Tiberius Gracchus* who deposed his colleague from office by revolutionary means. The killers of both these men won such glory that their names became famous throughout the world. No! The man I killed', Milo would dare to say, safe in the knowledge that he had freed his country at his own personal risk, 'was one whose unspeakable adultery,* actually committed on the sacred couches of the gods, was discovered by women of the highest rank. [73] A man whose punishment the senate repeatedly decreed to be necessary for the purification of the religious ceremonies that

he had defiled. A man whom Lucius Lucullus, after holding an investigation, declared on oath he had found guilty of the unspeakable crime of incest with his own sister.* A man who used the weapons of slaves to drive out a citizen* whom the senate, the Roman people, and all the nations had called saviour both of the city itself and of the lives of her citizens. A man who gave out kingdoms and took them away, and parcelled out the world to anyone he pleased.* A man who committed a great many murders in the forum, and who used armed force to confine an outstandingly brave and famous citizen* within his own home. A man who never saw anything wrong in any criminal deed or sexual outrage. A man who set fire to the temple of the Nymphs* in order to extinguish the official revision of the censors' register inscribed in the public records. [74] A man who respected no statute, no law, and no property boundary. Who went after other people's estates not by bringing false accusations against them or by submitting claims and deposits that were unjustified,* but by deploying camps, armies, and military standards. Who attempted to use weapons and camps to drive from their properties not just the people of Etruria, whom he had come to despise utterly, but this very juryman, Publius Varius,* a fine and valiant citizen. Who roamed around many people's country houses and suburban properties with architects and measuring rods. Who set the Janiculum and the Alps as the boundaries of the territory he hoped to acquire. Who, when he failed to induce the valiant and worthy equestrian Marcus Paconius* to sell him an island in Lake Prilius, suddenly took boat-loads of timber, lime, stone, and sand over to the island and, as the owner looked on from the shore, proceeded to erect a dwelling on land that was not his. Who had the nerve to tell Titus Furfanius* here (immortal gods, what a fine man!)—[75] for surely I do not need to mention that wretched woman Scantia* or the young Publius Apinius,* both of whom he threatened with death if they did not make over their suburban properties to him—who told Titus Furfanius that, if he did not give him the sum of money he demanded, he would plant a body in his house, and so destroy this admirable man's good name. Who in the absence of his brother Appius,* a man allied to myself by ties of the most loyal friendship, deprived him of the possession of his estate. And who, finally, set out to build foundations and construct a wall across his sister's forecourt* in such a way as not only to deprive her of the forecourt but to deny her access to and from her house entirely.'

[76] These acts of his had come to be seen as tolerable, even though they were directed equally against the state and against private individuals, against those far away and against those close to home, against strangers and against friends. Nevertheless, the amazing forbearance of our people, by being put to the test so often, had somehow become hardened and insensitive. But as for what was already upon us, and what was threatened, how could you possibly have either averted it or endured it? Suppose he had obtained military power.* I say nothing about the fate of our allies, foreign nations, kings, and tetrarchs: you would have been praying that he would hurl himself at them rather than at your own land, your houses, and your money. Money, did I say? Heaven is my witness, his lusts were so unbridled that he would not have refrained from assaulting your wives and children! Do you think I am making all this up? It is all plain to see, universally known, and established beyond doubt. Do you think I am making up the fact that he was on the point of enlisting armies of slaves within the city, and that he was going to use them to get his hands on the entire government of our country and on everybody's personal property?

[77] If, therefore, Titus Annius were to hold up his bloody sword and shout, 'Come and listen to me, citizens, if you will! I have killed Publius Clodius. With this blade and this right hand I have saved you from a man whose madness we were unable to curb by any laws or courts. I have thereby single-handedly ensured that justice and equity, law and liberty, and modesty and decency shall continue to exist in our country'—he would, I suppose, have reason to feel alarmed about how his fellow citizens might react! For, as things are, who does not approve of what he has done, who does not praise it, and who does not both declare and believe that Titus Annius has done more for this country than any other man in history,* and has brought the greatest joy to the Roman people, the whole of Italy, and all the nations of the world? I am not able to judge how joyful the happiness was that the Roman people experienced at various times in the past. But I can say that our age, too, has witnessed many famous victories won by generals of the highest distinction, but that none of these victories has occasioned such long-lasting and heartfelt celebration.

[78] Keep in mind what I am about to say, gentlemen. I trust that you and your children will enjoy many blessings in your public lives; but as you enjoy each one of them, please reflect that, if Publius Clodius had lived, none of them would have come your way. But as things are, I have high hopes—and, I believe, well-grounded ones—that, under this fine consul* that we now have, this year will turn out to be a good one for our country, and that disorder will be halted, unruly passions checked, and laws and courts established. Surely no one is mad enough to suppose that all this could be achieved if Publius Clodius were still with us? And again, if we were being ruled by a lunatic, do you think you could expect to enjoy any permanent right of possession over your own private property?

Members of the jury, I am not at all concerned that people might think I have been carried away by my own personal animosity towards my enemy, and that I am giving vent to my feelings about him with more zeal than truth. Even though I had more reason to hate him than others did, he was nevertheless so completely the enemy of everyone that the general hatred and my own amounted to much the same. Indeed, it is impossible to express, or even conceive, the extent of the criminality and destructiveness that existed in that one man.

[79] Look at it like this, gentlemen. I would like you to use your imaginations: after all, our minds range freely, and can see whatever they choose to, in just the same way as our eyes observe whatever we look at. Use your imaginations, then, to visualize what I propose—that I get you to acquit Milo, but only on condition that Publius Clodius comes back to life again. But why are you looking so terrified? In death, the mere thought of him has severely shaken you—so what effect do you think he would have on you if he were still living? Let me make another point. If Gnaeus Pompeius himself,* whose ability and good fortune have always enabled him to achieve what no one else can, if Pompeius, I repeat, could have had a choice between setting up an inquiry into Publius Clodius' death or bringing Clodius back to life, what do you think he would have chosen? Even if he had wished for friendship's sake to raise him from the dead, the national interest would have prevented him from doing so. You sit here, then, to avenge a man whose life you would never restore, if it were in your power to do so; and the law under which this inquiry was set up is one which, if it had entailed bringing this man back to

life, would never have been proposed. So if Milo were the killer of such a man as this, and admitted as much, do you really think he would have to fear punishment at the hands of those he had set free?

[80] The Greeks bestow divine honours on those who have killed tyrants.* What wonders I have witnessed in Athens and the other cities of Greece, what rituals ordained for these men, what music, what hymns in their honour! They are venerated with almost the same reverence and commemoration as the immortal gods. And will you not merely fail to reward a man who has saved so great a country and avenged so great a crime, but actually allow him to be led away to execution? If he had done the deed, he would admit—and admit, I tell you, proudly and willingly—that he had done for the freedom of all Romans a deed which ought properly to be not merely admitted, but actively gloried in. [81] And if he does not deny a deed* for which he seeks only pardon, would he hesitate to own up to a deed* for which he ought to seek to be rewarded with praise? Unless of course he had concluded that his preservation of his own life would be more agreeable to you than his preservation of yours! And of course by owning up to what he has done he would win the most generous rewards—if, that is, you chose to show your gratitude. But if his action should fail to win your approval (though how could anyone not approve of an action that has saved his life?), and if the bravery of an extremely courageous individual should fail to receive adequate recognition from his fellow citizens, then with a steadfast and unwavering spirit he would withdraw from his ungrateful country. And what more striking example of ingratitude could there be than for everyone else to rejoice, but for the man who gave them their reason for rejoicing to be himself, and he alone, plunged into mourning?

[82] All the same, when it comes to putting down traitors, we have always shared the view that, since the glory would be ours, the danger and the unpopularity that would also be incurred should be ours too. In my own consulship I undertook a bold venture* for the sake of yourselves and your children. But do you think I would really have deserved any praise for this if I had supposed that the venture which I was undertaking would not involve any great struggle on my part? Surely even a woman would have the courage to kill a wicked and pernicious citizen if she thought that there was no danger involved? No, the true hero is the one who knows that he faces unpopularity,

death, and punishment, but does not show any less vigour in acting to defend his country. It is right for a grateful people to reward citizens who have served their country well; and it is right for a man of courage not to be induced even by the prospect of execution to regret the courageous course that he has taken. [83] Titus Annius would therefore make the same admission that Ahala* did, that Nasica did, that Opimius did, that Marius did, and that I myself did. If the country showed its gratitude, he would be glad; but if it showed ingratitude, he would nevertheless in his misfortune derive satisfaction from the consciousness of having done right.

However, the fortune of the Roman people, your own good luck, and the immortal gods all claim your gratitude, gentlemen, for this blessing that you have received. No one could possibly think otherwise—unless there is anyone who does not believe in the existence of a divine power or force, or who remains unmoved by the sheer size of our empire, by the sun above our heads, by the movements of the sky and the heavenly bodies, by the world's ordered cycle of change, or (most important of all) by the wisdom of our ancestors, men who reverently observed the rituals, ceremonies, and auspices, and then handed them down to us, their descendants. [84] Yes, such a power does undoubtedly exist. It is inconceivable that there should exist in these weak and feeble bodies of ours something that has activity and consciousness, but that it should not exist in the great and wonderful workings of nature. Unless of course people do not believe in it because it cannot be viewed or discerned—as if we were capable of seeing or perceiving clearly the nature and position of our own minds, the minds which give us knowledge, foresight, and the ability to act and speak as I am doing now! It is accordingly this actual power, which has so often brought unimaginable blessings and prosperity to this city, that has now stamped out and eradicated that pernicious menace. It stirred up his mind and drove him to provoke and challenge with violence and the sword a man of supreme courage. He was vanquished; but had he been the victor he would have been free to do whatever he wished, without fear of punishment, for ever afterwards.

[85] It was not by human planning, gentlemen, nor by any ordinary attention on the part of the immortal gods that this event came about. No—by Hercules!—the very spot which witnessed that monster's fall appears to have roused itself and asserted its rights over

him. To you now, hills and groves of Alba,* to you I appeal and pray, and also to you, demolished altars of the Albans, associated with the religion of the Roman people and just as ancient—altars which that megalomaniac, after felling and levelling the most sacred groves, loaded with the gigantic pillars of the basement he was constructing. Yours was the sacred presence which exerted itself, yours was the force which prevailed against the criminal who had polluted it, and it was you, holy Jupiter, who from your lofty Latin hill did at last open your eyes to punish a man who had so often defiled your lakes, groves, and precincts with his many unspeakable immoralities and crimes. To you, yes, to you and in your very sight a long-delayed but just and richly deserved punishment has been paid. [86] Unless of course we are to put this also down to simple coincidence, the fact that it was in front of the actual shrine of the Good Goddess on the estate of Titus Sertius Gallus,* a conspicuously honourable and accomplished young man, in front of, I repeat, the Good Goddess herself that he initiated the fight, and so received that first wound by which he met his revolting death! And thus it was that he was shown not to have been acquitted by that scandalous verdict* but rather kept back for this glorious punishment.

And it was precisely the same divine anger which cast this madness that we have witnessed into his followers' minds and caused them to toss his charred corpse out into the street—without masks,* without dirges or games, without funeral rites, without weeping, without eulogies, without ceremony, covered in blood and dirt, and deprived of that final solemnity which even enemies invariably concede. Evidently the gods did not think it right that representations of his illustrious ancestors should lend a scrap of dignity to that disgusting murderer, or that his death should be dishonoured in any place other than the one in which his life had been condemned.

[87] As heaven is my witness, I had begun to think that the fortune of the Roman people was merciless and cruel, in that she had allowed that individual to trample on our country for so many years. He had sexually violated the most sacred of religious ceremonies. He had broken the most solemn decrees of the senate. He had openly used bribery to secure his acquittal when he was on trial. He had attacked the senate when he was tribune. He had cancelled measures that had been taken for the national security, and which had received the support of all the orders. As for me, he had driven me from my

country, plundered my property, burned down my home, and persecuted my wife and children. He had wickedly declared war on Gnaeus Pompeius. He had murdered magistrates and private citizens alike. He had set fire to my brother's home. He had devastated Etruria. He had turned many people out of their homes and taken their property. And he went on and on and on. Neither Rome nor Italy nor the provinces nor our dependent kingdoms could put a stop to his madness. At his own house laws were already being inscribed which would have made us subject to our own slaves.* Whatever property he coveted, he felt certain that he could get his hands on it within a year, no matter to whom it belonged. [88] His schemes were opposed by no one except Milo. As for the great man who could have resisted him, Clodius considered that person to be bound over to him by their recent reconciliation.* As for Caesar's power, Clodius said that belonged to him. And as for the feeling of the respectable classes, he had shown his contempt for them by his treatment of me. It was Milo, and Milo only, who stood up to him.

It was at this point that the immortal gods, as I said just now, put into that raving lunatic's head the idea of setting a trap for my client. There was no other way that that pestilential villain could ever have been got rid of. The state, with the powers it had, would never have taken its revenge on him. When he became praetor the senate would of course have kept him under control! But it failed to do so even in the days when it did take the necessary action, and when Clodius was merely a private citizen. [89] Or would the consuls have shown some courage and kept the praetor in check? In the first place Clodius, after killing Milo, would have had the consuls he wanted.* And secondly, what consul would have ventured to take a firm line with a praetor who, when only a tribune, had cruelly persecuted a brave ex-consul?* No, Clodius would have taken control, ownership, and possession of everything. Indeed, a new law was discovered at his house among the rest of his intended legislation, a law which would have made our slaves his own freedmen.* In short, if the immortal gods had not put it into his head to try to kill, effeminate sissy that he was, a real man of true courage, then today your country would no longer exist.

[90] If he had been praetor, if he had been consul (assuming these temples and the city walls themselves could have remained standing with him alive, and calmly waited for the year of his consulship!), if

he had been merely still living, do you really imagine he would have done no harm—considering that even when he was dead one of his followers* burned down the senate-house? Have we ever witnessed anything more sickening, painful, and distressing than that? The temple of sanctity and of majesty and of wisdom and of public deliberation, the very head of our city, the protection of our allies, the haven of every nation, the seat granted to a single order by a united people burned, destroyed, and desecrated—and all this done not by an ignorant mob, which would have been upsetting enough, but by a single individual? And if he dared to go so far when he was serving as a cremator for someone who was dead, what would he not have done as a standard-bearer for someone who was alive? Indeed, his purpose in throwing the body into the senate-house was so that Clodius in death should burn down the building which in life he had tried so hard to topple.

[91] And yet there are those who harp on about the Appian Way, but say not a word about the senate-house; who think that the forum could have been defended against a living man when the senate-house was unable to stand up to his dead body! Go on, then, raise him from the dead, if you can! But will you be able to oppose the violence of the living man when you are scarcely able to withstand the Furies of his unburied corpse? Unless of course you were successful in withstanding the men who converged on the senate-house with firebrands and on the temple of Castor with the rods of office,* and who overran the forum with drawn swords! You saw the Roman people massacred and a public meeting broken up at sword-point—a meeting at which people were listening quietly to the tribune Marcus Caelius,* a valiant defender of our country's interests, a determined advocate in each case that he undertakes, a devoted champion of patriotic causes and the senate's authority, and a man of outstanding, superhuman, and incredible loyalty to Milo in his present predicament or, one might say, his present good fortune.

[92] But I have now said quite enough about the case itself—and about what goes beyond that, perhaps even too much. So what is left, except for me to beg and beseech you, members of the jury, to extend to this man of courage the mercy for which he does not himself ask, but which I, against his wishes, both ask for and implore? If amid all our weeping you have seen not a single tear from Milo,* if you see his expression always the same, his tone of voice and his speech steady

and unchanging, then do not hold this against him. In fact I think this ought to make you all the more inclined to help him. In gladiatorial combats, involving men whose position and lot is that of the lowest class, we generally feel contempt for those who are cowardly and grovel and beg for their lives, while those who are brave and spirited and face their deaths undaunted we prefer to see spared. We feel more pity, in other words, for those who do not ask for our mercy than for those who beg for it. How much more will this be true, then, when the man in question is not someone of low class but one of our most courageous citizens!

[93] As for me, gentlemen, I feel bowled over and utterly destroyed by these words of Milo's which I am perpetually hearing and which surround me all day long. 'Farewell,' he says, 'farewell, my fellow citizens! May you be safe, prosperous, and happy. May this famous city still stand, and this country so dear to me, regardless of how she will treat me. May my fellow citizens enjoy peaceful government—without me, since I am not permitted to enjoy it with them, but nevertheless because of me. I shall retire and depart. If I shall not be allowed to enjoy good government, at least I shall be spared bad,* and the first well-ordered and free community* that I come to, there I shall take my rest.

[94] 'All my efforts', he continues, 'have been in vain! All my hopes have been dashed! All my dreams have come to nothing! When I was tribune of the plebs* and our country was being devastated, I devoted myself to the senate, which had been annihilated, to the Roman equestrians, whose power had been weakened, and to all loyal citizens, who had surrendered their authority in the face of Clodius' violence. Could I possibly have imagined, at that time, that these people would ever fail to support me? And when I had restored you* to your country'—Milo often says this to me—'did I ever imagine that there would be no place in that country for myself? Where is the senate now, whose followers we were? Where are the Roman equestrians,' he says, 'your very own equestrians?* Where is the support of the towns, where are the voices of Italy, and where, Marcus Tullius, is your eloquent advocacy, which has defended so many others in the past? Am I the only person it will fail to help, I, who have so often hazarded my life for your sake?'

[95] But he does not say these words, gentlemen, as I do now—with tears in his eyes. No, his expression remains just as you see it.

For he refuses to believe that the citizens on whose behalf he acted*
feel no sense of gratitude; although he does believe that they are
fearful and on the look-out for every kind of danger. As for the base
plebeian mob, led by Publius Clodius, which threatened your security, this, Milo reminds us, he made his own, to protect your lives.
And it was not just by strength of character that he controlled it: he
also used up his three inheritances in winning it over. Nor is he
worried that, when he has appeased the plebs with games, he should
then fail to win you over—by his outstanding services to our country.
The senate's goodwill towards himself, he says, has been demonstrated many times during these difficult days; and whatever course
his fortune takes, he will take away with him the greetings, support,
and kind words of yourselves and the orders which you represent.
[96] He also remembers that it was only the herald's formal
announcement, the thing he coveted least, that he failed to secure; it
was instead the unanimous vote of the people, the only thing he
desired, that declared him consul. And now, if these proceedings are
to go against him, he believes that it is merely the suspicion of some
evil intention* and not guilt on the present charge that will have
proved his undoing.

He further points out, correctly, that men who are brave and wise
do not pursue the rewards of right action so much as right action
itself; and that everything he has done in his life has been highly
meritorious—assuming, of course, that there is nothing more honourable than to deliver one's country from danger. Men who have
been honoured by their fellow citizens for such services are, he says,
happy; [97] while those who have performed greater services than
their fellow citizens are not unhappy. But of all the rewards that
virtue brings (if we must be calculating rewards), the greatest is
glory. It is this alone which makes up for the shortness of our lives,
through the recollection of future generations. It enables us,
although absent, to be present, and although dead, to live. In short, it
is this which supplies the steps by which men may seem to climb as
high as the gods.

[98] 'The Roman people', says Milo, 'shall always speak of me.
Foreign nations shall always speak of me. No age, however distant,
shall ever fall silent about what I have achieved. Even at this very
moment, although my enemies are lighting the fires of hatred against
me, my name is spoken of wherever people meet together, and grati-

tude and congratulations are the subject of everyone's talk. I say nothing of the festivals that have been celebrated or instituted throughout Etruria. Today is, I believe, the hundred and second day* since Publius Clodius' death. Not only has the news of that event now travelled all the way to the boundaries of the empire of the Roman people, but so has the public rejoicing. For this reason,' says Milo, 'I do not care where my body may be, since the glory of my name exists in every land, and will live there for all time.'

[99] That is how you speak to me away from the court, Milo, but here in court this is what I say to you. Your resolution I cannot praise highly enough. But the more superhuman your courage is, the more pain I feel at being separated from you. And if you are indeed taken from me, I will not even have the usual solace of being able to feel angry at those who are inflicting such a terrible wound on me. For it is not my enemies who will take you away from me, but my dearest friends, not those who have on occasion treated me badly in the past, but those who have always been good to me.

Gentlemen, you will never inflict on me a more painful blow than this—for what could possibly be as bad? But even this blow will not be enough to make me forget the high regard in which you have always held me. If, however, you yourselves have forgotten your regard for me, or if I have offended you in some way, why do you not make me, rather than Milo, pay the price for that? For if any disaster should happen to me before I see Milo suffer this awful fate, then my life will have been a glorious one.

[100] But as things are, Titus Annius, there is one consolation that sustains me—the thought that there is no duty of love, support, or devotion in which I have failed you. I have incurred the hostility of the powers that be* for your sake; I have exposed my body and my life many times to the weapons of your enemies; I have abased myself as a suppliant before many people for your sake; I have risked my own property and possessions, and those of my children, by throwing in my lot with yours; and today, if any violence has been arranged, or if there is to be any life and death struggle, then I claim it as my own. What, then, does that leave? What more can I do for you, to repay your services to me, except to consider your own fortune, whatever it may be, as my own? I shall not refuse it. I shall not say 'No'. And I beseech you, gentlemen, either to add to the kindnesses which you have bestowed upon me by saving my client, or to recognize that, if

instead you destroy him, all those kindnesses will have been for nothing.

[101] Milo remains unmoved by these tears: his strength of mind surpasses all belief. Exile, he thinks, does not exist, except where virtue finds no place. Death he regards as the natural end of life, not as a punishment. Let him keep this attitude: it is one that he was born with. But as for you, gentlemen, what will your attitude be? Will you cherish Milo's memory but expel his person? And is any place on earth more worthy to give shelter to his virtue than this one which gave it birth?* I appeal to you, valiant gentlemen, you who have shed so much blood in defence of our country. I appeal to you, centurions, and to you, soldiers of the lower ranks: a citizen, never before defeated, is facing the gravest danger! You are not mere onlookers: you are standing guard over this court and you have weapons in your hands. Will you allow such virtue as Milo's to be ejected, expelled, and banished from this city?

[102] How unhappy I am! What appalling luck I have had! You succeeded, Milo, in obtaining the help of these men in recalling me to my country; shall I be unsuccessful in obtaining their help to keep you in yours? What shall I say to my children, who count you as their second father? What shall I say to you, brother Quintus, who are now far away,* but who shared those difficult times with me? That, in attempting to protect Milo's welfare, I was unable to obtain the help of the very men who had enabled Milo to secure my own welfare? Unable in what sort of cause? One that was approved by all the nations of the world. Unable to protect Milo's welfare from whom? From those who had felt the greatest relief at the death of Publius Clodius. And on whose advocacy? My own.

[103] What terrible crime did I devise or what awful deed did I commit, gentlemen, when I tracked down, uncovered, exposed, and expunged those indications of our impending destruction?* All my troubles, and those of those close to me, derive from that source. Why did you want me to return to Rome? Was it so that I could watch the expulsion of those by whom my restoration was secured? I beseech you, do not let my return be more painful to me than my departure was! For how can I consider myself restored if I am to be separated from those who were responsible for securing my restoration?

How I wish that the immortal gods had arranged—forgive me, my country, for what I am about to say, since I am afraid that the words which I am obliged to utter in Milo's defence will constitute a criminal attack on you—how I wish that Publius Clodius had not merely remained alive but had become praetor, consul, even dictator rather than that I should have to witness such a spectacle as this! [104] But Milo will have none or it—immortal gods, what a brave man, and one, gentlemen, whom you would do well to save! 'No, no,' he says, 'it is right for Clodius to have paid the penalty he deserved: I am prepared, if necessary, to pay one that I do not deserve.' Shall this man, born to serve his country, die anywhere other than in his country—unless, perhaps, for his country? Will you hold onto the memorials of his spirit, but allow no funerary monument within Italy to be set up over his body? Will any of you use his vote to expel from Rome a man whom every other city will welcome with open arms? [105] Fortunate the land that shall accept this man! Ungrateful Rome, if she shall cast him out! Unhappy Rome, if she shall lose him!

But I must stop now. I can no longer speak for tears—and my client has ordered that tears are not to be used in his defence. But I beg and implore you, gentlemen, when you cast your votes, to be bold enough to vote the way you feel. Believe me, your courage, fairness, and good faith will be strongly approved by the man* who, when he picked this jury, was careful to select those who were the best, the wisest, and the most brave.

EXPLANATORY NOTES

Notes are cued to section numbers in the text. For recurring terms see the Glossary.

PRO ROSCIO AMERINO

3 *although ... abolished at Rome!*: this was the first murder trial since Sulla's proscriptions (§ 11). Cicero probably added this outspoken and abrupt remark when he published the speech.

6 *illustrious*: Cicero refers to senators as *clarissimi* and to *equites* (less commonly) as *splendidi*. This was a standard convention and in order to reproduce it in English I have translated these words throughout (when they refer to individuals) as 'illustrious' and 'worthy' respectively.

8 *You have been raised ... high character*: in 81 BC Sulla had added three hundred *equites* to the senate; he had then enacted a law that juries should consist exclusively of senators (previously they had consisted exclusively of *equites*). See note on § 139 below.

11 *when you presided ... before*: this was evidently some years earlier (Cicero says below and at § 28 that there had been no trials for murder for a long time); the court will therefore have been not the Sullan murder and poisoning court in which Roscius is being tried but its pre-Sullan predecessor, about which nothing is known. At that time Fannius would have been *iudex quaestionis* ('court judge'), and would presumably have been an ex-aedile.

15 *the Metelli, Servilii, and Scipiones*: the Caecilii Metelli were the most consistently distinguished family in Rome at this period (between 123 and 109 BC, six members of the family attained the consulship); in the year of Roscius' trial Quintus Caecilius Metellus Pius was consul with Sulla (and his first cousin Caecilia Metella, who died in 81, had been Sulla's wife). The following year, 79 BC, the consuls were Publius Servilius Vatia Isauricus and Appius Claudius Pulcher; Servilius was a first cousin of the Caecilia Metella who helped Roscius (§§ 27 (where see note), 147, 149), while Pulcher was her brother-in-law. (For a family tree of the Metelli, see J. Carcopino, *Sylla ou la monarchie manquée* (Paris, 1931), at end.) The Scipiones were another great family; their more recent members included Publius Cornelius Scipio Nasica Serapio, consul of 111, and Lucius Cornelius Scipio Asiaticus, consul of 83 (spared by Sulla).

16 *the recent civil disturbance*: the civil war between Sulla and the Marians (83–82 BC). The nobility were on Sulla's side.

18 *the baths of Pallacina*: near the Circus Flaminius at the southern end of

the Campus Martius (north-west of the forum), but the precise location is unknown.

20 *Volaterrae*: a hill-town in northern Etruria in which the Marians held out against Sulla for two years (82–80 BC); it was subsequently made a colony for Sulla's veterans.

bordered on the Tiber: a great advantage, allowing the produce of the farms to be transported to Rome by boat.

worthy: see note on § 6 above.

22 *although Sulla is 'fortunate'*: a play on the name 'Felix' ('the fortunate'), which Sulla had assumed upon the death of the younger Marius (son of the famous Marius) in 82 BC. Sulla also called two of his children Faustus and Fausta ('Lucky').

27 *Caecilia*: Caecilia Metella, the daughter of Quintus Caecilius Metellus Baliaricus, consul of 123, and sister of Quintus Caecilius Metellus Nepos, consul of 98; the Metellus who was consul with Sulla in the year of Roscius' trial (Quintus Caecilius Metellus Pius) was her third cousin, while the following year her brother-in-law and her first cousin were consuls together (see note on § 15 above). Her uncles (mentioned at § 147) were Lucius Caecilius Metellus Diadematus, consul in 117, Marcus Caecilius Metellus, consul in 115, and Gaius Caecilius Metellus Caprarius, consul in 113. Caecilia was a third cousin of the Caecilia Metella who was married to Sulla but died in 81.

29 *you . . . supreme authority*: the jury.

30 *sewn up in a sack*: the traditional punishment for parricide was to be stripped, scourged, sewn up in a sack together with a dog, a cock, a viper, and a monkey, and then thrown into a river or the sea to drown. The first reliably attested instance of this punishment dates from 102–101 BC (Livy, *Epitome* 68); it was also imposed by Cicero's brother Quintus when governor of Asia in 59 (*Epistulae ad Quintum fratrem* 1.2.5). In this speech Cicero speaks about the sack (see also §§ 70–2), but decides against mentioning the animals, perhaps for reasons of taste (cf. *Orat.* 107).

32 *You murdered my father*: Cicero speaks in Roscius' persona—an unusual and striking device repeated at §§ 94 and 145.

33 *Gaius Fimbria*: Gaius Flavius Fimbria was a prominent supporter of Marius, joining in his massacre at Rome in 87 BC. Cicero says he attempted to murder Scaevola (see next note) at Marius' funeral in 86; while he was alive, Marius had protected Scaevola, who was a relation of his by marriage. Later in 86 Fimbria went east against Mithridates under Lucius Valerius Flaccus, who had succeeded to Marius' place as consul; murdering Flaccus, he illegally assumed command, but committed suicide in 85 after his army had gone over to Sulla.

Quintus Scaevola: Quintus Mucius Scaevola, consul in 95 and *pontifex maximus* from 89. He served as an exemplary governor of Asia in 97

(or 94) and, besides being a famous orator, was the author of the first
systematic treatise on Roman law. He remained in Rome under Marius
and Cinna, surviving Fimbria's attempt to murder him (see previous
note), but was killed by the Marians in 82 to prevent him going over to
Sulla. Cicero implies below that he was trying to reconcile the two sides
in order to save the lives of the Marians. Cicero studied under Scaevola
from *c*.86 (*De amicitia* 1).

33 *'because he failed . . . chest'*: at the games, if the crowd shouted 'take the
sword' to a defeated gladiator, he was required to bare his chest to receive
the death-blow.

46 *no . . . knowledge of who your father is*: i.e. Erucius' mother was promiscu-
ous. Insults of this kind were part and parcel of ancient rhetorical
invective; there need not be any truth in them.

Caecilius: Caecilius Statius (d. 168 BC), the leading comic playwright
between Plautus and Terence, and a friend of Ennius. The play referred
to is his lost *Hypobolimaeus* (*The Supposititious Son*), which was adapted
from Menander. Cicero assumes a knowledge of the plot. Evidently
Chaerestratus, who lived in the city, was the supposititious son, and
Eutychus, who lived in the country, was the legitimate one preferred by
the father.

47 *the territory of Veii*: an agricultural district ten miles north-west of Rome,
named by Cicero *exempli gratia*. The Etruscan town of Veii no longer
existed, having been destroyed by the Romans in 396 BC.

48 *Umbria*: the region in which Roscius' home town, Ameria, was situated.

50 *Atilius*: the story was that one Atilius (perhaps Gaius Atilius Regulus,
consul in 257 and 250) was found sowing on his farm when he was called
on to undertake a military command, and hence acquired the nickname
'Serranus' (from *serere*, 'to sow'). The story will have been invented to
explain the unusual name. A similar tale was told of Lucius Quinctius
Cincinnatus, called from the plough to become dictator in 458.

55 *the Remmian law*: the *lex Remmia de calumnia* (Remmian law concerning
false accusation), of unknown date. The law imposed penalties for
malicious prosecution. See note on § 57 below.

56 *the geese on the Capitol*: these geese, which were sacred to Juno, had been
kept at public expense since 390 BC, when by their honking they raised
the alarm and so prevented the Capitol from being taken by the Gauls.

57 *they will tattoo . . . every month*: this passage implies that malicious prosecutors convicted under the Remmian law (see note on § 55 above) were
tattooed on the forehead with the letter K (the original initial letter of
calumniator, 'false accuser'). They would have been forbidden to undertake further prosecutions, and the tattoo would have ensured that any
application to prosecute which they might make would be rejected. (On
penal tattooing, see C. P. Jones, *JRS* 77 (1987), 139–55.) The letter K also
signified the Kalends (the first day of the month), on which the interest

on debts was due for payment. Cicero implies that Erucius has debts, and
has therefore taken a bribe to prosecute Roscius.

64 *Titus Cloelius from Tarracina*: on the name (wrongly given as 'Caelius'
at Valerius Maximus 8.1.abs.13) see T. P. Wiseman, *CR* NS 17 (1967),
263–4; Wiseman suggests that Cloelius may have been the same man as
the Titus Cloulius who was a moneyer in *c*.125 BC. Tarracina was 65 miles
south of Rome on the west coast of Italy (about half-way between Rome
and Naples). It had originally been a Volscian town with the name Anxur.

66 *sons ... to avenge their fathers*: Orestes (prompted by Apollo) killed
Clytemnestra to avenge Agamemnon; Alcmaeon killed Eriphyle to
avenge Amphiaraus. The Romans were familiar with these myths from
the plays of Ennius, Pacuvius, and Accius.

70 *Solon*: chief archon at Athens in 594–593 BC, and instigator of a wide
range of political, economic, and social reforms; he was traditionally
included among the 'Seven Sages' of Greece. His law code formed the
basis of classical Athenian law; this remained in force under the Romans
because of Athens' status as a 'free city' (*civitas libera*).

   parricides should be ... thrown into a river: see note on § 30 above.

72 *For what is so free ... a resting-place in death*: near the end of his life, in
46 BC, Cicero wrote disparagingly of this passage: 'What loud applause
there was when in my youth I spoke the following passage, one which
some time afterwards I began to feel was not nearly subdued enough
(*nequaquam satis defervisse*): [the passage is quoted]. This was the product
of a young man who was admired not so much for maturity and achievement as for promise and potential' (*Orat.* 107). It is nevertheless one of
Cicero's finest passages.

73 *even though it is my turn to speak*: the speeches of the prosecution, and
then those of the defence, were heard first without interruption; then the
evidence was taken; and finally a debate (*altercatio*) was held between the
two parties on the points in dispute. Cicero says here that he will allow
Erucius to debate with him now, without waiting until the *altercatio*.

77 *by offering their slaves for interrogation*: the evidence of slaves and others
was taken only after the speeches had been given (see previous note). As
at Athens, slaves could give evidence only under torture, since it was
believed that they could not be trusted to tell the truth unless it was
forced out of them; their evidence was then written down and read out to
the jury. However, slaves were not permitted to testify against their master, except in cases involving incest and in the specific case of the Catilinarian conspiracy (63–62 BC). Nor were masters required to hand over
their slaves to the court if they did not wish to (except in the cases just
mentioned): neither Cicero nor Fannius could compel Chrysogonus to
submit his slaves for interrogation.

   Publius Scipio ... Marcus Metellus: it is uncertain who these men
were, and 'Marcus' is a conjecture (the *praenomen* is omitted in the

manuscripts). Publius Scipio could be Publius Cornelius Scipio Nasica, praetor in *c*.93, and Metellus could be Marcus Caecilius Metellus, the praetor of 69.

82 *until the witnesses are heard*: see notes above on §§ 73 and 77 (first note).

83 *I should prefer to prosecute . . . to advance my career*: when a senator was convicted, his accuser, if a senator himself, acceded to his victim's rank in the senate, or if not a senator, took his victim's insignia of rank. Cicero means that, if he really wanted to advance his career by prosecuting, he would prosecute senators. Wisely he chose not to do this (until his prosecution of Verres in 70 BC): although prosecuting was an easy way for a young man to become noticed, it was also an easy way to make enemies.

84 *Lucius Cassius*: Lucius Cassius Longinus Ravilla, consul in 127 and censor in 125. He was famous for his use of the question *cui bono?* ('who stood to gain?'), and his strictness was proverbial (hence the popular name for his tribunal, *scopulus reorum* ('Defendants' rock', suggesting shipwreck), and the reference to 'Cassian jurors' in § 85). Cicero applies the principle *cui bono?* again at *Mil.* 32 and *Phil.* 2.35.

89 *the battle of Cannae*: this battle, in which a Roman army of 80,000 men was destroyed by Hannibal in 216 BC, is used here simply to indicate a great massacre. Cicero is referring to the period of Sulla's proscriptions, during which, he says, many prosecutors were killed. He claims that Erucius' survival gave him a prominence in the law courts which he would not otherwise have deserved.

lake of Trasimene . . . Servilian one: Lake Trasimene was the site of another defeat inflicted on Rome by Hannibal, in 217 BC. The Servilian 'lake' was a fountain in the forum, probably situated at the beginning of the Vicus Iugarius (the word *lacus* means both 'lake' and 'tank'); it was here (and also on the rostra nearby) that the severed heads of the proscribed were displayed.

90 *'Who was not wounded . . . Phrygian steel?'*: a quotation from a tragedy by Ennius (it is not certain which one); in the play, the words were spoken by the wounded Ulysses to Ajax after Hector had set fire to the Greek ships. 'Phrygian' stands for 'Trojan'.

a Curtius, a Marius . . . a Memmius: these prosecutors killed in the proscriptions cannot be identified with certainty. The words 'exempted from active service on grounds of age' explain that it was some time since the men had undertaken their prosecutions. They were presumably prosecutors active during the Cinnan regime.

that old Priam . . . Antistius: the identity of this further proscribed prosecutor, Antistius, is also uncertain. The reference to Priam (king of Troy) is mock-heroic, indicating Antistius' age and status; Cicero should really have chosen a Greek name in view of the quotation from Ennius, which described the wounding of Greeks by Trojans ('Phrygian steel'). The reference to Antistius' having been disqualified from fighting (that is, in the courts) because of the laws suggests that he had been convicted for malicious prosecution (see notes on §§ 55 and 57 above).

91 *he who had overall control*: Sulla. Cicero refers to the period of lawlessness which preceded Sulla's re-establishment of the courts in 81 BC.

94 *'But I was never there at all'*: see note on § 32 above.

96 *wife, and children*: it is a little strange that we hear nothing further about the elder Roscius' wife (the mother of Cicero's client). The reference to 'children' need not imply the existence of a daughter, since 'children' was sometimes written for 'child' (cf. Aulus Gellius 2.13).

98 *Automedon*: mock-heroic: Automedon was the charioteer of Achilles.

100 *the first major decoration*: literally, 'the first beribboned palm'. A palm branch, symbolizing victory, could be decorated with coloured ribbons to denote a particularly distinguished victory.

   I can even tell you . . . into the Tiber!: in mentioning Capito's murder of a man by throwing him from a bridge into the Tiber, Cicero jokingly introduces a reference to the festival of the Argei, which took place at Rome each year on 15 May. At this festival, twenty-seven straw effigies of 'Argei' (i.e. 'Greeks', the enemy nation at the time when the festival originated, in the sixth century) were thrown from the Sublician Bridge into the Tiber, in order to propitiate the dead. The Romans themselves explained the ceremony as a substitution for human sacrifice. But there was also a view, found in Festus (452 Lindsay) and alluded to by Ovid (*Fasti* 5.623–4, 633–4), that the festival was connected with the period after the sack of Rome by the Gauls in 390 BC, when men over 60 years of age were supposedly thrown from the bridge to prevent their becoming a burden on the city; hence the expressions 'thrown from the bridge' (*depontani*) and '60-year-olds off the bridge' (*sexagenarii de ponte*). Cicero's joke, then, is that the Romans of old would not have approved of the murder committed by Capito, because his victim was not old enough to be thrown from the bridge. On the festival of the Argei see B. Nagy, *AJAH* 10 (1985), 1–27.

102 *one of the two*: Magnus.

   his master: cf. § 17.

   The other one: Capito.

103 *Africanus*: i.e. Scipio Aemilianus (Publius Cornelius Scipio Aemilianus Africanus), the consul of 147 and 134, who destroyed Carthage in 146 and Numantia in 133. Europe, Asia, and Africa constituted the known world.

104 *my good friend*: Magnus again.

105 *Volaterrae*: see first note on § 20 above.

109 *the ten leaders of the council*: see § 25.

110 *if the prosecution . . . as witnesses*: only the prosecution had the power to require witnesses to give evidence; the defence had to rely on evidence

voluntarily given. The prosecution was thus able to intimidate witnesses for the defence from coming forward.

111 *in the execution of a trust*: a trust (*mandatum*) was a contract in which one person undertook to do or give something at another's request; it was entered into by mutual agreement, and without remuneration.

112 *Why accept a trust . . . advantage?*: Cicero is not addressing Capito, but an imaginary person who is not fit to act as a trustee.

     by no means . . . insignificant: the play on words, which is foreign to English, is characteristically Ciceronian. This sentence has been translated fairly literally because there are doubts about the text.

114 *convicted by an arbitrator*: civil suits concerned with matters of good faith were heard not by a judge (*iudex*) but by an arbitrator (*arbiter*), who based his decision on considerations of equity rather than law.

119 *I said earlier . . . for interrogation*: see § 77, with first note, above.

     I have . . . mentioned their names: at § 77.

     to offer himself . . . under torture: this would of course have been impossible, since Roscius was not a slave.

122 *at the outset*: § 35.

123 *at the beginning*: that is, of the part of the speech dealing with Magnus and Capito, i.e. § 83.

124 *that golden name*: a pun on Chrysogonus' name (*chrysos* means 'gold' in Greek), and an allusion to his profiteering during the proscriptions.

125 *the Valerian law or the Cornelian*: Cicero is referring to (and will shortly quote from) a single law, the law which set out the terms of the proscriptions. The uncertainty over the name of the law arises from the fact that it was proposed by Lucius Valerius Flaccus but framed by Sulla (82 BC): the law was unpopular and controversial, and it had evidently not yet been agreed whose name it should bear (see T. E. Kinsey, *Mnemosyne*, 21 (1968), 290–2). Cicero parades his ignorance of this law probably because he wants to distance himself from a law of which he disapproves; his disapproval was shared by the senate (§ 153). By 70 the law had come to be known as the Cornelian law, i.e. was regarded as Sulla's (*In Verrem* 2.1.123).

127 *this I will show later on*: Cicero does not return to this point, so it was presumably dealt with in the part of the speech which is lost (§ 132).

128 *we are being cheated . . . than we had realized*: i.e. the absence of a record of sale in the public accounts would confirm Cicero's suspicion that the sale never took place.

132 *the prosecution . . .* : in the gap which follows, to judge from the scholia, Cicero probably expatiated on the questions asked in § 130, and concluded that Roscius' property was never legally sold (cf. the reference forwards at § 127). The scholia state that he then proceeded to attack

Chrysogonus' power and wealth (in the passage beginning 'at this point I want those men to hear . . . ').

the territory of the Sallentini or the Bruttii: i.e. the heel (Calabria) or the toe (Bruttium) of Italy.

133 *the other one*: i.e. Chrysogonus.

135 *escorted by . . . citizens in togas*: Cicero is indignant that an ex-slave should be waited upon by free-born Roman citizens.

136 *good fortune*: see note on § 22 above.

139 *they will have to resign their distinctions*: Cicero is thinking of the law courts. Sulla had transferred the responsibility for providing juries from the *equites* to the senate (see note on § 8 above). Cicero hints that this change could one day be reversed, if the senate should abuse their privilege. Ten years later, Sulla's law was indeed overturned, and the *lex Aurelia* (70 BC) made juries henceforward two-thirds equestrian (i.e. one-third *equites* and one-third *tribuni aerarii*) and only one-third senatorial.

140 *who could not endure . . . the equestrian order*: the *equites* had provided the juries for the courts; this privilege was resented by the senate and withdrawn by Sulla (see previous note). Cicero was himself an *eques* at this date (later becoming a senator in 75 BC).

exercised in other fields: a reference to the proscriptions and the sales of confiscated property.

144 *the ring*: the gold ring which denoted equestrian rank.

145 *You are in possession of my farms*: see note on § 32 above.

something . . . than anyone else: because of his closeness to Sulla; but Cicero's words can also be understood ironically.

146 *You do an injustice*: i.e. to Sulla.

147 *Caecilia*: see note on § 27 above.

149 *Marcus Messalla*: probably Marcus Valerius Messalla Rufus, the future consul of 53 and nephew of the orator Hortensius. He is known from *Pro Sulla* 42 to have stood for the praetorship of 61, and since the minimum age for the praetorship was 39, he must have been born by 101 BC. This would make him 21 in the year of Roscius' trial—too young, as Cicero says, to speak for the defence (so there is no need to attribute his silence to political caution). During the year, Messalla's sister Valeria married Sulla; but whether this was before or after Roscius' trial is unclear. In 62 Messalla again asked Cicero to undertake a defence, this time of Sulla's nephew, Publius Sulla (*Pro Sulla* 20); the speech survives.

151 *'council of state'*: usually denotes the senate (as at § 153), but can also refer to a court of law.

153 *a new and far crueller proscription*: Roscius' father, of course, was not proscribed; but Cicero wants (even at the expense of consistency) to give his case a wider relevance. This passage (§§ 152–4) was probably revised or added by Cicero when he published the speech.

PRO MURENA

3 *the law on electoral malpractice*: Cicero's *lex Tullia de ambitu* (Tullian law concerning electoral malpractice), passed during the election campaign of 63 (see second note on § 67 below).

such severity during my consulship: Cicero's remarks on his severity, here and at § 6, are more readily applicable to his execution of the Catilinarian conspirators on 5 December (a week or two after Murena's trial) than to his expulsion of Catiline from Rome on 7 November. These passages may therefore have been introduced when the speech was written up for publication, at a time when Cicero was being criticized for the executions.

When property that has been formally sold: Cicero now compares himself to a seller who gives the purchaser (Murena) a guarantee of title to the property he is selling him (the consulship). Although rather involved, the analogy is a good one because it represents Cicero's duty to defend Murena as a contractual obligation.

4 *in some states*: it is not clear which states Cicero is thinking of.

a severe buffeting: the Catilinarian conspiracy.

two consuls . . . on the first of January: if Murena were acquitted, he and Decimus Junius Silanus would take office on 1 January 62; if he were convicted, only Silanus would take office, and he would then be occupied with arranging the election of Murena's replacement, leaving him no time to deal with Catiline. Cicero returns to this point at §§ 79–82.

6 *the severity I showed*: see second note on § 3 above.

by my words: i.e. by Cicero's *First Catilinarian*, delivered in the senate on 7 November.

8 *I feel that . . . to which they led*: these words are missing in the manuscripts; I have restored what I take to be the sense.

11 *Asia*: in 84 BC Sulla, who had hastily concluded the First Mithridatic War (88–85) so that he could return to Italy and recover Rome from the Marians, left the elder Murena in command of Asia. Murena resumed hostilities against Mithridates (the Second Mithridatic War, 83–81), was heavily defeated, and returned to Rome to celebrate a triumph (81). The younger Murena, Cicero's client, served under his father during these discreditable campaigns. The prosecution have accused him of succumbing to the temptations of wealth and luxurious living, for which Asia was notorious, during his service there.

Sons . . . at their father's triumphs: if they had not yet assumed the toga of manhood (on which see fourth note on *Arch.* 5), the sons of a triumphing general would ride on the horses which drew his chariot (unless they were too young to ride, in which case they would join their father inside the chariot—an illustration of the Romans' love of children); adult sons rode on their own horses behind the chariot.

15 *secession . . . to the Aventine*: secession (withdrawal) to a hill outside the
city boundary, generally the Aventine, was the traditional means by
which the plebeians in the early republic had sought to compel the patricians to redress their grievances; crucially, secession involved refusal to
enter military service. The first secession, which resulted in the institu-
tion of the tribunate, took place in 494 BC, and the last in 287; five
secessions are recorded.

both . . . were praetors: Murena's great-grandfather Lucius Licinius
Murena was praetor at some date before 146, and his grandfather of the
same name at some date before 100.

after capping . . . triumph: Murena's father was praetor in *c*.88. On his
triumph see first note on § 11 above.

16 *your noble birth*: there was a Servius Sulpicius Rufus who was military
tribune with consular power (equivalent to a consul) in 388, 384, and 383
from whom Sulpicius could have claimed descent, and also various
Sulpicii who held the consulship in the fifth century.

your grandfather . . . any brilliant deed: the wording implies that Sulpicius' grandfather was at least a senator.

in my own circle: being a new man himself, Cicero helped others in a
similar position who aimed at a political career. It must have been infuri-
ating for Sulpicius, as a noble and a patrician, to be told that Cicero had
befriended him because of his disadvantaged birth.

Quintus Pompeius: the consul of 141 and, in 131, the first plebeian censor.
Cicero compares him with Murena, who was also a soldier and lacked
noble birth (although he was not technically a new man, being descended
from a line of praetors (§ 15)).

Marcus Aemilius: Marcus Aemilius Scaurus, consul in 115, censor in 109,
and *princeps senatus* (leader of the senate). His family was patrician, but
not recently distinguished; Asconius (23 C; see p. 172 for explanation of
Asconius references) says he had to fight for office just as if he were a new
man (cf. § 36). Cicero is here comparing him with Sulpicius. But a comparison can also be made with Murena: in 116, Scaurus was prosecuted
for electoral malpractice by his unsuccessful rival for the consulship,
Publius Rutilius Rufus (see J. H. D'Arms, *Phoenix*, 26 (1972), 82–4). He
was acquitted, and immediately prosecuted Rutilius, unsuccessfully, for
the same offence.

17 *for I have often . . . and Coelius*: the text is corrupt; I have written what I
take to be the sense. The six men named by Cicero were all new men who
made it to the consulship. Manius Curius Dentatus was consul in 290,
275, and 274, and censor in 272; the elder Marcus Porcius Cato (the
great-grandfather of Murena's prosecutor) was consul in 195 and censor
in 184 (see second note on *Arch.* 16); for Pompeius, see fourth note on
§ 16 above. Gaius Marius was consul seven times between 107 and 86;
Titus Didius was consul in 98; and Gaius Coelius Caldus was consul in 94.

17 *for so many years*: the previous new man to attain the consulship was Gaius Norbanus in 83, and before him Coelius in 94.

newness of family: Murena was not in fact a new man (see fourth note on § 16 above); he was, however, not a noble.

Galba: Publius Sulpicius Galba. Cicero had six competitors at the election in 64: besides the patricians Catiline and Galba, there were the plebeians Gaius Antonius Hybrida (who was elected with Cicero), Lucius Cassius Longinus (the future Catilinarian conspirator), Quintus Cornificius, and Gaius Licinius Sacerdos. Antonius and Cassius were nobles; Cornificius and Sacerdos were not noble but came from senatorial families; Cicero alone was a new man. See Asc. 82 C.

18 *'Murena was a candidate . . . ahead of him'*: Murena and Sulpicius both stood successfully for the quaestorship in 75 BC. Quaestors were elected at Rome by the tribal assembly. After the votes of all thirty-five tribes had been recorded, the choice of each tribe was read out, and as soon as a candidate had a majority of the tribes he was declared elected (the procedure in the centuriate assembly, which elected consuls, praetors, and censors, was different: there, a magistrate with a majority would be declared elected even before all of the 193 centuries had cast their votes). Great importance was attached to priority of election, although Cicero tries to downplay its importance here (contrast *Man.* 2; *In Pisonem* 2; *Brut.* 321). In the years after Sulla, twenty quaestors were elected annually. They served either on the staff of a provincial governor, like Murena (whose province is not known) and Cicero himself (who served in western Sicily in 75), or in Rome or Italy; usually, they drew lots for their post. Sulpicius was allotted the administration of the port of Ostia. Cicero is probably correct in saying that this was an onerous job which (like most quaestorships, including Cicero's own (*Planc.* 64–5)) gave the holder no opportunity to win popular support. Famines were not the norm, and when they occurred the quaestor at Ostia might have his duties transferred to a more senior magistrate, as happened to Saturninus in 104 BC.

the Titian law: perhaps a law of Sextus Titius, tribune in 99.

19 *The period that followed*: i.e. 73–66 BC, the period between their quaestorships and praetorships.

20 *Lucius Lucullus*: Lucius Licinius Lucullus was consul in 74; from 73 until 67 he commanded the Roman forces against Mithridates (in the Third Mithridatic War, 73–63 BC). Murena was in some way related to him (*Att.* 13.6.4).

21 *'So . . . living in the forum?'*: Cicero's real view was the same as Sulpicius', that to become known to the electorate it was essential to remain in Rome and be seen in the forum (*Planc.* 66). But Murena's case requires him to take a different line here.

22 *how to keep off rainwater*: flooding caused by poor drainage often resulted in lawsuits.

24 *to check the frenzy . . . state handouts*: a reference to Cicero's defeat of the far-reaching agrarian bill of the tribune Publius Servilius Rullus at the beginning of the year. Cicero is of course thinking of himself throughout this passage on oratory.

25 *At one time . . . no calendar available*: legal business could only be trans-acted on certain days of the year; originally, only a few privileged people, such as priests, knew which days these were.

pecked out the crows' eyes: the expression was proverbial, and meant 'to catch out the watchful'. Crows watch for young or ailing animals, and peck out their eyes; they will look out for their opportunity, for example when a ewe is giving birth to a second lamb, and therefore temporarily unable to protect the first. Adult sheep can be seen today with only one eye, having been attacked by crows as lambs; this sight is becoming less common, however, now that ewes increasingly lamb indoors (information from Claude Berry). Gnaeus Flavius was a scribe of Appius Claudius Caecus (see second note on *Cael.* 33). He published a book of legal formulas (*Ius civile Flavianum*), and then the legal calendar to which Cicero refers here. These services won him the tribunate, followed by the aedileship of 304.

26 *to join hands*: i.e. in a symbolic struggle for ownership.

a Latin piper: pipers, traditionally Latins rather than Roman citizens, crossed from side to side when providing musical accompaniment for actors in plays.

when our ancestors wore beards: the Romans began to shave from 300 BC (in Flavius' time). Cf. *Cael.* 33.

27 *old men . . . secular marriages*: property at Rome was often encumbered with the expensive and tiresome obligation of performing religious cere-monies in honour of the family gods. Women property-owners who wished to rid themselves of this obligation might find a poor old man without heirs, and enter into a secular marriage with him (*coemptio*, literally the formal sale of a woman to a man). She would hand over her property, together with the obligations attached to it; he would immedi-ately return the property to her, but, as head of the family, would retain the obligations. The woman would pay the man a pension more than sufficient to cover the cost of the ceremonies; and when in due course he died, the family would technically die out with him, and thus the obligation to perform the ceremonies would cease.

were actually called 'Gaia': 'Gaia' was used for the woman's name in the formula of *coemptio*.

28 *extremely busy as I am*: Cicero was preoccupied with the Catilinarian threat.

the great Servius: i.e. Sulpicius. Cicero compliments his opponent on his knowledge, while nevertheless maintaining that such knowledge is valueless.

29 *the reed-pipe . . . the lyre*: the reed-pipe was a wind instrument, so the singer sang while someone else played; with the lyre, however, the performer played and sang simultaneously, a more difficult task. See J. T. Ramsey, *CP* 79 (1984), 220–5.

30 *that brilliant poet*: Quintus Ennius (see second note on *Arch.* 18). The quotations are taken from *Annales* 247–53 Skutsch.

they do not . . . join hands: cf. § 26 above (with first note).

31 *that war against Mithridates*: Cicero refers to the Third Mithridatic War (73–63 BC), in which Murena served under Lucullus (§ 20).

Manius Curius . . . Lucius Mummius: Manius Curius Dentatus defeated Pyrrhus of Epirus near Malventum in 275; Titus Quinctius Flamininus defeated Philip V of Macedon at Cynoscephalae in 197; Marcus Fulvius Nobilior defeated the Aetolians in 189; Lucius Aemilius Paullus defeated Perseus of Macedon (son of Philip V) at Pydna in 168; Quintus Caecilius Metellus Macedonicus defeated Andriscus, a pretender who claimed to be a son of Perseus, in 148; Lucius Mummius sacked Corinth in 146. These examples sound impressive, but do not in fact support Cicero's case: it will have been the Greeks of Asia Minor that Cato described as women, not those of Greece proper.

Antiochus: Antiochus III of Syria invaded Greece in 193, but was defeated by the Romans at Thermopylae in 191 and at Magnesia ad Sipylum (in Lydia) in 190. Lucius Cornelius Scipio Asiaticus served at Thermopylae and, as consul, won the victory at Magnesia. His more famous brother Publius Cornelius Scipio Africanus was the conqueror of Hannibal at Zama in 202; he accompanied his brother against Antiochus, but was unable to hold office himself since he had been consul in 194 (re-election to the consulship was normally permitted only after a ten-year interval). He was the first Roman general to take his *cognomen* from the country he conquered.

32 *Marcus Cato*: see first note on § 17 above. He also served at Thermopylae.

allowed Mithridates . . . in peace: in 85 BC Sulla made a generous treaty with Mithridates, the Treaty of Dardanus, because he needed to return to Rome quickly to recover it from the Marians. This treaty concluded the First Mithridatic War (88–85).

Lucius Murena . . . pursued him: in the Second Mithridatic War (83–81 BC). See §§ 11–12, with first note on § 11 above.

the forces of Sertorius: the rebel Quintus Sertorius held Spain against the central government from 82 to 72 BC. Mithridates offered him military support in return for recognition of his territorial claims. The date of this is uncertain; the winter of 76–75 has been suggested.

33 *both consuls were sent out*: the consuls of 74, Lucius Licinius Lucullus and Marcus Aurelius Cotta; Lucullus was given the command against Mithridates, Cotta the province of Bithynia. Hostilities did not begin, however, until 73. Lucullus relieved Cyzicus in 72; the victory off Tenedos

(near the mouth of the Hellespont) took place some time before the summer of 71.

making for Italy: Cicero makes the same claim at *Man.* 21. If they really were making for Italy (which seems unlikely), they had not got very far.

34 *the one that he fought against the king*: the battle of Nicopolis in Pontus (66).

the Bosporus: the Cimmerian Bosporus, connecting the Black Sea with the Sea of Azov (in the Crimea).

his kingdom: Pontus.

35 *But, you say . . . ahead of Murena*: Sulpicius and Murena were elected in 66 BC to praetorships for the following year. Praetors were elected by the centuriate assembly; on the procedure see notes on §§ 18 above (first note) and 38 below.

Euripus: the narrow strait between Euboea and the Greek mainland, notorious for its rapidly changing currents.

36 *Lucius Philippus . . . Marcus Herennius*: Lucius Marcius Philippus was defeated by Marcus Herennius, who may have been a new man, in the consular elections for 93 BC; he later became consul in 91.

Quintus Catulus . . . Gnaeus Mallius: Quintus Lutatius Catulus was defeated by the new man Gnaeus Mallius Maximus in the consular elections for 105 BC. He was also unsuccessful for 106 and 104, but became consul finally in 102. He was noted for his cultural interests, and encouraged the poet Archias.

Marcus Scaurus . . . Quintus Maximus: Marcus Aemilius Scaurus was defeated by Quintus Fabius Maximus Eburnus in the consular elections for 116 BC, but became consul the next year (see fifth note on § 16 above).

37 *his period of service*: when he was a legate under Lucullus in Asia.

for his triumph: Lucullus' command ended in 67 BC, but his triumph was delayed until 63 as a result of popular opposition.

38 *the vote of the first century . . . the final result*: Roman citizens, when voting in the centuriate assembly (see first note on § 18 above), were divided into 193 centuries, which were grouped into five classes based on wealth. The first century to vote was chosen by lot from the first (richest) class; its choice of candidate, when announced, had a strong influence on the choice of the remaining centuries, who were yet to vote.

40 *Lucius Otho*: Lucius Roscius Otho, when tribune in 67 BC, carried a law (the *lex Roscia theatralis*) reserving the first fourteen rows in the theatre for the *equites* (senators sat in the orchestra). At some point in 63 Otho was hissed in the theatre for this; Cicero reprimanded the objectors in a speech of which one fragment is extant.

Antonius' games: Cicero's consular colleague Gaius Antonius Hybrida had put on games during his praetorship in 66 BC (as Murena was to do as praetor the following year). Cicero's three sets of games (to Ceres,

Liber, and Libera, to Flora, and the Roman games) had been given when he was aedile in 69. It is not known whether Antonius was ever aedile.

41 *what you and Murena were assigned*: in 65 BC Sulpicius was praetor in charge of the embezzlement (*peculatus*) court, while Murena held the prestigious post of *praetor urbanus* (city praetor). The *praetor urbanus* was the praetor responsible for civil jurisdiction between Roman citizens; one of his duties was to put on games, a service which would in due course aid his election to the consulship. Newly elected praetors were assigned to the eight praetorships by lot.

42 *filth*: defendants wore shabby clothing and neglected their personal appearance in order to excite the pity of the jurors. Not to do so was a sign of arrogance; Milo refused, and was condemned (Plut. *Cic.* 35).

A favour from Sulla: Sulla had rewarded his veterans with confiscated land, and they were highly sensitive to the danger of it being returned to its previous owners.

Lucius Murena's province: after his praetorship he served as governor of Transalpine Gaul (64–63 BC).

the many tribes . . . Umbrian towns: consuls were in fact elected by the centuriate assembly, not the tribal assembly (see first note on § 18 above); but the general point that Murena obtained political support in Umbria is valid.

the support . . . turning down provinces: many people would support a candidate for office in the hope of receiving a lucrative post once the magistrate's year of office was over and he took up a provincial governorship.

45 *to drive a man from his country*: Cicero's *lex Tullia* added a ten-year exile to the penalties imposed by the *lex Calpurnia* (see next note).

46 *the . . . Calpurnian law*: the *lex Calpurnia* (67 BC), which imposed expulsion from the senate, permanent disqualification from public office, and payment of a fine. This law was stricter than its predecessor, the *lex Cornelia* (81?), which merely prohibited those convicted from resuming their candidature within ten years.

That law: the *lex Tullia*, passed in response to Sulpicius' demands. The rest of this paragraph discusses some of its provisions (actual or proposed).

47 *a stricter penalty for the masses*: for accepting bribes. The poor liked being given bribes: it was one of the perks of Roman citizenship.

The plea of ill-health: pleading ill-health was a legitimate means of avoiding court appearances. In the case of a trial for electoral malpractice, the defendant could feign ill-health until his year of office began, at which point, as a magistrate, he would be immune from prosecution. The plea was either disallowed or restricted in some way by a provision of the *lex Tullia*.

would also have to forfeit: i.e. if condemned by default and exiled. Cicero is saying that the abolition of the plea of ill-health had serious consequences for the genuinely ill. Either they would put their health at risk by going to court to stand trial (Murena was in fact ill himself: see § 86), or they would stay at home and be convicted in their absence.

had least to gain . . . himself: having reached the top of the political ladder, Cicero would not have to stand for election again.

You demanded that . . . votes be equalized: since the meaning is uncertain, I have kept the translation literal. Cicero here refers to (and perhaps exaggerates the revolutionary nature of) two demands made by Sulpicius but rejected by the senate and so not included in the *lex Tullia*. The first was that the class organization in the centuriate assembly (see note on § 38 above) be reformed in some way: this would have made it more difficult for candidates to target their bribery accurately (they would not have known in advance which centuries to bribe), and would also have had the effect of reducing the disproportionate voting power of the rich. See C. Nicolet, *The World of the Citizen in Republican Rome* (London, 1980), 312 f. (the translation of this passage given there is quite wrong, although correct in Nicolet's original French). The second demand concerns the Manilian law—not the famous law of 66 BC which gave Pompey his Asian command, but an earlier law of the same tribune, Gaius Manilius, which distributed the votes of freedmen among all thirty-five tribes (see first note on § 18 above) instead of confining them to the four urban tribes (where their voting power was reduced). This law was passed on the last day of 67, but immediately annulled by the senate on the first day of 66; Cicero claims that Sulpicius wished to revive it (the reading *promulgationem* is the conjecture of F. X. Ryan, *Gymnasium*, 101 (1994), 481 f.).

You also wanted . . . by the prosecution: the usual method (*sortitio*) of empanelling juries involved picking names by lot from an annual list; prosecution and defence would then each reject a number, and the total would be made up again by lot. But there was also an alternative method (*editio*), previously used in the *lex (Acilia?) repetundarum* (123 or 122 BC) and later to be used in the *lex Licinia de sodaliciis* (55), by which the prosecution themselves chose names from the list, their selection then being modified by the defence's right of rejection. Sulpicius wanted this second method to be prescribed by the *lex Tullia*, but this proposal, too, was rejected by the senate. The objection to it that Cicero gives below is that it would have allowed the prosecution to select the personal enemies of the accused, thus bringing private hostilities out into the open.

48 *Catiline*: Catiline was one of the candidates for the consulship of 62. Cicero argues that people were afraid that Catiline might win, realized that Sulpicius could not defeat him, and so voted for Murena (§ 53).

49 *my colleague*: Cicero's colleague in the consulship, Gaius Antonius Hybrida, had previously been an ally of Catiline. Early in 63, however, Cicero had bought his allegiance by exchanging provinces with him,

giving him the lucrative Macedonia in return for Cisalpine Gaul (which he afterwards renounced).

49 *colonists from Arretium and Faesulae*: Sulla founded colonies of veterans at Arretium and Faesulae in Etruria; some of these veterans had fallen into debt and supported Catiline (*In Catilinam* 2.20; Sallust, *Catiline* 28.4).

   those ruined in the time of Sulla: i.e. former Marians, having nothing in common with the rest of Catiline's supporters.

50 *to recoup . . . forfeited*: referring respectively to the veterans of Sulla who had fallen into debt and to the former Marians who had lost their property by proscription.

51 *if his own fortunes . . . by destruction*: i.e. if he should be successfully prosecuted, he would retaliate by destroying the state. In the ancient world fires were fought not just with water, but by demolishing the buildings in their path.

54 *the equestrian centuries*: see § 73. The eighteen centuries of *equites* belonged to the first (richest) class (see note on § 38 above), and their votes therefore carried weight.

   the decree of the senate: see §§ 67–8.

55 *the office*: the praetorship (§ 15).

56 *Servius Sulpicius*: i.e. Servius Sulpicius Rufus, the defeated candidate and main prosecutor.

   Servius Sulpicius: the assistant prosecutor.

57 *a circus rider . . . a four-horse chariot*: the driver of the four-horse chariot was as superior to the circus rider as the consular candidate was to the candidate for the praetorship. Postumius should not have involved himself with matters which were properly the concern of his superiors.

   (On the charges . . . young Servius): Cicero's reply to the charges of Postumius and the younger Sulpicius has been omitted, and this heading substituted, by Cicero himself (cf. *Pro Fonteio* 20; *Cael.* 19). See Pliny, *Epistulae* 1.20.7. Detailed discussion of the charges may have been of relatively little interest to a readership which read speeches mainly in order to appreciate great oratory.

58 *his impending tribunate*: Cato had been elected tribune for 62 (and would shortly be entering office, on 10 December).

   Publius Africanus prosecuted Lucius Cotta: Scipio Aemilianus (Publius Cornelius Scipio Aemilianus Africanus) was consul in 147 and 134, and destroyed Carthage in 146 and Numantia in 133. His prosecution of Lucius Aurelius Cotta (consul in 144), probably for extortion, is said here to have taken place after 133, yet is dated by Livy, *Epitome* 55 to 138. It therefore looks as if Cicero, unless simply mistaken, has altered the chronology for rhetorical effect. Cotta's acquittal was widely attributed to bribery.

59 *Servius Galba*: as governor of Further Spain in 150 BC, Servius Sulpicius

Galba massacred 8,000 Lusitanian tribesmen after they had surrendered. The following year the tribune Lucius Scribonius Libo, supported by the elder Cato (see first note on § 17 above), attempted unsuccessfully to bring him to trial; Cato afterwards included his speech on the subject in his *Origines* (cf. 'as history relates'). Galba went on to become consul in 144.

60 *'You do not make . . . put you right'*: Cicero quotes from an unknown play. Phoenix is addressing Achilles, it would seem.

61 *I am not making this speech before an ignorant rabble*: at *De finibus* 4.74 (written in 45 BC, after Cato's death), we find the following, spoken by Cicero to Cato: 'I will not joke with you now as I did when discussing the same subject in my defence of Lucius Murena, whom you were prosecuting. For my remarks on that occasion were spoken among the ignorant, and I also had to play to the gallery a little. But now the subject must be dealt with in a less superficial way.'

Zeno: Zeno of Citium (335–263 BC), the founder of the Stoic school of philosophy.

62 *The tax-farmers make some request*: we know of one such request, but it dates from two years after Murena's trial. In 61 BC the equestrian tax-farmers (*publicani*) who held the contract for raising revenues in Asia found themselves unable to collect the agreed amount, and appealed to the senate for a revision of their contract; the appeal was opposed by Cato (in accordance with his Stoic principles). If this is the incident to which Cicero is alluding here, the speech would have to have been revised for publication in or after 61, and would contain a glaring anachronism. It is more likely, therefore, that the reference is to some earlier clash between Cato and the tax-farmers which we do not know about.

63 *the 'mean'*: the doctrine of Aristotle that all virtues constitute a mid-point between two opposing extremes (e.g. courage the mid-point between rashness and cowardice). The doctrine has no connection with Plato, whose name Cicero has dragged in simply to impress his ignorant audience (Plato and Aristotle were much more prestigious figures than Zeno).

64 *better . . . or more just*: the four cardinal virtues were courage (*fortitudo*), self-control (*temperantia*), justice (*iustitia*), and wisdom (*prudentia*). In enumerating Cato's virtues Cicero has pointedly omitted wisdom.

guardians of the same year: Murena had been elected consul for 62, and Cato tribune.

66 *The great Scipio*: i.e. Scipio Aemilianus (see second note on § 58 above). On his cultural interests, and on his friends Laelius and Philus (mentioned below), see first note on *Arch.* 16.

Panaetius: a Stoic philosopher from Rhodes (*c.*185–109 BC); he was befriended by Scipio and lived with him in Rome, then from 129 until his death was head of the Stoic school at Athens. He revised Stoicism in the light of Platonic and Aristotelian philosophy, making it less inflexible and more suited to the tastes of Roman aristocrats. His *On duty* was to become the model for the first two books of Cicero's *De officiis*. Cicero naturally does not let on to his audience that the rigid doctrine of Zeno had been modified (moral perfection was no longer insisted upon); it may be, however, that Cato had a greater attachment than his contemporaries to the tenets of early Stoicism. Like Scipio, Cato kept a Stoic philosopher in his household, Athenodorus Cordylion, whom he had with difficulty persuaded to come to Rome from Pergamum.

66 *Gaius Galus*: Gaius Sulpicius Galus was consul in 166; he wrote a book on eclipses.

Can you think . . . Cato?: this is hilariously tongue-in-cheek. The elder Cato (see second note on *Arch.* 16) was notoriously aggressive and rude.

67 *by law*: Cicero's *lex Tullia*.

the senate . . . passed a decree: this decree of the senate was passed during the election campaign of 63 (as is shown by the references to candidates below). It served to clear up any ambiguity about what was and was not allowed under the existing law on electoral malpractice, the *lex Calpurnia* (see first note on § 46 above), by enumerating the practices which would be considered violations of it. (Evidently the *lex Tullia*, which was passed at Sulpicius' insistence (§§ 46–7), had not at that stage been passed: thus the *lex Tullia* can be dated to a later stage in the election campaign.)

68 *on his return from his province*: when Murena returned from Transalpine Gaul in 63.

69 *to escort . . . to the forum*: when a Roman boy came of age he assumed the toga of manhood (see fourth note on *Arch.* 5), and travelled to the forum accompanied by his family and friends; this passage shows that his patron might go too.

many of the jurors: Cicero is referring to the *equites* in the jury; the next question refers to the senators.

Lucullus' entire army . . . for a triumph: see second note on § 37 above.

71 *If poor people . . . whether or not they do vote*: poor people wishing to pay a favour to their patrons could vote for them when they stood for office, but such support counted for little because the voting system in the centuriate assembly was weighted in favour of the votes of the rich. See note on § 38 above.

the Fabian law . . . in the consulship of Lucius Caesar: the Fabian law, which is not attested elsewhere, evidently placed a limit on the size of escorts. The decree of the senate passed in the consulship of Lucius Julius Caesar and Gaius Marcius Figulus, i.e. 64 BC, is probably to be identified with the decree of 64 attested by Asconius (7 C) which abolished the *collegia* (political clubs). The omission of Figulus' name is contrary to the normal practice.

72 *lost us*: i.e. Sulpicius and his supporter Cicero (cf. § 7).

the forum: gladiatorial games were held in the forum and elsewhere (Rome had no permanent amphitheatre until 29 BC).

73 *a senatorial decree*: i.e. the one mentioned in § 67. Cicero's argument in this paragraph is very weak.

Lucius Natta: Lucius Pinarius Natta, Murena's stepson and the brother-in-law of Publius Clodius Pulcher. Cicero was proved wrong about him: he became *pontifex* in 58 and promptly consecrated the site of the exiled Cicero's house, to prevent it being re-occupied. This earned him Cicero's hatred (*Att.* 4.8a.3).

the equestrian centuries: see first note on § 54 above.

if a Vestal virgin . . . at the gladiatorial games: Vestal virgins (priestesses of Vesta; there were six) had reserved seats at the games. The charge is that Murena's relation (her identity and the relationship are unknown) had given him her seat so that he could offer it to someone else in return for political support.

74 *the originators . . . and speech*: Sparta was the chief city of Laconia (in the southern Peloponnese), and the speech of the Laconians was sparing or 'laconic'.

the latter . . . the former: the Cretans were conquered by Quintus Caecilius Metellus (who assumed the *cognomen* Creticus), but the war in fact lasted two years (68–67 BC). The Spartans were permitted to retain their own laws and institutions when Greece fell under Roman control in 146.

75 *Quintus Tubero*: Quintus Aelius Tubero was an aristocrat of the highest connections: his mother Aemilia was the daughter of Lucius Aemilius Paullus (see second note on § 31 above) and the sister of Scipio Aemilianus ('Publius Africanus': see second note on § 58 above). Despite this, he failed to secure election even to the praetorship (the year of his defeat is unknown): Cicero will explain why. Quintus Fabius Maximus was the son of Quintus Fabius Maximus Aemilianus, another child of Aemilius Paullus (and brother of Scipio Aemilianus); he had more success, and went on to become consul in 121, when he defeated the Allobroges and assumed the *cognomen* Allobrogicus. Scipio Aemilianus' death occurred in 129 BC.

Carthaginian couches: Tubero covered these with shabby goatskins instead of expensive embroidered cloth. It is debated whether the couches were of good quality and supplied by people other than Tubero or of inferior quality and supplied by Tubero. I take the former view: the previous sentence implies that Tubero was asked to provide covers but not the couches themselves, and it is Tubero's goatskins, and not the couches, that Cicero singles out when he recapitulates below (§ 76). It also seems unlikely that Tubero would have had enough couches of his own to accommodate 'the Roman people'. My guess is that the couches were plundered from Carthage and brought over to Rome by Scipio Aemilianus after he destroyed the city in 146 (cf. Isidore, *Etymologiae*

20.11.3); in any case, if the couches were of risibly poor quality, it is hard to see why anyone should have put themselves to the expense of transporting them to Rome. The view that Carthaginian couches were of good quality is supported by Pliny (*Naturalis historia* 33.144), who says that couches of this type were inlaid with silver. The only evidence pointing the other way is from Seneca (*Epistulae* 95.72–3). Seneca classes the couches together with the goatskins and the Samian crockery, but he may have misinterpreted our passage (perhaps deliberately, to reinforce his point); alternatively, a type of couch regarded as of good quality in 129 BC may well have been despised by Seneca's time (and Seneca was a man of colossal wealth).

75 *Samian crockery*: cheap earthenware; silver or Corinthian bronze (an alloy of gold, silver, and copper) would have been more appropriate.

Diogenes the Cynic: Diogenes of Sinope founded the Cynic school of philosophy in the fourth century BC; he was famous for his squalid but true-to-nature way of life. Stoicism developed out of Cynicism.

76 *you will be put in charge of me*: in 62 Cato would be tribune, and Cicero would no longer be a magistrate. Cato had evidently approached Cicero before the election to ask for his support.

77 *a prompter*: a prompter (*nomenclator*) was a slave who accompanied his master and informed him of the names of those he met.

But if you do ... you did not know them?: the text and sense of this sentence are very uncertain.

78 *supposition ... lack of wisdom*: yet the Stoic wise man never supposes anything (§§ 61–3). Cicero implied earlier that Cato lacks wisdom (see first note on § 64 above); now he says so explicitly.

79 *in the Campus Martius*: Cicero's prevention of Catiline's intended massacre at the consular elections of July 63 was alluded to at § 52.

in the forum: a reference to Cicero's *Second Catilinarian*, delivered on 8 November.

even in my own home: the Catilinarians Gaius Cornelius and Lucius Vargunteius had attempted to murder Cicero at his home on 7 November.

80 *a pernicious distribution*: e.g. a land bill like that of Rullus (see note on § 24 above).

81 *a tribune designate*: Quintus Caecilius Metellus Nepos, an enemy of Cicero's; like Cato, he was about to take up office as tribune. Cato had initially refused to stand for the tribunate, but changed his mind when he heard that Nepos was standing. At the end of the year Nepos was to attack Cicero's execution of the Catilinarian conspirators and veto his retiring speech; he went on to become consul in 57.

Gnaeus Piso: Gnaeus Calpurnius Piso held an extraordinary command in Nearer Spain from 65 BC until his murder there the following year. Subsequently he was accused by Cicero of having associated with

Catiline; Cicero claimed (absurdly) that Catiline and Piso had plotted to murder the senate on 5 February 65 (before Piso set out for Spain).

82 *those men*: i.e. the Catilinarians generally.

   the vacant consulship: i.e. the consulship that would be made vacant by Murena's conviction. The surviving consul, Decimus Junius Silanus (Cato's brother-in-law), would have to arrange for the election of a replacement for Murena. According to Cicero, the Catilinarians are confident that they could induce one of the new tribunes to veto the election, leaving the state with only a single consul.

83 *the most distinguished orders*: senators and *equites*.

84 *we must also acquire fresh ones*: yet 'There is no longer any place from which we can restore our strength'. This passage is emotional rather than logical.

   the Anio: a river which joins the Tiber 3 miles north of Rome, and was a source of the city's water. The Anio was the closest that Hannibal came to Rome during the Second Punic War, in 211 BC.

   my most valiant colleague: Cicero's fellow consul Gaius Antonius Hybrida. His forces destroyed Catiline's army early in 62 BC, but Antonius himself took no part in the battle.

86 *exhausted . . . by physical illness*: by referring to Murena's illness, Cicero not only excites pity for Murena but also points to the harshness of the law under which he is being tried. The *lex Tullia* disallowed or restricted the plea of ill-health: see notes on § 47 above.

   the congratulations: that is, on his election to the consulship.

   an extremely ancient town: Lanuvium.

   dressed in filth and rags: see first note on § 42 above.

88 *the mask*: wax portrait-masks (*imagines*) of ancestors who had held curule office were kept in cupboards within the *atria* of the houses of the leading families, and were displayed and adorned on special occasions (as here on Murena's election to the consulship). Murena's father had held the praetorship (§ 15), a curule magistracy, and had therefore earned the 'right to a mask' (*ius imaginum*), i.e. the right to be represented after his death among his family's masks. Masks were a sign of high social status: Murena would have had several at his house, but Cicero, being a new man, would have had none.

89 *the penalty of the new law*: the *lex Tullia* imposed a penalty of exile for ten years (cf. § 45).

   Gaius Murena: Murena had left his brother Gaius in charge of Transalpine Gaul when he departed for Rome to stand for the consulship earlier in the year.

90 *Juno Sospita*: Juno Sospita ('Juno the Saviour') was the chief deity of Murena's home town Lanuvium (cf. § 86). She was given a temple at Rome in 194 BC; the obligation on the consuls to sacrifice there is not

mentioned anywhere else. Terracotta fragments from her temple at
Lanuvium (*c.*550 BC) are in the collection of Leeds City Museum.

PRO ARCHIA

1 *Aulus Licinius*: to establish Archias' Roman credentials at the outset,
Cicero refers to him by his Roman names, without the addition of
'Archias'.

3 *a most excellent man*: the ancient scholia on this passage (175 Stangl)
reveal that the praetor in charge of the court was Cicero's brother Quintus. After his praetorship he governed Asia from 61 to 58.

4 *Antioch*: Antioch in Syria, the most important city in the Greek east after
Alexandria. It did not become part of the Roman empire until 64 BC.

5 *Italy*: southern Italy is meant.

   when Marius was consul with Catulus: Gaius Marius and Quintus Lutatius
   Catulus were consuls in 102, Marius for the fourth time. Marius had
   concluded the Jugurthine War in 105, and in 102 defeated the Teutoni at
   Aquae Sextiae. The following year Marius and Catulus defeated the
   Cimbri at Vercellae (see second note on § 19 below). Catulus was noted
   for his cultural interests, and two short poems written by him survive.
   Cicero's method of naming the consuls here deviates from the usual
   formula to give greater prominence to Marius.

   The Luculli: Lucius Licinius Lucullus and his brother Marcus Terentius
   Varro Lucullus. Lucius was the consul of 74, who fought against Mithridates from 73 until his replacement in 67 (see note on § 21 below);
   Marcus was consul in 73. Their father Lucius Licinius Lucullus (praetor
   in 104 and commander in Sicily in 103) was condemned for misconduct
   in Sicily and went into exile, probably in 102, the year of Archias' arrival
   in Rome.

   when the toga of boyhood is worn: *praetextatus* means 'of an age to wear the
   purple-bordered toga'. Roman boys wore the purple-bordered toga (*toga
   praetexta*, also worn by curule magistrates) until their mid-teens, when
   they formally assumed the toga of manhood (*toga virilis*). It is impossible
   to believe that Archias had been honoured by Greek states at so early an
   age, and Cicero said above (§ 4) that Archias had already 'grown out
   of childhood' before he began his tour. Cicero is therefore overstating
   Archias' youth. He is also misleading the jury over Archias' nationality
   at this time: since he was not yet a Roman citizen, he would not have
   worn a toga of any type.

6 *Quintus Metellus Numidicus and his son Pius*: Quintus Caecilius Metellus,
consul in 109, fought against Jugurtha, king of Numidia, from 109 until
his replacement by Marius in 107; in 106 he celebrated a triumph and
assumed the *cognomen* Numidicus. In 100 he was exiled for refusing to
swear to observe Saturninus' agrarian law, but was recalled in 98 as a

result of the efforts of his son, also named Quintus Caecilius Metellus, who consequently acquired the *cognomen* Pius ('Dutiful'). Pius was the praetor of 89 from whom Archias received Roman citizenship (§ 7); he afterwards became consul in 80. He was dead by the time of Archias' trial.

Marcus Aemilius: Marcus Aemilius Scaurus, consul in 115, censor in 109, and *princeps senatus* (leader of the senate). Cicero admired him as a man who had risen to the highest seniority without the advantages of birth and wealth (see fifth note on *Mur.* 16).

Quintus Catulus and his son: the father has been mentioned above (§ 5); the son, also named Quintus Lutatius Catulus, was consul in 78 and censor in 65.

Lucius Crassus: Lucius Licinius Crassus, consul in 95 and censor in 92. He was a famous orator and an important influence on Cicero, who cast him as the principal speaker in his dialogue *De oratore*.

Drusus, the Octavii, Cato, and . . . the Hortensii: Marcus Livius Drusus was a pupil of Lucius Crassus; as tribune in 91 he proposed a series of reforms which led to his assassination and precipitated the Social War. The Octavii included Gnaeus Octavius, the consul of 87. Cato was the brother-in-law of Drusus and father of the famous Cato who committed suicide in 46. The Hortensii included Quintus Hortensius Hortalus, Cicero's oratorical rival and, later, partner.

Marcus Lucullus: see third note on § 5 above. The date and purpose of his visit to Sicily are unknown. The Servilius who was prosecuted, perhaps in 91, by Marcus and his brother Lucius is not likely to have been the same man as the Servilius who was praetor in Sicily in 102, and it is therefore unlikely that Marcus was travelling to Sicily to collect evidence for his prosecution, as has been suggested. See E. Badian, *Klio*, 66 (1984), 301–6.

Heraclea: in the centre of the instep of Italy, in Lucania. Its treaty with Rome was granted in 278 BC (cf. *Pro Balbo* 21, 50).

7 *IF ANY PERSONS . . . SIXTY DAYS*: a quotation from the *lex Plautia Papiria* (89 BC), carried by the tribunes Marcus Plautius Silvanus and Gaius Papirius Carbo. The main law by which Rome conceded the citizenship to her Italian allies was the *lex Iulia* (90 BC). The *lex Plautia Papiria* was a supplementary law which extended the citizenship to men in Archias' position, that is, honorary citizens of federate states not resident in those states but nevertheless resident in Italy. The *lex Iulia* evidently did not provide for such cases. See A. N. Sherwin-White, *The Roman Citizenship*[2] (Oxford, 1973), 150–2.

Quintus Metellus: Pius (see first note on § 6 above).

8 *Italian War*: i.e. the Social War (91–87 BC), the war between Rome and her Italian allies (*socii*); it resulted in the extension of Roman citizenship to all Latin and Italian communities south of the Po.

9 *the board of praetors*: there were at this date six praetors each year. Four (of 89 BC) are named below: Appius, Gabinius, Metellus (Pius), and Lentulus. It appears from this passage that declarations of citizenship could be made before any of them (therefore at § 7 *PRAETOREM* has been translated as 'A PRAETOR', not 'THE PRAETOR').

Appius: Appius Claudius Pulcher (consul in 79), the father of Cicero's enemy (from 61 BC onwards) Publius Clodius Pulcher.

Gabinius: Publius Gabinius, convicted some time before 70 of extortion when governor of Achaea (*Divinatio in Caecilium* 64).

Lucius Lentulus: Lucius Cornelius Lentulus, evidently praetor in charge of a *quaestio de civitate* (court concerning citizenship).

10 *Locri*: Locri was not mentioned at § 5 when Cicero listed the towns which gave Archias their citizenship: it may have dropped out of the manuscripts there, or been wrongly added here.

the general granting of Roman citizenship: i.e. the *lex Iulia* (see first note on § 7 above).

the Papian law: the *lex Papia* (65 BC). This was the law under which Archias was being tried. It was carried by the tribune Gaius Papius, and sought to expel from Rome all non-citizens who did not have a fixed residence in Italy.

11 *the Roman census lists*: the census list was a register of all adult male citizens, compiled by the censors in theory every five years, but in practice at irregular intervals. The first census after Archias' enfranchisement was that of Lucius Julius Caesar and Publius Licinius Crassus in 89, but it was abandoned. The next was in 86; this time it was successfully completed (463,000 citizens were listed), but Archias was not included because he was abroad with Lucius Lucullus (see third note on § 5 above), who was serving under Sulla in the eastern Mediterranean. The next census was in 70 (910,000 citizens): Archias was again with Lucullus, on campaign in Asia. Further censuses were attempted in 65 and 64, but Cicero ignores them because they were abandoned.

14 *desperate men*: an allusion to the Catilinarian conspirators.

16 *the younger Africanus*: Publius Cornelius Scipio Aemilianus Africanus, the destroyer of Carthage (146) and Numantia (133), consul in 147 and 134, and censor in 142. He was noted for his cultural interests and his philhellenism, as were his friends Gaius Laelius (consul in 140) and Lucius Furius Philus (consul in 136). Cicero's dialogue *De republica* idealizes the society of Scipio and his friends, thus giving rise to the notion of a 'Scipionic circle', an idea now downplayed by scholars. Laelius is given the leading part in Cicero's *De amicitia*.

the elder Marcus Cato: Marcus Porcius Cato, consul in 195 and censor of notorious severity (censors had the power to expel unworthy members of the senate) in 184. He was a famous orator and a stern moralist, and was opposed, in spite of his Greek learning (reflected especially in his

historical work), to the rapid hellenization which Roman society underwent during his lifetime. He is the central figure in Cicero's *De senectute*,
in which Scipio Aemilianus and Laelius also appear.

17 *Roscius*: Quintus Roscius Gallus, a famous actor of tragic and, particularly, comic parts. Cicero hopes that the jury's fondness for Roscius will
dispose them favourably towards Archias, although the two men were
artists of quite a different kind, and Archias was a Syrian by birth. Early
in his career Cicero had spoken in civil cases on behalf of Roscius'
brother-in-law (*Pro Quinctio* 77) and, later, Roscius himself; both
speeches survive, *Pro Quinctio* and *Pro Roscio comoedo*.

18 *improvise . . . words and expressions!*: Archias' powers of improvisation are
mentioned by Quintilian (*Inst.* 10.7.19); but this passage will be the
source of his information.

    Ennius: Quintus Ennius (239–169 BC), from Rudiae in the heel of Italy
(§ 22), the greatest of the early Latin poets. He was brought to Rome by
the elder Cato and befriended by the Fulvii Nobiliores, who took him
on campaign with them and obtained Roman citizenship for him (cf. the
Luculli and Archias). Ennius' greatest work was the *Annales*, an epic
poem on Roman history down to the elder Scipio Africanus.

19 *Rocks and deserts . . . tracks*: evoking the myths of Orpheus and Amphion.
Orpheus charmed animals, trees, and stones with his music; Amphion
with his caused the walls of Thebes to arise.

    the Cimbri: a German tribe which migrated from north Jutland towards
Italy, defeating Roman armies in 113, *c.*109, and 105 before being
destroyed by Marius at Vercellae in 101 (see second note on § 5 above).

20 *Lucius Plotius*: Lucius Plotius Gallus was the first person to teach declamation in Latin (*c.*92 BC). The young Cicero was prevented from studying under him because his mentors (men such as Lucius Crassus: see
fourth note on § 6 above) thought that his rhetorical training should be
Greek (Suetonius, *De grammaticis et rhetoribus* 26).

21 *The Mithridatic War*: i.e. the Third Mithridatic War (73–63 BC), fought
against Mithridates VI of Pontus. Lucius Lucullus relieved Cyzicus in
72, conquered Pontus between 72 and 70, and took control of part of
Armenia in 69, after which he lost the loyalty of his troops. The victory
off Tenedos (near the mouth of the Hellespont) took place some time
before the summer of 71; Cicero ignores the fact that it was won by
Lucullus' legate Gaius Valerius Triarius, not by Lucullus himself (Mem-
non 33.1). Cicero makes no mention of Pompey, who concluded the war
between 66 and 63, after Lucullus had been relieved of his command in
67. In view of the hostility between Lucullus and Pompey, Archias' poem
must have stopped short of Pompey's appointment, and Cicero will
therefore be being over-generous to Lucullus in claiming that Archias
treated the war 'in its entirety'.

22 *the elder Africanus*: Publius Cornelius Scipio Africanus, the conqueror of

Hannibal (202), consul in 205 and 194, and censor in 199. The tomb of
the Scipios still exists, about a kilometre out of Rome on the Appian Way.
Although there was accommodation inside for at least eighteen Scipios,
only three individuals had their statues on the outside of the tomb: the
elder Africanus, his brother Lucius, and Ennius. See Livy 38.56.4;
L. Richardson, *A New Topographical Dictionary of Ancient Rome*
(Baltimore and London, 1992), 359 f.

22 *our Cato*: i.e. the younger Marcus Porcius Cato (tribune this year, later
praetor in 54), the man who joined in Murena's prosecution and who
committed suicide at Utica in 46. For his great-grandfather Cato the
censor, see second note on § 16 above.

  Maximus, Marcellus, and Fulvius: other men who were eulogized in the
Annales of Ennius. Quintus Fabius Maximus Verrucosus (consul in 233,
228, 215, 214, and 209, censor in 230, and dictator in 221 and 217) was
one of the leading generals in the Second Punic War, noted for his successful policy of avoiding direct confrontation with Hannibal (hence his
nickname 'Cunctator', meaning 'Delayer', alluded to by Ennius in the
line 'One man by delaying restored our country to us', *Annales* 363
Skutsch). Marcus Claudius Marcellus (consul in 222, 215, 214, 210, and
208) also fought against Hannibal, and was most famous for his capture
of Syracuse from the Carthaginians in 211. Fabius and Marcellus were
called the 'shield of Rome' and the 'sword of Rome' respectively. Marcus
Fulvius Nobilior (consul in 189 and censor in 179) took Ennius with him
when fighting the Aetolian War during his consulship (§ 27); see second
note on § 18 above.

24 *the man whom we today call Great*: Pompey, i.e. Gnaeus Pompeius, called
'Magnus' ('Great') from 81 BC; he took the historian Theophanes of
Mytilene with him during his Mithridatic campaign (66–63 BC).

25 *the property he was engaged in selling*: the reference is to the proscriptions
of 82–81 BC, in which Sulla's political enemies were killed and their
property sold at auction.

26 *Corduba*: the capital of the province of Baetica (in southern Spain).
Seneca and Lucan came from Corduba in the first century AD.

27 *Decimus Brutus*: Decimus Junius Brutus Callaicus, the consul of 138. He
won victories in Iberia in 138–136 and was the patron of Lucius Accius
(170–*c*.85 BC), the tragic poet, whom Cicero knew in his youth. Accius
wrote the dedication for the temple of Mars built by Brutus to com-
memorate his Spanish victories.

  the great Fulvius: see third note on § 22 above.

28 *a poem on which Archias has now started work*: Archias' poem on Cicero's
suppression of the Catilinarian conspiracy (63 BC) seems never to have
come to fruition (*Att.* 1.16.15).

PRO CAELIO

1 *on a day of festivities and public games*: Cicero was speaking on 4 April, the first day of the *ludi Megalenses* (Megalesian games), which lasted until 10 April.

   there is a law: the *lex Plautia de vi* (Plautian law concerning violence), of *c*.70 BC. See note on § 70 below.

   someone he has prosecuted . . . again: Lucius Calpurnius Bestia, the father of Atratinus, whom Caelius had unsuccessfully prosecuted for electoral malpractice on 11 February.

   by a prostitute: Clodia.

2 *some other person*: Clodia again.

3 *Marcus Caelius*: the father.

4 *before these jurors . . . myself as advocate*: two-thirds of the jurors were equestrian, and Cicero was from an equestrian family.

   filth: see first note on *Mur.* 42.

5 *Praetuttians*: Caelius came from Interamnia (Teramo) in the Praetuttian territory, in Picenum (on the eastern side of Italy, north-east of Rome).

7 *the kindness . . . your father*: Cicero had defended Atratinus' father, Lucius Calpurnius Bestia, five times, and was now preparing to defend him a sixth time.

9 *the toga of manhood*: see fourth note on *Arch.* 5.

10 *a friend of Catiline*: in §§ 10–15 Cicero attempts to explain away the embarrassing fact that Caelius had been a friend of Catiline. This was a damning point against Caelius, and it was particularly awkward for Cicero to have to defend him on this count since Cicero had been unequivocal in his condemnation of Catiline and his supporters over many years.

    was standing for the consulship: in 64 BC.

    later on: in 63 BC.

    when I was praetor: 66 BC.

    praetor in Africa: Catiline was governor ('praetor' is used loosely for 'propraetor') of Africa in 67–66.

    Catiline was tried for extortion: in 65; he was acquitted, allegedly as a result of collusion with the prosecutor Publius Clodius Pulcher. Cicero had considered defending him (*Att.* 1.2.1), despite believing him to be guilty (*Att.* 1.1.1).

11 *standing for the second time*: in 63.

    keeping our arms inside our togas: trainee orators were forbidden to gesticulate in the way that experienced orators did.

    when we wore our tunics: this detail is added purely for the contrast with togas. The reader will detect many other such contrasts.

12 *a great many indications of the highest qualities*: in this extraordinary (and famous) passage (§§ 12–14), Cicero argues, in stark contrast to the view he takes everywhere else (e.g. in his *Catilinarians*), that Catiline had good qualities as well as bad, and that this enabled him to fool people (like Caelius) into giving him their support. This is in fact the characterization that we find in Sallust's *Catiline*: there Catiline possesses many traditional Roman virtues, but has been corrupted by the times in which he lived; born several centuries earlier, he might have become a great patriotic hero. One suspects that the more complicated and interesting picture that we find in these sections and in Sallust is closer to the truth than the usual picture we have of Catiline.

13 *men of high rank*: definitely a reference to Crassus and Caesar.

14 *on one occasion*: see sixth note on § 10 above.

15 *a charge of conspiracy*: in April 59 BC Caelius successfully prosecuted Gaius Antonius Hybrida, Cicero's colleague in the consulship of 63, on a charge connected with his governorship of Macedonia (62–60), probably extortion. Cicero defended him, since Antonius had been the general nominally responsible for the defeat of Catiline. Antonius, however, was believed to have been a Catilinarian sympathizer (he absented himself from the final battle), and Cicero's reference here to 'a charge of conspiracy' implies that Caelius had brought up this point against Antonius in his prosecution. On the trial, see E. S. Gruen, *Latomus*, 32 (1973), 301–10. We have a lively extract from Caelius' speech, quoted by Quintilian (*Inst.* 4.2.123–4); it seems to me to be modelled on Cicero's *Verrines* (no doubt every prosecutor for extortion took these speeches as his model).

16 *the question of . . . bribes*: the prosecution have accused Caelius of bribery at an election, but we do not know which one. The likeliest guess is that it was at his own election to the quaestorship, which he probably held in 58 or 57—although Cicero strangely makes no mention anywhere of his tenure of this office. See G. V. Sumner, *Phoenix*, 25 (1971), 247 f. The suggestion that the election was the one in 57 at which Lucius Calpurnius Bestia stood unsuccessfully for the praetorship can be ruled out: Atratinus would hardly have incriminated his father, who was facing a second prosecution for this very offence.

another person: the references to 'another person' and 'someone else' (the same word in Latin, but English demands some variety) are all to Lucius Calpurnius Bestia, whom Caelius had prosecuted unsuccessfully for electoral malpractice on 11 February (Cicero defending), and was now prosecuting again.

17 *have adjusted . . . his purpose*: i.e. have exaggerated the rental income from the property in order to help Clodius achieve a better sale. The property was on the Palatine, the rich and fashionable area overlooking the forum where Cicero himself lived.

18 *in a political case*: his prosecution of Antonius (see note on § 15 above).

our houses: Cicero may be referring to Crassus' house as well as his own.

by his own people: by his friends and his clients, since he aspired to a political career.

'Would that never in Pelion's forest . . . ': this and the following quotations are from the opening lines of Ennius' *Medea* (*trag. fr.* 103 Jocelyn). Crassus was referring (as Cicero says) to the arrival of Ptolemy XII Auletes in Rome in 58 BC: this was the first in a series of events which led ultimately to the murder of Dio and the prosecution of Caelius.

Medea of the Palatine: Atratinus had rashly called Caelius a 'pretty-boy Jason', *pulchellus Iason* (Fortunatianus, *Ars rhetorica* 3.7 (=124 Halm)); he must have referred in some way to the golden fleece. This prompted Crassus and Cicero to quote from Ennius' *Medea*, and allowed Cicero to trump Atratinus by comparing Clodia to Medea, a terrifying woman driven by her passion to take excessive revenge against the man who had rejected her.

19 *a senator*: Quintus Fufius Calenus, a friend of Clodius and later a prominent enemy of Cicero's. He became consul in 47.

that very fountain-head: Clodia.

(On the witness Fufius): as at *Mur.* 57 (where see second note), Cicero has chosen to leave some original material out of the published speech. Here, however, it is questionable whether he himself wrote the heading which is substituted in its place, since this heading gives the name of the senator, whereas Cicero in § 19 carefully preserves his anonymity.

23 *about Dio*: i.e. about the murder of Dio, the leader of the Alexandrian deputation, killed at the house of Titus Coponius in Rome at the instigation of King Ptolemy Auletes.

or even admits his responsibility: Cicero is conjecturing, not stating, that Ptolemy admits responsibility for Dio's murder. The wording seems intended to confuse.

Publius Asicius: Publius Asicius was prosecuted for the murder by Gaius Licinius Macer Calvus and successfully defended by Cicero; Calvus' speech survived to Tacitus' time, but was not much read (Tacitus, *Dialogus* 21.2). Caelius was accused of having been in league with Asicius.

26 *He claimed . . . for the praetorship*: Herennius' complaint is that Caelius was a friend of Lucius Calpurnius Bestia (the father of Atratinus), supporting him in the praetorian elections of 57, but that he afterwards betrayed him, prosecuting him for electoral malpractice on 11 February 56 (when Cicero secured his acquittal), and then bringing a second prosecution (cf. § 56).

I am not troubled . . . in the Luperci: Herennius' complaint here is that Caelius has in some way failed to show him the loyalty expected of a fellow-member of a religious association, the Luperci; Cicero turns the charge around by pointing out that to prosecute one's fellow-member is hardly an act of loyalty, and that Herennius, instead of alluding to his connection with Caelius in his speech, ought more properly to feel ashamed of having prosecuted him. Rome had many religious associations (*sodalitates*), and their members were always expected to help and support one another. The Luperci were an ancient fraternity of primitive origins; at the Lupercalia (15 February) they were required to dress only in girdles made from the skins of sacrificed goats and run round the Palatine whipping female bystanders with goatskin thongs. In spite of this, the Luperci boasted some high-ranking members, including Mark Antony; the festival survived until AD 494, when it was turned into the feast of the Purification of the Virgin.

27 *Publius Clodius*: the prosecutor, not the famous Clodius who was Cicero's enemy.

    Balbus: i.e. Lucius Herennius Balbus. Cicero sometimes calls him 'Herennius' and sometimes 'Balbus'.

    Baiae: a fashionable coastal resort to the west of Naples. Many rich Romans owned houses there, and the place had a reputation for luxury and decadence.

30 *There are two charges . . . poison*: Cicero has now dismissed all the charges except the two which he wants to concentrate on, because they concern Clodia. These are: (i) the charge that Caelius borrowed gold from Clodia under false pretences, intending to bribe Lucceius' slaves to murder Dio at Lucceius' house (§§ 51–5); (ii) the charge that Caelius, when Clodia had found out what he intended to do with the gold, attempted to poison her with the help of her own slaves (§§ 56–69). Cicero's vagueness about these charges is of course deliberate.

32 *Gnaeus Domitius*: the presiding magistrate, a man not otherwise known, but possibly praetor in 54 (unless he is Gnaeus Domitius Calvinus, who was praetor this year; but praetors did not usually preside over violence cases).

    I mean her brother: Cicero implies that Clodia is guilty of incest with her brother Clodius. The allegation was made against all three of Clodius' sisters, but originally only against the youngest of them, Clodia Luculli; Catullus (79) also accused his 'Lesbia' (one of the Clodia sisters: it is not known which) of incest with Clodius. See T. P. Wiseman, *Catullan Questions* (Leicester, 1969), 52–5. Cicero's joke is in bad taste; it is also very funny, and very revealing of his hatred of Clodia and her brother.

33 *masks*: see note on *Mur.* 88.

    the famous Caecus: Appius Claudius Caecus, censor in 312 and consul in 307 and 296, and the earliest clear-cut personality in Roman history. As censor he commissioned the Appian Way from Rome to Capua and the Aqua Appia, Rome's first aqueduct. In 280, when he was old and blind (hence the *cognomen* Caecus ('Blind'), and Cicero's joke in the next sentence), he dissuaded the senate from making peace with Pyrrhus.

34 *Quintus Metellus*: Quintus Caecilius Metellus Celer, a legate of Pompey in Asia in 66 (and perhaps 67), praetor in 63, governor of Cisalpine Gaul in 62, and consul in 60; as consul he opposed Clodius' transfer to the plebs.

He was Clodia's cousin as well as her husband; they married in *c*.79. They did not get on, and when he died in 59 she was suspected of having poisoned him (cf. §§ 59–60). We have a letter from Metellus to Cicero (*Fam.* 5.1), written in 62; it is haughty and insulting.

the famous Quinta Claudia: when the sacred image of Cybele was being transported from its temple at Pessinus in Phrygia to Rome in 204 BC, the ship carrying it became grounded in the Tiber; Claudia, however, pulled the ship free, thereby demonstrating her chastity, which had been questioned.

the famous Vestal virgin Claudia: when her father (or perhaps brother) Appius Claudius Pulcher as consul in 143 wished to celebrate a triumph for his victory over the Salassi but was prevented by a tribunician veto, Claudia saved the triumph by the action which Cicero describes. On Vestal virgins see fourth note on *Mur.* 73.

36 *your youngest brother*: Clodius.

he always used to sleep ... sister: see second note on § 32 above.

Why do you ... of nothing?: a line from a comic poet, perhaps Caecilius Statius (see second note on *S. Rosc.* 46).

37 *Caecilius*: see second note on *S. Rosc.* 46. Nothing is known of the comic fragments quoted in this paragraph; they are all assumed to be from Caecilius, but Cicero says only that the first one is. We lose much by not knowing the contexts.

Why did you go ... aware of her allurements?: these words are not in verse, and are not therefore from a comedy (attempts have been made, however, to emend them into verse); the words which follow are snatches of verse.

38 *her own brother ... unkind gossip*: see second note on § 32 above.

'He has broken ... be mended': a quotation from Terence, *Adelphi* 120–1.

that woman: Clodia.

39 *Camillus, Fabricius, and Curius*: Marcus Furius Camillus (dictator in 396, 390, etc.) destroyed Veii in 396, doubling Rome's territory; Gaius Fabricius Luscinus (consul in 282 and 278, and censor in 275) won victories in southern Italy in the war against Pyrrhus, and expelled an ex-consul from the senate for possessing 10 pounds of silver tableware; Manius Curius Dentatus (consul in 290, 275, and 274, and censor in 272) defeated Pyrrhus near Malventum in 275. Fabricius and Curius were famed for their frugality and incorruptibility.

40 *times have changed for Greece*: the Greeks lost their freedom to Rome in 146 BC.

41 *For there are some*: Cicero refers to the Epicureans, the Academics and Peripatetics, and the Stoics respectively.

43 *any valiant ... personage*: Cicero may be thinking of Caesar, among others.

45 *as a prosecutor*: Caelius had prosecuted Lucius Calpurnius Bestia on

11 February and Gaius Antonius Hybrida back in 59 (see note on § 15 above). Cicero had been his teacher, hence the remark about not wishing to boast.

47 *a prosecution against an ex-consul*: another reference to Caelius' prosecution of Antonius.

maintain . . . a struggle: another reference to Caelius' prosecutions of Bestia, and to the present trial.

that neighbourhood: the Palatine, where Caelius and Clodia lived.

49 *her blazing eyes*: Cicero refers to Clodia as 'Ox Eyes' (Boöpis) in his letters to Atticus; the word is an epithet applied in the Homeric poems to Hera, who was significantly both the wife and the sister of Zeus.

50 *when I was away*: in exile (58–57 BC).

51 *First there is the gold . . . Clodia's death*: cf. § 30, with note, above.

Lucius Lucceius: Dio's host in Rome, until Dio moved on to stay with Titus Coponius. Lucceius was a friend of Cicero; he prosecuted Catiline unsuccessfully in 64 and supported Cicero in 63. In the 50s he took up writing history, and Cicero in a famous letter of 55 BC (*Fam.* 5.12) begged him to glorify his achievements. See also *Fam.* 5.13–15, letters to and from Lucceius in the 40s.

52 *that Venus of yours*: Cicero claims that Clodia had a statue of Venus on which she kept items of jewellery given to her by her lovers. Unless invented, this information will have come from Caelius.

54 *For I have . . . a most impressive witness*: contrast the line taken at §§ 22 and 66.

55 *whether an impetuous . . . conscientiously*: the text as it stands is of course illogical. It could be made logical by the insertion of a 'not' (' . . . has not given his evidence conscientiously'); 'not' is a word easily omitted by scribes. But Cicero is quite capable of arguing along the lines of 'Heads I win, tails you lose'.

56 *the charge about poison*: cf. § 30, with note, above.

To avoid being accused?: of the attempted murder of Dio at Lucceius' house. Clodia would have been a witness to his guilt, so Caelius would have had a motive for murdering her.

And would anyone . . . himself?: i.e. no one would ever have thought of connecting Caelius with the attempted murder of Dio were it not for the fact that Caelius had prosecuted Lucius Calpurnius Bestia twice, and his son Atratinus had consequently been in need of a charge to bring against him.

Caelius has now brought . . . been acquitted: Caelius' first prosecution of Bestia for electoral malpractice on 11 February was unsuccessful, and he had now brought a second prosecution on the same charge. The charge had been lodged but the case had not yet come to court.

so horrific a crime: the attempted poisoning of Clodia.

an extremely serious charge: the attempted murder of Dio. Cicero says that this charge was fabricated simply to provide a motive for the main charge, the attempted poisoning of Clodia.

59 *Quintus Metellus*: the husband of Clodia. He died in 59 BC, and Clodia was suspected of having poisoned him. See first note on § 34 above.

how terrible a storm . . . threatened the state: a reference to the tribunate of Clodius and exile of Cicero in 58 BC.

Quintus Catulus: Quintus Lutatius Catulus, son of the consul of 102 and himself consul in 78 and censor in 65. He was the leader of the conservatives in the senate in the 70s and 60s, opposing the *lex Gabinia* in 67 and the *lex Manilia* in 66; he also opposed Caesar in 63. His death in 61 or 60, like that of Metellus in 59, was a serious blow to Cicero and the conservative cause.

60 *his deranged cousin*: Clodius, whose mother was a sister of Metellus' father. Cicero goes on to mention Metellus' opposition to Clodius' activities in 60 BC; this is a reference to Clodius' intended transfer to the plebs, which took place in the following year.

the celerity: a malicious pun on the name of Metellus Celer.

61 *that explains the tears*: a quotation from Terence, *Andria* 126; the phrase became proverbial.

62 *her usual one-penny transaction*: a *quadrans* (a low-value copper coin, here translated 'penny') was the usual price of admission to the baths; but here Clodia is supposed to have received the fee in return for her sexual favours rather than paid it as an admission charge. The main point of the joke, however, is that it connects with a remark that Caelius had made in his speech: he had memorably described Clodia as 'the one-penny Clytemnestra' (*quadrantaria Clytaemestra*), i.e. a husband-murderer who sells her sexual favours cheaply (Quint. *Inst.* 8.6.53; cf. Plut. *Cic.* 29.4 for the origin of Clodia's nickname 'Quadrantaria' (with note on § 71 below)).

64 *an experienced poetess . . . to her credit*: it is possible that Cicero's words are to be taken literally, that Clodia did indeed write for the stage (cf. *Sest.* 116).

Licinius: Cicero's frequent repetition of the name emphasizes the farcical absurdity of the situation.

65 *So here . . . up goes the curtain*: mime was a crude and makeshift form of comic drama, akin to pantomime or vulgar farce; it enjoyed great popularity. Clappers (*scabilla*) were hinged boards operated with the foot to beat time for dancers (for an illustration of them in use see T. P. Wiseman, *Cinna the Poet* (Leicester, 1974), pl. 2a). The stage-curtain was lowered at the beginning of a performance and raised at the end; while a play was in progress, it lay concealed in a trough set into the floor.

68 *It must mean . . . pay-off*: i.e. it must mean either (i) that the slaves were being rewarded for having helped to frame Caelius, or (ii) that the

prosecution wished to remove all possibility of the slaves being interrogated under torture and revealing Caelius' innocence (although there was no legal obligation on Clodia to submit her slaves for interrogation (see first note on *S. Rosc.* 77), not to do so was seen as an admission of guilt (as Cicero says at *S. Rosc.* 120), and so it was better to free them), or (iii) that the slaves were being rewarded for their silence regarding Clodia's crimes and immoralities.

69 *that fictitious box ... indecent story*: Cicero now makes a connection between the box in which the poison was allegedly contained and an obscene story which was afterwards told against Clodia. The story is unknown: not even T. P. Wiseman is able to recover it (*Cinna the Poet*, 170–5). But it must have reflected very badly on Clodia, given that Cicero brings it up at such a prominent point in the speech (the end of the argumentation, immediately before the conclusion). As for the box (the word *pyxis* denotes a small sealed jar or pill-box), we know from Quintilian (*Inst.* 6.3.25) that Caelius produced a *pyxis* during one of his speeches and used it to make an obscene joke (Quintilian thought such behaviour undignified). The speech was no doubt Caelius' own defence speech; but what the joke was, and how it connects with the story Cicero alludes to here, we simply do not know.

a pennyworth of scandal: a pun on Clodia's nickname 'Quadrantaria' (see note on § 62 above). In the Latin the pun is contained in the word 'square' (*quadrare*), but it is not possible to reproduce it in the translation there, so I have instead introduced it here (where the Latin says merely 'a certain amount of scandal').

70 *The law concerned ... of the conspiracy*: Cicero points out the absurdity of Caelius' being brought to trial under a law designed for use in national emergencies such as the insurrection of the consul Lepidus in 78–77 BC and the Catilinarian conspiracy in 63–62 BC. He refers to an otherwise unattested *lex Lutatia* carried by Lepidus' opponent and fellow consul Quintus Lutatius Catulus (see third note on § 59 above) in 78. The Catilinarian trials, however, are known to have been held under a different violence law, the *lex Plautia* (*c*.70 BC). The easiest way of explaining how Cicero can treat these two separate violence laws as one and the same is to assume that the *lex Lutatia* was an *ad hoc* measure whose provisions were later incorporated into the *lex Plautia*, and that it was the *lex Plautia* under which Caelius was tried: see D. H. Berry (ed.), *Cicero: Pro Sulla* (Cambridge, 1996), 14–16.

71 *Marcus Camurtius and Gaius Caesernius*: these men are not otherwise known, and the identity of the Vettius mentioned below is also unknown; this paragraph is as obscure to us as § 69. It appears that the prosecution had cited the conviction of Camurtius and Caesernius under the *lex Plautia de vi* as a precedent for the trial of Caelius under the same law. It seems that Camurtius and Caesernius had committed a homosexual assault on Vettius to punish him for some offence committed against

Clodia. That offence may well be the one described at Plut. *Cic*. 29.4, when one of her lovers sent her a purse of copper coins instead of silver, this being the origin of the nickname 'Quadrantaria' (see note on § 62 above); cf. 'that veteran tale about the coppers' below ('veteran', incidentally, is a play on 'Vettius'). Essentially Cicero is asking how the prosecution can have the stupidity or the cheek to cite the case of Camurtius and Caesernius when Clodia had instigated the crime for which they were condemned.

72 *nor indeed . . . just censure*: i.e. there is no parallel with the case just cited. The law referred to is the *lex Plautia de vi* (see note on § 70 above).

older men: Crassus and Cicero himself.

73 *Quintus Pompeius*: Quintus Pompeius Rufus, praetor in 63 and then governor of Africa from 62 until (at the latest) 59. (He is not to be confused with the Quintus Pompeius Rufus who was tribune with Caelius in 52 and was afterwards successfully prosecuted by him.)

74 *Gaius Antonius . . . did him harm*: on Caelius' prosecution of Gaius Antonius Hybrida, see note on § 15 above. The signal service was Antonius' defeat of Catiline (in fact achieved in Antonius' absence by his subordinate Marcus Petreius); the intended crime was his suspected involvement with the conspirators.

76 *a friend of mine*: Lucius Calpurnius Bestia, successfully defended by Cicero on 11 February.

78 *a senator of consular rank*: Antonius again.

someone already acquitted of bribery: Bestia again.

Sextus Cloelius: the leader of Clodius' gang. He was narrowly acquitted on an unknown charge in March 56 BC. The prosecutor was probably Titus Annius Milo. On Cloelius see T. P. Wiseman, *Catullus and his World: A Reappraisal* (Cambridge, 1985), 39–41.

set fire to a sacred temple: the temple of the Nymphs (in the Campus Martius). At *Mil*. 73 Cicero refers to Clodius as 'a man who set fire to the temple of the Nymphs in order to extinguish the official revision of the censors' register inscribed in the public records' (the crime was presumably authorized by Clodius and carried out by Cloelius). Clodius' motive in seeking to destroy 'the official revision of the censors' register' is uncertain, but C. Nicolet (*The World of the Citizen in Republican Rome* (London, 1980), 199) has made the attractive suggestion that the revision referred to may have been one undertaken by Pompey in his capacity as superintendent of the grain supply (57–52 BC). If this revision excluded those who had benefited under Clodius' grain law (58 BC), Clodius would have had a good reason for wishing to destroy it.

knocked down . . . that of my brother: when Cicero had gone into exile in 58 BC, Clodius demolished his house on the Palatine together with the adjoining portico of Quintus Lutatius Catulus (see second note on *Arch.*

5) and consecrated the site (in an attempt to prevent rebuilding); the following year he set fire to the house of Cicero's brother Quintus.

78 *her brother and husband*: see second note on § 32 above.

PRO MILONE

3 *inasmuch as . . . citizens*: Cicero pretends that all the Clodians are slaves.

7 *Marcus Horatius*: Marcus Horatius killed three Alban champions, the Curiatii, in single combat, thereby securing Rome's dominance over neighbouring Alba Longa; when his sister wept for one of the Albans, to whom she had been betrothed, he killed her and was sentenced to death, but was freed on appeal to the people. The story was set in the regal period (*c.*670 BC).

8 *Publius Africanus . . . lawfully killed*: Tiberius Sempronius Gracchus was the tribune of 133 BC whose controversial agrarian bill and unprecedented attempt to secure re-election to office led to his murder and that of his supporters at the hands of the *pontifex maximus* Publius Cornelius Scipio Nasica Serapio (in 133). Publius Africanus (i.e. Publius Cornelius Scipio Aemilianus Africanus, the consul of 147 and 134, who destroyed Carthage in 146 and Numantia in 133) was Gracchus' cousin, brother-in-law, and political enemy; as Cicero says, he was deliberately put on the spot by the Gracchan tribune Gaius Papirius Carbo at a public meeting (in 130), but was not afraid to express an unpopular opinion.

Servilius Ahala . . . beyond the pale: Gaius Servilius Ahala was famous for having killed Spurius Maelius in 439 BC on the grounds that he was aiming at tyranny; Nasica was the killer of Tiberius Gracchus (see previous note); Lucius Opimius was the consul of 121 who suppressed the reformer Gaius Gracchus; Gaius Marius as consul suppressed Lucius Appuleius Saturninus and Gaius Servilius Glaucia in 100; and in 63 the senate recommended execution of the five captured Catilinarian conspirators (notice how Cicero transfers responsibility for this from himself to the senate).

one who killed his mother: Orestes killed his mother Clytemnestra to avenge his father Agamemnon. According to Aeschylus in the *Eumenides*, he was tried by the Areopagus, with a majority of one for condemnation; Athena then equalized the votes and pronounced his acquittal (Cicero's version differs slightly and is rhetorically neater). The story had also been dramatized by Roman tragedians (cf. *S. Rosc.* 66, with note).

9 *The Twelve Tables*: the first collection of Roman statutes, compiled in 451–450 BC.

A military tribune: Gaius Lusius, a nephew of Marius. The incident took place in 104 BC, and was frequently cited in the rhetorical schools as an illustration of justifiable homicide.

12 *this scorched tribune of the plebs*: the Clodian tribune Titus Munatius

Plancus Bursa, who brought Clodius' body into the forum on 19 January, from where it was taken into the senate-house and burnt, together with the senate-house itself. Asconius (42 C) says that Plancus addressed the crowds outside the senate-house and continued speaking until driven away by the flames. Cicero mockingly pretends that Plancus sustained burns in the process.

13 *his sacrilege and immorality*: a reference to Clodius' profanation of the rites of the Bona Dea, when he had infiltrated an all-female festival disguised as a woman in order (so it was suspected) to commit adultery with Caesar's wife Pompeia (62 BC). He was narrowly acquitted the following year, despite Cicero's having disproved his alibi in court (this was the origin of the hatred between the two men). The senate had wished the jurors to be nominated by the praetor, but in the event they were chosen in the usual manner by lot.

the assault on Marcus Lepidus' house: shortly after Clodius' death, the gangs of Milo's rivals for the consulship, Quintus Metellus Scipio and Publius Plautius Hypsaeus, attacked the house of the *interrex* Marcus Aemilius Lepidus (the future triumvir) when he declined to hold the consular elections (Asc. 43 C). (Asconius tells us that ancestral masks, a sofa, and some looms were smashed.)

14 *Tiberius Gracchus . . . Saturninus*: see first two notes on § 8 above.

that demented tribune of the plebs: Plancus. In fact two tribunes interposed their veto (see next note).

The motion . . . by a purchased veto: a composite motion was proposed by Hortensius, but Quintus Fufius Calenus called for it to be taken in two parts. The first part, that the killing of Clodius, the burning of the senate-house, and the assault on Lepidus' house were against the interests of the state, was passed, and so became the decree of the senate which Cicero has been discussing since § 12. The second part, that a trial should be held under the existing laws but with special priority, was vetoed by Plancus and his fellow tribune Gaius Sallustius Crispus (the historian Sallust). See Asc. 44–5 C.

15 *the letter . . . of condemnation*: jurors were given wax tablets with 'A' (*absolvo*, 'I acquit') inscribed on one side and 'C' (*condemno*, 'I convict') inscribed on the other. They erased one or other of the letters (or both, to abstain) before casting their vote.

16 *Marcus Drusus*: Marcus Livius Drusus, who as tribune in 91 proposed a series of reforms intended to solve all of Rome's major problems and increase the power of the senate. The reforms were almost universally opposed, Drusus was assassinated, and the Italian allies, whom Drusus had proposed to enfranchise, declared war on Rome (the Social War, 91–87 BC).

Publius Africanus: i.e. Scipio Aemilianus (see first note on § 8 above). Hostile to the agrarian commission which had been set up by Tiberius

Gracchus, he succeeded in 129 BC in limiting its powers, and was soon afterwards found dead; murder was suspected but not proved.

17 *the famous Appius Caecus*: Clodius' ancestor Appius Claudius Caecus, the man who commissioned the Appian Way from Rome to Capua (see second note on *Cael.* 33). The road was lined with tombs; evidently there were some Claudian ones close to the spot where Clodius was killed.

18 *Marcus Papirius*: killed by Clodius in 58 BC. Asconius (47 C) describes the circumstances: Clodius had removed the prisoner Tigranes (son of the king of Armenia) from Pompey's custody in Rome and was hoping to put him on the throne of Armenia; Papirius, a friend of Pompey, was one of a number killed in a scuffle on the Appian Way while trying to recapture him.

to murder Gnaeus Pompeius: Asconius (46 C) supplies the date of this incident, 11 August 58 BC. The temple of Castor was at the south-west corner of the forum.

21 *his past reconciliation with Clodius*: in 56 BC.

22 *Lucius Domitius*: Lucius Domitius Ahenobarbus, the consul of 54 and a strong conservative (also great-great-grandfather of the emperor Nero). As quaestor in 67, he used violence to oppose the law of the tribune Gaius Manilius on the votes of freedmen (see fifth note on *Mur.* 47), to the delight of the senate (Asc. 45 C, with B. A. Marshall's commentary *ad loc.*); it is this to which Cicero is alluding at the end of the paragraph ('ever since your youth'). In the 50s and 40s he was a prominent opponent of Caesar.

24 *the previous year's elections . . . delayed*: the elections for the praetorships of 53 ought to have been held in the summer of 54, but were delayed until July or August 53. Clodius originally intended to stand in 54 for 53 ('his proper year', i.e. the first year for which he was eligible), but changed his mind for the reason Cicero gives and chose to stand instead for 52.

Lucius Paullus: Lucius Aemilius Paullus, elder brother of the triumvir Lepidus, praetor in 53, and consul in 50.

25 *acted as agent*: for bribery.

a new Colline tribe: the Colline was one of the four urban tribes. Cicero's words are best explained by L. R. Taylor: 'I interpret this to mean that Clodius, who already had a band of followers from the Collina, levied a new band from the same tribe' (*The Voting Districts of the Roman Republic* (Papers and Monographs of the American Academy in Rome, 20; Rome, 1960), 145 n. 50). The common assertion that the Colline tribe was composed of the lowest class of citizens is demonstrably false.

by the . . . Roman people: on the occasions when an election had been started but not completed.

26 *Marcus Favonius*: opponent of Clodius in 61, aedile in 53 or 52, praetor in 49; he was an imitator of Cato. It is not clear whether he gave evidence in the trial.

27 *to nominate a priest*: of Juno Sospita, the town's chief deity (see note on *Mur.* 90). This duty fell to Milo in his capacity as dictator (chief magistrate) of Lanuvium (Asc. 31 C).

a rowdy public meeting: Asconius (49 C) tells us that this meeting was held on 18 January and he names his source, the *acta senatus* (*Proceedings of the Senate*). Cicero, on the other hand, both here and at § 45, is deliberately vague as to whether the meeting was on 17 or 18 January: he would like the jury to suppose that Clodius actually tore himself away from the meeting (hence the ambiguous word *relinquere*, 'abandon') rather than leaving Rome, as he did, the day before it took place. An interpolation awkwardly inserted into the text (referring to the meeting) reads 'which was held on that same day', i.e. 17 January, an incorrect statement. Clark rightly deleted this (and two other interpolations in this section) in his 1895 edition, but seems to have lost his nerve when he came to publish his Oxford Classical Text.

28 *that day*: the day of the rowdy public meeting, 18 January.

this bandit here: Milo (ironic). The account of the ambush which now follows should be carefully compared with that of Asconius (31–2 C). Cicero's account is a breathtaking fiction.

29 *at around 3 p.m. or thereabouts*: Asconius (31 C) places the incident earlier, at around 1.30 p.m., the time cited by the prosecution (Quint. *Inst.* 6.3.49). Cicero judged it helpful to his case to pretend that the murder occurred close to nightfall, at a time too late for Clodius to consider returning to Rome (§ 49).

32 *Cassius' famous test*: see note on *S. Rosc.* 84.

consuls: Milo's rivals for the consulship Quintus Metellus Scipio and Publius Plautius Hypsaeus.

33 *the Palladium*: the sacred guardian-statue of Pallas Athena, rescued from Troy (according to Roman tradition) by Aeneas. A statue reputed to be the Trojan Palladium was preserved at Rome in the temple of Vesta.

That shining light of the senate-house: the primary meaning is 'glory of the senate-house' (as if Cloelius were a distinguished senator, which he was not); the secondary meaning, a reference to Cloelius' responsibility for the burning of the senate-house on 19 January, is more obvious. For Cloelius see third note on *Cael.* 78.

masks: see note on *Mur.* 88. They were carried in procession at aristocratic funerals.

35 *Clodius . . . Plautian law*: Milo had made two unsuccessful attempts to prosecute Clodius under the *lex Plautia de vi* (Plautian law concerning violence: see note on *Cael.* 70) in 57 BC. Cicero's contention that Milo wished to secure Clodius' conviction flatly contradicts the argument he has just put forward (§ 34) that Clodius' continuing presence in political life was in Milo's interest.

36 *when I departed from Rome*: into exile (58 BC).

36 *who had been saved . . . by my quick thinking*: when Cicero suppressed the
Catilinarian conspiracy in 63 BC. Cicero is saying that he chose to go into
exile in 58 in order to prevent Rome becoming embroiled in violent civil
strife.

37 *Quintus Hortensius . . . acting in my support*: Hortensius was accompanying a deputation which attempted unsuccessfully to intercede on Cicero's
behalf with the consuls and the senate before Cicero went into exile (Dio
38.16.2–5).

Gaius Vibienus: otherwise unknown, except from an inaccurate interpolation at Asc. 32 C. See, however, T. P. Wiseman, *Mnemosyne*, 16
(1963), 275–83 on Gaius Vibienus the Arretine potter.

a dagger which . . . Pompeius: see § 18, with second note, above.

a dagger which . . . Papirius: see §§ 17–18, with notes, above.

a dagger which . . . outside the Regia: the incident referred to is uncertain.
Asconius (48 C) tentatively connects it with a fight between the sup-
porters of Milo and Hypsaeus on the Sacred Way in 53 BC. The Regia or
'Royal Palace', traditionally the home of King Numa, was the official
headquarters of the *pontifex maximus*; it was situated where the Sacred
Way enters the forum.

38 *Publius Sestius*: Publius Sestius and Quintus Fabricius were tribunes with
Milo, and Lucius Caecilius Rufus was *praetor urbanus* (city praetor), in
57; all were active in promoting Cicero's recall.

on that day: 4 August 57 BC.

39 *Publius Lentulus*: Publius Cornelius Lentulus Spinther, consul in 57,
worked hard to secure Cicero's recall and the restoration of his property.
The other consul, Quintus Caecilius Metellus Nepos, was Clodius'
cousin and an old enemy of Cicero's. He was eventually induced to agree
to Cicero's recall.

There were seven praetors . . . supported me: Cicero failed to receive the
support of one praetor, Appius Claudius Pulcher (Clodius' eldest
brother), and two tribunes, Sextus Atilius Serranus Gavianus and
Quintus Numerius Rufus.

40 *Twice . . . to court*: see note on § 35 above.

Milo . . . by Publius Clodius: Milo's year as tribune ended on 10 December
57; in February 56 he was then prosecuted by Clodius (who was by now
an aedile) for misconduct during his year of office. The case was
disrupted by violence and came to nothing.

Marcus Antonius: Mark Antony, the future triumvir. He returned from
Gaul in 53 to stand for the quaestorship (of 52), and supported Milo
against Clodius, coming close to killing him in the incident which Cicero
describes below (and again in more detail at *Phil.* 2.21, 2.49). At Milo's
trial, however, he was one of the prosecutors. His quaestorship (served
under Caesar in Gaul) did not take place until 51.

42 *the highest office*: the consulship.

44 *Quintus Petillius*: not otherwise known (not mentioned by Asconius).

   within three days: at § 26 Cicero said 'within three days, or four at the most'. There was also no mention there of Petillius.

45 *the dictator of Lanuvium*: see § 27, with first note, above.

   But on which day?: i.e. on which day did Milo (not Clodius) leave Rome? Answer: on the day of the public meeting, 18 January. Clodius left Rome the previous day, 17 January (§ 27, with second note, above). In this paragraph, as at § 27, Cicero is determined to confuse his audience.

46 *Titus Patina*: unknown.

   on that very day: untrue: Milo was to have nominated the priest on the following day, 19 January (Asc. 31 C). It is strange that Cicero should falsify the chronology here when elsewhere on matters of chronology he has told the truth (although in a misleading manner). I therefore wonder if the words 'on that very day' (*illo ipso die*) are an interpolation; the same words were judged an interpolation at § 27. This speech overall seems quite heavily interpolated (all the interpolations having a similar character and thus probably being the work of the same scribe).

   Quintus Arrius: an ex-praetor (there is uncertainty over his identity). His designation as Cicero's friend is most likely ironic.

   Gaius Causinius Schola of Interamna: an *eques* (Asc. 31 C). Asconius (49 C) tells us that it was Causinius who had provided Clodius with his false alibi at his Bona Dea trial in 61 BC (see first note on § 13 above). This information is also provided by our interpolator later in the sentence; I have omitted the words, with Clark.

   Cyrus the architect: Vettius Cyrus, a Greek architect employed by both Cicero and his brother.

   Gaius Clodius: a well-known plebeian (Asc. 31 C), unknown to us.

47 *those abandoned ... individuals*: the tribunes Quintus Pompeius Rufus and Gaius Sallustius Crispus (Asc. 49–50 C). The first 'someone' referred to in the previous sentence will be Pompeius. At *Phil.* 2.22 (44 BC) Cicero says that no one at the time accused him of being behind Clodius' murder; this passage proves him wrong.

48 *he had named ... as his heirs*: only at a later period did it become illegal for heirs to act as witnesses.

49 *What was Clodius' reason ... into the night?*: at § 29 (where see note) Cicero misrepresented the time of the murder in order to prepare for this argument.

51 *Why, then ... at nightfall?*: i.e. Milo (if he planned to ambush Clodius at all) would have chosen to do so either before Clodius reached his estate at Alba or at a spot between Alba and Rome, not at Alba itself (where the murder took place).

52 *nothing of the kind was ever heard from Milo*: not according to Cicero at *Att.* 4.3.5 (57 BC).

53 *at least a thousand ... megalomaniac scheme*: it appears that Clodius was
enlarging his building by creating a basement floor and supporting the
floor above it on pillars or arches (cf. Sallust, *Catiline* 13.1; Horace, *Car-
mina* 3.1.33–4); this grandiose project is referred to again at § 85 as
having involved the obliteration of some ancient altars. Cicero implies
that Clodius' workmen were available for violence against Milo. An alternative interpretation of this sentence would have the basement specially
constructed in order to accommodate the thousand strong men; this
seems much less plausible.

54 *'He was calling in at Pompeius' house'*: Clodius and Pompey were reconciled in 56 BC (cf. § 21).

55 *each been selected by his fellow*: i.e. each man was as disreputable as the
next. The reference is to a traditional method of selecting a picked body
of men for military service; it was later employed by Augustus to
reconstitute the senate.

a woman ... among men: a witty allusion to Clodius' profanation of the
rites of the Bona Dea, when he had been by contrast a man who had fallen
among women.

57 *I suppose ... on the Appian Way!*: ironic. Cicero wants to refute the
suggestion that Milo freed his slaves to prevent them giving evidence
which would damage his case (the defence particularly wished to conceal
the fact that Clodius had been killed in cold blood on Milo's order).
Slaves could give evidence only under torture. However, they were not
permitted to testify against their master (§ 59), nor were masters required
to hand over their slaves for interrogation if they did not wish to, except
in some special cases (see first note on *S. Rosc.* 77). Nevertheless, it was
better to free them, as Clodia did hers, since to refuse to hand them over
for interrogation was seen as an admission of guilt (see note on *Cael.* 68).

59 *the Hall of Liberty*: this was the headquarters of the censors; its site is not
known, but it was near the (later) Forum of Caesar (and therefore close to
the forum). To us there seems a cruel irony in a hall of liberty being used
as a place for torturing slaves.

'Appius': the prosecutor. He was the elder son of Clodius' brother Gaius
Claudius Pulcher (Asc. 34 C, 41 C), and went on to become consul in 38.
He made a good job of his prosecution (Asc. 54 C).

Clodius ... acts of sacrilege!: Cicero has pointed out that it is Clodius'
slaves who have been interrogated, not Milo's (Milo's had been freed),
and he now gives two reasons why he regards this situation as absurd.
First, it is generally only in cases with religious implications (e.g. cases of
sacrilege) that slaves are permitted to testify against their master. This
objection is nonsense since the slaves were examined against Milo, not
Clodius; its purpose seems simply to provide a context for a further
reference to Clodius' profanation of the rites of the Bona Dea. (Cicero
seems to suppose for a moment that Clodius is the defendant; cf. 'did
Clodius set a trap for Milo?', § 60.) The second reason for the absurdity

of the proceedings, on the other hand, is valid (and is made much more of, taking up the rest of §§ 59–60): the prosecution would obviously have no difficulty inducing their own slaves to incriminate Milo.

60 *did Clodius set a trap for Milo?*: Cicero gives a humorous parody of the proper procedure. The questioner was not allowed to ask leading questions.

61 *when the senate-house was on fire*: Clodius' body was taken into the senate-house and burnt at Cloelius' instigation on 19 January, the day after the murder; the senate-house also caught fire. Milo returned to Rome that evening (Asc. 33 C).

the power of him: i.e. of Pompey.

63 *to submit to the laws*: i.e. by leaving Rome and retiring into exile (as Cicero did in 58 BC).

64 *Ocriculum*: a town on the border of Umbria, forty miles north of Rome. The weapons (it was alleged) had been brought down the Tiber to Ocriculum from some place further north.

66 *one senator*: Publius Cornificius (Asc. 36 C).

that most sacred temple: the temple of Jupiter Best and Greatest.

67 *loud enough for you to hear me*: Pompey was sitting in front of the treasury (temple of Saturn), at the north-west corner of the forum (Asc. 41 C). It is at this point in the speech (beginning of § 67) that criticisms of Pompey start to appear, implying a date of composition some time after Milo's trial (most likely January 51 BC); see notes on §§ 70, 73, 77, 79, and 88 below. The added part, which Asconius (41 C) shows did not feature in the original trial speech, begins properly at § 72. §§ 67–71 are transitional, but seem to me to be either wholly or largely hostile to Pompey (therefore reflecting the later revision).

68 *that pestilential scourge*: Clodius.

his tribunate: 57 BC.

that he had later . . . for the praetorship: on the criminal trial, see second note on § 40 above; Pompey acted as a character witness for Milo. Milo's praetorship was in 55 BC.

Magnus: Pompey (see note on *Arch.* 24).

70 *Gnaeus Pompeius is an expert in . . . politics*: Pompey was in fact notorious for his ignorance of such matters (see e.g. Aulus Gellius 14.7.1–3; also *Pro Balbo* 14–15, which I failed to cite in the article referred to below). This passage must therefore be ironic, introduced when the speech was revised for publication after the trial. I have argued elsewhere that Cicero is most likely recalling Pompey's unconstitutional behaviour at the trial of Titus Munatius Plancus Bursa in (probably) January 51; the reference would therefore provide us with a date for the revision of the speech (*Historia*, 42 (1993), 502–4).

'to see that the state comes to no harm': Cicero quotes the wording of the

emergency decree (*senatus consultum ultimum* or 'ultimate decree of the senate'), a senatorial decree passed in national emergencies exhorting the consuls to take whatever measures they deemed necessary to ensure the safety of the state (the responsibility for any action taken lay, however, with the consuls, not with the senate). The decree was passed early in February 52 BC in response to the rioting which followed Clodius' death. Cicero is also thinking here of the passing of the emergency decree during his own consulship in 63. He executed the Catilinarian conspirators because they were guilty; Pompey has not executed Milo (the argument runs), therefore must consider him innocent.

71 *yesterday's public meeting*: on the previous afternoon (6 April) the tribune Plancus had held a public meeting at which he urged the people to turn up the next day and make their feelings known to the jurors as they cast their votes (Asc. 40 C).

72 *The charge . . . no cause for concern*: the part of the speech which was added when the speech was revised for publication begins at this point (see note on § 67 above). This is the defence which Cicero might have made but chose not to, that Clodius' murder was justified by the public interest (Asc. 41 C).

    Suppose that I were not prepared: the Latin sentence which begins here ends at the end of § 75. A translator has no option but to chop it up.

    Spurius Maelius: a wealthy plebeian who used his own means to relieve a corn shortage in 439 BC, was suspected of aiming at tyranny, and was killed by Gaius Servilius Ahala.

    Tiberius Gracchus: see first note on § 8 above. He secured the deposition of his fellow tribune Marcus Octavius when Octavius refused to withdraw his veto of Gracchus' agrarian bill.

    whose unspeakable adultery: the reference is to Clodius' suspected adultery with Caesar's wife Pompeia at the festival of the Bona Dea in 62 BC.

73 *incest with his own sister*: see second note on *Cael.* 32. Lucius Licinius Lucullus divorced his wife Clodia (the youngest of Clodius' three sisters, all of whom were called Clodia) for adultery in 66 BC.

    a citizen: Cicero, exiled by Clodius in 58 BC. It was by suppressing the Catilinarian conspiracy in 63 that Cicero was considered to have saved the city from fire and the citizens from slaughter.

    gave out kingdoms . . . to anyone he pleased: when tribune in 58, Clodius had secured the passage of bills bestowing the title of King on Brogitarus of Galatia, deposing King Ptolemy (younger brother of Ptolemy XII Auletes of Egypt) from the throne of Cyprus, and assigning the provinces of Macedonia and Syria to the consuls Piso and Gabinius.

    an outstandingly brave . . . citizen: Pompey (§ 18). The description of him as 'outstandingly brave' can be taken ironically as suggesting that Pompey showed cowardice in failing to stand up to Clodius.

set fire to the temple of the Nymphs: see fourth note on *Cael.* 78.

74 *by submitting claims and deposits that were unjustified*: i.e. by making legal claims on property to which he was not entitled (a deposit was required, to be forfeited if the claim was unsuccessful). Clodius did not bother to go to court to obtain property that he wanted: he simply took it by force.

Publius Varius: identity uncertain.

Marcus Paconius: not otherwise known. Lake Prilius was on the coast of Etruria, near Rusellae.

Titus Furfanius: Titus Furfanius Postumus, a friend of Cicero's and governor of Sicily in 45.

75 *Scantia*: unknown.

Publius Apinius: unknown.

his brother Appius: Clodius' eldest brother Appius Claudius Pulcher. As praetor in 57, he took his brother's side against Cicero's. He then became consul in 54, governor of Cilicia from 53 to 51 (to be succeeded by Cicero, who was appalled by his rapacity), and censor in 50. Cicero forced himself to remain on good terms with him (when he says 'a man allied to myself . . . ', he seems to forget that it is Milo who is supposed to be speaking). Clark in his commentary remarks that 'Appius has gone down to posterity as the only augur who took his art seriously'.

his sister's forecourt: the reference has not been explained. Clodius lived on the Palatine, and had ambitions to unite the neighbouring properties (the houses of Quintus Seius Postumus and Cicero, and the portico of Catulus: see fifth note on *Cael.* 78) with his own. This involved rebuilding the portico of Catulus, possibly extending it across the front of the several properties. Beyond the portico of Catulus was, first, the house of Catulus (*Cael.* 59), and then the house of Clodius' middle sister Clodia Metelli. If Clodius planned to construct a wall across his sister's forecourt, this projected wall may (I suggest) have been a further extension of the rebuilt portico of Catulus.

76 *Suppose . . . military power*: Clodius had been standing for the praetorship at the time of his death.

77 *Titus Annius . . . any other man in history*: a thinly veiled slight to Pompey and Caesar (as is the final sentence of this section).

78 *this fine consul*: Pompey.

79 *If Gnaeus Pompeius himself*: the rest of this paragraph subtly underlines Pompey's hypocrisy in setting up a court to punish a deed which he could not in all honesty have regretted.

80 *The Greeks . . . killed tyrants*: Harmodius and Aristogiton killed Hipparchus at Athens in 514 BC; Timoleon killed his brother Timophanes at Corinth in the mid-360s BC, and overthrew tyrannies in Sicily.

81 *deny a deed*: the killing of Clodius in self-defence.

own up to a deed: the deliberate murder of Clodius, to save his country.

82 *a bold venture*: Cicero's suppression of the Catilinarian conspiracy, involving the illegal execution of five of the leading conspirators (63 BC).

83 *Ahala*: see second note on § 8 above.

85 *hills and groves of Alba*: Cicero now appeals to the hills and groves of Alba (the place where Clodius was killed), the altars of the Albans which Clodius had demolished in the course of his building works (see note on § 53 above), and Jupiter Latiaris. The town of Alba had been destroyed many centuries before, but its ancient cults were preserved at nearby Bovillae. Jupiter Latiaris ('of Latium') was worshipped on the Mons Albanus (the 'lofty Latin hill' mentioned below), the ancient religious centre of the Latins.

86 *Titus Sertius Gallus*: unknown.

that scandalous verdict: Clodius' acquittal in the Bona Dea ('Good Goddess') trial in 61 BC.

without masks: see note on *Mur.* 88. They were carried in procession at aristocratic funerals. (Cicero is repeating what he said at § 33 but making a different point.)

87 *At his own house . . . our own slaves*: this was a proposal (previously put forward by the tribune Gaius Manilius in 67 BC: see fifth note on *Mur.* 47) to distribute the votes of freedmen among all thirty-five tribes instead of merely the four urban tribes (Asc. 52 C). See S. Treggiari, *Roman Freedmen during the Late Republic* (Oxford, 1969), 49–50, 164–6. Cicero says that Clodius was so confident of the law being passed (even though he had not yet been elected to the praetorship) that he was already having the text inscribed on bronze. At § 89 he adds that Clodius was also proposing a large-scale manumission of slaves, with the new freedmen becoming clients of himself rather than of their former masters.

88 *As for the great man . . . reconciliation*: Pompey and Clodius were reconciled in 56 BC (cf. § 21). The tone here is critical of Pompey for failing to stand up to Clodius (cf. § 73).

89 *the consuls he wanted*: Quintus Metellus Scipio and Publius Plautius Hypsaeus. The reference is slightly scathing.

a brave ex-consul: Cicero.

a new law . . . his own freedmen: see note on § 87 above.

90 *one of his followers*: Cloelius.

91 *the rods of office*: the *fasces* (bundles of rods, usually with an axe, carried by lictors before a magistrate as a symbol of his authority). Their seizure by the Clodians is mentioned by Asconius (33 C). The temple of Castor was at the south-west corner of the forum.

Marcus Caelius: Marcus Caelius Rufus, defended by Cicero in 56 BC. He and Cicero worked together during 52–51, defending Milo's supporters in court and prosecuting Clodius'.

92 *not a single tear from Milo*: Milo refused to wear shabby clothing and

neglect his personal appearance, as custom required (and as he had done at Publius Sestius' trial in 56 BC (*Sest.* 144)), but remained fearless and defiant. Plutarch says that this was not the least cause of his condemnation (*Cic.* 35). In this paragraph we see Cicero trying to make amends.

93   *at least I shall be spared bad*: i.e. Rome would have had bad government if Clodius had lived. The meaning does not seem previously to have been understood.

      well-ordered and free community: Massilia. This passage was patently written after Milo had gone into exile.

94   *When I was tribune of the plebs*: in 57. Milo's and Clodius' gangs fought each other, and Milo twice attempted to prosecute Clodius for violence.

      you: Cicero. Milo worked for his recall from exile.

      your very own equestrians: Cicero always cultivated the *equites*, the class from which he himself came. He regarded himself as their guardian, and sought to promote harmonious relations between them and the senate (*concordia ordinum*, 'harmony between the orders').

95   *on whose behalf he acted*: the argument assumes that the killing was intentional. This is consistent with the argument of §§ 72–91, but not that of §§ 1–66. §§ 92–105 therefore belong with §§ 72–91 (the added part), and will not have featured in the original trial speech in this form.

96   *some evil intention*: against Pompey.

98   *the hundred and second day*: Cicero has miscalculated: it was actually the 101st (7 April). See J. S. Ruebel, *TAPA* 109 (1979), 245–7.

100   *the powers that be*: Pompey.

101   *this one which gave it birth*: Milo was actually born at Lanuvium, not Rome.

102   *who are now far away*: with Caesar in Gaul (54–52 BC).

103   *those indications . . . destruction*: a colourful way of referring to the Catilinarian conspiracy (63 BC). In this paragraph Cicero refers to the conspiracy and its corollary, Cicero's exile and recall (58–57 BC).

105   *by the man*: Pompey.

GLOSSARY

acta senatus the *Proceedings of the Senate*, an official record of senatorial proceedings begun in 59 BC.

aedile the third of the annual magistrates, below consul and praetor. There were four aediles, two curule and two plebeian; they were responsible for city administration, the corn supply, and for putting on public games. Cicero was aedile in 69 BC, and gave three sets of games.

allies the *socii* or 'federate states', native Italian communities linked to Rome by treaties of alliance; they provided Rome with troops and received certain benefits in return. In 91–87 BC they rebelled against Rome in the Social War (the war against the *socii*) and won their goal of Roman citizenship and incorporation within the Roman state.

as a copper coin (plural, *asses*).

augur a member of the college of augurs, the official interpreters of religious auspices. As with the college of pontiffs, there were fifteen members, all high-ranking aristocrats. Cicero was elected to membership in 53 (or 52) BC.

Campus Martius the 'Field of Mars', a flood plain to the north-west of the city, between the Capitol and the Tiber. It was used for military training, for elections, and as the place where the census was taken. In Cicero's time it was already starting to be built over.

censor one of two magistrates elected every five years for a maximum period of eighteen months. They conducted the census (register of names, ages, and property of all adult male citizens), and revised the list of senators and *equites* by excluding the unworthy; they also leased out the right to collect taxes and acted as guardians of public morals. The office was of great importance and prestige, and was normally held by ex-consuls.

centuriate assembly the *comitia centuriata*, an assembly consisting of all Roman citizens divided into 193 'centuries' (military units); it elected the consuls, praetors, and censors, and occasionally passed legislation (it passed the law recalling Cicero from exile in 57 BC). The centuries were unequally composed so as to give greater voting power to the rich, and the voting system also favoured the rich. A result was usually declared before the poorest citizens had had the opportunity to vote.

colony a town, usually in Italy, founded by official authority and settled by Roman citizens.

consul the most senior of the annual magistrates. The two consuls held office for the calendar year, which (in the absence of any numerical system) was named after them. Ex-consuls were called 'consulars' and were influential in the senate. Cicero was consul in 63 BC.

curule magistrates consuls, praetors, censors, and curule aediles were known as curule magistrates and enjoyed special privileges, including the right to sit on an ivory 'curule' chair (*sella curulis*).

dictator in the early republic, an extraordinary magistrate with supreme powers appointed in an emergency for a maximum of six months. He appointed a deputy who was called Master of the Horse. In the later republic, Sulla and Caesar revived the office for their own ends, Caesar taking it for life. In some other communities, such as Lanuvium, the dictator was simply the chief magistrate.

equites the members of the Roman upper class who were not senators (originally, the *equites* were the cavalry); there was a property qualification of 400,000 sesterces. Unlike senators, *equites* were permitted to engage in trade, and some were involved in tax-farming (leasing the right to collect taxes for the state). The singular is *eques* ('an *eques*'), the plural *equites*; it is often translated 'knight', but in this translation 'equestrian' is preferred ('an equestrian', 'the equestrians', 'the equestrian order'). Cicero came from an equestrian, not senatorial, family, and viewed himself as a representative of the *equites* and defender of their interests; but, as a senator, he wished to minimize conflict between the two groups and promote 'harmony between the orders' (*concordia ordinum*).

federate states, *see* **allies**.

freedman an ex-slave. A freedman/freedwoman would normally remain a dependant of his/her former master.

interrex a magistrate appointed from among the patricians to hold office for five days if there was no consul; after each five days, a new *interrex* ('between-king') would be appointed until new consuls were elected. The office dated from the regal period, when the patrician senators would take it in turns to hold office for five days until a new king was chosen.

legate a senator serving as an assistant to a general or provincial governor.

magistrate the holder of a public office (technically, however, tribunes of the plebs were not magistrates). They are listed in T. R. S. Broughton's *The Magistrates of the Roman Republic* (see Select Bibliography).

new man a *novus homo*, the first man of a family to reach the senate. Cicero was therefore a new man, but Murena, being descended from praetors, was not. The senate contained many new men, but few rose high (in the first half of the first century BC, only four besides Cicero reached the consulship).

noble a direct descendant of a consul through the male line. Plebeians as well as patricians might be noble. Cicero was not a noble; his son was.

patricians members of a select group of Roman clans (*gentes*). The distinction dated back to the regal period: it was believed that the patricians were descended from the 100 fathers (*patres*) chosen by Romulus to form the original senate. In early Rome, the patricians monopolized the priesthoods and the political offices, but by the late republic the offices had long been opened up to the plebeians (i.e. non-patricians) and, from a practical point of view, patrician birth brought more disadvantages than advantages (patricians were ineligible for the offices of tribune of the plebs and plebeian aedile: Clodius had to be adopted into a plebeian family to become tribune). At the end of the republic, only fourteen patrician clans were still in existence. Cicero was not a patrician.

plebeians, *see* **patricians.**

pontifex a member of the college of pontiffs in charge of Rome's religious affairs. There were fifteen members, holding office for life, and their head was called the *pontifex maximus* ('chief pontiff'). Caesar was *pontifex maximus* from 63 BC until his death. The office of *pontifex maximus* still exists: it is held by the Pope.

praetor the second most senior of the annual magistrates. In the late republic there were eight praetors each year. The city praetor (*praetor urbanus*) handled civil suits between citizens and the foreign praetor (*praetor peregrinus*) civil suits between citizens and non-citizens; the remaining six praetors presided over the permanent criminal courts (not all the criminal courts were presided over by a praetor). Cicero was praetor in 66 BC, and presided over the extortion court. After their year of office, praetors regularly went out to govern a province as propraetors (consuls did the same as proconsuls).

Proceedings of the Senate, see *acta senatus.*

proconsul a magistrate who was not a consul but was given a consul's authority in order to command an army or govern a province.

quaestor the most junior of the annual magistrates and the first stage in the 'sequence of offices' (*cursus honorum*); election to the quaestorship brought entry to the senate. Twenty quaestors were elected annually; the two city quaestors were in charge of the treasury, while the rest were officials, mainly dealing with financial matters, in Italy and the provinces. Cicero was quaestor in 75 BC, in western Sicily.

rostra the speaker's platform in front of the senate house in the forum. It was named after the *rostra*, the bronze prows which adorned it, taken from Latin warships captured in 338 BC.

senate the supreme council of the Roman state, consisting of all ex-magistrates (except those expelled as unworthy by the censors). The senate passed decrees, advised the magistrates, assigned provinces, negotiated with foreign embassies, and voted funds, but could not legislate. Its most famous (and controversial) decree was the emergency decree (*senatus consultum ultimum*, 'ultimate decree of the senate'), passed at moments of civil crisis. The 600 or so senators enjoyed a very high social status (and were forbidden to engage in trade), but only a minority were influential in politics: a small number of families predominated. The senate-house was at the north-east corner of the forum, but the senate sometimes met elsewhere.

sesterce a silver coin, the equivalent of four *asses*.

tribal assembly the *comitia tributa*, an assembly consisting of all Roman citizens divided into thirty-five largely territorial 'tribes' (four urban and thirty-one rural); it elected the curule aediles, quaestors, and lower officers, and passed some legislation.

tribesman, *see* **tribal assembly**.

tribune (of the plebs) one of ten annual officers (their year of office began on 10 December, not 1 January) elected to protect the interests of plebeians (the office was closed to patricians). A tribune could initiate and veto laws and senatorial decrees, powers which gave the office great political importance. Tribunes of the plebs are not to be confused with military tribunes (senior officers in the legions) or with *tribuni aerarii*.

tribuni aerarii 'treasury tribunes', originally treasury officials, but from 70 to 46 BC one of the three classes of jurors, after senators and *equites*. They may be considered as *equites*; probably there was a lower property qualification.

triumvir capitalis one of three annual officers responsible for executions.